D1356619

Leonard Bernstein

The Infinite Variety of a Musician

——————— *Peter Gradenwitz* ———————

Leonard Bernstein

The Infinite Variety of a Musician

With personal contributions by
LEONARD BERNSTEIN
YEHUDI *and* DIANA MENUHIN, CHRISTA LUDWIG,
DIETRICH FISCHER-DIESKAU, ISAAC STERN,
NIKOLAUS HARNONCOURT, ANTAL DORATI, LUKAS FOSS,
FREDRIC R. MANN, VIRGIL THOMSON, HANS NOVAK, ABBA EBAN,
STEPHEN WADSWORTH *and* BURTON BERNSTEIN

OSWALD WOLFF BOOKS
Berg Publishers
Leamington Spa / Hamburg / New York
Distributed exclusively in the US and Canada by St. Martin's Press, *New York*

An Oswald Wolff book, published in 1987 by
Berg Publishers Limited
24 Binswood Avenue, Leamington Spa, CV32 5SQ, UK
Schenefelder Landstr. 14K, 2000 Hamburg 55, FRG
175 Fifth Avenue/Room 400, New York, NY 10010, USA

© Copyright Peter E. Gradenwitz 1987

This is the author's own revised and updated version of the German edition,
published in Germany as *Leonard Bernstein. Unendliche
Vielfalt eines Musikers.* © Atlantis Musikbuch 1984
First published by Atlantis Musikbuch-Verlag
Dr Daniel Bodmer, Zurich

British Library Cataloguing in Publication Data

Gradenwitz, Peter
    Leonard Bernstein.
    1. Bernstein, Leonard   2. Musicians—
    United States—Biography
    I. Title
    785′.092′4   ML410.B566

    ISBN 0–85496–510–6

Library of Congress Cataloging-in-Publication Data

Gradenwitz, Peter, 1910–
    Leonard Bernstein.

    "With personal contributions by Leonard Bernstein,
    Yehudi and Diana Menuhin, Christa Ludwig, Dietrich
    Fischer-Dieskau, Isaac Stern, Nikolaus Harnoncourt,
    Antal Dorati, Lukas Foss, Fredric R. Mann, Virgil
    Thomson, Hans Novak (Vienna Philharmonic), Abba Eban,
    Stephen Wadsworth, and Burton Bernstein."
    "Oswald Wolff books."
    Bibliography: p.
    Filmography: p.
    Discography: p.
    Includes index.
    1. Bernstein, Leonard, 1918–   . 2. Musicians—
    United States—Biography.   I. Title.
    ML410.B566G713   1986   780′.92′4 [B]   86–26326
    ISBN 0–85496–510–6

Printed in Great Britain by OUP Printing House

Contents

Contents

Illustrations

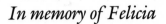

In memory of Felicia

Acknowledgements

The publishers are grateful to the following for permission to reproduce photographs: Amberson Enterprises Inc., on pages 103, 254, 255; Amberson Enterprises and G. Schirmer Inc., on pages 156, 189, 197, 208; the author, on pages 46, 56, 66, 84, 124, 277 (upper and lower), 288; Bayerische Staatstheater, on page 50; Columbia Records, on pages 96–7 (photo by Hunstein), 110; Christa Cowrie, on page 284; Ellinger, Max Reinhardt-Gedenkstätte, Salzburg, frontispiece; Deutsche Grammophon, on pages 112 and 286 (photos by Lauterwasser), 147 (photo Grossman), 270; Hamburg Staatsoper, on page 228 (photo Thomas Kaiser, Hamburg); Houston Grand Opera, on pages 239, 241; Israel Philharmonic Orchestra, on pages 44 (photo by R. Weissenstein), 45 (photo by Triest, Tel Aviv), 62–3, 158 (photos by Isaac Berez, Tel Aviv); Jalni Publications Inc., New York, on page 243; Kim, on page 78; Naftali, Ein Gev, on pages 18, 41; New York Philharmonic Orchestra, on page 36; Prior, Tel Aviv, on page 68; Teatro alla Scala, Milan, on pages 71, 73.

About this Book

A composer of successful Broadway shows who writes symphonies, a world-famous conductor who composes operas, a ballet composer who teaches at universities and gives lectures on TV — such a musician does not fit easily into the concepts of traditional musicography. But what about a personality whose talents encompass every possible sphere of creative music and interpretation — conducting his own musical on Broadway, conducting the Vienna Philharmonic Orchestra at the Salzburg Festival and operas at the Teatro alla Scala, Milan, and the Viennese Staatsoper, travelling around the world with the New York and the Israel Philharmonic Orchestras, writing operas himself and acquainting a public of many millions over TV with classical and contemporary music: this might seem to border on the impossible. Leonard Bernstein, to whose work and personality the present study is devoted, is a phenomenon of spiritual and musical versatility, at the same time always searching, always trying to discover the hidden meaning that lies beneath the surface of matter and appearance, behind words and music. In one of his books he speaks of 'The Infinite Variety of Music'; infinite variety characterises his own personality and in music there is for him no difference between 'serious' and 'light': 'For me every music is serious', reads one of his statements in one of his many self-critical essays.

A considerable number of articles and books have already been written about Leonard Bernstein, most of them of a predominantly anecdotal character; a recent book set out to intrude into his privacy, indelicately exposing some anomalies of which no extraordinary personality may be entirely free, and which have no bearing on the undisputed significance of his contributions to performing style, musical composition, and music education. Some aspects of his musical work have formed the subject of dissertations written at American universities. On his compositions, both Leonard Bernstein himself and his assistant of many years' standing, Jack Gottlieb, have published valuable commentaries for concert programme notes and record sleeves. Of invaluable service is the detailed catalogue of Bernstein's works, with an introductory chronicle of the different stages in his life and career, together with lists of recordings, writings, films and video tapes, the honours he has received and analyses of his compositions, as compiled by Jack Gottlieb (Amberson Enterprises, Boosey & Hawkes, New York).

The starting point of the present study is a close acquaintance of forty years with Leonard Bernstein's work and career, as well as a personal friendship. Though the present author has, from the very first meeting, been fascinated by the musician and his musicianship as well as by his personality — as are people all over the world — he has tried to offer in this book as objective as possible a picture of the man Bernstein and a critical evaluation of his works, musical and literary, and thought. The music industry and the media of the modern world have done much wrong to Leonard Bernstein by featuring him as a glamorous 'world star', surrounding him with a propaganda image behind which a broad public of music lovers will not always immediately detect artistic depth. The 'infinite variety' of his personality and his work opens up in all its scope and depth if his interpretations are listened to seriously and his writings read carefully.

The manifold aspects of Leonard Bernstein's life, activities and creative work necessitate that in this study biographical details and chronological data are sometimes repeated in different contexts. In the biographical chapter the musical works are mentioned in the chronological order of their composition, while description and analysis are to be found in the chapters dealing with the different musical spheres in which he has been creative.

The author wishes to thank all those who have contributed memories, experiences and evaluations of their own to this book in personal conversations, letters and recorded talks, and most especially to Leonard Bernstein himself who throughout many years has helped to build a picture of his versatile personality and his thinking in innumerable hours of very personal informative talks and exchange of ideas.

We also thank the various music publishers, institutions, orchestras, libraries and archives throughout the world which have provided documentary and informative material and photos and have also kindly permitted the use and reprinting of excerpts protected by copyright law.

Last but not least the author wishes to thank Ms Juliet Standing for her most valuable cooperation in preparing the updated manuscript for publication.

July 1987

[2]

1

Music in America — American Music

We have been writing music in this country for only
fifty years, and half of that fifty years the music has
been borrowed clean out of the pockets of Brahms and
Company . . . .
Leonard Bernstein, November 1954

When, in 1943, 25-year-old Leonard Bernstein made his sensational concert debut, stepping in at the last moment for the indisposed Bruno Walter at Carnegie Hall as conductor of the New York Philharmonic Orchestra, he was announced as a 'full-fledged conductor who was born, educated, and trained in this country' — the first of whom this could be said. Hardly anything was known then to the American public of the role of their own native musicians in the development of musical life in the country and few musicians were aware of American musical history. Most prominent musicians conducting and performing in the United States had been born in Germany, France, Italy, Hungary or Russia, or at least had obtained their formative musical education in a European country. In Europe, on the other hand, few names of musicians active in the Western hemisphere were known. American composers were hardly played on either side of the Atlantic. 'American music' to Europeans meant negro spirituals, jazz and George Gershwin's *Rhapsody in Blue*, which Paul Whiteman and his orchestra had brought over in 1924. George Antheil's opera *Transatlantic* had its world premiere in Frankfurt in 1930 but disappeared from the operatic stage very quickly. Only thirty-six years later two German opera houses attempted, independently, to revive the interesting work. Names of American composers appeared in the 1920s and 1930s here and there, mostly as authors of film scores.

Two years after his first startling success conducting the renowned

[3]

New York Philharmonic, Leonard Bernstein made his first appearance in 'Old Europe', and here he surprised conservative audiences — and critics — not only by his unusual drive and musical insight, but also as a promoter of new American music. His first European concerts took place in Prague and London in the spring of 1946; he was twenty-seven years old at the time. His programmes contained music by William Schuman, Samuel Barber, Roy Harris, Aaron Copland, George Gershwin and his own First Symphony, *Jeremiah*.

The symphonic works Leonard Bernstein had chosen for his programmes were all composed between the years 1936 and 1942 — with the exception of Gershwin's *Rhapsody in Blue* — and the majority of listeners then heard for the first time music from the 'New World'. The oldest composer represented was Roy Harris (born 1898), whose Third Symphony, one of the most important works of new American music and one of the great symphonies in the twentieth-century orchestral repertoire, had been completed in 1938. Aaron Copland and William Schuman were both born in 1900; Copland's *El Salón Mexico* (1936) and Schuman's *American Festival Overture* (1939) had distinctly American musical traits; *Essay No. 2* (1942) was composed by the 32-year-old American musical lyricist, Samuel Barber. None of the composers presented by Leonard Bernstein to his European audiences were numbered among those musicians described in his essay, 'Whatever happened to that Great American Symphony?' (November 1954, reprinted in *The Joy of Music*, New York, 1954), of whom he says that their music 'has been borrowed clean out of the pockets of Brahms and Company'. In dating the beginnings of an 'American music' around the early years of the twentieth century, he looks back to a generation of composers characterised by names such as John Knowles Paine (1839–1906), George W. Chadwick (1854–1931), Edgard Stillman Kelley (1857–1944), Arthur Foote (1853–1937), Horatio Parker (1863–1919), Mrs H.H. Beach (1867–1944), and Henry F. Gilbert (1868–1928) — the so-called Boston or New England Group. A contemporary of these composers was Edward MacDowell (1861–1908), known as 'America's Grieg', the first American composer to gain recognition in Europe. The 'Bostoners' were followed by a post-Romanticist generation of composers, such as Frederick Shepherd Converse (1871–1940), Henry Hadley (1871–1938), Daniel Gregory Mason (1873–1953) and David Stanley Smith (1877–1920); or Impressionists such as Charles Martin Loeffler (1861–1935) and Charles Tomlinson Griffes (1874–1954). It was only with the works of Charles Ives (1874–1954) (whose importance was discovered and appreciated long after the bulk of his work had been written) and of the composers born towards the end of the nineteenth century, that music written in America gained characteristic traits of its own.

Leonard Bernstein's promotion of American composers, his choice of significant works for his programmes and his study of the development of American music went a long way towards compelling music historians to ask once again: is there such a thing as music that may be termed national and uniquely characteristic of a certain nation or people? Do national characteristics find expression in the musical creations of a nation's composers? Analysts and historians have distinguished between a spiritual–national and folkloristic–national approach in the case of composers eager to be regarded as musical representatives of their countries. Attempts have also been made to detect national strains in the music of composers of more cosmopolitan, universal leanings and to doubt the inclusion of folk elements in the music of composers who expressed their national-mindedness in words. The entire question seems anachronistic at a time when technology and the media make music of every kind and description familiar all over the world with the help of satellite transmissions, radio and television — music of all countries and peoples, of all historical periods and styles, showing different techniques, means of expression, forms and structures is available. In previous epochs of history, musical nationalism has played a major role in various countries especially during a time of national renascence in those countries which had not yet found a place in world cultural history. Romanticism and musical–national Romanticism often develop side by side and have survived even such turbulent times as the second half of the twentieth century. Cultural nationalism is a natural phenomenon in a country like the United States of America, a melting-pot of civilisations and cultural inheritances, where a continual immigration of newcomers wishing to become American citizens and not just to hold a US passport, are seeking a unifying identity.

American composers themselves have often asked whether a typically American music exists: answers have been very different. Virgil Thomson, the important critic, chronicler and composer, has said: 'The way to write American music is simple. All you have to do is to be an American and then write any kind of music you wish'. A similar opinion has been expressed by Aaron Copland, who in his early compositions used folkloristic material and jazz-style, but later said: 'I no longer feel the need of seeking out conscious Americanism. Because we live here and work here, we can be certain that when our music is mature it will also be American in quality'. Among the most pointed sayings on nationalism in music is a remark by Heitor Villa-Lobos: 'A

[5]

truly creative musician is capable of producing, from his own imagina-
tion, melodies that are more authentic than folklore itself'. Leonard
Bernstein's own opinion seems to follow that of the composer Edward
MacDowell, who wrote at the turn of the century:

> Before a people can find a musical writer to echo its genius it must first
> possess men who truly represent it — that is to say, men who, being part of
> the people, love the country for itself: men who put into their music what the
> nation has put into its life. What we must arrive at is the youthful optimistic
> vitality and the undaunted tenacity of spirit that characterize the American
> man. That is what I hope to see echoed in American music.

Leonard Bernstein, in his television programmes for young people,
during his fourth talk, asked 'What makes music American?'

> Think of all the races and personalities from all over the globe that make up
> our country. What our composers are nourished on is a folk music that is
> probably the richest in the world, and all of it is American, whether it's jazz,
> or square-dance tunes, or cowboy songs, or hilly-billy music, or rock'n'roll,
> or Cuban mambos, or Mexican huapangos, or Missouri hymn-singing. It's
> like all the different accents we have in our speaking; there's a little Mexican
> in some Texas accents, and a little Swedish in the Minnesota accent, and a
> little Slavic in the Brooklyn accent, and a little Irish in the Boston accent.
> But it's all American, just like Copland's *Billy the Kid*, which also has a
> Mexican accent here and a Brooklyn accent there . . . . And hearing all these
> accents you can feel strongly what it means to be an American — a
> descendant of all the nations of the earth (*Leonard Bernstein's Young People's
> Concerts for Reading and Listening*, New York, 1962, pp. 96f.).

When Leonard Bernstein, at the age of forty, became Music Director
of the New York Philharmonic Orchestra in 1958, he started a series of
performances of works written during the past hundred years by
American composers; he also initiated preview talks on the concert
programmes. The earliest symphonic works in his programmes were
chosen from what he called 'the kindergarten phase of American
music'. He drew the attention of both musicians and the general public
to early attempts of composers to create consciously conceived national
music, without however playing the very earliest specimens of this kind
— music that is indeed of little inherent interest, but has some historic
importance because of its influence on later developments in American
music.

Such national sentiments were shown by a composer living in Kentucky at the beginning of the nineteenth century, who later moved to

[6]

cities with Amerindian populations. In April 1822, John R. Parker, in his *Euterpiad*, called him 'the Beethoven of America'. The composer in question was born in Bohemia in 1781 as Anton Philip Heinrich, came to America by way of Malta and changed his first name to Anthony. Only a few years after immigration, he already felt himself to be an American composer. In his book *Dawning of Music in Kentucky, or The Pleasures of Harmony in the Solitudes of Nature* (published in 1820) Heinrich wrote that it 'has been one of the chief motives, in the exercise of his abilities . . . to create but one single Star in the West [and] no one would ever be more proud than himself, to be called an American Musician'. His works bear such titles as *The Wildwood Troubadour, a musical Auto-Biography, The Indian Carnival or The Indian's Festival of Dreams, Gran sinfonia misteriosa indiana, The Treaty of William Penn with the Indians — Concerto grosso — An American national dramatic divertissement* . . . . Heinrich was proud to have received a letter from Heinrich Marschner, dated 10 May 1849, which praised 'the originality, the deeply poetic ideas' developed in his compositions, which other musicians often criticised as eccentric and bombastic. While his music no longer holds much interest, there can be no doubt that his preoccupation with Indian music and the use of Indian folklore in his works exerted an influence on American composers of later generations. Anthony Philip Heinrich died in New York in 1861, aged eighty; some two hundred of his compositions, many of them printed, are preserved in the Library of Congress in Washington, D.C.

The oldest composer from the 'kindergarten phase' included in Leonard Bernstein's concerts, was William Henry Fry, who has gone down in history as the creator of the first publicly performed opera by an American-born composer. His *Leonora* was staged in June 1845 in Philadelphia: critics of the time said it was an opera of the Bellini school. Bernstein has played Fry's *Santa Claus Symphony* (1853) and thus William Henry Fry (born circa 1815, died 1864) at last achieved a place in a New York Philharmonic concert. When the Philharmonic Society of New York was founded in 1842, many composers hoped that their works would be performed at its concerts, but most were disappointed: Fry was one of the composers who complained bitterly at the time that his symphonies were not given a hearing in the Philharmonic concerts. Discontent among composers grew when one of the first — out of very few — works by American composers to be performed was in fact one written by George F. Bristow, concert master of the Philharmonic. The founder and first conductor of the orchestra was American-born Ureli Corelli Hill (1802–75), who as a violinist had studied for a time under Louis Spohr in Germany. Thus the founder-director of the Philharmonic was, in fact, a native American.

One of the most characteristic early works of American music with a folk background was the fantasy *Nights in the Tropics* by Louis Moreau Gottschalk, famous in his day as pianist and composer; his piano pieces are still played. Born in 1829 in New Orleans, with an English Jewish father and a Creole mother, at the age of thirteen he went to study in Paris and there became a pupil of Hector Berlioz, who was enthusiastic about his youthful talents as a pianist. Chopin predicted that he would become a 'king of pianists'. In 1853, Gottschalk returned to America to embark on a series of concert tours, and was acclaimed wherever he played. He died in Rio de Janeiro in 1869. His incorporation of Negro tunes and Creole melodies into his compositions exerted on American composers an even deeper influence than had the music of Anthony Philip Heinrich. In his concerts Bernstein sought out works by early American composers with a leaning towards the folk tradition and Gottschalk's music was given its due place.

Compositions by the Boston Group that figured in Leonard Bernstein's survey of American music were George Chadwick's *Melpomene*, first performed in 1891, the *Suite on Negro Themes* by Henry Gilbert, premiered in Boston in 1911 when the composer was forty-three years old, and the *Indian Suite*, op. 48, by Edward MacDowell, first given in 1896. Further programmes included music by American composers who had become independent of 'Brahms and Company', who belonged to the generation born between 1874 and 1900, and composers of the twentieth century proper.

The wide-ranging versatility of Bernstein's taste and the thoroughness with which he studied American musical history are evident from the works which, under his directorship, the New York Philharmonic played in various series of concerts. There were compositions with which he had become familiar long before his appointment to the important position of Music Director, music that he unearthed from the archives, new works and music that influenced his own style of writing. One of the first modern works which Bernstein performed with the New York Philharmonic was the Second Symphony by Randall Thompson. This was in fact the very first orchestral piece that he ever conducted professionally, for his conducting teacher Fritz Reiner had assigned this work to him as his first task as a student at the Curtis Institute of Philadelphia in 1939; Randall Thompson (born 1899), had been a composition student of Ernest Bloch. The symphony, written in 1931 and first performed at Rochester in 1932, was the work of a composer who — in his own words — argued that 'a composer's first responsibility is, and always will be, to write music that will reach and move the hearts of his listeners in his own day' and who wished to express America's own genuine musical heritage in its every manifestation, every inflection, every living example'. His symphonic music has no 'programme' and aims to be as 'primarily melodious and objective as the symphonies of the Eighteenth Century'. Yet the melodic invention points to influences of American folklore from various regions of the country, while jazz shines through in the fast movements and a blues mood reigns in some parts of the slow movement. There can be little doubt that the artistic credo of Randall Thompson, who was teacher as well as friend to Leonard Bernstein, and his way of musical expression, went a long way towards shaping the younger man's own style of composing. The Second Symphony, the first work Bernstein had thoroughly studied and successfully conducted, not only appeared in his New York Philharmonic series, but also in future programmes.

A far more demanding work from his New York programmes was to turn Bernstein the composer in the direction of modern American musical theatre. This was *The Mother of Us All*, Virgil Thomson's opera, written in 1947 to a text by Gertrude Stein, who had died in Paris the previous year. At the age of twenty Bernstein had written the first of his pieces connected with the stage, incidental music for a production of Aristophanes' comedy *The Birds*, which he conducted at Harvard University. Soon afterwards he led from the piano a performance of the satirical opera *The Cradle Will Rock* (1936) by Marc Blitzstein (born 1905). In 1942, he produced Aaron Copland's school opera *The Second Hurricane* (1937) at the Institute of Modern Art in Boston. 1944 saw the premiere of his own first complete work for the stage, the ballet *Fancy Free*, which he conducted at the New York Metropolitan Opera; its music combines elements of blues, jazz, folklore and romantic sentiment. His first great opera experience came when Sergei Koussevitzky entrusted him with the American première of Benjamin Britten's operatic tragedy *Peter Grimes* at the Tanglewood Festival in August 1945, two months after the world première at Sadler's Wells Theatre in London under the baton of Reginald Goodall. In 1952, Leonard Bernstein wrote the libretto and music of a one-act operatic comedy, *Trouble in Tahiti*; in 1956 he set to music the Lillian Hellman version of Voltaire's *Candide*, and in 1957 there came *West Side Story*. In October 1958, he assumed the post of Music Director of the New York Philharmonic Orchestra, which he was to occupy for eleven years.

The Mother of Us All was Virgil Thomson's second opera; the first had been *Four Saints in Three Acts* (1928). Gertrude Stein's libretto is based on the life and work of the suffragette Susan B. Anthony and personalities from various epochs of American history are brought face to face

with each other to support the heroine's ideas. Sharp musical characterisation and a certain impersonal romanticism are the main traits of
Thomson's style and the music, though permeated with Americanisms,
distinctly reflects the influence of Thomson's eight Parisian years
during which he collaborated with Gertrude Stein and had much
contact both with French and emigré poets, artists and musicians. The
composer admits that in words and music there is something nostalgic,
something of nineteenth-century rural America; 'sophisticated simplicity' was a description coined for his music at the time. The very first
performances of the opera, in May 1947 at Columbia University, New
York, were given by students and professionals under the direction of
Otto Luening, and the composer was astonished and delighted that the
fairly difficult score was mastered by college students. In 1949, Sir
Thomas Beecham wanted to perform the work in celebration of his
seventieth birthday, but the British Broadcasting Corporation rejected
it. For Leonard Bernstein, himself an outspoken emotionalist, the
appeal of Thomson's opera lies as much in its nostalgia, as in its
sophistication, as much in its Americanism as in the inherent charm of
the melodic lines with their deceptively easy-going simplicity. The
Parisian elements in Virgil Thomson's music were familiar to Bernstein mainly through Francis Poulenc's opera *Les mamelles de Tirésias*
(1947), whose American premiere he conducted at Brandeis University
in June 1953 — only a short time before he was called to conduct
Cherubini's *Medea* at the Teatro alla Scala, Milan, with Maria Callas
in the title role.

Among the symphonies of American composers given in Bernstein's
Philharmonic concerts there was one work of especial significance. The
New York Philharmonic had already performed it under Leonard
Bernstein's direction eight years before he became its Music Director:
the occasion was the world premiere of a symphony written fifty years
earlier by a composer now aged seventy-seven who had never heard
most of his music performed. This was the Second Symphony of
Charles Ives, born in 1874, whose importance as the creator of an
idiomatic American music and of new structures, new sounds and new
means of style and expression in twentieth-century music, well in
advance of European composers, was only recognised long after Ives
had ceased writing. The emancipation of dissonance, as brought about
by Arnold Schoenberg, the liberation of melody from symmetrical
rhythm and clearly-defined harmony, open form and microtonality are
some of the features of Charles Ives' music, practised decades before
European composers introduced them. Charles Ives remained lonely,
virtually unknown in his own time, and if musicians read or heard any

of his music, they thought it abstruse. His most significant compositions were written between the years 1890 and 1916: they included
chamber music, two large-scale sonatas for the piano and four symphonies; there followed a number of songs, music for quarter-note piano or
two pianos with different tunings. In the 1920s he stopped writing
music altogether. Some conductors who had heard about Ives asked
him to send them scores, but no performances resulted and some of the
original scores were lost. In 1910, Gustav Mahler asked to see the score
of Ives' Third Symphony (composed 1904); apparently he intended to
conduct it in Europe. However Mahler died soon afterwards and the
original score appears to have been lost. One of the few of Ives'
orchestral works to reach Europe — though even this was only after his
death in 1954 — is *The Unanswered Question*, composed as early as 1908
and with a subtitle no longer often mentioned: *A Cosmic Landscape*. This
work has often been performed by Leonard Bernstein in concerts the
world over, he has not only identified himself deeply with this music
and imparted to it an interpretation and meaning of his own but used
its title as heading and leading idea of his six Charles Eliot Norton
lectures given at Harvard University in 1973.

Charles Ives' *The Unanswered Question*, first published forty years after
its composition, is a 'cosmic landscape'; it is played by a chamber
orchestra whose members are placed at a distance from each other,
producing what today would be called a stereo effect. A small group of
string players — Ives directed that they should play behind the concert
stage or at its furthest end — represents 'the silence of the seers who,
even if they have an answer to the Perennial Question of Existence,
cannot reply'; they play very softly and slowly, in concordant harmony
and with notes widely spaced. Their quiet playing continues throughout the entire piece. On stage the Question is asked by a solo trumpet,
assisted by a group of wind instruments which try to find an answer, in
a predominantly dissonant texture which becomes ever sharper as the
work develops. The trumpet repeats the Question over and over while
'The Fighting Answerers [flutes and other people] run about trying in
vain to discover the invisible, unattainable reply to the trumpet. When
they finally surrender the search they mock the trumpet's reiteration
and depart. The Question is then asked again, for the last time, and the
silence sounds from a distance undisturbed' (Henry and Sidney Cowell,
Charles Ives and His Music, New York, 1955, p. 177). The work thus ends
quietly, with consonant chords, as from another world, in pure G major.

In his fifth Harvard Lecture, printed in his book *The Unanswered
Question*, Leonard Bernstein asks: 'Is that luminous final triad the
answer? Is tonality eternal, immortal? Many have thought so, and

some still do. And yet, that trumpet's question hangs in the air, unresolved, troubling our calm. Do you see how clearly this piece spells out the dilemma of the new century — the dichotomy that was to define the shape of musical life from then to now? On the one hand, tonality and syntactic clarity; on the other, atonality and syntactic confusion' (*The Unanswered Question*, p. 269). In Alban Berg's Violin Concerto, dating from 1936, Leonard Bernstein sees a compromise solution, the 'great twelve-tone work has found its resting place' when ending in a clear B flat major, but does this mean, he asks, that 'the ultimate ambiguity was solved once and for all?' (ibid., p. 312). At the end of his sixth and last Harvard lecture, he draws his conclusion from his analyses of musical works and the contemporary state of music, enabling us to look into his own mind, into his creative disposition and creed, and to understand the foundations of his mature compositions. He has himself experienced how troubling it may be for a composer to decide whether and how to apply musical grammar, so to speak, to inspiration and musical invention, how to set in opposition and how to unite the divergent powers of consonance and dissonance, tonality and pantonality, determined and free musical syntax, harmonically orientated and twelve-tone melodic themes. 'I believe that Ives' *Unanswered Question* has an answer . . .', says Bernstein at the end of his lectures, 'I'm no longer quite sure what the question is, but I do know that the answer is *Yes*' (ibid., p. 424).

Charles Ives put *The Unanswered Question* in 1908 — decades earlier than composers who were to gain much more fame than he ever did. The unanswered question — resounding in 'a cosmic landscape' — preoccupied even in Ives' lifetime Gustav Mahler, much later both Igor Stravinsky (after his dodecaphonic period in which he turned to twelve-tone music somewhat rigorously in the 1950s), and also Arnold Schoenberg in the compositions of his American years. The ideological–musical and structural foundations, the oscillation between tonal, free-tonal and tonally undetermined melodic lines that characterise the music of Charles Ives exerted a decisive influence on Leonard Bernstein the composer. From his earliest essays to his Harvard lectures, the problem of tonality occupies a central part of his writing. The struggle between chromatic melodic themes, which in his later compositions assumed dodecaphonic character, and tonal 'answers' in melody and harmony is present in almost all of Bernstein's musical works, most clearly in those written since the mid-1960s. In a deeply serious manner, it shapes the nocturne *Halil* for flute, string orchestra, and percussion (1981), while in lighter mood it appears in the orchestral *Divertimento* of 1980.

Leonard Bernstein first conducted Charles Ives' important Second Symphony as guest conductor of the New York Philharmonic at a concert on 22 February 1951. Hardly any of the audience had ever heard of the composer, who lived at Danbury, Connecticut, and still fewer knew any of his works. Characteristically, this was the world première of a work completed in 1902. Two of its five movements were based on organ music written by Ives to be played in church and the final movement was an adaptation of an earlier symphonic overture entitled *American Woods* in which — according to Ives — 'over a Stephen Foster tune the old farmers fiddled a barn dance with all of its jigs, gallops and reels'. Ives, the son of a military band leader, had been taught music professionally in his youth, but then decided to practise his art only as a passionate sideline. A successful businessman working in insurance, he was able to afford complete independence from the professional and commercial music establishment. He never did anything to promote his work, while musicians or conductors who read his scores argued that they were impossible to perform. The struggle between realities and ideals in his nature led to a physical collapse in 1918, when Ives was forty-four; he spent his remaining thirty-six years in solitude and only sporadically composed small-scale works, mainly songs and quarter-tone piano pieces. He arranged for a few of his compositions to be printed privately, but not until 1927 was any of his music first performed publicly, when the conductor Eugene Goossens chose excerpts from Ives' orchestral pieces at an International Referendum Concert (attended by Darius Milhaud amongst others) in New York's Town Hall. In 1930, the Boston Chamber Orchestra played Ives' *Three Places in New England* under the direction of Nicolas Slonimsky and repeated the work on its subsequent concert tour; Slonimsky also conducted Ives' works in various European cities. It took a long time for the musical world to recognise the importance of this composer. One of his first admirers was Arnold Schoenberg; among the documents he left, his widow found a paper which she sent to Mr and Mrs Ives. It read: 'There is a great man living in this country — a composer. He has solved the problem how to preserve one's inner self and learn. He responds to negligence by contempt. He is not forced to accept praise or blame. His name is Ives' (Cowell, *Charles Ives*, p. 114).

Leonard Bernstein had done much to advance the knowledge of Charles Ives' music among musicians and public. For the first performance of the Second Symphony, he invited the composer to come to New York; Ives had once said that he would bring himself to attend if his Second Symphony were played at New York's Carnegie Hall — he always doubted whether a performance would be proficient enough to satisfy him and whether it would meet a friendly reaction. In the end he declined Bernstein's offer, although it was promised that he could listen to rehearsals whenever he wished and could sit quite alone in the darkened hall. Mrs Ives, however, made the trip to New York and attended the concert together with their daughter and son-in-law, sitting in a box near the stage. It was obvious that the audience was initially somewhat puzzled by the first hearing of this novel kind of music, but the extraordinarily intensive and eloquent reading of conductor and orchestra, Bernstein's complete identification with the expressive work, captivated the audience — the conductor's youth was probably an additional factor — and at the end of the performance there was cheering and clapping for many minutes. Henry Cowell (ibid., p. 135) reports that the warmth and excitement reached Mrs Ives and she said in a heart-breaking tone of pure surprise, 'Why, they like it, don't they?'

Charles Ives himself heard the Bernstein performance on radio shortly after the Carnegie Hall premiere and found it better than he had expected; Henry Cowell (ibid., p. 136) says this seems to have been the only unqualified pleasure in an orchestral performance that Ives ever had. He died before Leonard Bernstein, as the New York Philharmonic's music director, again conducted his Second Symphony.

The case of Ives deserves mention in the attempt to analyse the stages of Leonard Bernstein's development as a practising musician and as a composer. The fate of Charles Ives — the long neglect and late discovery of his musical greatness and originality — is not very different from that of his contemporary Gustav Mahler, another genius who foreshadowed the future of music. In Mahler's case, too, it needed the insight and enthusiasm of Leonard Bernstein to bring about understanding and wider playing of his music. Both these composers felt themselves to be misunderstood: when, in 1949, during one of the few interviews Ives ever gave, Howard Taubman — then music editor of the *New York Times* — pointed out that he was regarded as the composer who had anticipated the innovations of all the famous men of the day, the 75-year-old Ives retorted spontaneously 'That's not my fault' (ibid., p. 136).

Gustav Mahler's symphonies, which opened up a new chapter in musical history, were composed between 1895 and 1910, the same years as Ives was writing his most important works. Arnold Schoenberg was fully aware of Mahler's significance, just as later he recognised Ives' pioneering spirit and greatness. Mahler's symphonies were performed by a few conductors from the 1920s onward on rare occasions; some were recorded after the Second World War. But it was only Bernstein's glowing enthusiasm and personal identification with the music that brought about a veritable Mahler renaissance; in 1967 he recorded all nine symphonies (on fifteen CBS long-playing records) demonstrating the natural affinity — based on a shared Jewish heritage, temperament and a twofold vocation as composer and conductor — between the present-day American and the last symphonist of the European Romantic period. Like Charles Ives and Gustav Mahler, Leonard Bernstein is moved by questions and doubts, by worldly grief and joy; he longs for quiet and solitude in the midst of social turmoil; he ponders on the confrontation of dissonance and consonance, of free chromatic and harmony-bound melody and of asymmetric against symmetric rhythmic dance patterns and must decide on transparent polyphonic structures or compact tone colours. Mahler, in a letter to the conductor Bruno Walter, said that he dreaded 'a confluence' of real life and dreams — this would mean for the artist 'that we would suffer for the laws of the one world in the other'. 'Strangely enough', he wrote in the same letter, 'when I listen to music — during my conducting as well — I hear certain answers to my questions, and I am quite clear and sure. Or rather, I feel that these questions are no questions at all.' Ives says, in his *Essays before a Sonata* (1919); 'The nearer we get to the mere expression of emotion, the further we get away from art . . . . Should not the intellect have some part?' And Arnold Schoenberg demands the right proportion of heart and brain for a genuine work of art. Charles Ives has other pointed comments in *Essays before a Sonata*, such as: 'Even vagueness may be, at times, an indication of truth' and: 'Dissonances are becoming beautiful'.

For American music, Charles Ives' theory and practice of incorporating 'local colour' in a musical work took on a quite special importance. Like Mahler, Ives longed for the naive in art, and in many of his works used church tunes or folklore or created his own themes echoing traditional music: 'If local colour, national colour, any colour, is a true pigment of the universal colour, it is a divine quality. And it is a part of substance in art, not of manner'. In this context, Bernstein is seen to follow older composers in only a limited way. The tunes of Indians and Negroes were not heard or noted by composers in these people's original reserves; Indians and Negroes living in great cities lose their cultural heritage rather quickly. Leonard Bernstein regards jazz as the real folk music of America; it is the result of a genuine amalgamation of American negro music and European music after the first World War. Folklore and local colour play only partly a role in his own music — apart from the Hebrew liturgical psalmody, which sometimes finds echoes even in compositions that have no real Jewish thematic connection, and resemblances to folk-dance tunes and rhythms in some of his theatre works.

Not only did Gustav Mahler and Charles Ives influence Bernstein's development as a composer, but also other American composers whose works were included in his programmes, first and foremost among them Randall Thompson and Virgil Thomson. Some composers introduced into his New York concerts with first performances of their works were Edgar Varèse (1885–1965), Wallingford Riegger (1885–1961), John J. Becker (1886–1961) — who became known for his experiments in new combinations of music, dance, and dramatic action — Carl Ruggles (1876–1971), Aaron Copland (born 1900) — a personal friend, whose musical language was of special impact on Bernstein's work — Walter Piston (1894–1976), Roy Harris (1898–1979) — whose masterly Third Symphony Bernstein often performed — Roger Sessions (1896–1985) and one of the youngest American composers at that time, Ned Rorem (born 1923), whose Third Symphony he premièred in 1959.

During Bernstein's first season with the New York Philharmonic (1958/9) he also gave the first performances of works by two still younger composers: *Elegy* by Kenneth Gaburo (born 1927) and *The Titans*, a symphony by William Joseph Russo (born 1928), a jazz musician commissioned to write the work by the Koussevitzky Foundation at the request of Leonard Bernstein. In later years, American compositions given included *Connotations for Orchestra* and *Inscape* by Aaron Copland, symphonies and a violin concerto by David Diamond (born 1915), four works by William Schuman (1910), a piano concerto by Ben Weber (1916–79), *Relata II* by Milton Babbitt (born 1916), Concerto for Orchestra by Elliott Carter (born 1908), *Hymn and Fuguing Tune* No. 16 by Henry Cowell (1897–1965), the biographer of Charles Ives (this work was performed a year after the composer's death), and a work produced by the two composers Otto Luening and Vladimir Ussachevsky, *Concerted Piece for Tape Recorder and Orchestra* (1960). In 1967, Bernstein conducted the world premières of *Triplum* by Gunther Schuller (born 1925) and *Phorion* by Lukas Foss. He had already, in 1960, premièred the latter's *Introductions and Goodbyes* and *Time Cycle* at the Philharmonic. Foss, born in Berlin in 1922, had come to America in 1937 via Paris. Like Bernstein he was a pianist, composer and conductor, and the two had been fellow-students at the Curtis Institute and worked with Koussevitzky at Tanglewood. Foss became one of Bernstein's closest friends and a frequent piano soloist in his concerts and recordings.

The list of names and compositions appearing in the New York Philharmonic's concerts under Leonard Bernstein's direction reads like a compendium of American musical history — in all its different tendencies and styles of composition. Only one single curious figure in the history of American symphonic music seems to be missing, the composer of a *Lincoln Symphony*, a *Centennial Overture*, celebrating the one hundredth anniversary of American independence, and of some operas. This was Silas Gamaliel Pratt (1846–1916) who even conducted his symphonic works in Berlin and London; in Bayreuth he met Liszt and Wagner and is reported to have said to Wagner (in 1875, when Pratt was not yet thirty!) 'Herr Wagner, you are the Silas G. Pratt of Europe!'

The 'kindergarten' phase of American music, the Boston Group, the innovators in the first half of the twentieth century and the young composers were all represented by characteristic works in Bernstein's concerts. Among the composers of the second half of the century, many of them influenced by Edgar Varèse and Charles Ives, who were less concerned with the problems of how to create music reflecting the American spirit than with looking for links with universal movements seeking new means and styles of expression as developed in Western Europe, only a few have written concert music for orchestra; their work thus lies somewhat outside the scope of Leonard Bernstein's search for new American music for the Philharmonic — such as music by John Cage (born 1912) or his students and friends such as Morton Feldman (1926), Christian Wolff (1934), and some other younger musicians who have experimented with new combinations of sound effects and playing, unusual groupings of instruments, the production of sounds basically alien to instruments and trying out all kinds of percussive contrivances. These composers contribute a great deal to the colourful kaleidoscope of the American continent, and to music throughout the world, and exert their influence on musicians of their own and a still younger generation. Leonard Bernstein has studied their music thoroughly and with great interest, but his own music has not been affected by such experiments.

Leonard with his father Samuel and sister Shirley in Israel, May 1947

2

Leonard Bernstein — Youth, Education, Development and Progress

My son a *klesmer* — a sort of wandering minstrel little
better than a beggar? Never!
Samuel Bernstein

I suppose I could have made a passable good rabbi.
However, there was no question of it, because music
was the only thing that consumed me.
Leonard Bernstein

There were no artists or musicians in the Bernstein family or among
the Resnicks, Leonard's ancestors on his mother's side, before Leonard
was born in 1918; yet both his sister Shirley and his brother Burton
have artistic leanings and talents. Burton, younger than Leonard by
thirteen years, has written interesting and successful novels and biogra-
phies; in his book *Family Matters. Sam, Jennie, and the Kids* (New York,
1982) he has vividly narrated the story of his family, including many
facts and hitherto unknown details from the life of his famous brother.

The Bernsteins had lived in the Russian province of Volhynia, where
Jews were segregated by the authorities within a small zone and
suffered severe restrictions. Family tradition has it that they settled
there in the early nineteenth century and their name may have derived
either from amber (*Bernstein*) merchants or from the little town of
Beresdiv where they lived. It is also possible that there once existed a
place named Bernstein; there is an Austrian city of Bernstein in the
Burgenland (which made Leonard an honorary citizen on the occasion
of his visit there). Earlier forebears had been rabbis and biblical
scholars, but Leonard's great-grandfather (born about 1840) was a
blacksmith, the subject of numerous legends, who perished in his

[19]

thirties when fire broke out in his workshop. The blacksmith, Bezalel Bernstein, had not followed the family rabbinical tradition but his son Yudel took it upon himself to restore the reputation of the Bernsteins as teachers and scholars and became an ultra-orthodox rabbi. At the time of his father's tragic death he was twelve; he remained with his impoverished mother in Beresdiv, while his brothers went to live with relatives elsewhere. Yudel married Dinah Malamud from the nearby city of Koretz; her brothers Herschel and Shlomoh were to play an important role in the life of couple's eldest son, Shmuel Yosef, born on 5 January 1892.

Shmuel Yosef grew up in the narrow world of the ghetto at a time when antisemitism had reached a dangerous pitch in the neighbouring Russian towns and villages, and the Jews of the *shtetl* were subject to many murderous attacks. Shmuel Yosef wanted to become a rabbi like his ancestors and many of his nearest relatives, but he was also plagued by tormenting doubt. When he was just eleven years old, he learned that Herschel, his mother's youngest brother, had escaped conscription by a daring flight from the country — the despised Jews were good enough as soldiers for the Tsar and many Jews risked their lives by illegally leaving their homeland, rather than serve in the Russian army. In a letter to the family, Herschel reported that he had found work as apprentice in a barber shop in the United States and had earned some dollars. This letter made young Shmuel Yosef yearn to escape the narrowness of the *shtetl* and try to find an existence in the world outside. When his uncle Herschel sent him some money from Hartford, Connecticut, some years later, he at once made up his mind and set out on an adventurous and daring journey to the coast in the hope of finding a ship to America. This was in 1908, Shmuel was just sixteen years old, and on a hard, tiring march on foot, only occasionally relieved by hitch-hiking a ride, he got to Danzig. From there he sailed to Liverpool where he found a place on a ship full of emigrants to America. Uncle Herschel was waiting for him at New York harbour and assisted him with the immigration formalities; Shmuel Yosef became Samuel Joseph. Herschel Malamud had already changed his name and was now Harry Levy.

Uncle Herschel now had a barber's shop of his own, but as he could not yet afford to employ an apprentice or assistant, Samuel — called Sam for short — had to look for work elsewhere. Like thousands of other poor immigrants he began cleaning fish for twelve hours a day six days a week. The two years of dirty and frustrating work in New York's fish market he later called his 'university years'. But then his uncle's shop began to prosper and Sam was able to join him and learn the trade. One day a travelling salesman came to the shop and, watching Sam busily cleaning and putting things in order, was so impressed with the industrious young man that he invited him to come to Boston to work in a business providing barber shops with cosmetics of all kinds. Sam accepted the offer and thus started on a commercial career in which he became so successful that he could found a company of his own, the Samuel Bernstein Hair Company. He was a hard worker and it was his fervent wish that he would one day have children to continue his life's work and develop the flourishing company still further.

On 28 October 1917 Samuel Bernstein married Jennie (originally Charna) Resnick, born 1898 in Schepetovka (not far from the Bernsteins' town of Beresdiv), who had lived in America since she was seven. She had reached the USA on no less an adventurous journey than Sam, but she came with her family. Jennie's family were also religious Jews, though less inclined towards rabbinical mysticism and hassidism than were the Bernsteins. Her ancestors were craftsmen; the father was a smith and famous as a fascinating story-teller. Young Jennie led a rather miserable life as a factory-worker and had only enough free time to attend evening school to learn English and acquire some general knowledge. The family lived at Lawrence, some twenty-five miles north of Boston, and there Sam met her in 1916, while on a trip with a friend. After the wedding in Lawrence, Sam took his young wife with him to Boston, but when she was expecting her first child she wished to be with her family. Leonard was born at Lawrence on Sunday, 25 August 1918. On 3 October 1923 there followed Shirley Anne, and Burton was born on 31 January 1932 — both in Boston.

The firstborn of Samuel and Jennie Bernstein was originally named Louis after Jennie's grandfather, and this remained his legal name until he was sixteen and had it changed to Leonard. At home he had always been called Leonard or Lenny. His brother, Burton, whose family chronicle we have followed, is unable to explain this. Louis/Leonard was a weakly child, plagued by asthma attacks and hay fever, who often had to be taken to the doctors and given injections. In addition he suffered from the continual change of apartments within the Boston area, as well as from the lack of harmony he felt between his parents. Leonard was shy and had little contact with children of his own age, especially because the family frequently moved from place to place. He was happiest when left alone at home; he felt safe and protected there. He did not take part in games or sport with other children, who often teased him. The parents were extremely worried about all this, but they felt somehow that there was something special in him. For in spite of his physical handicap and weakness he was always the best in school and was full of original ideas. When he was ten years old he became interested through his history lessons in the constitution of ancient Rome. Together with a classmate he invented a country called Rybernia (the name was made up from his own surname and that of his friend Eddie Ryack). The two boys appointed themselves consuls of this land and conversed in their own concocted Rybernian language, intelligible only to the 'citizens' of that country. Other children could apply for citizenship in Rybernia and learn the language. To this day, among themselves the three Bernsteins, Leonard, Shirley and Burton, have fun with this language, which nobody else can understand.

In Leonard Bernstein's life there have been many coincidences, important events that decisively influenced his development and career. The first such event was the almost simultaneous invention of the imaginary land of Rybernia — a 'country' where he did not feel lonely — and the discovery of music as a power to save him from his youthful anxieties. At the age of eight, he had been moved to tears on hearing organ music and choral singing in the local synagogue; whenever the family visited relatives or friends who had a piano, he always tried to steal away from the party and put together sounds and melodies at the piano. One day the ten-year-old Lenny came home from religious school and to his great astonishment and delight saw a piano standing in the living room; there had never before been a musical instrument in the Bernstein's apartment. Samuel Bernstein's sister Clara, who had been living in the neighbourhood, had moved to New York, and as she never really played herself had decided to leave the piano with her brother Sam. She knew that Sam's eldest boy loved music but could not possibly foresee what a turning point the appearance of a piano in the Bernstein household would mean for Lenny. The boy felt this himself immediately; in one of our talks Leonard Bernstein described to me the impact of his discovery of music:

I was unhappy until I discovered music at the age of ten. Because I was a very sickly boy, I was small and pale, weak and always had some bronchitis or something and when I was ten years old this thing happened with Aunt Clara and the piano. And suddenly I found my world; I became very strong inside and strangely enough around the same period I grew up very tall and I became athletic and was very strong, and I won medals and cups for diving. It all happened together and that changed my life. Because you see the secret of it is I found a universe where I was secure, where I was safe — that's music. And I was at home and nobody could touch me. My father couldn't hurt me, nobody could hurt me when I was in my world of music, sitting at that piano. There I was protected, I was at home. This was my *Sicherheit*.

[22]

Leonard soon started to improvise at the piano and to arrange for himself a system of harmonies. Whenever he had a free moment, he sat at the piano. 'My father worried. He loved me. He wanted the best for me. He wanted me to have a life of security either to become a rabbi or a businessman — to take his business over. But not a musician. Because a musician means to be a *klesmer* — and he did not want me to be a beggar.' And his mother? 'My mother was very sympathetic but she did not have much to say in the family. She used to listen and cry. She loved to listen when I played. But my father was the boss.' Sam Bernstein believed that the piano-playing only diverted Lenny from his homework for school and he would interrupt him when he thought his son had played long enough. Once the family was awakened late at night by the sound of the piano. His father stormed into the room and shouted, 'Lenny, don't you know what time it is? It's two o'clock. What in heaven's name are you doing?' Lenny answered firmly, 'I have to do this. The sounds are in my head and I have to get them out!' (David Ewen, *Leonard Bernstein*, 1967, p. 20).

It was only natural that Lenny soon asked if he could have piano lessons. A neighbour, Frieda Karp, was prepared to teach him for one dollar a lesson and father Samuel did not object. The teacher came to the Bernsteins once a week. For a year Lenny was satisfied with his progress but after that became unhappy with her method of teaching. He went by himself to the New England Conservatory of Music and asked whether he could be recommended a good piano teacher. He was given the name of Miss Susan Williams. But when Leonard told his father that he would like to study with another teacher, who was asking three dollars for a lesson, Samuel became furious — not so much because of the money but because he feared that lessons with a really professional teacher would endear music to Lenny even more and so increasingly estrange him from the family business. Although his mother tried to support her son's request, his father was determined not to pay three dollars under any circumstances. Lenny, however, was not so easily defeated: he found it possible to earn the necessary money by occasionally playing in bands and by teaching what he was learning to children of his own age or younger. For two years he financed his piano lessons with Miss Williams in this way and made good progress.

In time his father learned to bear with his son's piano playing but still did not give up hope that one day he would get tired of it and win interest in the business. He even took Leonard, now aged fourteen, to a concert — the first that Samuel Bernstein himself had ever attended. The Boston Pops Orchestra left an unforgettable impression on both father and son; they particularly enjoyed Maurice Ravel's *Boléro*. Soon afterwards Samuel and Leonard went to a piano recital by Sergei Rachmaninov; for Leonard the great experience of the evening was his first acquaintance with a late Beethoven sonata, music that remained a closed book to father Sam.

At this time Leonard, together with a music-loving friend, believed that he should continue his studies under a really eminent pedagogue, first asking the German-born Heinrich Gebhard, the best piano teacher in Boston, to invite the boy for an audition. They knew that for an audition Gebhard demanded a fee of twenty-five dollars and fifteen dollars for a lesson — at that time these were astronomical amounts of money. However, it was arranged that Gebhard should receive 14-year-old Leonard for an audition. Gebhard recognised his great talent but found that he had little command of basic piano technique. He suggested that Leonard should study with one of his young assistants; this made things easier for Leonard, since the fee would be only six dollars a lesson. So began a musical association, both friendly and professional, with Helen Coates, first as Bernstein's piano teacher and since 1944 his knowledgeable, capable and faithful secretary who has for many years organised his professional schedules and helped him in his manifold activities.

After four years of study with Helen Coates, Leonard was ready for Heinrich Gebhard and the commitment to a career as a professional musician. His father was still unhappy about this development, while his mother liked to accompany him to Boston Symphony Orchestra concerts. Samuel Bernstein was glad when his son played lighter music from time to time, especially when he entertained at public functions and earned applause. However he was still convinced that piano-playing was no proper work and could not possibly be the ultimate aim in life for the son of Samuel Bernstein; he was certain that Leonard would fail utterly if he chose music as his profession. He tried once again to interest Lenny in his flourishing business and to his great delight found his son ready to work there for six weeks one summer. However Lenny says that the work was 'horrible' and he had no desire to continue further.

Sam Bernstein was a warm-hearted father, anxious to provide independence and security for his children's future. He had inherited from his forebears high moral and religious standards, accompanied by a great esteem for learning and knowledge. In his early American years he had experienced poverty and a life of drudgery; he had seen dirt and filth, distress and misery. His own diligence, sense of duty and skill had made him a successful and well-to-do businessman; dexterity and luck had even helped him to survive the years of depression, which had not harmed his business at all. Now he had three well-educated and talented children — and was none of them to continue his life-work and take over his company? He could not accept this thought and felt desperately unhappy. After his son Leonard had become world-famous and mention was made of the difficulties which his father had tried to put in his way, Sam was quoted as saying: 'How could I know that my son Leonard Bernstein would one day become *the* Leonard Bernstein?'

There was an opportunity to get to know Samuel Bernstein when, with his children Leonard and Shirley, he visited Jewish Palestine in 1947. Leonard then for the first time conducted the Palestine Orchestra, later to become the Israel Philharmonic Orchestra. Samuel's warmth of feeling, his enthusiasm and also his good-hearted humour quickly earned him friends: one of the high points of his stay in the country was a speech in which he addressed the members of an agricultural settlement in the Jesreel Valley. Among the numerous settlers in the kibbutz were many immigrants from Samuel's former homeland, with whom he could talk in Russian and Yiddish. He gave his short address in Yiddish, already tinged with an American accent, and won all hearts. And when Lenny spoke, interspersing his English with some words and phrases in Hebrew, the assembly recognised that the great artist they had admired that evening was also a friend sharing their own ways of thought.

In 1935, aged sixteen, Leonard Bernstein graduated from Boston Latin School. His pursuit of music had not affected his general education, as was shown by his excellent marks. Samuel was proud of his son and happy to see him playing the piano as soloist with the school orchestra. Lenny had also composed the melody of a school hymn, with words written by himself and Lawrence F. Ebb. His good school record meant that he could continue his studies at university. Before this he had undergone a further decisive experience, listening to the radio relay of a concert by the Boston Symphony Orchestra conducted by Sergei Koussevitzky. The programme included Sergei Prokofiev's *Symphonie classique* and Igor Stravinsky's *Sacre du Printemps*. This made him 'suddenly discover that music had a future': one outcome of this 'discovery' was his attempt to write himself a sonatina for piano in 'this modern musical language'.

It was impossible to halt Leonard Bernstein in his pursuit of music and even in his teens he showed an extraordinarily varied and manifold artistic talent. At the age of fourteen he organised a performance of Bizet's *Carmen* at the Bernsteins' summer house at Sharon, by a lake south of Boston. In this performance, the men and boys — all neighbours — sang the women's parts, while the girls took the male roles. A

[25]

schoolmate, already sporting a beard, was Micaëla and Lenny himself sang Carmen; a girl of whom he was fond, Beatrice Gordon, acted and sang Don José and another posed as Escamillo. When Lenny was on stage as Carmen a young girl played the piano; otherwise he accompanied the singing himself. Nine-year-old Shirley recited a prologue written by her elder brother. Stage, costumes and actors had great success in the small community and two summers later Lenny staged there the Gilbert and Sullivan operetta *The Mikado* — however this time the sexes were not 'exchanged'. Again Lenny acted and sang a main role, Nanki-Poo, and Shirley, now almost twelve, was brilliant as Yum-Yum. This show too was enthusiastically received and the following year another Gilbert and Sullivan piece was chosen, this time *H.M.S. Pinafore*. For this performance Leonard choreographed a special ballet, inventing a dance sequence to the ballet music from Verdi's *Aida*, with Shirley and a pair of twins of the same age appearing as 'Egyptian belly-dancers'. The experience gained by the young producer, director and conductor in these amateur entertainments helped him greatly when he later produced a performance of Gilbert and Sullivan's *The Pirates of Penzance* at a summer camp. On this occasion he met for the first time a young lad from the Bronx, Adolph Green, who played the Pirate King. The two became close friends and Green was later to collaborate with Leonard in the texts of the musicals *On the Town* and *Wonderful Town*.

Samuel Bernstein could not help being amused by his son's productions, though they were not in keeping with his puritan spirit; he did not like to see 'artist types' in his house. Leonard himself has always preserved a certain bourgeois disposition and has inherited from his father a serious approach to all things in life and art; he has often said that there is 'something of a rabbi' in him. Is it true, we asked him, as his many friends and contemporaries maintain time and again, that there is still some puritanism in his thinking and philosophy of life? 'Well, the puritan morality comes from a combination of this talmudic father of mine and the city of Boston where I grew up, you can imagine, the home of puritanism is Boston, Massachusetts, so I had this double influence. I suppose I could have made a passable good rabbi. However, there was no question of it, because music was the only thing that consumed me.'

Having graduated from school with high marks, Lenny was accepted at seventeen as a student at Harvard University in Cambridge, Massachusetts. His father was pleased that his son would at last embark on serious studies. Apart from music, Leonard's main interests lay with philosophy and aesthetics, literary history, philology and linguistics.

[26]

Returning to Harvard in 1973, almost thirty-five years after gradua-
tion, to deliver his Charles Eliot Norton Lectures, he told the students
of his first experience in scientific study and understanding: he recognised that the important matter for him then — and for his entire life —
was the opening of the mind to the validity of interdisciplinary learning; the best way to understand a problem was the recognition of its
relationship to other spheres of knowledge. 'The principal thing I
absorbed', he wrote in 1973, 'was a sense of interdisciplinary values —
that the best way to *know* a thing is in the context of another discipline'
(*The Unanswered Question*, p. 5).

One of his early papers for a class in aesthetics was concerned with
Aaron Copland's *Variations for Piano* (1930), a work that he had heard
in 1937 for the first time and fell in love with: 'It seemed so fierce and
prophetic, and utterly new' (ibid., p. 3). Copland's piece also introduced him to the world of a composer whom he met on 14 November
1937 — Copland's thirty-seventh birthday — and with whom he
developed a close musical and personal friendship. Bernstein was also
very much influenced in his music by the style and expression of the
older composer's work.

Leonard Bernstein's teacher in composition at Harvard was Walter
Piston, the American composer (1894–1976), himself a former Harvard graduate who had studied with Nadia Boulanger in Paris; he was
among the most prominent composers and teachers of his generation
and his textbooks on harmony (1941) and counterpoint (1947) are still
used by students of composition, since they provide the foundations of
a sound training in musical theory. *The Incredible Flautist*, one of Piston's
best-known works (composed in 1938) was performed under Leonard
Bernstein's direction on many occasions; in June 1948 we heard him
conduct Piston's *Sinfonietta* as part of the concerts given at the
Amsterdam-Scheveningen Festival of the International Society for
Contemporary Music.

Apart from taking his Harvard studies very seriously, Leonard was
engaged in many side activities. He wrote music reviews for the university journal *The Advocate*, where his first published article was a review
of a concert of the Boston Symphony Orchestra conducted by Sergei
Koussevitzky: the same orchestra that had so greatly impressed the
sixteen-year-old over the radio and with the conductor who was to
become Bernstein's greatest mentor, friend and adviser. In April 1939
Leonard made his debut as a conductor. He conducted the incidental
music he had composed for a performance in Greek of Aristophanes'
comedy *The Birds*; some passages with jazz rhythms he later used in his
first musical, *On the Town*. A month later he conducted from the piano a

performance of Marc Blitzstein's political-satirical portrait of the American depression, *The Cradle will Rock*, having persuaded his sister Shirley to appear in one of the roles. Blitzstein attended the performance and a friendship quickly developed between the two musicians. At the Harvard Music Club, Leonard often entertained professors and students alike; when Sergei Eisenstein's film *The Battleship Potemkin* was screened, he accompanied it on the piano with music by Copland and Stravinsky and improvisations on Russian folk songs.

The year 1937 — the penultimate year of study — was a memorable one for Leonard Bernstein: not only did it mark the beginning of his friendship with Aaron Copland, but also an encounter that was to be the most decisive for his future life. The great conductor Dimitri Mitropoulos came to Boston as guest conductor of the Boston Symphony and the Harvard Helicon Society arranged a tea-party for him. Leonard was among the invited guests. He had almost forgotten the invitation, but at last arrived with his mother who had at first planned to drive him home. The young man was introduced to the famous maestro, who had already heard from other guests that there was a promising music student at Harvard whom he should, if possible, meet. Asked by Mitropoulos to play for him, without hesitation Leonard sat down and performed a Chopin nocturne and part of his own piano sonata. Mitropoulos at once invited him to attend his orchestral rehearsals, which proved an exciting experience. Leonard was asked to lunch by Mitropoulos, who called him 'genius boy' and encouraged him to study conducting seriously. The performances of the Boston Symphony Orchestra under Mitropoulos impressed Leonard profoundly and he especially admired his interpretation of Robert Schumann's Second Symphony and the way in which Mitropoulos directed a piano concerto as soloist from the piano. The Schumann symphony has since then been among Leonard Bernstein's favourite works and he often conducts it. Moreover, from the beginning of his career he has played piano concertos, above all those of Mozart, Beethoven, Ravel and George Gershwin, directing them from the keyboard.

In June 1939, Leonard Bernstein graduated from Harvard *cum laude*. His father made a last attempt to win him over to the family business. He allowed his son to go to New York for one summer, convinced that in the big city Leonard would see how difficult and how insecure the life of a musician would prove, while a leading position in the Samuel Bernstein Hair Company would guarantee him security for his entire life. Sam gave Lenny only a small amount of money and expected that he would soon return home. Lenny looked for a cheap room in New York and found one in Greenwich Village. There he met Adolph Green again, working in a night club cabaret, writing satirical songs in collaboration with Betty Comden, later to work with him on Bernstein's musicals *On the Town* and *Wonderful Town*. The two engaged Lenny as piano accompanist at the club and he earned a few dollars there. The rules of the Musicians' Union did not, however, allow him to take on regular work and he was forced to return to Boston when he ran out of money. But he had used his time in New York well from a professional point of view. He heard many interesting concerts, he met Aaron Copland regularly, and had frequent meetings with actors, artists and musicians.

Hardly was Leonard back in Boston when he learned that Mitropoulos, who was in New York, was about to leave for Europe. Two years had passed since he had met the maestro in Boston. To see him now seemed to Lenny his very last hope. Borrowing some money, he took the first possible train to New York, where Mitropoulos received him in a very friendly manner, showed great understanding for his problems and firmly endorsed his desire to devote his life entirely to music. He suggested to him that he should study music seriously at the Curtis Institute of Music in Philadelphia and asked Fritz Reiner, chief conductor of the Pittsburgh Symphony Orchestra, to give Bernstein an audition. Reiner asked him to play Brahms' Academic Festival Overture at the piano from the full orchestra score and was so impressed by the ability of the young musician, who had never seen the score or heard the work before, that he immediately agreed to take him as a student at the Curtis Institute.

Leonard Bernstein studied there for two years. Fritz Reiner instructed him in conducting, Isabelle Vengerova was his demanding piano teacher, Renée Longy Miquelle taught score reading and Randall Thompson, the composer and director of the Curtis Institute, introduced him to the fundamentals of orchestration. At first, Bernstein did not feel at all comfortable there. He remembers:

When I first came there, the atmosphere around me was bad. This was because I was there the only college graduate. Everybody at the Curtis Institute had come into the school eight years old, with short pants, playing very fast, and the thing was to be playing faster than anybody else, Paganini Etudes or Chopin Etudes or what else. I didn't have anybody to talk to. They hated me because they thought I was a snob, I was a Harvard graduate, an intellectual. My only friends there were people at the faculty, Fritz Reiner, Randall Thompson, Renée Longy — my very dear friend, who taught *solfège* and score reading — these were my friends. But after six months or so, it was okay, and I made friends with the students.

[29]

Nevertheless, a mentally deranged Curtis student was once found carrying a pistol, intending to shoot Leonard Bernstein, Thompson and Reiner. He was, of course, immediately required to leave the school. It did not take long for the students to come to terms with Lenny, to appreciate his talents and the brilliance of his mind, and even to begin admiring him.

In his very first term at the Curtis Institute, Leonard Bernstein was assigned a major task. For the first time, he was to conduct a real symphony orchestra and the work chosen was a contemporary composition so far unknown to him. Moreover, it was the Second Symphony of his tutor and director of the Institute, Randall Thompson, with whom he had become very friendly. True, Fritz Reiner had once asked him to try and conduct one movement from a Brahms symphony, but this had been in class. Leonard prepared himself thoroughly for Thompson's Second Symphony, but when the day came suffered stage fright; yet the performance went so smoothly and was so successful that he felt it was 'the most natural thing in the world' to stand on a podium and conduct an orchestra.

The 20-year-old Leonard commanded a good professional piano technique and became even more proficient while studying with Isabelle Vengerova. He had tried his hand at composition and received acclaim from friends and musicians when he played them his first piano pieces. Fritz Reiner was satisfied with the success of his performance of Randall Thompson's symphony. Music must remain his vocation and the centre of his life. How should he continue? Which paths could he possibly pursue? He entered various competitions that seemed to hold out the chance of progress or possible engagements, but without success.

Considering the present fashion for competitions of all kinds and the attraction for artists in trying to win prizes for singing, piano playing, conducting or composing, because managers wish to engage prize winners, it is ironical to contemplate the career and standing of some of today's greatest creative and performing artists who either never took part in international competitions, or were never considered worthy of a medal or prize. Leonard Bernstein never won an award in any competition, apart from one single instance: he 'won' a weekend at Tanglewood — as a second prize — where he was going in any case as a student conductor, together with the right to conduct the Boston Pops Orchestra in a performance of Richard Wagner's prelude to *Die Meistersinger*. As a composer, he failed to win a prize when, after copying for many days and nights, he managed to deliver the score of a symphonic work for a competition at the New England Conservatory of

Music in Boston, just a few minutes before the deadline: this was his 'Jeremiah' Symphony.

Leonard Bernstein came to Tanglewood in the summer of 1940 during the vacation after the first year at the Curtis Institute. Dimitri Mitropoulos and Fritz Reiner had warmly recommended him to Sergei Koussevitzky, the great conductor and patron, promoter of contemporary composers and young musicians, who had decided to establish a summer music school in connection with the Berkshire Symphony Festival. This Festival had come into being in 1934 on the initiative of the composer and conductor Henry Hadley (Kimball), born 1871, of the second generation of New England composers; he organised the first summer festival in the Berkshires at Stockbridge, Massachusetts. The following year, Sergei Koussevitzky began his series of summer concerts in the green and hilly scenery of Tanglewood, where he also built his summer residence, calling it Seranak after the names Sergei and Natalia, his first wife. Flanking a stretch of green lawn, two shell-shaped, open concert auditoria were erected, one large and holding about six thousand people, the other more intimate and used for the performance of choral works and chamber music. Tanglewood became the summer home of the Boston Symphony Orchestra; Koussevitzky conducted concerts for a few weeks each summer from 1935 to 1940. He then enlarged the scope of the festival by adding the summer school for young performing artists and talented young composers. The musicians chosen could study for six weeks with great composers and eminent teachers, and had a chance to conduct student orchestra groups and choirs and to hear their own compositions performed. Koussevitzky opened the Berkshire Music Center on 8 July 1940; he was organiser and director, Aaron Copland vice-director. In later years, he invited as teachers the composers Paul Hindemith, Arthur Honegger, Olivier Messiaen and Darius Milhaud; he gave a master class in conducting and invited three young and aspiring conductors to work with the students' orchestra. It was not difficult for Leonard Bernstein to be accepted for one of these posts as he brought with him recommendations from Mitropoulos and Fritz Reiner. Between Koussevitzky and Leonard, then not yet twenty-two, there soon developed a close friendship; the older man liked the temperament and verve of Lenyushka, as he was soon calling him, and recognised his versatile music talents. Soon after the beginning of the concert weeks, Bernstein was allowed to conduct the work he had been assigned as his first conducting task at the Curtis Institute, the Second Symphony of Randall Thompson. He prepared himself meticulously in private lessons and rehearsals with the orchestra and achieved a resounding success.

[31]

Leonard Bernstein spent the summers of 1940 and 1941 at Tanglewood as student conductor; he had finished his studies at Curtis before the summer of 1941. In 1942 Koussevitzky appointed him as his assistant and he then began teaching. The six or seven weeks of the Berkshire Music Festival were so organised that three weeks were devoted exclusively to tuition in various departments — conducting, chamber music, choir, ensemble playing, composition and opera; during the remaining weeks, classes went on but there were festival concerts for which music-lovers came to Tanglewood from near and far, especially at weekends.

In the winter of 1941/2 Bernstein lived in New York and tried to settle down there as a piano teacher. But the times were not favourable for that profession; with the Japanese attack on Pearl Harbor, war came to America. Because of this, the summer of 1942 saw the suspension of the Tanglewood Festival, and it was not restarted until after the end of the Second World War. Leonard had no choice but to look for a regularly paid job. He had meanwhile composed a sonata for clarinet and piano and begun to write a vocal piece based on the original Hebrew text of a passage from the *Lamentations of Jeremiah* — a composition that later became the final movement of his 'Jeremiah' Symphony (his First Symphony), the work that failed to win a prize in the composers' competition of the New England Conservatory.

Leonard finally found a job with the music publishing company of Harms Inc. He was engaged to prepare and edit piano arrangements for printing and he managed to get some tunes of his own published; for these he chose the pen-name Lenny Amber, 'amber' being the English for 'Bernstein': the name crops up again much later in Leonard Bernstein's management and publishing organisation, Amberson Enterprises. Otherwise he has remained faithful to his name. His younger brother tells how their father was very much afraid Leonard would turn his back on Judaism because Koussevitzky, like Sam born a Russian Jew, had embraced Christianity, and might exert an influence on Lenny (Burton Bernstein, *Family Matters*, p. 137). Indeed, Koussevitzky did suggest one day that 'Lenyushka' should change his name to Leonard S. Burns (S. for Samuelovich, son of Samuel), but Lenny declined. Curiously enough, some years before, a conductor of German origin named Bernstein had emigrated to America and had changed his name to Byrns because a music impresario had told him 'It is impossible to make a career in America with a name like Bernstein': this was in the 1930s . . . .

Although there was no Tanglewood Festival in 1943 because of the war, 'Lenyushka' visited his friend and mentor Koussevitzky at Seranak and learned there that the newly-elected musical director and chief conductor of the New York Philharmonic Orchestra, Artur Rodzinski, would like to meet him. Rodzinski spent the summer on a farm at nearby Stockbridge. On Leonard's twenty-fifth birthday, 25 August 1943, he went there and, to his great astonishment, was told by Rodzinski that, having heard Leonard conduct the Tanglewood students' orchestra the summer before he was so impressed that he had decided to offer the young man the post of assistant conductor of the New York Philharmonic and that no audition was necessary.

The post was quite well paid, but an assistant conductor only rarely gets the chance to conduct a concert; nevertheless, his name appears on all printed programmes alongside that of the chief conductor. However, Leonard Bernstein had some promising engagements in the near future elsewhere: for January 1944, Fritz Reiner had reserved for him one of his own orchestral concerts in Pittsburgh and promised that the 'Jeremiah' Symphony could be performed as part of this concert. Koussevitzky, who at first glance had not liked this symphony, nevertheless agreed that 'Lenyushka' should conduct the work a few months later in Boston. Moreover, in New York the magnificent singer Jennie Tourel was to present the first performance of a song cycle by Leonard Bernstein, with the composer accompanying her at the piano, at her début in the city's Town Hall.

Jennie Tourel and Lenny Bernstein had first met at Tanglewood and Jennie once told us how their friendship and musical collaboration actually began. Like Koussevitzky, she was of Russian descent; although she sang excellently in many languages — especially French, English, Italian, German and Hebrew, in addition to Russian — her original accent was noticeable in conversation. On one occasion, Koussevitzky asked her to go to Lenyushka's studio and ask him whether he could accompany her at a public function. Jennie described this first encounter with great gusto:

> I knocked at the door of the studio, went in, and found Lenny sitting at the piano studying a score. He hardly looked up. 'I come to ask you to accompany me in a recital; Koussevitzky wants me to sing with you!' Lenny looked at me somewhat sceptically and I went to the piano to examine the music he had been immersed in. There was the manuscript of songs lying on the piano. 'May I have a look at the songs?', I asked. 'Oh, these are songs you have composed? May I try to sing them?' Lenny parodied my accent mockingly: 'You — ssing my ssongs? Impossible! These arre Amerrrican ssongs — and you with yourr Rrrussian accssent?' Whereupon I grasped the manuscript and started singing. Lenny sat down at the piano and played. I sang one song of the cycle after the other and when we had finished he

jumped up and embraced and kissed me. We have been friends ever since.

Jennie Tourel became Leonard Bernstein's favourite interpreter of his own vocal compositions and as a soloist in his symphony concerts, where she particularly excelled in the solo parts in Gustav Mahler's symphonies. His moving tribute to her on her death in 1973 has been reproduced in the collection of his writings, *Findings* (New York, 1982, pp. 306ff.): 'Wherever she stood to sing', he concluded, 'that stage was the Holy of Holies. And when she opened her mouth in praise of music, she was a High Priestess, and each phrase was the Name of God; and that moment was the Sabbath of Sabbaths . . . Jennie sang God's Name up to the last possible moment'.

The song cycle Jennie had found on the piano was *I Hate Music*, five *Kid Songs*, for which Lenny Bernstein had written words and music in 1943. At Lenox, Massachusetts, a little town not far from Tanglewood, Jennie Tourel sang the first performance of the cycle with Bernstein at the piano on 24 August 1943, the day before the composer's birthday and his portentous meeting with Artur Rodzinski. The important New York premiere was scheduled for 13 November, shortly after Leonard Bernstein had taken up his post as assistant conductor with the New York Philharmonic. Lenny thought his New York debut as pianist and composer so important that he asked his family to come from Boston to be in the audience. Before the concert was due to start, Leonard had a rather exciting visit. Bruno Zirato, member of the New York Philharmonic's managing board, had come to tell him that Bruno Walter, the guest conductor of the forthcoming series of concerts, was suffering from severe influenza in his hotel and might not be able to conduct the Sunday afternoon symphony concert. Under normal circumstances, Artur Rodzinski, the chief conductor, would have stepped in for an ailing colleague, but although he had already been informed of the situation, he was in Stockbridge and so much snow had fallen during the week that he could not possibly reach New York in time. Bernstein must therefore be prepared to conduct the concert if Bruno Walter's health did not improve by Sunday morning.

Leonard Bernstein had to hide his excitement and devote all his attention to the important recital at Town Hall. With Jennie Tourel, he scored extraordinary success as pianist as well as composer: the *Kid Songs* amused and delighted the audience. His parents were more than happy. They returned to their hotel, while Lenny and some friends celebrated the evening with Jennie Tourel in her apartment until early morning. Bruno Zirato, Bruno Walter and the Philharmonic were quite forgotten; in any case Bernstein was not at all afraid of what might happen. He knew the works to be played at the Sunday concert, since among his duties as assistant was to be always in attendance and he had been present at Bruno Walter's orchestral rehearsals.

Early on Sunday morning, Lenny had just gone to bed when he was awakened by the telephone. It was Bruno Zirato, who told him 'Bruno Walter feels miserable. He cannot conduct this afternoon and Artur Rodzinski cannot get to New York'. Leonard Bernstein had to conduct and there was no possibility of arranging an orchestral rehearsal. After a short talk with Bruno Walter in his hotel bed, Leonard Bernstein appeared on the stage of Carnegie Hall and conducted a concert carried by radio networks into American homes all over the country — that night has passed into American musical history. When Bruno Zirato announced that Bruno Walter had regrettably fallen ill, but that 'we are going to witness the debut of a full-fledged conductor who was born, educated, and trained in this country', there was at first some indignant murmuring in the hall and some people actually left. 'Then Lenny came out on stage', his brother remembers. He wore a grey suit and was 'looking much younger and less elegant than the orchestra musicians. He sort of hopped onto the podium'. There was some applause and the concert began.

Bruno Walter's programme was given unchanged: Schumann's *Manfred Overture*, *Theme, Variations and Finale* by Miklós Rósza, an emigrant to the USA from Hungary, *Don Quixote* by Richard Strauss and Wagner's *Meistersinger Prelude*. The applause for Leonard Bernstein grew from one piece to the next and the members of the orchestra joined in the audience's acclaim. 'When the concert ended', remembers Burton Bernstein, 'the house roared like some giant animal in a zoo. It was certainly the loudest human sound I have ever heard — thrilling and eerie' (ibid., pp. 146f.). 'I can hardly hear that story any more: "he substituted for Bruno Walter"', said Lenny some years later when we talked about his first professional appearances. But the story became decisively important for him and his future life. 'It's a good American success story' declared the *New York Times* in an editorial entitled 'A Story Old and Ever New' of 16 November 1943:

> There are many variations of one of the six best stories in the world: the young corporal takes over the platoon when all the officers are down; the captain, with the dead admiral at his side, signals the fleet to go ahead; the young actress, fresh from Corinth or Ashtabula, steps into the star's role; the junior clerk, alone in the office, makes the instantaneous decision that saves the firm from ruin. The adventure of Leonard Bernstein, 25-year-old assistant conductor of the Philharmonic, who blithely mounted the podium at

[35]

THE PHILHARMONIC-SYMPHONY SOCIETY
1842 OF NEW YORK 1878

CONSOLIDATED 1928
ARTUR RODZINSKI, Musical Director

1943   ONE HUNDRED SECOND SEASON   1944

CARNEGIE HALL

SUNDAY AFTERNOON, NOVEMBER 14, 1943, AT 3:00

4025th Concert

Under the Direction of

~~BRUNO WALTER~~

LEONARD BERNSTEIN   Substitute

PROGRAM

SCHUMANN   Overture to "Manfred," Op. 115

MIKLOS ROZSA   Theme, Variations and Finale, Op. 13

INTERMISSION

STRAUSS   "Don Quixote" (Introduction, Theme with Variations and Finale) ; Fantastic Variations on a Theme of Knightly Character, Op. 35
Solo 'Cello: JOSEPH SCHUSTER
Solo Viola: WILLIAM LINCER

WAGNER   Prelude to "Die Meistersinger"

ARTHUR JUDSON, Manager   BRUNO ZIRATO, Associate Manager
THE STEINWAY is the Official Piano of The Philharmonic-Symphony Society
———————— COLUMBIA AND VICTOR RECORDS ————————

ORCHESTRA PENSION FUND—*It is requested that subscribers who are unable to use their tickets kindly return them to the Philharmonic-Symphony Offices, 113 W. 57th St., or to the Box Office, Carnegie Hall, at their choice either to be sold for the benefit of the Orchestra Pension Fund, or given to the uniformed men through the local organizations instituted for this purpose. All tickets received will be acknowledged.*

"Buy War Bonds and Stamps"

The concert programme for 14 November 1943

Carnegie Sunday afternoon when Conductor Bruno Walter became ill, belongs in the list. The corporals and captains must be brave, the young actress beautiful and talented, the clerk quick on his feet. Likewise, Mr. Bernstein had to have something approaching genius to make full use of his opportunity. It's a good American success story. The warm, friendly triumph of it filled Carnegie Hall and spread far over the air waves.

Burton Bernstein recalls that the media, always hungry for sensational news, also carried gossipy items: thus, for instance, the *Boston Post*, under the headline 'Father in Tears at Boy Conductor's Triumph. Boston Merchant Calls Son's Accomplishment "My Contribution to an America That Has Done Everything for Me"', went on to say that 'Papa Bernstein spent over £12,000 for Lennie's [sic] education, but it was worth it' (ibid., p. 150). Did Samuel Bernstein say something like this to a journalist?

Lenny Bernstein's first triumph as conductor in totally unforeseen circumstances was followed by two more unexpected appearances. Two weeks after the historic 14 November, Rodzinski asked him to conduct *Poèmes Juifs* by Ernest Bloch and on 16 December he once more had to deputise, this time for Howard Barlow who had fallen ill. In the spring of 1944 he again conducted the New York Philharmonic and other American orchestras invited him as a guest conductor.

As a composer, Lenny, as he was soon affectionately called by anybody and everybody, had so far appeared only before smaller audiences. In April 1942 his Sonata for Clarinet and Piano had had its first performance in Boston and his amusing song-cycle had been successful at the New York Town Hall the night before his surprise appearance with the Philharmonic. His first large-scale composition, the 'Jeremiah' Symphony, rejected by the Boston Conservatory jury, was premiered on 28 January 1944, with the composer conducting the Pittsburgh Symphony Orchestra and Jennie Tourel singing the mezzo-soprano solo in the final movement. He was now acclaimed by public and press as a conductor as well as a composer of talent and originality; the work was awarded the New York Critics' Circle Award of 1944. Only three months after the première of his first symphony, the musical world was startled by a Bernstein composition of quite a different kind: on 18 April 1944, at the New York Metropolitan Opera House, he conducted the world première of a Jerome Robbins ballet for which he had written the music.

This was *Fancy Free*, composed for the Ballet Theater (now called American Ballet Theater) and, like so many of Lenny Bernstein's successes, its composition stemmed from a lucky coincidence. It is possible to put together the story of how it came about from recollections of Lenny Bernstein himself and of the conductor Antal Dorati, at that time musical director of the Ballet Theater.

'One day', recalls Antal Dorati in a letter he sent me on 8 September 1982, 'Jerome Robbins came to me with the idea of a new ballet about three sailors on shore leave. I liked the story very much and set out to look for a composer to set it to music. Hardly did I have time to think about whom I could commission, when Jerry came back with the news that he had found the composer: young Leonard Bernstein.'

How Jerome Robbins and Bernstein came together, I heard from Lenny himself. He was working at the piano in his studio at Carnegie Hall when there was a knock at the door. It was Oliver Smith who, together with Lucia Chase, had founded the Ballet Theater and was producer and designer for it. He brought with him the choreographer Jerome Robbins, who wished to speak about the plot of a ballet he planned to perform with the Ballet Theater. The two had just met in Central Park and Robbins had mentioned that a composer he had commissioned for the music of his ballet had not written as expected and he did not like the music at all. Oliver Smith then proposed they should see Bernstein, as Carnegie Hall was so near the Park. 'The story of the ballet impressed me immediately', says Lenny, 'and I improvised some themes at the piano. After a few minutes Jerry said spontaneously that I was the composer for him.'

Antal Dorati tells the sequel:

Leonard Bernstein's name was not unfamiliar as the new assistant conductor of the New York Philharmonic. We musicians already had the word that he was a most promising conductor and we also heard that he was composing. Very soon after he gave ample proof of both qualities, but just then all this was, as said, a promise.

As I had not met him yet, I asked Robbins to bring him over to my place for a talk.

Within a few days both appeared at my modest apartment at 108 East 82nd street — N.Y. N.Y. of course — Leonard with some music paper, on which the first scene of the prospective ballet was already sketched.

He played for us on the piano what he wrote, suggestively and brilliantly, and improvised some more of what was to follow. After that 'audition' he had a commission from me and we had a drink to celebrate it.

A few months later *Fancy Free* was composed, staged and performed with the success that is now history. It was — I do not like the word, but there is no better — a hit.

Lenny himself conducted the first performance at the old Metropolitan Opera House in N.Y. and also a good number of subsequent performances there as well as the Boston premiere and more.

His conducting was — as we know it now: as competent as it was breathtaking. His music, as can now be heard on records and I hope also soon in another staged revival, exciting, immediate, and refreshing.

The novelty created great interest, as it emerged. I remember that Rodzinski — Leonard's boss at the Philharmonic — sat in at rehearsals and many of the young music-world of New York were around.

This happened very close to the time, when Leonard's 'Jeremiah' was first heard and when he made his sensational substitution for the ailing Bruno Walter that changed the course of his life — and that of American music history.

And Maestro Dorati adds (1982): 'It is hard to believe that almost forty years have passed since — memories of those days are as fresh as the flowers that grow in my garden now. Here I picked some of them to bind them in a bouquet for his anniversary. I send them with an affectionate, friendly embrace'.

It had nevertheless not been very easy for Leonard Bernstein to complete his ballet score and to synchronise his music in accordance with the demands of the threatre and of Jerome Robbins himself. Before accepting the commission to write the music for *Fancy Free* he had already been engaged to conduct various orchestras in different cities, Jerome Robbins was on tour with the Ballet Theater and Oliver Smith was in Mexico. As soon as various parts of the score were ready, they were sent from one place to the other, music was recorded and played to the producers over the telephone and it took a considerable time before everything was coordinated. However, music and or-chestrations were ready in time for the New York premiere on 18 April 1944.

The warm audience and press reaction that had greeted Leonard Bernstein's 'Jeremiah' Symphony at its Pittsburgh première in January 1944 was still fresh in the memory when, only three months later, the composer surprised the public with so different a score as *Fancy Free*. He had written a sophisticated jazzy work to an original choreographic plot, and the ballet critic of the *New York Times*, John Martin, expressed a general opinion in describing the work as 'a rare little genre master-piece'; Edwin Denby wrote in the *New York Herald Tribune* that *Fancy Free* was 'a perfect American character ballet'. So great was the success of the work that it drew about two hundred full houses during its first year, and was sold out for two weeks at the Hollywood Bowl. The composer conducted a good number of performances himself, whilst at the same time travelling to conduct orchestral concerts in various American cities, sometimes also appearing as piano soloist. Since then he has scarcely ever ceased to live a hectic life — conducting, composing, teaching, lecturing — and only rarely has he taken time off for a real rest, a genuine holiday. On 14 May, only a month after the *Fancy Free* premiere, at a benefit concert in Boston, he gave the first public performance of his set of piano pieces written the previous year and entitled *Seven Anniversaries*, birthday greetings and souvenirs for seven of his closest friends.

In the midst of the eventful year of 1944, Leonard Bernstein was compelled to interrupt his activities to undergo an operation. However, chance that has so often played a major role in his life brought about the creation of a new work. He learned that his friend Adolph Green had also just been brought to the same hospital department and that they could be given adjoining rooms. Thus they could have long talks and exchange ideas. Shortly before this chance meeting, they had thought of turning the plot of *Fancy Free* into a full-scale musical comedy. Bernstein was enthusiastic about the chance to compose a genuine Broadway musical. While in hospital, the two friends discussed the libretto (which Adolph Green was to write with Betty Comden) and the musical style and after their discharge they set to work and soon completed writing the musical. After a preview in Boston two weeks earlier, the New York première of *On the Town* took place on 28 December 1944; George Abbott directed, Oliver Smith and Paul Feigay produced the show and the choreography was by Jerome Robbins; Max Goberman conducted. *On the Town* was immediately successful, with a run of 463 performances.

Interviews, engagements, commissions and letters flooded in on Bernstein, now suddenly famous. The relatively few conducting engagements and commissions that he could actually accept provided him with a considerable yearly income, but secretarial assistance was essential. His former piano teacher Helen Coates, who had meanwhile become a close friend, was ready to move to New York from Boston; she has remained his secretary since 1944. The string of successes as composer and conductor began to overwhelm Bernstein, who at the time of the premiere of *On the Town* was only twenty-six. But even with success and fame mounting from year to year, he remained modest at heart. An early biographer once heard him say, 'I couldn't believe that all this was happening to me. I didn't really believe it was me at all. *Me* — a celebrity!' (David Ewen, *Leonard Bernstein*, London, 1967, p. 83).

In order to have more freedom to move, he gave up his post as associate conductor of the New York Philharmonic after only one year and accepted guest engagements in many American cities. However, he subsequently agreed to become chief conductor of a fairly new orchestra in New York: in 1944 Mayor Fiorello La Guardia and the conductor Leopold Stokowski had founded the New York City Symphony Orchestra and Leonard Bernstein, asked to take it over, was attracted by the possibility of planning programmes to his own liking. He conducted this orchestra for three years in succession and devised interesting series of concerts; in particular, he performed contemporary masterpieces. Stravinsky, Bartók, Alban Berg, Hindemith, Darius Milhaud, Aaron Copland, Carlos Chavez and Mark Blitzstein were among the composers whose works were featured in his programmes. His work with this orchestra also allowed him some spare time as a guest conductor in other American cities.

In the spring of 1946 Leonard Bernstein left America for the first time and went to Europe to conduct concerts in Prague and London. On 15 and 16 May, he participated in the Prague International Music Festival celebrating the fiftieth anniversary of the Czech Philharmonic Orchestra. He was invited there to represent the United States of America; other countries were represented by veteran conductors such as Charles Munch for France and Sir Thomas Beecham for England. Bernstein's first programme opened with William Schuman's *American Festival Overture* and also included *Essay No. 2* by Samuel Barber, the Third Symphony of Roy Harris, *El Salón Mexico* by Copland, and George Gershwin's *Rhapsody in Blue* with Eugene List as solo pianist. In the second concert the symphonic works, but not the Gershwin, were repeated and Bernstein conducted his own 'Jeremiah' Symphony.

In the palm grove at Ein Gev, May 1947

[41]

Leonard Bernstein had hardly returned to New York before setting out again to fulfil engagements in London from mid-June to the first week of July. The month spent in London is still vivid in his memory. 'I had a very hard time there', he told us:

I arrived in the beginning of June. I was to conduct the London Philhar-monic Orchestra. The orchestra was half-demobilised only, the soldiers hadn't come back from army service yet, so it was not very good, and London was in a terrible shape after the war in 1946. There was very little to eat or wear, and it was very difficult to give concerts there because there wasn't a hall — Queen's Hall had been bombed, the new hall hadn't been built yet, the Festival Hall, there was only Albert Hall. The orchestra couldn't play in tune because there were so many substitutes. There were no newspapers to announce the concerts even, often the newspapers had only two pages. It was a very bad situation. And I remember I arrived in London on the first of June; I had left New York in a heat wave, very hot, and when I arrived in London it was freezing, like the North Pole, and it stayed that way for the whole month of June. And in that month I·tried to work with the London Philharmonic, very young kids in the orchestra, and I tried to play American music which they had never heard of, of course, and *Appalachian Spring* was one of the things — it was so difficult to try to teach them these rhythms, and it's not so difficult a piece now because we people play it like a Haydn symphony. But I remember it was so cold and there was nowhere I could buy a scarf or a pair of gloves or a sweater — nothing — because I had left New York with summer clothes, it was so hot, and in England it was so freezing cold for a whole month. This was my first longer time in Europe, I got sick and felt sick all the time. Finally after two weeks I got a sore throat and was really so sick that I thought we had to cancel everything and to hire a substitute (I believe Leinsdorf) to conduct. There was nobody to be able to give me something warm to wear, there wasn't anything, nobody had anything, and the orchestra couldn't help. At last I was in bed with tremendous fever. I was then one of the first people in England to have penicillin which had just been invented. The army got me penicillin. Gloves they couldn't get me but penicillin saved my life, as I was so very very sick in the Hyde Park Hotel. So this was my first attempt to make American music in Europe [i.e. after Prague]; it was a terrible feeling.

Appalachian Spring was the only piece I was allowed to play, to try here. In order to fill the hall they had to have things like the Grieg Concerto with Eileen Joyce, then we got Marjorie Lawrence in a wheelchair to sing the *Liebestod* — that was the only way to get the audiences to come; for *Appalachian Spring* they wouldn't come or whatever else I was playing, Schubert or Schumann etc. It had to be Grieg, *Liebestod*, with these names, because I was unknown, so how would you get public to come with no newspapers to advertise, no announcements. And the orchestra was very bad, so out of tune, I can't tell you how hard I worked, especially on *Appalachian Spring* to try to get this piece learned . . . .

[42]

So far Leonard Bernstein's own recollections. His two concerts took place on 16 and 21 June and research has revealed that there were some newspaper write-ups despite the severe curtailing of space. *The Times* of Monday 17 June carried a short review of the Sunday concert. Headlines in that issue were:

'Austria and Germany to be discussed. Talks on Italian Treaty', at a conference of the British, American, Russian and French Foreign Ministers in Paris; 'Atomic Production for Peace', at Oakridge, Tennessee, USA; 'Trade within Germany — Exchange of Goods between Two Zones'; 'British Soldier Killed in Gaza', in a clash with Arabs; 'Middle East Security — Lord Montgomery's Talks in Jerusalem'; 'B.O.A.C. Record Flight — New York to London in 11 Hours 24 Minutes' — and also 'Opera in English — A New Policy for Covent Garden — Mr. Rankl Appointed Musical Director': this was also the subject of one of the three leaders in the paper.

The Times reviewed the Bernstein concert as follows (anonymously, as was usual at the time):

The Sunday concert of the L.P.O. at the Stoll Theatre was conducted by Mr. Leonard Bernstein of New York.

The first part of the programme consisted of music by composers still alive, the second of operatic music in which Mrs. Marjorie Lawrence, the distinguished dramatic soprano from the Metropolitan, took part. All of it involved a large orchestra, with augmentations up to four each of the wind in addition to four saxhorns for Wagner, which the L.P.O. generously provided for its patrons.

Mr. Bernstein is plainly a Wagnerian conductor by temperament, and it was indeed an exciting experience to hear again after seven years the closing scene of *Götterdämmerung* built up to climax and consummation under his impulsive direction. He gave vivid performances too of Walton's Portsmouth Point' overture, Strauss's 'Till Eulenspiegel', and a work new to us, the ballet, 'Appalachian Spring', by his fellow-countryman and contemporary, Aaron Copland. But like all conductors who scorn the use of a baton he threw away the last degree of tautness and brilliance — this was particularly noticeable in the overture; for however expressive shoulders and hands may be they are not an instrument of precision as a stick is. Orchestras are suggestible and responsive, but they can only give a firm outline to what they play if without looking they can see where they are.

Copland's ballet has a Quaker-grey kind of austere beauty. Its subject is a Puritan dedication of their house by Pennsylvanian pioneers and its themes suggest, without actual quotation, Genevan psalm tunes . . . . [The work] is distinctively American — the America of New England — in the originality and restraint which are alike proper to its source of inspiration.

[43]

At a performance of *Jeremiah*, Israel, 1947

This programme, containing music from *Götterdämmerung*, marked the first time that Wagner's music had been played in Britain since the war against Nazi Germany. After Leonard Bernstein's London debut as a conductor, there immediately followed his first appearance there as a composer: the Ballet Theater had been invited to Covent Garden, where *Fancy Free* was performed, conducted by the composer.

In that same year, 1946, the Berkshire Music Center reopened and the Tanglewood Festival was again held. There, on 6 August, Leonard Bernstein conducted the American première of Benjamin Britten's opera *Peter Grimes*. Commissioned by the Koussevitzky Foundation, which had agreed to the world premiere being given at Sadler's Wells (June 1945). In the summer of 1947, for the first time Koussevitzky asked 'Lenyushka' to conduct two gala concerts of the Boston Symphony Orchestra at Tanglewood — he had never permitted any other conductor to take over one of these concerts; Bernstein had, however, conducted the Boston Symphony in Boston a few times since 1944. It was always a great event for himself and for his family when he 'came home' to Boston.

From 1948 onward, Bernstein devoted more time to guest conducting; the New York City Symphony Orchestra had had to be disbanded for lack of funds, so that for ten years he had no orchestra 'of his own'. Koussevitzky frequently invited him to conduct in Boston, with com-

Leonard Bernstein talking in the communal hall at Ein Charod — Tel Yosef, May 1947

plete freedom in the choice of programmes; he often included performances of contemporary music by European and American composers. On the one hand, Leonard Bernstein was sorry to be without his own orchestra but on the other hand the freedom from fixed dates and regular engagements made it possible for him to devote more time to composition. Since the 'Jeremiah' Symphony (1942), *Fancy Free* and *On the Town* (1944) he had completed only one large-scale work, his second ballet for Jerome Robbins, *Facsimile* (1946). 1948 saw the beginning of a prolific period of creative work.

Meanwhile, however, Leonard Bernstein, not yet thirty years old, had two stirring experiences that were diametrically opposed to each other in both their musical and emotional impact, the one elevating and heart-warming, the other shattering and deeply moving. In the spring of 1947, one year before the State of Israel came into being, he visited Jewish Palestine for the first time. A year later he accepted an invitation to conduct in Germany and, after a concert in Munich, visited two camps for Displaced Persons. There he met survivors of the Holocaust and played with an ensemble of instrumentalists from a concentration camp orchestra that had been formed by order of the Nazis in the death camps.

[45]

At the Sea of Tiberias: 'Rosie, don't you know how to dance a conga?'

The first of these emotional experiences came when, in April 1947, Leonard Bernstein travelled to Tel Aviv with his father Samuel and his sister Shirley. Ten years and six months earlier, the first great symphony orchestra in Palestine had come into existence, founded by the violinist Bronislaw Huberman. He had assembled first-desk instrumentalists from European countries where they were threatened by the antisemitic regimes and had thus saved many lives. The Palestine Orchestra as it was known — later to become the Palestine Philharmonic and, with the foundation of the State of Israel, the Israel Philharmonic Orchestra — had been launched in December 1936. The first conductor had been Arturo Toscanini, who had declined to conduct in fascist countries, and now made a generous gesture to Huberman and the all-Jewish orchestra. Many prominent European and American musicians had conducted or played in this orchestra; Leonard Bernstein came as a young unknown but preceded by his reputation as a versatile musician. When he arrived in Tel Aviv in the last week of April, Charles Munch was guest-conducting the Philharmonic; the last concert of his series was given on 24 April and the first of Bernstein's series of concerts was scheduled for 27 April. In order to satisfy the demand of subscribers, the orchestra had (and still has) to repeat its concerts several times in Tel Aviv and also in Jerusalem and Haifa. The concert series beginning on 27 April had been planned to present Robert Schumann's Second Symphony, the Concerto in G for Piano by Maurice Ravel (with Bernstein doubling as pianist and conductor), and the 'Jeremiah' Symphony. However, the orchestral parts for the Bernstein symphony had not arrived in Tel Aviv in time for the first concert, and Mozart's 'Linz' Symphony (C major, K.425) was played instead. The music for Jeremiah arrived in time for subsequent rehearsals and concerts, and the final movement, 'Lamentation', set to the biblical Hebrew verses, was for the first time sung in the country where Hebrew is the national language. The Tel Aviv contralto Edith Goldschmidt had been chosen as soloist for the vocal movement and sang the solo in all concerts. Public and press were enthusiastic about Leonard Bernstein as conductor, pianist and composer.

He is one of the most talked-of personalities and popular visitors for years [I reported to the *New York Times*]. The enthusiasm of the audience at his first concert with the Philharmonic Orchestra knew no bounds, and not since the days of Arturo Toscanini has a conductor been recalled so many times and given a similar ovation . . . . The Philharmonic has never been better. Its musicians were fascinated by Mr. Bernstein . . . . The concerts . . . were the climax of the orchestra's tenth season.

[47]

In an interview with the Jerusalem daily, *The Palestine Post* (now the *Jerusalem Post*) on 2 May 1947, Bernstein said that he could feel the public every second, even with his back to the hall — 'they rise with the *crescendi* and sink down with the *descrescendi* — they are like a barometer — there is nothing more subtle in the world'.

Concert tours in Palestine were a difficult and dangerous undertaking. The British Mandate government had convened one commission after another to bring about a partition of Palestine into an Arabic and a Jewish country, but no decision acceptable to all parties had been possible. Arab ambushes on the country's roads, attacks on Jewish settlements and acts of sabotage in Jerusalem occurred almost daily and in many places the British authorities had to impose a curfew, so that concerts, especially in Jerusalem, had to be given in the afternoons. Often the orchestra was compelled to travel from one city to the other in armoured buses and cars, yet the public never missed its concerts and hardly any were cancelled. One of Leonard Bernstein's orchestral concerts took place in an agricultural settlement in the Yesreel Valley, opposite the Gilboa mountains which are so well-known from biblical history. After the concert at E'in Harod on 10 May 1947, the Bernstein family, with guests from Tel Aviv and orchestra members, were invited to meet settlers from the Kibbutzim E'in Harod and Tel Yosef. Leonard and Samuel Bernstein addressed the party in short and very personal speeches: Leonard in English and Hebrew, his father in Yiddish. They also visited E'in Gev on the shore of Lake Tiberias (the biblical Sea of Galilee or Genezareth) which Sergei Koussevitzky, on a later journey to Israel, regarded as an ideal place for an Israeli counterpart to Tanglewood. A Festival Hall was built there, but the music centre envisaged by Koussevitzky never materialised.

Leonard Bernstein, soon Lenny to everyone, made many friends among musicians and music-lovers, most of whom remained in touch with him. At the time of his first visit there was not yet the turmoil and commotion that was to become a fact of life for him as a world-famous sought-after celebrity. At one of the many small informal parties in the Tel Aviv studio of the dance teacher Katya Michaeli, he sat down at her small upright piano late at night and started playing and singing the final scene from Richard Strauss' *Der Rosenkavalier*. Rosi Gradenwitz, not a professional singer, who nevertheless knew the opera well, stood up and joined him in the duet. As though entranced, Lenny concluded the scene and said wistfully: 'I could become such a good opera conductor, but they don't let me . . .'. Though he had conducted *Peter Grimes* a year earlier, his real career as an opera conductor began with an imposing debut in December 1955, conducting Cherubini's

Medea at the Teatro alla Scala in Milan with Maria Callas in the title role. At the New York Metropolitan Opera, his first opera was Verdi's *Falstaff* in March 1963; in 1966 he was invited by the Vienna Staatsoper to conduct the same opera and in April 1968 *Der Rosenkavalier*.

At another private meeting later on it was possible to experience the deep roots of creative inspiration. In my modest private apartment there was a pause while the dessert was fetched from the kitchen. Lenny looked around the dining room, which was also the library and music room. On one of the shelves he noticed the vocal score of a very recently published opera. As though drawn by a magnet, he rose and took the volume from the shelf, sat down at the piano, opened it, and began to play. It was the 'Good Night' scene from Benjamin Britten's *Rape of Lucretia*, which had had its world première at Glyndebourne in July 1946. This is the final scene of the First Act: the voluptuous Prince Tarquinius has found a night's shelter in the house of Lucretia; Lucretia has not dared to deny him and the servants Blanca and Lucia have to prepare a room for him. The music for this scene, lyrically tender and cool at the same time, is dominated by a mystically sinister mood presaging tragedy. Ten years after Lenny's visit to our home *West Side Story* excited the musical world: in its Balcony scene between Maria and Tony, the beautiful lyrical duet 'To-night' is heard; here too a mysterious undertone pervades the music and in the reprise towards the end of the First Act it is sung to the counterpoint of preparation for a tragic struggle. It is interesting to note that the instrumental introduction to the balcony scene in *West Side Story* is based on the same four melodically descending intervals followed by melodic ascent and downward sequence heard in the instrumental accompaniment to Britten's 'Good Night' and both sequences are performed pianissimo. Did Lenny's inspiration stem from looking at the Britten score that night? He remembers the evening and says that *Lucretia* fascinated him then for the second time: the year before he had heard some rehearsals in England for the world premiere of Britten's opera, just before leaving London after the concerts with the London Philharmonic and the *Fancy Free* performance at Covent Garden.

In Tel Aviv, Leonard Bernstein also took part in a concert organised by the local branch of the International Society for Contemporary Music. In the second part of that concert (the first part comprising music by the local composers Mordechai Starominsky, who later changed his name to Seter, and Oedön Partos) he accompanied the clarinettist Klaus Kochmann in his own Clarinet Sonata and gave a short talk on 'Nationalism in Music'. He then played his piano arrangement of Aaron Copland's *El Salón Mexico* and took the piano part

ayerifche Staatstheater

ᴧATSOPER PRINZREGENTENTHEATER

München, Sonntag, 9. Mai 1948

6. KONZERT
DER MUSIKALISCHEN AKADEMIE

Das Bayerische Staatsorchester

Musikalische Leitung:

LEONARD BERNSTEIN

(New-York) a. G.

Roy Harris: 3. Symphonie

Maurice Ravel: Konzert f. Klavier u. Orchester in G-dur
Solist: Leonard Bernstein

Robert Schumann: Symphonie II, C-dur, op. 61

Flügel aus dem Pianohaus Lang · Landsberger Straße 336 · Fernruf 8 02 31

Die für den 10. Mai vorgesehene Wiederholung dieses Konzertes fällt aus; gelöste Eintrittskarten können an der Tageskasse der Bayerischen Staatstheater, Maximilianstraße zurückgegeben oder gegen noch vorhandene Eintrittskarten für 9. Mai umgetauscht werden.

Anfang **17** ^{1}|2 Uhr   **Pause nach Ravel**   Ende gegen **20** Uhr

Kartenvorverkauf
der Opernkasse der Bayer. Staatstheater, Maximilianstr., täglich von 9 bis 15 Uhr, Samstag und Sonntag von 9 bis 13 Uhr, und bei den üblichen Vorverkaufsstellen.
Die Abendkasse im Prinzregententheater ist jeweils dreiviertel Stunden vor Vorstellungsbeginn geöffnet.

Eintrittspreise C: 4.— bis 10.— RM

Gegeben unter der Zulassungsnummer 1444 der Nachrichten-Kontrolle der Militärregierung

Druck: Rischmöller & Meyn, München

Concert in Munich, 9 May 1948

in a performance of Darius Milhaud's *La Création du Monde* with members of the Philharmonic led by Josef Kaminski.

In June 1948 we met again in the Dutch spa of Scheveningen where some concerts were being given as part of the annual festival of the International Society for Contemporary Music. The Kursaal of Scheveningen and its fashionable public seemed a somewhat peculiar choice for modern music programmes. The centre of the hall was occupied by bewildered spa guests; delegates from countries East and West, representing national sections of the ISCM, were seated around them, along the walls. New American music included recently composed works by Roger Sessions and Walter Piston. Leonard Bernstein was impressed by a *Lullaby* for twenty-nine strings and two harps by Andrzei Panufnik, conducted by the Polish composer (born 1914) himself; the orchestra was the Residentie Orkest which Bernstein had conducted in concerts at The Hague a year before. In July the new season began at Tanglewood and in October Bernstein returned to Israel for another visit.

In May 1948, Leonard Bernstein had one of the most moving experiences of his entire life, visiting DP camps near Munich. The American Army authorities were ready to grant him his wish to see survivors at a camp but requested that he should at the same time conduct a concert in Munich. Georg Solti (now Sir Georg Solti) had become music director of the Bavarian State Opera in the summer of 1946; opera performances and concerts were given at the Prinzregenten-Theater. Even three years after the end of the war, singers and musicians were working under most difficult conditions. There was little to eat, no warm clothes and no proper heating in winter. Strikes were common and theatre and opera performances had often to be cancelled as singers, actors and musicians became ill or fainted on stage because of undernourishment. At the time of Bernstein's visit there were also transport problems arising from a tram strike.

Georg Solti had arranged a concert for Leonard Bernstein. When he arrived for his first rehearsal he found the musicians rather unwilling to work, especially with a conductor who was young, unknown, an American and a Jew at that. Thirty-four years later, Lenny vividly remembers this first — and for a long time last — visit to Germany. 'You don't know that story?' he said, 'It's incredible. I didn't want to conduct German orchestras. You know, feelings were very tense and tight. But I wanted to see the DPs, and there were two DP camps outside of München. I had no relationship like the one Yehudi [Menuhin] had with Furtwängler . . . .' Yehudi Menuhin had played with Furtwängler in Berlin in 1946 and 1947 and explained: 'I much wanted

[51]

to go, as a Jew who might keep alive German guilt and repentance, and as a musician offering something to live for' (Yehudi Menuhin, *Unfinished Journey*, London, 1976, p. 224). Jewish and Israeli circles criticised his attitude at the time because of his attitude to Furtwängler.

For me all this was brand new territory [said Leonard Bernstein]: I wanted to see these DP camps in Landsberg and Feldafing near Dachau. The only way I could get there was to accept through the American Army, which was running everything in München, to conduct the *Staatsorchester* at the Prinzregenten-Theater. So I had to go to München and to conduct this all-Nazi orchestra (they had probably all been Nazis) in order to get to the other thing. And I remember that at the first rehearsal they wouldn't even look up from their music. But after a half hour they were licking my shoes and holding my coat and lighting my cigarette — it was, you know, such a revelation about the German character, the two sides of the coin, the slave and the master: the master race and on the other hand they've been brought up to obey orders absolutely and click their heels and be slaves.

And suddenly this orchestra was slaves. We had a lot of difficulties to go through the strikes, *Strassenbahnstreik, Orchesterstreik, Lebensmittelstreik*. It was terrible. But we finally got the concert done and it was a big success.

The programme consisted of the Third Symphony by Roy Harris, the Ravel Piano Concerto (with Bernstein as soloist and conductor), and Robert Schumann's Second Symphony. The concert took place on a Sunday afternoon, 9 May. The State Opera House had been closed for one week because a great many singers and musicians had been ill and the State Orchestra had had to cancel its participation at the festive opening of the German Press Exhibition on 5 May, four days before the Bernstein concert. 'For the first time since the war an American conductor appeared before the public', wrote the renowned critic Hans Pringsheim in the *Süddeutsche Zeitung* (Tuesday 11 May, p. 3),

Leonard Bernstein, not yet thirty years old, is regarded as one of the most remarkable personalities among the young generation of American conductors. Since . . . his sensational success at Carnegie Hall in 1943 his career has been extraordinary and all who attended last Sunday's concert will agree that he fully deserves his success. For this young artist is steeped in music, it gushes out of his eyes, his lips, the suggestive gestures of his arms and hands and his entire body, he transmits music to the keys of the piano as much as to the musicians and the fascinated audience. Bernstein is one of those conducting phenomena who, gifted with the finest sense of sound and filled with outstanding rhythmic vitality, sweep the orchestra entrusted to them along with them and achieve from it beauty of sound and flexible subtlety of the highest order.

[52]

The same reviewer pointed especially to unexpected beauty of detail in the Schumann symphony and the impressiveness of the Roy Harris Third Symphony. The highlight was the Ravel Piano Concerto which Bernstein conducted from the piano.

The musical *élan*, the playful mastering of the unusual technical difficulties (which were not felt as such here at all), the emotional rendering of the lyrical piano sections, the almost unbelievable security in his uniting piano solos and orchestra in such a difficult solo work — all this must be considered as unique, as peerless. The public success was thus enormous for him as well as for the orchestra whose idealism had made this extraordinary event possible.

Die Neue Zeitung, an American journal in German for the German population — like other Munich papers, appearing only twice a week — described Leonard Bernstein in its issue of 13 May as 'a musician of astounding, demonic gifts, a wizard of the orchestra as were Liszt and Paganini on their instruments . . . his virtuoso craftsmanship is matched by spiritual-emotional sympathy'. The reviewer Fritz Brust notes that the enormous applause compelled Bernstein to encore the third movement of the Ravel Piano Concerto. The *Münchner Merkur* of 10 May found in Leonard Bernstein's appearance and interpretations the answer to the question of what may be typical of American music: 'This young American radiates freshness, vitality and inexhaustible musical power and he has nothing in him of academism or lack of refinement . . . . His interpretations surprise by their immediacy and illumination'.

'I was on my way to Israel again. I was there twice that year, once in spring after Munich (when Israel became a State) and I came again in autumn', Lenny recalls.

But the day after the Munich concert I went out to Landsberg and conducted an orchestra of sixteen people, called the Dachau Symphony Orchestra, this was all that was left from what was once an orchestra of sixty-five players — only sixteen were left, all the others were killed. The survivors had this little thing called The Dachau Symphony Orchestra; it played for the DPs and I conducted them — it was so touching, I can't tell you. The programme had to be only that music they had, that they had written out by hand — the material, the parts they had written. Whatever they had, I had to play: *Rhapsody in Blue* for some reason, and I played this twice in one day for five thousand DPs in Landsberg and five thousands DPs in Feldafing. It was the same hall, they came and went, and in both concerts it was so unbelievable that the whole Nazi orchestra from München came and filled the first three rows. They came with their *Intendant*, I still remember a woman called Frau Fichtmüller who had been the *Intendant* of this orchestra throughout the entire *Nazi-Zeit*.

Frau Hedwig (Hedi) Fichtmüller is listed in the archives of the Bavarian Staatstheater as an opera singer and superintendent of the artist's management office; she was also responsible for the supervision of evening performances. She held the titles of professor and *Bayerische Kammersängerin*. At the time of Leonard Bernstein's concerts she was fifty-four years old; she died in December 1975 at the age of eighty-one, having worked in the opera from 1917 to 1952.

Bernstein went on:

They all came and they were all on their knees and they had come with flowers, with roses, and put them on the stage, it was such a *Busse*, you can't imagine, it was an atonement like Yom Kippur for them, for this German orchestra, which had hated me in the first rehearsal. And they had now become my slaves and they just wanted to atone somehow. Can you imagine they came to listen to this little orchestra, I can hardly tell you what this orchestra was, it was with one viola, no bassoon, one clarinet, you know whatever was left. Jewish survivors, all DPs. When I was telling them I was going to Israel, they were screaming 'Take us with you! Take us with you!' because they were stuck in these camps, and I was terribly wounded — I can't tell you what it was like to conduct this little orchestra . . . . I remember some of this orchestra I go out. It was one boy, Chaim something, sixteen years old, I got him to Philadelphia, he played the violin and he is still in the Philadelphia Orchestra, and I got another one to Israel. And a third one I got somewhere else. They were especially good players.

This is a day I can never forget in my life. Because to have in the audience a hundred people of a Nazi orchestra with whom I had played a Schumann Symphony, I mean their most treasured German music, I, an American-Jewish boy, under thirty years old, to come and play Schumann was *nicht erlaubt* you know, and then I come and they get all very excited. We also played Bartók's *Music for Strings*, rather difficult music for them. So I won them as partisans, and they all followed me out to Feldafing and Landsberg. I never forget how they dropped flowers and how Frau Fichtmüller came and knelt down in front of me — unbelievable this big woman who had seen the orchestra through the whole *Hitlerzeit*, and I remember her saying 'Not since Abendroth has one heard such a Schumann Symphony'. I never heard about him so I didn't know what she was talking about. Since then I heard, but this was new for me then. And then she added that the days of Bruno Walter had come back . . . .

'Do you think all the members of the Munich Orchestra were Nazis?'
— 'They must have been':

The experience of these ten thousand DPs was unforgettable. After the concert they gave me a gift, the most precious gift they could give me. It was the concentration camp striped uniform with the number of the leader of the orchestra who had founded it, Walter something; he was a flautist, founder of the Dachau Symphony Orchestra. He was killed and they gave me his uniform, which had so *gestunken*, for years lying there, and this was the biggest present they could give me. And I had it for years in New York. I didn't know what to do with it. I had it cleaned, fifty times, I couldn't get the smell off. It was the smell of death you know. And finally somebody threw it out without asking me. I'm sorry because I wanted to save this . . . but the housekeeper or somebody threw it away. But this was the most precious gift I have ever been given because it really came from the heart and liver and *Eingeweide* of these people.

In his excitement, remembering the DP camp visit thirty-four years later, his story was interspersed with German words.

It was all so moving. I thought I would never return to Germany. And I never conducted a German orchestra again until a special *Amnesty* concert with the Bayerisches Rundfunk-Orchester with Claudio Arrau as soloist in October 1976. For almost thirty years I was not there. On the 1948 trip I also went to Vienna. I had big success but I also didn't go back for almost twenty years. I couldn't stand it, there was so much falsity and intrigue, I hated it. They had made me there — without my wanting it at all — a figure in a *Dirigentenstreit*.

I had been engaged to conduct the Wiener Symphoniker. I arrived on a train from Budapest where I had conducted the night before, with a success that was unbelievable — one of these stories — the audience carried me on their shoulders back to the hotel, one of these things, because I played Bartók in Budapest and they said, the Hungarians, they had never heard Bartók like that, they said they were out of their mind. So I arrived on the train to Wien the next day and I was met by a committee of the orchestra that said before I was even getting out of the train: 'Please, listen, we heard already on the telephone about your big success in Budapest with this Bartók. Could you please change your programme and put this Bartók in the programme here in Vienna because the other orchestra which has for its conductor a certain Mr. Karajan played with him this Bartók piece and everybody started to fight, people left the hall, it was empty at the end of the piece, they hated it'. This was 1948, I had never heard the name Karajan before. I was to conduct the Symphoniker and he conducted the Philharmoniker — this was the other orchestra of which they were talking. And they said: 'Now, if you had such a success with Bartók and *you* could play the

[55]

Sergei Koussevitzky at his villa, Tanglewood, 1948

piece with *our* orchestra, we will have *Triumph* and *Siegheil* and they wanted to draw me into a *Dirigentenkrieg*. And this against a conductor I had never heard of. So I told them I wouldn't change the programme, I don't want to get involved with these intrigues. Yet they tried again and said it would mean so much to them and would put their orchestra on the map as really superior to the other orchestra. I refused and played my proper programme and it was a tremendous success. But I didn't go back, I hated the whole spirit of intrigue.

Yet another incident had infuriated Leonard Bernstein. He had left the complete orchestral material of Gustav Mahler's Ninth Symphony in Vienna, marked with his own personal annotations and markings. This material was handed over to 'the other conductor', who used it for concerts and a recording. Only after the performance and recording was a telegram sent to Leonard Bernstein in New York with the request to allow the material to be kept for another week. 'This was an additional chapter in the *Dirigentenkrieg* and another reason why I did not want to go back to Vienna. Why always *Konkurrenz?*'

After the stirring events of the spring of 1948 — Vienna, Munich, the proclamation of the State of Israel — there was the June festival of the International Society for Contemporary Music at the Scheveningen Kursaal prior to Leonard Bernstein's return to America. I had attended the ISCM congress and festival as delegate of the Israeli section — representing the newly established State — and had been invited by Aaron Copland to lecture at the Berkshire Music Center at Tanglewood. There one of my first experiences was a talk Leonard Bernstein gave to performing musicians and composers on the subject on Beethoven's Fifth Symphony. This lecture was expanded and developed in the context of his later television programmes and the essays collected in book form and published in many languages. At the time, professionals and students at Tanglewood were fascinated by the original approach of young Bernstein to the analysis and appreciation of music. Playing Beethoven's various sketches for the first theme of the symphony, he demonstrated that from a logical musical development of the themes set down in the early drafts there could never have been created a gigantic composition such as Beethoven then developed out of the four-note motif. Almost the entire faculty of the Tanglewood summer school was present and admired the analytical insight, the logic of the argument and the freshness of presentation that characterised Leonard Bernstein's talk.

[57]

For all visitors to Tanglewood at that time the great affection Sergei Koussevitzky had for his young protegé was obvious but so too was the fact that many musicians looked enviously towards Lenny Bernstein. Some of the most talented among the young composers became Bernstein's closest friends, among them Lukas Foss (four years younger) who had in 1944 become the 'house pianist' of the Boston Symphony Orchestra, and Irving Fine (born 1914), a sensitive musician and writer who died all too young in 1962. As early as 1945, in Bernstein's twenty-seventh year, Fine had described Lenny's period of study at Harvard University 'with great nostalgia' and analysed the style of his earliest compositions such as the Clarinet Sonata, *Seven Anniversaries* for piano, *Jeremiah, Fancy Free* and *On the Town* (Irving Fine, 'Young America: Bernstein and Foss', in *Modern Music*, XXII, 4, 1945). He described Bernstein's work with insight as blending 'sophistication and naïveté' combined with 'a strong dramatic sense', also remarking that his 'mind is agile and intuitive, if not overly introspective'. *Jeremiah* had already been written, it is true, but the deeper roots of Leonard Bernstein's soul-reaching would only find expression in much later compositions. Fine also gave a warning that the attempt to write in 'a truly modern popular style' might include 'attendant dangers for the composition of serious music. When dramatic effectiveness is emphasized refinements may fall by the wayside . . . . In the improvisational élan of the music, hiatuses in the harmony go unheeded, as do occasional lapses of taste. But in such a work as *Jeremiah*, these defects seem insignificant in relation to the loftiness of the conception'.

Irving Fine's characterisation of the early work of Leonard Bernstein and its note of warning hold good for much of the composer's music before lyricism, popular leanings, drama and artful elaboration came together in his mature works. Leonard Bernstein himself said in a much later interview that he feels himself to be first and foremost a dramatist; Irving Fine had already argued in his 1945 article that 'Bernstein's talents appear most appropriate to the theatre. The gift for brilliant improvisation, the flair for striking and not too subtle contrasts, the free rein he gives to sentiment, his relative objectivity — does this not all suggest the theatre composer?', he asked at a time when *On the Town* and *Fancy Free* had just been written. The article concludes by conceding that 'it is dangerous to make any prediction about this young man. He can be anything he wants to be, providing he wants it hard enough'.

Apart from the young musicians and composers at Tanglewood, there were older masters who took much interest in Lenny the conductor and Lenny the composer. In 1948, Darius Milhaud held a master class there; Bernstein's erstwhile composition teacher Walter Piston watched his development; Aaron Copland observed all his activities at the Berkshire Music Center. In Lenny's studio I met the singers Nan Merriman (who had even before Jennie Tourel recorded the 'Lamentation' of the 'Jeremiah' symphony) and Ellabelle Davis — both were soloists in a performance of Gustav Mahler's Second Symphony which Leonard Bernstein conducted for an audience of more than ten thousand.

Among professional musicians and critics, many expressed doubts and warnings on the future of the all-too-fascinating young Bernstein with his manifold talents. Virgil Thomson, the composer and much-feared critic of the *New York Herald Tribune*, wrote on 19 October 1947 that:

Whether Bernstein will become in time a traditional conductor or a highly personal one is not easy to prophesy. He is a consecrated character, and his culture is considerable. It just might come about, though, that, having to learn classic repertory the hard way, which is after fifteen, and in a hurry, he would throw his cultural beginnings away and build toward success on a sheer talent for animation and personal projection. I must say he worries us all a little bit. It would be disappointing if our brightest young leader should turn out to be just a star conductor in an age when bluff, temperament, and show-off are no longer effective on the concert stage. They have become, indeed, the privilege of management. Success, today and tomorrow, even financial success, depends on any artist's keeping his ego down to reasonable size. One of the best ways of accomplishing this is to keep one's mind on both the sound and the sense of music one is playing. All the available knowledge there is about these matters constitutes the tradition. Neglecting to buttress his rising eminence with the full support of tradition is about the biggest mistake an American conductor in this generation could make (Virgil Thomson, *Music Right and Left*, New York, 2nd ed. 1969, p. 180).

In May 1982, I asked Virgil Thomson what he thinks now about the warnings he expressed almost thirty-five years earlier. He replied:

Leonard Bernstein, I am happy to say, has developed from a merely gifted young conductor to a master of his art with few rivals. He still poses on the concert platform and mimes transports a bit, but these faults are entirely absent when he conducts in an opera pit. Actually he is a conductor of enormous repertory, the most effective parts of which are, in my opinion, the French and the American. Bernstein is also a highly accomplished composer, whose chief successes have been in the domain of light music (letter to the author, 21 May 1982).

The ecstatic gesticulations of Leonard Bernstein on the concert podium have baffled many critics and listeners ever since he started conducting: they are not widely understood as part of his complete surrender to a musical work and his innermost reaction to the meaning and significance, the content and expression of the composition the orchestra must follow him to interpret. Like Gustav Mahler before him, Leonard Bernstein says that as a conductor he feels he must identify himself with a composer's work as if he himself had created it. Among his sharpest critics in his early years was Claudia Cassidy, reviewer of the *Chicago Tribune*; she did not like the music or the person of this young 'upstart'. I witnessed one incident which quickly made the rounds in Tanglewood. A few minutes before the scheduled beginning of a Koussevitzky concert with the Boston Symphony Orchestra, six thousand people filled the open auditorium and some eight to ten thousand sat or lay on the lawns around. The Orchestra was waiting for the Maestro Koussevitzky, who usually drove in his elegant car from his villa Seranak accompanied by a cavalcade of motor cycles. It was like a princely procession and when the maestro stepped down from his car and was about to enter the shed, a fanfare was sounded and no further movement was allowed in the hall. Listeners held their breath and thunderous applause greeted the conductor as he mounted the rostrum. On that afternoon the trumpet had just sounded when a lady hastily tried to make her way in and hurry past the ushers. The ushers prevented her from entering. 'But I am Claudia Cassidy of the *Tribune*', she protested, only to receive the retort, 'No matter who you are, you don't get in, even if you were Leonard Bernstein in person!' Claudia Cassidy turned and left, never to be seen again at Tanglewood.

Unforgettable memories of that Tanglewood summer of 1948 include not only Mahler's Second Symphony with Leonard Bernstein, but also the first acquaintance with 28-year-old Isaac Stern, who played Sergei Prokofieff's First Violin Concerto, as well as Koussevitzky's performance of Paul Hindemith's 'Mathis der Maler' Symphony. Unique, too, were Koussevitzky's public addresses given on the special Tanglewood on Parade day of celebration; he described them as 'manifestations' and delivered them in his own self-coined, unmistakable brand of English, filled with humanity, inspiring his listeners to approach all music with deep love and the desire for understanding: he had a deep affection for the young people coming to Tanglewood to widen their horizon and to learn. I came to know the generous champion of new music and patron of young composers and musicians still better when he came to Israel as guest conductor of the Israel Philharmonic Orchestra.

Leonard Bernstein's visit to Israel in the months of October and

November 1948 was memorable for a number of events. In his concerts with the Israel Philharmonic, which had just taken its new name after the birth of the new State, he gave Aaron Copland's important Third Symphony, Gustav Mahler's Second Symphony, with Eytan Lustig's Tel Aviv Choir and Josefa Schocken and Emma Shaver as vocal soloists, and his own music from *Fancy Free*. In addition, he took part in the world premiere of his most recent composition. While travelling over the past few months, he had been hard at work on his Second Symphony, inspired by Wystan Hugh Auden's *The Age of Anxiety*; the Koussevitzky Foundation had commissioned the work and the first performance was scheduled for the spring of 1949, so that even while flying he had to work on the score. A central movement of the symphony, opening the second part of the work, and entitled 'Dirge', was almost ready when Leonard Bernstein arrived in Tel Aviv, and he completed it between rehearsals and concerts. The orchestral parts were hastily copied and on 28 November 'Dirge' was premiered in the Habimah Theatre hall, as part of a gala concert given by the Israel Philharmonic Orchestra to say farewell to Leonard Bernstein. Between George Gershwin's *American in Paris* and Franz Joseph Haydn's 'Farewell' Symphony in F sharp minor, the conductor-composer stepped down from the rostrum and sat down at the grand piano to play the solo part in his own 'Dirge' from *The Age of Anxiety*, conducted by Georg Singer, an Israeli of Czech descent. I had the opportunity to observe Bernstein closely at the piano as he had asked me to turn the pages of the hastily-written score. When Koussevitzky conducted the première of the entire work in Boston on 8 April 1949, the composer again played the piano solo part. However, in the recording later made with the Israel Philharmonic, Bernstein conducted throughout, entrusting the piano solo to Lukas Foss.

Another event during this visit will not easily be forgotten. In the last week of Bernstein's sojourn in Israel — marked by forty concerts in two months, in thirty-two of which he doubled as piano soloist — on the morning of 20 November, he travelled to the town of Beersheba on the edge of the Negev desert. On his own initiative, a concert was arranged there for an Israeli brigade which had just succeeded in driving enemy invaders out of the Negev and liberating the town and the surrounding country. Thirty-five members of the Philharmonic went with him in two buses; at the time it took some hours to get from Tel Aviv to Beersheba and the journey was not without danger. Even a piano was brought along, for Lenny wanted to play concertos by Mozart and Beethoven as well as *Rhapsody in Blue*. Soldiers and civilians were excited at the prospect of the visit. The United Nations had ordered the

Leonard Bernstein at the piano, with members of the Israel Philharmonic Orchestra, Beersheba, after the town's liberation in 1948

State of Israel, then only a few months old and attacked on all sides, to evacuate Beersheba and surrender the town; nobody in Israel took this seriously. The evening before, Leonard Bernstein had wanted to play a concert at the nearby kibbutz of Negba, but it had been impossible to get a piano there. Now at half past three in the afternoon, thousands of listeners sat on the sandy desert ground, on stools brought with them or on the excavated walls of the biblical town, and listened to Bernstein playing and conducting Mozart, Beethoven, and Gershwin. On the way back a foreign journalist exclaimed, 'This must have been the first time that Mozart has ever been played in Beersheva'; another seriously enjoined: 'Are you talking about this piece that we have just heard?' to which the first replied smartly: 'Not at any rate since Abraham's time'.

The colourful scene was enhanced by the audience — Arab sheiks and camel-drivers, thousands of farmers, soldiers, and airmen joined the inhabitants of the war-weary town. For the first time, Arab listeners heard classical Western music that sounded strangely foreign in the oriental surroundings, even to concert habitues. An oboe solo in the Beethoven work lured a camel to the scene, with apparent astonishment on its sleepy face. As in other cities where Bernstein had conducted concerts, air-raid warnings sounded, but neither conductor nor orchestra interrupted the concert even when bombs or shells fell nearby.

From Israel, Leonard Bernstein flew back to New York, stopping in Rome to conduct the renowned Santa Cecilia Academy orchestra. A month after the world première of *The Age of Anxiety* in Boston he was back in Israel, and conducted the same work from the piano on 9 May 1949. The following day his soloist in a Philharmonic concert was Jascha Heifetz and he also conducted the Roy Harris Third Symphony. A few weeks earlier, in March, Koussevitzky had visited Israel for the first time — under him the Israel Philharmonic had played symphonies by Tchaikovsky and Prokofiev. This visit and another in October/November 1950 led to Koussevitzky's consenting to direct the Israel Philharmonic on its first extensive tour of the United States at the beginning of 1951. That tour was conducted partly by Koussevitzky himself and partly by Leonard Bernstein. Israel owes to Sergei Koussevitzky two important initiatives apart from his magnificient work with the Philharmonic. I had taken him to E'in Gev on the shores of Lake Tiberias, the kibbutz which Leonard Bernstein had also visited with me, and it was Koussevitzky's advice that influenced the New York philanthropists Mr and Mrs Frank Cohen to make it possible for the settlement to build a concert hall for festival performances. Ethel Cohen and Richard Tetley, the US cultural attaché, had travelled there with us by jeep (!) after which the Esco Foundation (headed by the Cohens) chose E'in Gev instead of another spot that had been contemplated. Koussevitzky envisaged a music centre in the style of Tanglewood, with a regional school serving settlements in the Jordan Valley and Galilee: E'in Gev, however, concentrated on the more commercial possibilities of annual festivals and no music centre came into being. The other debt owed to Koussevitzky was for his valuable advice, in conjunction with architect friends, for the building of a concert hall to serve the Israel Philharmonic in Tel Aviv. The generosity of the philanthropist Fredric R. Mann made it possible to build the auditorium; it was named for him and was opened in his presence on 2 October 1957; the gala opening concert was conducted by Leonard Bernstein with Arthur Rubinstein, Paul Tortelier and Isaac Stern as soloists.

For the first American tour of the Israel Philharmonic — in 1951 — Sergei Koussevitzky and Leonard Bernstein brought the music of Israeli composers to America for the first time. The orchestra and US management had originally proposed programmes from the classical and romantic repertoire. However, when I asked Koussevitzky as tour director why he, a life-long champion of contemporary composers, had not insisted on the inclusion of Israeli works for the American concerts, he answered in his heavily accented English, 'Dere arr none'. When I asked who said so, he replied, 'Dee Orkestra'. 'And you believe that?' We arranged that the maestro should be shown some scores and a few days later he asked us to visit him at the hotel, saying 'Look at the telegram I received from New York'. He had cabled to the New York organisers of the tour, telling them he would change his programmes to include an Israeli composition in each concert. If they disagreed he would resign from the direction of the tour. So what was their reaction? 'Read that: ten minutes of Israeli music agreed. What do you say to that?' He banged the table and said scornfully, 'So I shall make twelfph!'

During the extended tour of the Israel Philharmonic Orchestra in America, Koussevitzky alternately conducted two symphonic works by Israeli composers: *Psalm* by Paul Ben-Haim, the central movement from his First Symphony, and two movements from the David Symphony by Menahem Avidom (originally Mahler-Kalkstein). Leonard Bernstein conducted the folk-based rhapsody *Emek* by Marc Lavry and *Song of Praise*, a concerto for viola and orchestra by Oedön Partos, himself an outstanding violist who played the solo part. Bernstein and

1025 Park Ave.
NYC
11 May 49

Dear P:
Just time for a few notes:
1) A great joy to receive our book, & many thanks for the sweet dedication.
2) The Age of Anxiety was a walloping success, & I thought of you often in preparing it. Everyone adored it, which amazed me.
3) Doesn't look so good for you + Tanglewood this summer. I have very little to do with it this year — just a token appearance: and I've taken a farm 45 miles away from it! Have you heard from them?
4) I'd love to see the "Bernstein article". The Variations you saw remain about the same.

My love to you + Rosi & the kids, & from Helen — Sorry this is too short — I'm rushed with plans for a new show: Lenny

AIR
MAIL

A letter to the author, 11 May 1949: 'our book' — the author's *The Music of Israel*, New York, 1949, which was dedicated to Leonard Bernstein; 'Bernstein article' — in *The Music Review*, vol. X, 1949

Partos had tried to shorten this twenty-minute work, in order to remain within the bounds of twelve minutes. But since it could not be done the tour managers had to accept it and, like the other Israeli compositions, the work was very well received by American press and public.

The American tour started on 8 January 1951 and rehearsals with Koussevitzky and Bernstein had begun in Israel two months before, in December 1950. But though the New Year opened with great success for Bernstein, it later brought him deep grief, for Koussevitzky died on 4 June. The Berkshire Music Center appointed Bernstein successor to his friend and mentor as director of the orchestra and the conducting department, a post he held till 1955. However, the committee of the Boston Symphony Orchestra did not ask him to succeed Koussevitzky, although, as far back as 1949, the latter, on relinquishing his musical directorship, had recommended Leonard Bernstein for the post. Instead, Charles Munch was chosen. But the year ended on a happy note, for on 9 September 1951 Leonard was married in Boston to Felicia Montealegre Cohn, four years younger than himself.

They had decided to marry while in Tanglewood in the summer of 1951, but Lenny and Felicia had already known each other for some years. 'On 6 February 1946, Claudio Arrau had played with me the Brahms D minor concerto in New York', Lenny recalls. 'After the concert he said: "I have a party in my house. Please come!" And I went with him and there I met this little girl called Felicia and I heard it was her birthday also — it was Claudio Arrau's birthday, I knew. It was her twenty-fourth birthday. And that's where we fell in love.' Lenny has never quite overcome Felicia's too early death and he talks of her with loving affection and deep sorrow in his voice.

Felicia was born in Costa Rica but the family moved to Chile when she was one year old. With her great musical talent she was accepted by Claudio Arrau — himself a Chilean — as a student. She also studied acting but when Arrau went to New York she followed him there to continue studying with him. Her father was Roy Ellwood Cohn, a Jew who did not even know he was Jewish; he had nothing to do with this, though he had this name Cohn. His grandfather had been the Chief Rabbi of Albany, New York, and then was sent to San Francisco to become Chief Rabbi there. His son was a brain surgeon, a very famous brain surgeon who changed his religion. So Felicia's father was born on the West Coast. He was like a cowboy. He read comic books and he was not an intellectual, he was not a thinking man. He was a geologist and he worked for some company which sent him to South America to investigate mines, tin and copper, you know, and that's how he came to Costa Rica, and he met Clemencia Monteallegre who was one of twelve children of this great Monteallegre family — a very ancient Spanish family

[67]

With his wife Felicia, Tel Aviv, 1957

that lived in Costa Rica — and he married her. After Felicia was born he was sent to Chile, and they had two more daughters. The three daughters were always called 'the Cohn sisters' and all of a sudden, with the Hitler time in Germany, suddenly everybody realised Cohn was something different and special. Jews were suddenly told they were Jewish, which they had not known before — many Germans had that experience. So Felicia was half Jewish, but she was raised as a Catholic, because her mother did the raising. She went to a convent, she was raised by nuns and she rebelled against all this. When she came to America actually she was trying to get away from all that — and when she married me she had to go through a conversion service, to become Jewish. Our children are, of course, Jewish. They are very Jewish, you should imagine, four weeks ago [March 1982] we all celebrated Passover *Seder* together, all the children came, Jamie came from California, with my mother in Boston, my mother's sister, my brother, my sister, my brother's children, altogether, and you should have heard my children sing *Shechi'anu*, it was just wonderful, they love it — in the house of my mother's sister.

After their meeting at Claudio Arrau's house, Lenny invited Felicia to come to Boston to meet his parents and at the end of 1946 they announced their engagement. However, in the following summer, they apparently decided that they were not ready for marriage and the engagement was broken off. They did not see each other for some time, though Felicia remained in touch with Lenny's sister Shirley. They met again in her house and there came a day when 'it became apparent to them that if they were ever going to marry, it would be to each other' (Bernstein, *Family Matters*, p. 183). They got engaged for the second time during the Tanglewood season in the summer of 1951, five years after the first engagement, and on 9 September they were married at a Boston synagogue. Leonard's parents, especially his father, were at first not very happy about his choice, but they came to like Felicia and were overjoyed on the arrival of grandchildren: Jamie Anne Maria was born on 8 September 1952, Alexander Serge (after Koussevitzky) on 7 July 1955, and Nina Maria Felicia on 28 February 1962. Felicia had meanwhile given up all idea of becoming a professional pianist, but continued to study acting and became a successful television actress. She also appeared with her husband in performances of stage work; for example taking the reciter's part in Arthur Honegger's oratorio *Jeanne d'Arc au Bûcher* and in Bernstein's 'Kaddish' Symphony. She succumbed to a malignant disease when only fifty-six.

In the year of his marriage Leonard Bernstein became Professor of Music at Brandeis University, Waltham, Massachusetts; there he lectured from 1951 to 1954, in 1952 conducting the première of his short opera *Trouble in Tahiti*, whose characters were to appear again later in the full-length opera first called *Tahiti II*, but then renamed *A Quiet Place* (1983). In order to be able to complete the libretto and music of *Trouble in Tahiti*, soon after his wedding he looked for a quiet, secluded place. He found it at Cuernavaca in Mexico, where he retreated with his young wife, refusing to conduct anywhere until the opera was finished. But the peaceful life dedicated to creative work was not to last very long. Charles Munch was ill in Boston, and Bernstein was urged and implored to take over Munch's concerts with the Boston Symphony Orchestra. Despite this interruption he managed to complete his opera and the first performance took place at Brandeis University on 12 June 1952. Soon after he had a visit from his old friends Betty Comden and Adolph Green. They had received a commission to turn *My Sister Eileen* (a comedy by Joseph Fields and Jerome Chodorov, based on Ruth McKenny's short stories originally published in the *New Yorker*), into a Broadway musical; they had only four weeks to accomplish the work, as the management wanted to cast Rosalind Russell as the star, but she would not come from Hollywood unless the première were in January 1953. Betty Comden and Adolph Green wrote the lyrics and Lenny Bernstein, who knew their style so well from their previous collaboration, wrote very witty and amusing music for them. After feverish work, everything was ready for the January première, after a preview season at New Haven, Connecticut, (starting January 1953); *Wonderful Town* opened at the New York Winter Garden Theatre on 26 February and ran for 550 performances. I remember vividly that Henry Levinger of the then popular music magazine *The Musical Courier* told me that he met Lenny strolling in the street with his dog the morning after the Broadway première: Lenny embraced him, exulting: 'At last we shall be rich now!'

Among the events of the next few years, 1953 to 1957, in Bernstein's life and work, one of the most memorable was his debut as opera conductor at the Teatro alla Scala, Milan; now too came the beginning of his television talks, composition of his *Serenade* for violin solo and small orchestra and the operetta *Candide*. All this was before *West Side Story* opened in September 1957 — the work that revolutionised the music theatre scene.

In December 1953, when Leonard Bernstein was on tour in Italy, an urgent call reached him from the directorate of the Teatro alla Scala. The great Italian conductor, Victor de Sabata, who was to conduct the opening night of the season, had fallen ill and would be unable to prepare or conduct the new production of Cherubini's *Medea*, with the

TEATRO ALLA SCALA

(ENTE AUTONOMO)

'appr. N. **2**   STAGIONE LIRICA 1953 - 54   N. **1** del Turno **A**
N. **2** degli abbonati alle "Prime,,

GIOVEDI 10 DICEMBRE 1953 - alle ore 21 precise

PRIMA RAPPRESENTAZIONE

di

MEDEA

Opera in tre atti di F. B. HOFFMANN

Musica di

LUIGI CHERUBINI

NUOVO ALLESTIMENTO

Personaggi e interpreti

Medea	MARIA MENEGHINI CALLAS
Neris	FEDORA BARBIERI
Glauce	MARIA LUISA NACHE
Giasone	GINO PENNO
Creonte	GIUSEPPE MODESTI
Prima ancella	ANGELA VERCELLI
Seconda ancella	MARIA AMADINI
Un capo delle guardie	ENRICO CAMPI

Maestro concertatore e direttore

LEONARD BERNSTEIN

Regia di MARGHERITA WALLMANN

Maestro del coro VITTORE VENEZIANI — Direttore dell'allestimento scenico NICOLA BENOIS

Bozzetti e figurini di SALVATORE FIUME

Scene realizzate da CARLO IOHINA - MARIO MANTOVANI - ANTONIO MOLINARI - VINCENZO PIGNATARO

Capo del servizio macchinismi di scena: AURELIO CHIODI - Capo del servizio elettrico e luci: GIULIO LUPETTI - Capo del servizio sartoria: ARTURO BRAMBILLA
Attrezzi: Ditta E. RANCATI & C. di SORMANI e PIAZZA SORMANI - Calzoleria: Ditta PEDRAZZOLI - Parrucche: Ditta FELICE SARTORIO

PREZZI

'oltrona di platea (ingresso compreso) L. **8000**	Palchi . . . . esauriti in abbonamento
'oltroncina di platea (› ›) L. **5000**	Ingresso ai palchi . . . . L. **2500**

Galleria (ingresso compreso) Poltroncina centrale di I galleria L. **1500**
Numerato di I galleria » **900** - Ingresso L. **300**
Numerato di II galleria » **600** · Ingresso » **200**

A tutti i prezzi suesposti va applicato il diritto erariale 15°'₀ e I'I. G. E. 3°'₀

IN PLATEA NON VI SONO POSTI IN PIEDI
È prescritto l'abito da sera per la Platea e per i Palchi

Durante l'esecuzione dello spettacolo è vietato accedere alla Platea e alle Gallerie. È pure vietato muoversi dal proprio posto prima della fine di ogni atto.
Gli indumenti e gli altri oggetti depositati alle guardarobe non possono essere ritirati che negli intervalli tra gli atti o alla fine dello spettacolo.
Il pubblico è pregato di uniformarsi alle disposizioni che vietano i "bis,,.
Per disposizione prefettizia è assolutamente vietato agli spettatori di accedere a qualsiasi posto della Sala, (Platea o Gallerie), con cappelli, soprabiti, pellicce, bastoni, ombrelli e simili
Per disposizioni del regolamento sulla vigilanza dei teatri il pubblico può lasciare la sala, alla fine dello spettacolo, da tutte indistintamente le porte d'uscita

Il Teatro si apre alle ore 20.30 - Le Gallerie si aprono alle ore 20.15.

Debut at the Teatro alla Scala, Milan: *Medea*, with Maria Callas title role sung by Maria Callas. Leonard Bernstein hesitated. He had a severe bronchitis, he did not know the opera and there were only ten days left before the planned première performance. He asked for the score, yet when it arrived he was even more hesitant about accepting the responsibility. The score was very old, badly worn, and parts of it were hardly readable. It was tempting indeed to conduct a major work at the most famous opera house in the world, with Maria Callas, the greatest soprano of the day. Yet his alarm was intensified by Callas's reputation as a difficult, volatile and temperamental prima donna. Moreover, he found an aria in *Medea* which he would like to cut if he were to conduct the performance. How could he possibly demand of a world-famous singer that one of her effective arias should simply disappear? However, at long last he overcame his doubts and fears and accepted the request. After all, he had been able to replace Bruno Walter at much shorter notice.

Of the rehearsals and performance at the Scala, some vivid eye-witness reports have been preserved. Maria Callas's biographer Arianna Stassinopoulos (*Beyond the Callas Legend*, London, 1980) tells how dust rising from the torn score made Bernstein's eyes water; it certainly took some time before prima donna and conductor came to a good mutual undertanding. Callas found Bernstein irresistible with his combination of sharp-wittedness, dramatic instinct and good manners. For his part, while working with her Leonard forgot his coughing, sneezing and running eyes. But then came the anxiously-dreaded moment of discussion about the aria that was to be cut; Bernstein was greatly surprised when the singer immediately grasped the dramaturgi-cal necessity of omitting it, together with certain changes in the sequence of scenes and numbers in the opera. 'She understood every-thing I wanted and I understood everything she wanted — it was marvellous', Bernstein recalled (ibid., p. 137).

Medea opened to an enthusiastic and jubilant public on 10 December 1953. La Callas was 'pure electricity', in Bernstein's words, and he had now gained international fame as an opera conductor, having been the first American to conduct at the renowned Milan opera house. He returned there in March 1955 to conduct Bellini's *La Sonnambula* and Puccini's *La Boheme*, not only the first American but also the youngest conductor to appear at the Teatro alla Scala. Yet it was not until 1963 that he was asked for the first time to conduct at the New York Metropolitan Opera, where he led ten performances of Verdi's *Falstaff*. When, three years later, the Wiener Staatsoper invited him to conduct six performances of *Falstaff*, he returned to Vienna, although at one time he had said that he would never go there again. In 1968, at the

With Maria Callas after a performance of Bellini's *La Sonnambula* at the Teatro alla Scala, March 1955

same opera house, there followed *Der Rosenkavalier* and in 1970 he conducted Beethoven's *Fidelio* at the Theater an der Wien, where the work had received its first performance in the composer's lifetime, when the theatre was known as the Theater an der Wieden.

In the 1950s Leonard Bernstein also became active as a composer in many different fields. In 1954 he wrote a symphonic score for Elia Kazan's film *On the Waterfront*, and a year later developed it into a concert work. Less known are other works from this period: incidental music and songs for performances of J.M. Barrie's *Peter Pan* (1950), *The Lark* by Jean Anouilh, adapted for the American stage by Lillian Hellman, and Oscar Wilde's *Salome* (both 1955). In the winter season of 1956, the comic operetta *Candide* was first staged. The piece, based on Lillian Hellman's dramatic version of Voltaire's satire, was not very successful, though Bernstein's sparkling overture became a favourite concert offering. In later years, both text and music were rewritten and reworked several times.

Leonard Bernstein's first symphonic work after *The Age of Anxiety* (the Second Symphony, dating from 1949) was the *Serenade* for solo violin, string orchestra, harp and percussion, premiered by Isaac Stern on 12 September 1954 at the Teatro Fenice in Venice under the composer's baton. Like *The Age of Anxiety*, the *Serenade* had been commissioned by the Koussevitzky Foundation. *The Age of Anxiety* had been dedicated in tribute to Sergei Koussevitzky; the *Serenade* was dedicated 'to the beloved memory of Sergei and Natalie Koussevitzky'. The *Serenade*, one of the few musical compositions inspired by philosophy, being based on the characters and dialogues in Plato's *Symposium*, has even attracted the attention of choreographers. In June 1959 the American Ballet Theater presented it in a choreography by Herbert Ross at the Spoleto Festival of Two Worlds. In 1950, Jerome Robbins had choreographed *The Age of Anxiety* in New York with the New York City Ballet.

'We are going to try to perform for you today a curious and rather difficult experiment. We're going to take the first movement of Beethoven's Fifth Symphony and rewrite it.' So began Leonard Bernstein's first television lecture on 14 November 1954 in CBC's *Omnibus* programme:

> Now don't get scared; we're going to use only notes that Beethoven wrote. We're going to take certain discarded sketches that Beethoven wrote, intending to use them in this symphony, and find out why he rejected them, by

[74]

putting them back into the symphony and seeing how the symphony would have sounded with them. Then we can guess at the reason for rejecting these sketches, and, what is more important, perhaps we can get a glimpse into the composer's mind as it moves through this mysterious creative process we call composing (Leonard Bernstein, *The Joy of Music*, New York, 1959, II, no. 1).

In this first talk, relayed to an immense television audience and interspersed with numerous musical illustrations, we recognise the lecture young Lenny Bernstein had given six years earlier to just a small group of musicians and students at Tanglewood. In the expanded talk, probing deep into 'the mysterious creative process' in an easily comprehensible language, Bernstein tried to make his viewers and hearers understand 'the key to the mystery of a great artist: that for reasons unknown to him or to anyone else, he will give away his energies and his life just to make sure that one note follows another inevitably. It seems rather an odd way to spend one's life; but it isn't so odd when we think that the composer, by doing this, leaves us at the finish with the feeling that something is right in the world, that something checks throughout, something that follows its own laws consistently, something we can trust, that will never let us down'.

This first illuminating talk — throwing light on Bernstein the pedagogue and thinker as well as on his own approach to the art of composition — was followed by six television lectures on various topics up to March 1958. In November 1959 the seven scripts were published in the first edition of his book *The Joy of Music*, together with three 'Imaginary Conversations' and a short description of the atmosphere in the film studio when his music to *On the Waterfront* was being produced. Further television programmes with Leonard Bernstein were regularly shown from 1958 onward, among them talks for young listeners and later the six Harvard lectures (1973). Many of the telecast scripts were printed in Bernstein's later books, in magazines and journals and were translated into other languages.

Leonard Bernstein was already well-known in the musical world as a composer of symphonic music, chamber music, songs and piano pieces, and ballets and Broadway shows, as a guide to music for a televison audience and as a conductor and pianist, when he made musical theatre history with the tragic realism, social criticism and high drama of the emotionally charged *West Side Story*. It was 1957 and he was thirty-nine years old. His old friend and collaborator Jerome Robbins had had the idea for the plot, Arthur Laurents wrote the book and Stephen Sondheim the lyrics for the songs. On 19 August the first preview was staged at the National Theatre, Washington, DC; the New

York première was on 26 September 1957. The film version was released in 1961 and the musical was performed in many countries in different languages. Leonard Bernstein dedicated the work to his wife Felicia, 'with love'.

Only six years after *West Side Story*, Leonard Bernstein completed a new large-scale symphonic work, the Third Symphony, entitled *Kaddish* and, like earlier compositions, commissioned by the Koussevitzky Foundation. The work is scored for soprano solo, choir, narrator, boys' choir and orchestra. The world première on 10 December 1963 by the Israel Philharmonic Orchestra, was conducted by the composer, with Jennie Tourel as soloist and the first lady of the Hebrew theatre, Hannah Rovina, as narrator. The choirs were conducted by Abraham Kaplan and Yizhak Graziani and the première was held in Tel Aviv's new Fredric R. Mann Auditorium. The American première was conducted by Charles Munch with the Boston Symphony Orchestra on 10 January 1964; Jennie Tourel was again the solo singer and the narrator was Felicia Monteallegre Bernstein. In 1977, the composer revised his score and recorded the new version with the Israel Philharmonic Orchestra; Montserrat Caballé sang the soprano soli and Michael Wager was the narrator; the Viennese Jeunesse Chor sang under the direction of Günther Theuring and the Vienna Boys' Choir was conducted by Uwe Christian Harrer.

Early in 1957, Leonard Bernstein was appointed co-director of the New York Philharmonic Orchestra by its Musical Director, his old friend and supporter Dimitri Mitropoulos. A year later Mitropoulos resigned and Leonard Bernstein became Musical Director. On 3 October 1958 he conducted his first concert in that capacity, a post he retained for eleven years. He began a series of performances of symphonic works by American composers, instituted a 'preview' series with introductory talks and took the orchestra on world tours to South America, Europe, the Near and Far East, Australia, New Zealand, Turkey, Poland, Yugoslavia and Soviet Russia, and from coast to coast in the United States. His last concert as Musical Director in May 1969 marked the 939th that he had conducted with the New York Philharmonic; his 1000th was reached on 15 December 1971. The NYPO conferred on him the title 'Laureate Conductor'. His programmes were always interesting, unusual and original in many respects; he conducted forty world premières and many American first performances with the orchestra.

Bernstein's most exciting tour was to Soviet Russia, his parents' native country. This was in August and September 1958, a year after he became Musical Director of the New York Philharmonic. Before the

USSR tour, he had taken the orchestra to Salzburg, where the conservative audience at the Festival — accustomed to the magnificent Wiener Philharmoniker and its classical music tradition — had given the Americans a remarkable ovation. One characteristic press review spoke of 'almost tumultuous enthusiasm for the debut of the orchestra under Leonard Bernstein. The ovation came not only from the sportive applause of American lady tourists who invaded the Festival Hall. The Austrians were enraptured as well'. Samuel Barber, Dimitri Shostakovich and Leonard Bernstein were the composers on the Salzburg programme, 'a modern Russian-American musical mixture, which resulted in an ideal, or at least ideally revealing, marriage of sounds' wrote one reviewer. Bernstein's *Age of Anxiety*, with Seymour Lipkin as piano soloist, was not liked by all reviewers; one described it as 'uninhibited self-advertisement'. The conductor was described very vividly:

> As sportive and matter-of-fact-like, the forty-year old Bernstein, gracefully tough, at first faces his army, so determined and powerful, so effective and dramatic he leads his men.
> His sinewy, sun-tanned hands do mostly without the birch-tree wooden stick in the right hand (this became *chic* from Stokowski to Karajan); they modulate the streams of sound rather in free air. The entire wiry man bends and twists under the pain-lust waves or he seems to ride on water skis or to swing rumba-rattles and mix cocktails, to sip invisible rapture attempts. A Shaman from Lawrence, Massachusetts! Orpheus of Carnegie Hall 59 (Heinrich Lindlar, *Deutsche Zeitung*, Stuttgart, 20 August 1959).

Salzburg's press and public, together with musicians from all over the world, fêted the New York Philharmonic and their conductor after the concert at a party given by the US Consul-General at the Hotel Österreichischer-Hof, where Leonard Bernstein also met Dimitri Mitropoulos and Herbert von Karajan.

A tour of Soviet Russia by an American orchestra would not have been possible during the Cold War, that is, up to the mid-1950s. Towards the end of the decade, the relationship between the super powers took a turn for the better and a concert tour of the New York Philharmonic was arranged, in order to demonstrate the possibilities for cultural exchange; the orchestra also visited Poland. For Leonard Bernstein this tour meant a new and exciting challenge. He also hoped he could see his relatives who had remained in Russia and might perhaps persuade his father to travel with him. Samuel Bernstein hesitated a long time before he could decide whether he really wanted to go to the country of his birth: nor was it easy to obtain a visa for a

Warsaw, 1959

former illegal emigrant. Jennie, his wife, was not at all interested in seeing her homeland again. Samuel applied for a visitor's visa, but when at last it arrived (after his son had already left with the orchestra) he decided not to come after all. Shortly after reaching Moscow Lenny, accompanied by his wife, met his own uncle and cousin, Shlomoh Bernstein and Michoel Zvainboim; Shlomoh had come from Novosibirsk and Michoel from Dnepropetrovsk, after both had had to overcome extraordinary bureaucratic procedures before being granted permission to travel. Together with Shlomoh Lenny put through a telephone call to his father in Boston, so that the brothers Shlomoh and Sam could talk to each other for a few minutes. Sam was overwhelmed; he took a plane to Paris and thence flew to Moscow, not without further troubles with his Soviet visa. When he arrived, it soon transpired that the brothers no longer had much in common; living in different worlds, they found it difficult to talk to each other. The situation was saddening for Leonard: his father stayed only a few days in Moscow, where the concerts and his son's success held much more interest for him than his family.

Russian audiences gave a demonstrative welcome to the New York Philharmonic and its conductor. In Moscow Bernstein had included the Shostakovich Fifth Symphony in his first concert on 22 August and from the piano he conducted Mozart's G major Piano Concerto K.453 — something completely new for the Russian public. On 24 August 1959, the eve of his birthday, he conducted a programme that was sensational for Soviet Russia. It included *Le Sacre du Printemps* by Igor Stravinsky and Charles Ives' *The Unanswered Question*. Stravinsky's music had long been taboo in the USSR; after having turned his back on Russia in 1914, the composer did not visit his homeland again until 1962. In a short address to the audience, Leonard Bernstein reminded his listeners that *Le Sacre du Printemps* had 'created a musical revolution five years before your revolution . . . then five years after your revolution he created another revolution by turning to neoclassic form'. The story goes that the interpreter distorted Bernstein's meaning by using the Russian word *skandal*, which signifies not 'revolution', but an uproar (John Briggs, *Leonard Bernstein. The Man, his Work and his World*, Cleveland and New York, 1961). Again, Bernstein preceded the playing of *The Unanswered Question* by a talk on Ives and his work; the music was then so enthusiastically received by the audience that he performed it again as an encore, which was severely criticised by the magazine *Sovjetskaja Kultura*.

Leonard Bernstein has a great talent for languages and was able to speak a few words in Russian; after concerts he used to acknowledge applause by saying 'Bolshoieh spasibo' ('Thank you very much'). In Moscow he met many artists and musicians, among them the composers Shostakovich and Aram Khatchaturian, the violinist Leonid Kogan, the pianist Vladimir Ashkenazy and the poet and novelist Boris Pasternak, whom Felicia and Leonard visited in the village to which he had retired. For the last concert of the tour, on 11 September 1959, Pasternak came to Moscow and it is said that his farewell words to Bernstein were: 'Thank you for taking us into heaven. Now we must return to earth' (Ewen, *Bernstein*, p. 145). Pasternak died only a few months after this meeting, which had been as exciting for him as for Leonard Bernstein.

Apart from Moscow, the New York Philharmonic also visited Kiev and played in Leningrad; shortly before their departure a film was made to be shown on US television a few weeks later. On returning home Leonard Bernstein talked of his trip in fascinating detail, including his many meetings with the younger generation of Russian musicians and composers. One such anecdote concerned a young Soviet composer, who had brought him the score of a work based on a theme from Bernstein's youthful Clarinet Sonata and written in his honour. Bernstein has reported that he told the young man: 'Your piece is better than your theme' (ibid., p. 143).

Apart from the concerts in the Soviet Union the New York Philharmonic also played in Athens and Thessaloniki, Baalbek in the Lebanon, Istanbul, Salzburg, Warsaw, Scheveningen, Luxemburg, Paris, Basle, Belgrade and Zagreb, Venice and Milan, Oslo, Helsinki and Turku, Stockholm and Göteborg, London and in six German cities, including Berlin. Out of fifty concerts, Leonard Bernstein conducted thirty-seven, the others being led by Thomas Schippers and Seymour Lipkin. Back in the United States, the Philharmonic gave a 'Welcome' concert in Washington and opened the winter season in New York on 16 October. The streets around Carnegie Hall and the concert hall itself were gaily decorated and signs all along 57th Street proclaimed 'Welcome Home International Heroes' (ibid., p. 146).

Highlights of the years following the Russian 'adventure' and the extended concert tour were the first Gustav Mahler Festival with the New York Philharmonic in January 1960, a concert series on *Twentieth Century Problems in Music*, a *Spring Festival of Theater Music* (March to May 1960), an orchestral concert of Bernstein compositions (February 1961), the inaugural concert at the new Philharmonic Hall at Lincoln Center (23 September 1962), a tour to Britain where the New York Philharmonic took part in London's salute to the Royal Philharmonic Orchestra on its 150th anniversary, Bernstein's successful debut as a conductor at the New York Metropolitan Opera House (6 March 1963) and the first performance of his 'Kaddish' Symphony (Tel Aviv, 10 December 1963). At the beginning of the winter season 1962/3 Leonard Bernstein's second book *Young People's Concerts for Reading and Listening*, containing the scripts of his televised youth concerts, appeared in New York. He had not created any important musical work between *West Side Story* and *Kaddish*. Two short pieces were performed: he had written them for the staging of Christopher Fry's play the *The Firstborn*. These were the 'Israelites' Chorus' and 'Tensret's Song' for voice and percussion, but they have not been published. On a tour of Japan in the spring of 1961 Bernstein surprised his listeners when he introduced his assistant Seiji Ozawa in a short speech in Japanese. Ozawa later became chief conductor of the Boston Symphony Orchestra.

In the autumn of 1964, Leonard Bernstein took sabbatical leave, interrupted only by guest conducting engagements in Denmark and at the Casals Festival in Puerto Rico (in May and June 1965) and by conducting the first performance of his own new *Chichester Psalms* in New York on 15 July 1965. The work is based on the Hebrew texts of psalms and on this occasion the Camerata Singers participated under the direction of Abraham Kaplan: John Bogart was the boy soloist.

During his sabbatical year, Bernstein, as a composer, had experimented with modelling music on twelve-note rows, adhering strictly to dodecaphonic elaboration, but did not find any satisfaction in this work. In the *Chichester Psalms* tonality reigns supreme. At the time, Bernstein also contemplated writing a new musical work for the stage. But in this field he was greatly disappointed with his prospective authors. 'Some of my collaborators did not dare anything — thought my plans were not commercial enough for Broadway', he told me. 'They did not have any courage to do something new and original'. He had wanted to turn Thornton Wilder's *The Skin of our Teeth* into a musical and worked on a libretto with his friends Jerome Robbins and the Comden–Green team, but gave it up after many months of endeavour. Another literary work contemplated for adaptation as a musical was Bertold Brecht's *The Exception and the Rule*; he worked on this with Jerome Robbins, Stephen Sondheim and Jerry Leiber and even wrote some music for it. But, dissatisfied with this project too, he abandoned it. 'For *West Side Story* everyone of us had the same idea, it was so wonderful, there was complete agreement. But now my colleagues did not go along with me.' It was the difficulty in finding a like-minded team which later led to the catastrophic flop of *1600 Pennsylvania Avenue* in 1976:

The original concept was so exciting [Bernstein says], so interesting, so original, but they did not have the courage to follow me. They cut and changed it, to make it charming. Cut it to shreds. Nothing what I started out to write. I wanted to stop the show from coming to New York. I did everything I could to stop it in Washington and not let it come to New York. I was not successful. They insisted on bringing it to New York where it ran for four days and closed and it was just humiliating — it was one of the worst experiences of my life.

'Is there nothing you can do in such a case?' I asked. 'Not if you have collaborators, that's the problem on Broadway. You have directors, producers, choreographer, the book writer, the lyric writer, all these people who contribute to the show. You can't be in charge just yourself.'
'Didn't you have a similar experience with a film?'

Yes, I worked for two years with Franco Zeffirelli on a film musical on St Francis of Assisi. It was an incredible idea. It would happen both in the twelfth century and now. I wanted to write music also like this — anachronistic. It was very interesting. And then he got scared. He was afraid it would not succeed commercially and he wanted to make it more pietistic, more religious, and so I gave it up, after two years, and he made a film with some folk or rock composer, a terrible film, called *Brother Sun and Sister Moon*, which is a very bad film. A lot of this music I wrote I used in *Mass*, as for instance the 'Simple Song', the 'Sanctus', a lot of the music.

Apart from *Mass*, some of the St Francis music was also used in *1600 Pennsylvania Avenue* and the orchestral overture *Slava!*; *Mass* was written in 1971, *Slava!* (for Mstislav 'Slava' Rostropovich) in 1977. 'I have given up Broadway', said Lenny, 'and I am now writing only for the opera house.' His first full-length opera, *A Quiet Place* (*Tahiti II*) was composed during 1982 and 1983.

In his sabbatical year, Leonard Bernstein wrote a mock report in rhyming verse for the *New York Times* (repr. in *The Infinite Variety of Music*, pp. 143ff.). With much humour and some nostalgia he speaks of his attempts to use modern composing techniques and how he gave them up and finally wrote the 'simple, modest and tonal' *Chichester Psalms*. The verses tell of his trip to England to hear his new work performed at Chichester Cathedral, where the Dean, the Very Rev. Walter Hussey, had commissioned the Psalms. Bernstein conducted the performance on 31 July 1965, two weeks after the New York première.

In September 1965, Leonard Bernstein returned to the New York

[82]

Philharmonic Orchestra and his work as Musical Director. As a central theme for two concert seasons he chose *Symphonic Forms in the Twentieth Century*. On 14 March 1966 there followed his first appearance as opera conductor in Vienna, when Dietrich Fischer-Dieskau sang Falstaff at the Wiener Staatsoper, Bernstein also conducted the Vienna Philharmonic in a series of concerts; this became one of his favourite orchestras with which he subsequently made numerous recordings. In November 1966 his third book, *The Infinite Variety of Music*, was published. In June 1967 he conducted a memorial concert in Florence to mark the centenary of the birth of Arturo Toscanini, with whom the young Leonard had had some connections. At that time the Six-Day War broke out in Israel, when the young state had to defend itself against Arab armies about to attack the country. The ancient Old City of Jerusalem and the newer parts, separated for eighteen years by walls and barbed wire, were once again united; devout believers of the three great religions, Christianity, Islam and Judaism, could now freely make the pilgrimage to their shrines and holy places. Leonard Bernstein hastened to Israel and on an historic Sunday afternoon in July 1967 conducted a stirring performance of three movements from Gustav Mahler's 'Resurrection' Symphony with the Israel Philharmonic Orchestra, soloists, and chorus. The setting of the concert was Mount Scopus, cut off from Jerusalem before unification, and the audience had a breathtaking view of the city as well as the stony desert lying between Jerusalem, Jericho and the Dead Sea. Just before this, the whole of Mahler's Second Symphony had been performed in Tel Aviv; at the open-air concert it was not possible to play more than the Scherzo, 'Urlicht' and the finale ('The Great Call'). The Israel Philharmonic was supplemented by musicians from the Jerusalem Radio Symphony Orchestra; Jennie Tourel and Netania Davrat were the solo singers, together with the Philharmonic Choir. The Symphony was preceded by Felix Mendelssohn-Bartholdy's Violin Concerto in E minor played by Isaac Stern. A film, *Journey to Jerusalem*, was produced at the time and the concert was recorded for CBS, but the record seems to be no longer in the catalogues.

From Israel, Leonard Bernstein travelled to Italy where he spent an extended summer holiday with his wife and children in a villa in Ansedonia, a village dating back to the Roman Empire, on the shores of the Tyrrhenian Sea. 'Lenny . . . was both exalted and exhausted', reported John Gruen, who stayed in Ansedonia while the Bernsteins were there and wrote a lively book about his holidays and talks with them.

[83]

New Year's greetings from the Bernstein family

Exalted because the experience of conducting in Israel on such an occasion moved him deeply, exhausted because yet another New York Philharmonic season had recently ended. His back was giving him great trouble — a problem of long standing . . . and he looked pale and drawn . . . . While the object of the summer was rest and leisure, Lenny was full of projects. First and foremost, he wished to compose. He feels he has not yet begun to do so . . . . 'I have not even scratched the surface' he kept saying . . . and there was Strauss' *Der Rosenkavalier* to think about; he would conduct it in the spring at the Vienna Opera . . . . But swimming and diving resuscitated him both physically and spiritually (John Gruen and Ken Hyman — Fotos —, *The Private World of Leonard Bernstein*, New York, 1968).

On 1 September 1967 the Bernsteins had to leave the Italian idyll and return to New York. Leonard felt refreshed and looked much better; hardly had the New York season begun than he took the Philharmonic on a tour to nine Canadian cities.

On 13 April 1968, Bernstein conducted *Der Rosenkavalier* at the Wiener Staatsoper; Christa Ludwig, who became one of his favourite singers, sang the Marschallin. In the autumn of that year he embarked on yet another tour with the New York Philharmonic, again to Europe and to Israel; he had in May already conducted the Israel Philharmonic Orchestra in a series of festival concerts to celebrate the twentieth anniversary of the State of Israel. A year later, on 17 May 1969, came the last concerts to be conducted by Bernstein as Musical Director of the New York Philharmonic; eight days later, he conducted Beethoven's *Missa solemnis* in celebration of the Wiener Staatsoper's centenary.

Leonard Bernstein was now fifty years old. He was mourning the death of his father who had died on 30 April 1969. In spite of all the difficulties he had raised in opposition to a musical career, Lenny had a very deep affection for his father, who had always only wanted the best for his son. He never saw in his father a towering and domineering figure — as has sometimes been maintained — but a head of family in the best Jewish tradition, a father who felt obliged to care for his children in the best possible way, as he saw it. He knew that he owed to Samuel Bernstein a thorough education, an example of diligence and industriousness and a proper sense of tradition and that gratitude, friendship and devotion were his due. 'We're a funny family', Samuel Bernstein said a short time before his death, 'My grandfather, Bezalel, became a blacksmith instead of a rabbi like his father. My father became a rabbi instead of a blacksmith. I ran from the *shtetl* to be a businessman in America. Now my own kids won't have anything to do with my work and my life . . . Who knows what your kids and Lenny's

[85]

will turn out to be?' (Bernstein, *Family Matters*, p. 199). Samuel Bernstein died at the age of 77. When Leonard conducted the *Missa solemnis* in Vienna three weeks after his father's death, he must have felt the performance to be a memorial tribute.

In May 1970, he was in Vienna again for the festival commemorating Beethoven's bicentenary; he conducted *Fidelio* in the theatre where it had received the first performance in Beethoven's own time. Before that he had produced the first of over a hundred television concerts, conducting Verdi's *Requiem* at St Paul's Cathedral in London with Martina Arroyo, Josephine Veasey, Plácido Domingo and Ruggiero Raimondi, with the London Symphony Orchestra and Chorus; the performance was also recorded by CBS. Later television and video productions included some of Bernstein's own compositions, all the symphonies of Gustav Mahler, together with his *Lied von der Erde* and a Brahms lieder recital with Christa Ludwig, accompanied by Bernstein on the piano, and Daniel Benyamini of the Israel Philharmonic as solo violist in the two Brahms songs with viola.

The next memorable date was 8 September 1971, with the first performance of *Mass*, a work commissioned from Bernstein by the family of John F. Kennedy for the opening of the Kennedy Center for the Performing Arts. The composer describes *Mass* as 'A Theatre Piece for Singers, Players and Dancers', based on liturgical texts from the Roman Catholic Mass with additional words by Stephen Schwartz and Leonard Bernstein. The first performance was conducted by Maurice Peress and Alvin Ailey was the choreographer. *Mass* was the first large-scale work since the *Chichester Psalms* (written six years earlier). From the *Mass* Leonard Bernstein extracted three numbers as 'Meditations' for violoncello solo and small orchestra (or piano). In 1974 he composed another ballet — for Jerome Robbins' choreographic version of *The Dybbuk*, the classic Jewish legend — and conducted the first performance by the New York City Ballet, given on 16 May 1974. In November 1976, at Avery Fisher Hall (formerly the Philharmonic Hall), Bernstein conducted the first performance of four symphonic songs later incorporated in the cycle *Songfest*; an additional song dedicated to the First Lady, Mrs Rosalynn Carter, was premièred at the Carter Inaugural Gala in Washington on 19 January 1977. On 12 October 1977 I attended the second of a series of four concerts in Washington, D.C. in which the complete *Songfest* was performed; the composer had conducted the whole cycle for the first time on the previous evening and this second night was attended by President Jimmy Carter and his wife. At the beginning of this all-Bernstein programme, Mstislav Rostropovich, newly appointed Chief Conductor of the National Symphony Orchestra (in succession to Antal Dorati, who had held the post for seven years), conducted the Symphonic Suite from the music to the film *On the Waterfront*; afterwards playing the cello solo in the 'Three Meditations from *Mass*' conducted by the composer. As an overture to the concert proper, the orchestra played Leonard Bernstein's friendly tribute to 'Slava' Rostropovich, entitled *Slava!* After the interval, *Songfest — A Cycle of American Poems for Six Singers and Orchestra* was given. Clamma Dale, Rosalind Elias, Nancy Williams, Neil Rosenshein, John Reardon and Donald Gramm were the singers and Bernstein conducted. Among the poems was one by the Puerto Rican Julia de Burgos (died 1953) translated into English by Jamie, Leonard Bernstein's daughter. After the concert, there was some annoyance backstage since, although the song 'To my Dear and Loving Husband', dedicated to America's First Lady, was included in *Songfest*, Jimmy and Rosalynn Carter had not come round to speak to the singers, Rostropovich or Bernstein. Rostropovich was disappointed, Bernstein was furious and exclaimed 'How rude of him!'

Nevertheless, Lenny was pleased with the succes of his new work. He had another reason for happiness, though in this he was sadly deceived. On 30 September I had met him in New York, when he was in despair about Felicia's failing health and the pain she suffered through her malignant disease. However, she had attended the first performance of *Songfest*. 'She was so beautiful, so beautiful', Lenny exclaimed, 'it is a miracle!' Felicia, however, died a few months later.

On 22 December 1979, soon after *Songfest* had been given in Germany and Austria, the choreographer John Neumeier produced dance versions of *Songfest* and *Age of Anxiety* at the Hamburg State Opera. Deutsche Grammophon released a recording of the song cycles' Washington performance. For a large part of 1980, Bernstein stayed at Fairfield, Connecticut, and concentrated on composing. In the summer he completed his *Divertimento* for orchestra, a work full of wit and humour but complex and interesting in its musical artfulness. The Boston Symphony Orchestra had requested him to write a composition for its hundredth season of 1980/1 and so he dedicated *Divertimento* to it with these words:

When Stravinsky wrote his *Symphony of Psalms*, commissioned by the Boston Symphony Orchestra, in honour of its fiftieth birthday, he dedicated the work 'To the glory of God and the Boston Symphony Orchestra'. This dedication elicited a witty reaction at the time: 'That is what you call making the best of two worlds at once'. If I dared to put myself in Stravinsky's league, I'd follow his example by having the double dedication: 'To the Boston Spymphony Orchestra and my Mother', or I might even go him one better by offering a triple dedication: 'To the Boston Symphony Orchestra, my Mother, and Boston, my old home town'.

The dedication and the occasion, the hundredth anniversary of the BSO, are documented in the score of *Divertimento*; all eight movements of the work are based on the motif of the interval B–C, from which all the musical themes are developed: B–C stands for Boston Centenary.

Bernstein's next compositions, completed before he devoted all his time and efforts to writing the opera *A Quiet Place*, were *Halil — Nocturno for solo flute, string orchestra, and percussion* and the piano piece *Touches*. The score of *Halil* was finished in New York on 13 April 1981; *Touches* was written at Fairfield, Connecticut, in July 1980. *Halil* was first played publicly on 27 May 1981 by Jean-Pierre Rampal and the Israel Philharmonic Orchestra in Tel Aviv, the composer conducting; the *Divertimento* and other orchestral works by Bernstein were also performed in Israel at that time and recorded live by Deutsche Grammophon which released them on two LPs in 1982. Julius Baker was the solo flautist in the later New York première. The Nocturne is dedicated to the memory of a young Israeli flautist unknown to Leonard Bernstein personally, killed in his tank in the Sinai at the age of 19 while defending his country in 1973. *Halil* is the Hebrew for flute and the dedication reads 'To the Spirit of Yadin and to his Fallen Brothers'. In this lyrical work, which becomes dramatic only in some passages, the listener may discern some sounds of struggle; the composer hears in it 'like in much of my music', a 'struggle between tonal and non-tonal forces', mirroring 'that struggle involving wars and the threat of wars, the overwhelming desire to live and the consolations of art, love, and the hope for peace. It is a kind of diatonic final cadence, is an ongoing conflict of nocturnal images; wish-dreams, nightmares, repose, sleeplessness, night-terrors — and sleep itself, Death's twin brother . . .'.

Since Leonard Bernstein had relinquished his commitments as music director of an orchestra, it had become easier for him to plan his schedules so as to divide his time between conducting, teaching (through television and in 1973 as Charles Eliot Norton Professor of Poetry at Harvard University) and composing. From time to time, he conducted the New York Philharmonic as Laureate Conductor both in America and abroad. Mostly, however, during the 1970s and 1980s he conducted two 'favourite orchestras', with which he also made many recordings and television appearances. These were the Vienna Philharmonic and the Israel Philharmonic Orchestra.

On 25 June 1973, *Mass* had its first European performance at the Vienna Konzerthaus under the conductor John Mauceri; the performance was recorded for television. Yale University students and Viennese choirs took part in this performance. Seven years later on 16 February 1980, Leonard Bernstein conducted a performance of *Mass* at the Wiener Staatsoper. In June 1973, the day following the Viennese première, he had conducted *Mass* at the New York Metropolitan Opera House; he had seen the Yale University performance and agreed to its being taken to Vienna. In November 1973 he began his Harvard lectures and in January 1976 they were released for television and ultimately seen in many countries.

In the summer of 1974, Bernstein conducted two concerts in memory of Sergei Koussevitzky, whose centenary fell on 13 June. One concert was given at Tanglewood with the Boston Symphony Orchestra, the other in Central Park, New York, with the New York Philharmonic. After a concert tour with the New York Philharmonic and after the disappointment of *1600 Pennsylvania Avenue*, he returned to Munich after twenty-eight years to conduct a German orchestra: on 15 and 17 October he conducted concerts by the Bavarian Radio Symphony Orchestra as a benefit for Amnesty International; Claudio Arrau was the solo pianist.

February 1976 saw the first Bernstein Festival: the Butler University, Indianapolis and the State of Indiana designated the period 17 to 22 February as Bernstein Week. In March and April 1977 the Israel Philharmonic celebrated thirty years of association with Leonard Bernstein by playing with him a series of his compositions. Between 14 and 21 August 1977, Bernstein and the IPO took part in the Carinthian Summer Festival at Ossiach in Carinthia, where Marcel Prawy, *Chefdramaturg* of the Viennese Opera, had issued invitations to the 'First European Leonard Bernstein Festival', which included lectures, film shows and concerts. An illustrated programme booklet was published for the occasion, containing a 'small Bernstein portrait' by Franz Endler, then music editor of the Viennese daily *Die Presse*. Lukas Foss came from the USA as solo pianist in *The Age of Anxiety*, together with an opera ensemble from Indiana University for an evening called *Bernstein on Broadway*, including *Trouble in Tahiti* and excerpts from musicals. On 25 August 1978, Leonard Bernstein's sixtieth birthday was celebrated in Washington with a concert by the National Symphony Orchestra, in which Isaac Stern, Claudio Arrau, Aaron Copland and Mstislav Rostropovich took part.

After the pause in creative activity of 1980, Leonard Bernstein

[89]

embarked on one of his most challenging tasks as a conductor —
concert performances of Richard Wagner's *Tristan und Isolde* coupled
with television and gramophone recordings. Having prepared himself
over many months of study, he had come to think that *Tristan* could
more convincingly be interpreted in the concert hall than on the opera
stage, where, he felt, nothing much happens and the visual effect only
distracts from the music. On 11 January 1981, the first act of *Tristan and
Isolde* was sung by Hildegard Behrens, Peter Hofmann, Yvonne Minton
and Bernd Weikl, with the Bavarian Radio Symphony Orchestra. Act
Two followed in April and Act Three on 10 November. Between these
concerts and recordings, Bernstein gave a benefit concert at the Vatican with the orchestra of the Academia di Santa Cecilia and soloists
from the Israel Philharmonic; the programme included his own *Halil*
and 'Three Meditations'.

Throughout the years of a hectic life, of hard and responsible work, of
great successes and a number of disappointments, of family joy and
mourning, Lenny has preserved an astonishingly youthful vitality,
displaying his incomparable memory in recalling events of his life and
work, and conducting classical masterpieces and complex contemporary music. In his conversation, however, there may be sensed a certain
'wisdom of age', as well as some nostalgia and the fear that fate may
not allow him to accomplish all the tasks he has set himself. When, in
August 1981, he learned that the conductor Karl Böhm was seriously
ill, he wrote to him with a wish for his speedy recovery; however, Böhm
died before the letter arrived. In the opening sentences of his letter,
dated 13 August 1981, Bernstein said that Böhm's 'years of physical
age have mounted close to ninety, and even I, on the eve of my 63rd
birthday, can feel their weight and the concomitant pain at time
running out before all our works can be finished'.

In commemoration of Karl Böhm's encouraging criticism of his
Tristan interpretation some months before, Leonard Bernstein completed his recordings of the music drama in November 1981. In the
spring and summer of 1982 he conducted concerts in America and
Europe to mark the centenary of Igor Stravinsky. In Israel he was
prominent in a Stravinsky Festival with the Israel Philharmonic Orchestra, conducting the music of a composer whose works had exerted
a decisive influence on his own style. After a concert tour with the
Vienna Philharmonic in the autumn of 1982, he retired from concert
life in order to be able to complete his new opera, *A Quiet Place*, in time
for the planned world première at Houston, Texas, in June 1983. The

last composition before the completion of the opera was a piece for piano solo: *Touches* — Chorale, eight Variations, and Coda — written for the Sixth International Van-Cliburn Piano Competition at Fort Worth, Texas, and dated Fairfield, Connecticut, July 1980.

A Quiet Place, to a libretto by Stephen Wadsworth, opened on 17 June 1983 at the Jones Hall for the Performing Arts, Houston, Texas. Since it was conceived as a sequel to the early chamber opera *Trouble in Tahiti*, showing the same characters thirty years later, *Trouble in Tahiti* was performed as a curtain-raiser to the new opera. However, composer, librettist, audience and critics were more or less unanimous in finding the combination unsuccessful. Wadsworth and Bernstein decided to revise and partly rewrite the words and music, and to incorporate *Trouble in Tahiti* into *A Quiet Place* as a textual and musical flashback.

The revision of the opera occupied Leonard Bernstein for many months after the series of Houston performances. Meanwhile his sixty-fifth birthday in August 1983 was approaching, and he wished to mark it by organising a world-wide demonstration of support for a 'mutual and verifiable nuclear weapons freeze'. A circular letter was sent to musicians and music-lovers, and to his personal friends throughout the world — in the United States, in Western and Eastern European countries, in South America, Japan and Israel. With the circular went a piece of sky-blue cloth and the recipients were asked to wear armbands of this material on 25 August, wherever they were on that day, 'while playing concerts (symphonic, rock, chamber, recital, or cocktail), taking tickets, selling records, or even at the beach . . . to show their individual support . . . in testimony to this vital cause, which will help ensure many more happy birthdays for us all'.

The initiative was praised by a world-wide community of friends and well-wishers and the blue armbands were seen in many countries and cities. Leonard Bernstein himself wore one at the dedication ceremonies of the Leonard Bernstein Section of Heritage State Park in Lawrence, Massachusetts, the city of his birth, where he conducted a group from Musicians Against Nuclear Arms. In Budapest, where the present author happened to be on that day, a festive concert took place in the Matthias Church in Buda, the church where the Habsburg kings had been crowned; orchestra members and visitors had received the blue cloth and wore it as a sign of sympathy with the Bernstein who had regularly journeyed to Budapest and conducted immensely successful concerts there.

In November 1983 Leonard Bernstein visited Europe again for concerts and recordings. In January 1984, he opened a concert tour

with the Vienna Philharmonic Orchestra, performing a Mozart programme as part of the annual *Mozartwoche* in Salzburg. The tour went
on to many cities of the United States; in Chicago he stumbled and fell
while descending the podium and had to be taken to hospital, but he
recovered so quickly that the tour could continue as scheduled. At the
end of March, he conducted the New York Philharmonic in a spring
concert with music by Copland, Robert Schumann and Stravinsky.
After a series of guest appearances with the Israel Philharmonic in
Israel and for the Maggio Musicale Fiorentino, he went to Milan to
help prepare the première of the revised version of *A Quiet Place,* at the
Teatro alla Scala, directed by the author Stephen Wadsworth; John
Mauceri was chosen by Bernstein to conduct the work. On 22 July
1984, a month after the Scala première, the new version of the opera
was given in the Opera House, Kennedy Center, Washington DC, as
the start of a series of performances. Though the opera was quite
favourably received both in Italy and America, the authors decided on
further changes. The resulting revised version was brought by an
American cast to Vienna in April 1986 for six performances at the State
Opera House, while the Staatsoper company were touring Japan. On
this occasion the opera was conducted for the first time by Bernstein
himself; the orchestra was the Austrian Radio Symphony Orchestra. In
April 1987 a slightly shortened version of *A Quiet Place*, in a German
translation by Paul Esterhazy, was premiered at the Theatre of
Bielefeld in West Germany under the title *Ruhe und Frieden* (Quiet and
Peace). It was staged by John Dew and conducted by Rainer Koch.

The London Symphony Orchestra organised a Leonard Bernstein
Festival at the Barbican Centre in London, from 29 April to 11 May
1986, with Bernstein himself, John Mauceri, Lukas Foss and Jeffrey
Tate as conductors. A US concert tour by the Israel Philharmonic
Orchestra, conducted by Zubin Mehta and Leonard Bernstein, followed in August–September 1986 and at the end of September Bernstein opened the celebrations in Jerusalem and Tel Aviv marking the
fiftieth anniversary of the Israel Philharmonic, for which occasion, he
had promised the orchestra a new composition. The new work, *Jubilee
Games*, was premièred on the tour and in Tel Aviv and Jerusalem on 27
and 28 September. Another new composition was readied for the
festive re-opening of the refurbished New York Carnegie Hall, a *Prayer*
on Hebrew liturgical benedictions, for baritone and small orchestra;
Leonard Bernstein conducted the premiere performance and incorporated the work in *Jubilee Games* in 1987.

In the midst of the busy 1985/6 schedule of composition and appearances Leonard Bernstein completed television portrayals of two important composers. The first was a 90-minute film on Gustav Mahler, with whose work he had been deeply associated from his early days, and the second on Richard Wagner, the great musician but of dubious character. In the first programme, Bernstein, in his own words, 'delved into Mahler's Jewish roots, his deep ghetto origins and his ambiguity towards Christianity', and found that the composer's musical language undoubtedly sounds German or Austrian, echoing influences from Bach, Mozart, Schubert and Bruckner. Nevertheless, his works present overtones of the Jewish diaspora, the suffering of the Jews in many countries and throughout many centuries; Bernstein believes that this is especially felt in the vocal works with orchestra, the nucleus of Mahler's entire musical work. 'Questionable but masterly' were the words of the German literary critic Marcel Reich-Ranicki on this TV essay ('Feuilleton', *Frankfurter Allgemeine Zeitung*, 31 July 1985, p. 22).

The Wagner film was filmed and recorded at the house of Sigmund Freud in Vienna, indicating Bernstein's intention of analysing the man and musician Wagner in all the seemingly diametrically opposed facets of his life, ideas and compositions: 'I sat there waiting to unburden myself over my Wagneritis', Bernstein said in an interview in August 1985.

In May 1985, the Philadelphia Fellowship Commission conferred upon Bernstein its National Fellowship Award; on that occasion he recalled the time of his studies at the Curtis Institute there, his early association with Fredric R. Mann, and also the failure of his show *1600 Pennsylvania Avenue* which had had its pre-Broadway try-out at Philadelphia's Forrest Theatre. The 'failure still haunts my soul', he said then, 'I loved this show the most of all . . . it is the show I worked the hardest on . . . it was about my beloved America . . . it was written to rescue patriotism from the clutches of the selfish and ill-advised'. He announced that he was taking a West European Youth Orchestra to Hiroshima on the fortieth anniversary of the dropping of the first lethal atomic bomb: 'I am going there to apologize for man's inhumanity to men'.

The programme of the Peace Tour concerts with the Youth Orchestra included Bernstein's own 'Kaddish' Symphony, with all the choirs singing in Hebrew, and a Japanese composition. On the return to Europe the programmes were also given in Budapest and Vienna; there some twelve thousand people massed outside the State Opera

House and witnessed the performance of 'Kaddish' on a giant television screen. Immediately after the series, he took the Israel Philharmonic Orchestra on a tour of Japan and the USA after spending his
sixty-seventh birthday in Tel-Aviv, rehearsing for the tour. In 1985,
too, one of his most cherished dreams was realised, the release of a
recording of *West Side Story* with opera singers in the main roles, Kiri te
Kanawa as Maria and José Carreras as Tony, Anita sung by Tatiana
Troyanos, while Marilyn Horne sings 'Somewhere': in dialogue passages, Leonard Bernstein's youngest daughter Nina and his son Alexander speak the lines of Maria and Tony respectively. The producer for
Deutsche Grammophon was Hanno Rinke.

Apart from preparing his new orchestral work *Jubilee Games*, for a
first performance by the Israel Philharmonic Orchestra in their 1986/7
jubilee season, Leonard Bernstein began to think of a new operatic
work, again with a libretto by Stephen Wadsworth, along the lines of
his own thoughts and ideas. Three commissioning bodies await the
new opera for premieres in 1988: the Chicago Lyric Opera, the Vienna
State Opera, and the Jerusalem Foundation which hopes to present the
work at the International Jerusalem Festival. Librettist and composer
were reluctant to disclose details of the content and shape of their new
work: however, in the summer of 1985 Bernstein indicated that he
wants to set it against the background of the last dramatic fifty years,
the scenes being set in different cities, the first being Vienna before the
Nazi invasion. The opera would be multilingual with also disturbing
scenes in the ghettoes of Eastern European and in Soviet prisons: 'This
work will prove to show that the world has not learned anything from
history in about half a century'. Late in 1986 it became known that
work on the opera was interrupted, as Stephen Wadsworth apparently
found it difficult to handle the Holocaust theme. Leonard Bernstein has
said that he is deeply depressed about the set-back as he wishes so
much to give musical expression to the drama of humanity as he sees it.
The horrors of the past have not stopped him hoping for a brighter
future: 'All the world is a stage', he was reported as saying at the
Philadelphia reception in his honour in May 1985 (Michael Elkin,
Jewish Exponent, 10 May 1985), 'with audiences searching for the perfect
play . . . . We may not reach perfection — this is not a utopian world
— but all of us can strive toward that perfection . . . . To do that: *Keep
rehearsing!*'

3

The Conductor and Interpreter of Music

> The conductor must not only make his orchestra play;
> he must make them want to play. He must exalt them,
> lift them, start their adrenalin pouring, either through
> cajoling or demanding or raging. But however he does
> it, he must make the orchestra love the music as he
> loves it.
> *Leonard Bernstein,* December 1955

When 25-year-old Leonard Bernstein stepped in for Bruno Walter at that historic concert on 14 November 1943, he was introduced as a 'full-fledged conductor who was born, educated, and trained in this country'. As a composer and performing musician, he was a product of America, the country where European musicians had always been valued more than native artists. American concert audiences were accustomed to celebrated European conductors — Arturo Toscanini, Bruno Walter, Sergei Koussevitzky, Leopold Stokowski, Dimitri Mitropoulos, Eugene Ormandy, Arthur Rodzinski and Fritz Reiner were its favourites in the 1930s and 1940s. The public at large disliked the music of contemporary composers as much as its counterparts at the subscription concerts of orchestras in Berlin, Vienna or London, and American music was a closed book for concertgoers. It is thus quite understandable that the Carnegie Hall audience on that Sunday afternoon in November 1943 should have been sceptical when a young and perhaps inexperienced 'Boston boy' took over the concert from the beloved Bruno Walter. All the greater was the surprise when young Bernstein justified his description as a fully-fledged conductor and led the renowned New York Philharmonic through a demanding programme with astounding success. Public and press followed the young man's career thereafter with ever-mounting interest and saw how he also succeeded in introducing a basically conservative public to the

The conductor rehearsing for a recording session

world of contemporary music and evoking interest and acceptance for the works of American composers past and present.

Historically speaking, Leonard Bernstein was not the very first American conductor at the helm of the New York Philharmonic. Its founder, Ureli Corelli Hill, was a native New Yorker (born 1802), whose father was a music teacher in Boston and New York. When Hill founded the Philharmonic Society of New York in 1842, a clause was incorporated in its constitution (23 April 1843) which read: 'If any grand orchestral compositions such as overtures, or symphonies, shall be presented to the society, they being composed in this country, the society shall perform one every season, provided a committee of five appointed by the government shall have approved and recommended the composition' (John Tasker Howard, *Our American Music*, New York, 3rd ed., 1946, p. 248).

During the early years of the Philharmonic's existence directors and conductors took no notice of this commitment. In an article written in 1852 for the journal *The Musical World*, the composer William Henry Fry (circa 1815–64) deplored the fact that the American public, and especially the critics, decried native compositions and sneered at native artists. In reply George Frederick Bristow (1825–1898), a violinist with the Philharmonic from its inception and himself a composer, wrote in *The Musical World*:

> As it is possible to miss a needle in a hay-stack, I am not surprised that Mr. Fry had missed the fact, that during the eleven years the Philharmonic Society has been in operation in this city, it played once, either by mistake or accident, one single American composition, an overture of mine. As one exception makes a rule stronger, so this single stray fact shows that the Philharmonic Society has been as anti-American as if it had been located in London during the Revolutionary War, and composed of native-born British tories . . . .

George Bristow was forced to resign in the wake of this protest and it was pointed out by the Society that during the first four years of its existence no American composition at all had been suggested to the committee for performance. During the next seven years several works were performed at concerts or at public rehearsals. Bristow was later reinstated, but American music played only a minor role in the Society's programmes ever after. Leonard Bernstein's innovation, when he became Music Director of the New York Philharmonic a hundred and sixteen years after its foundation, of playing an American composition in almost every programme and introducing the works in special preview concerts, went a long way towards the acceptance of new music by the public. This was a success for contemporary music that could not have been foreseen, especially as a great deal of criticism and objection had been heard in the early stages.

There had been American conductors before Bernstein, among them a few musicians who had also gained recognition in European countries. The most prominent were John Bitter, Alfred Wallenstein, Arthur Fiedler, Werner Janssen and Rudolph Dunbar. Arthur Fiedler was born in Boston in 1894 and had studied in Berlin before the first World War. Alfred Wallenstein was of German descent, born in Chicago in 1898, and studied in Europe between 1920 and 1922. Werner Janssen, born in New York in 1899, studied in Boston, won the Prix de Rome of the American Academy in 1930 and made his conducting debut in Rome; in 1934 he returned to America. Rudolph Dunbar, born in 1907, came to New York from British Guiana in 1919, but he also studied in Europe. These conductors, born between 1890 and 1907, and so belonging to the generation before Bernstein, became chief conductors in various American cities. However, despite audience success and good publicity, they were unable to compete in public favour and general acclaim with the attraction of the prominent European who conducted the great American orchestras. Accordingly, much critical comment warned Leonard Bernstein not to succumb to the initial enthusiasm roused by his spectacular New York debut. Mark Schubart sounded a characteristic note in his article in *The New York Times*:

> Bernstein's friends and well-wishing critics realize full well that the youthful musician's success represents, in a sense, the most serious obstacle he must overcome in maturing as a composer and as a conductor. His 'Jeremiah' Symphony, for example, was generally regarded as the work of a talented young man, rather than that of a finished musician; and it is no easy feat for Bernstein, in view of his spectacular career, to give such opinion serious consideration. Yet it is generally agreed that Bernstein must overcome his success in order to achieve a position in the world of music which will be less striking, perhaps, but much more durable (28 January 1945).

The development of Leonard Bernstein as composer and performing musician has shown that success with the public and critical acclaim have certainly always delighted him but never distracted him from further study, research, introspection and self-control, nor from trying to deepen his understanding of music and to enlarge his horizon. He has often said that before the interpretation of a musical masterwork, even the most familiar, he must study and restudy its score and more often than not he detects traits in it that he may previously have

[99]

overlooked. It is his main concern to put technical knowledge and craftsmanship to the service of purely artistic creativity and creative interpretation. Among the many talks he has given on his ideals as a performing musician, his televised 'The Art of Conducting' on 4 December 1955 contained the following basic statements:

> The conductor must be a master of the mechanics of conducting. He must have an inconceivable amount of knowledge. He must have a profound perception of the inner meanings of music, and he must have uncanny powers of communication . . . . But the conductor must not only make his orchestra play; he must make them want to play . . . he must make the orchestra love the music as he loves it . . . . When one hundred men share his feelings, exactly, simultaneously, responding as one to each rise and fall of the music, to each point of arrival and departure, to each little inner pulse — then there is a human identity of feeling that has no equal elsewhere. It is the closest thing I know to love itself . . . . And perhaps the chief requirement of all is that he be humble before the composer; that he never interpose himself between the music and the audience; that all his efforts, however strenuous or glamorous, be made in the service of the composer's meaning — the music itself, which, after all, is the whole reason for the conductor's existence (Bernstein, *Joy of Music*).

Twenty-six years later, in 1981, Leonard Bernstein, in his preface to Franz Endler's book on Karl Böhm (Hamburg, 1981), expressed admiration for Böhm because he was a musician who, quite contrary to Bernstein's own practice, could conduct a performance of *Ariadne* without having to study the score once again and still endeavoured always to interpret music in a pure and spontaneous spirit. In his letter of 13 August 1981 to the dying Böhm, Bernstein wrote that he was always 'somewhat amazed at the warmth and musical closeness of our relationship. After all, you were born in the realm of Mozart, Wagner and Strauss, with full title to their domain; whereas I was born in the lap of Gershwin and Copland, and my title in the kingdom of European music was, so to speak, that of an adopted son'. It had been an exciting experience for Leonard Bernstein when Karl Böhm came up to his podium in Munich after a 'not very well polished run-through' of the First Act of *Tristan*, and 'his eyes aflame, his cheeks ablaze', said 'Na Bernstein, jetzt hab' ich endlich zum ersten Mal im Leben *Tristan* gehört'. 'I was in heaven', wrote Bernstein, 'not only because of this unbelievable imprimatur from the Wagnerian pope himself, but also because I was watching a mystical, quasi-Faustian rejuvenation.' Leonard Bernstein admired Karl Böhm the musician; he seems not to have been aware of the conductor's uncritical collaboration in Nazi

Germany.

Interestingly, Karl Böhm's verdict on Bernstein's *Tristan* parallels the view of American and English critics that Bernstein, at barely thirty, was an ideal interpreter of Wagner's music: Dietrich Fischer-Dieskau, however, is of the opinion that Leonard Bernstein, whom he greatly admires, 'magnificently errs in his interpretation of Wagner' (letter to author, 20 June 1982).

While previous American composers and conductors invariably studied in European countries, Leonard Bernstein did not go to Europe, although his teachers Fritz Reiner, Dimitri Mitropoulos and Sergei Koussevitzky were great representatives of European musical traditions. For his development as a performing musician, it was an invaluable asset that, during his college and university studies, he could exploit the many opportunities to gain experience in all spheres of classical, popular and contemporary music. Hardly any European conductor of quality rose to a top position with a prominent stage or symphony orchestra without first working in small provincial halls and theatres conducting all kinds of music — opera, operetta, symphony or light music. For Leonard Bernstein this kind of gaining of experience was provided by the amateur and partly-trained musicians in his school and college. His youthful opera and operetta productions ranging from *Carmen* to Gilbert and Sullivan, his improvisations for dance and cinema performances and his thorough study of score-reading laid the foundations for his technical musical education; studies at Harvard opened his eyes to the diversity of the human thirst for knowledge and scholarship. His musical interpretations, therefore, mirror knowledge, understanding and extensive experience. The most eminent Haydn scholar of our times, H.C. Robbins Landon, valued Leonard Bernstein's recordings of Franz Joseph Haydn's symphonies far above those of most other conductors. Hearing Bernstein conduct Schumann's Second Symphony for the first time, I found his identification with the spirit of German Romanticism and Schumann's own poetry quite astounding. The ability to identify with the composer's spirit derives from Bernstein's own knowledge of composing; he had said that when conducting Beethoven and Mahler he often feels that he composed their symphonies himself. Perhaps a creative musician can indeed penetrate more deeply into the secret world of a composer than a performer who has no talent or no urge to compose.

The success Leonard Bernstein enjoys with orchestral musicians as well as with the public has been aptly described by Robert Layton,

Music Talks producer of the British Broadcasting Corporation: 'His command does not purely rest on the exceptional quality of musicianship he is fortunate enough to possess, though without this nothing could be accomplished. It is rather that in addition to his rhythmic vitality, sensitivity to detail, and feeling for texture, he conveys rare generosity of feeling' (from the brochure for Deutsche Grammophon to accompany the album of the three symphonies and *Chichester Psalms*, 1978).

The dichotomy arising from the desire to conduct and the urge to compose may be overcome, says Bernstein, by thinking of the wise biblical proverb 'To everything there is a season, and a time to every purpose under the heaven' (Ecclesiastes III, 1). At the age of thirty, he said:

> It is impossible for me to make an exclusive choice among the various acitivities of conducting, symphonic composition, writing for the theatre, or playing the piano. What seems right for me at any given moment is what I must do, at the expense of pigeon-holing or otherwise limiting my services to music. I will not compose a note while my heart is engaged in a conducting season; nor will I give up writing as much as a popular song, while it is there to be expressed, in order to conduct Beethoven's Ninth. There is a particular order involved in this, which is admittedly difficult to plan; but the order must be adhered to most strictly. For the ends are music itself, not the conventions of the music business; and the means are my own personal problem.

This statement recalls somewhat similar confessions from two great composer-conductors of the early and late Romantic period — Felix Mendelssohn-Bartholdy and Gustav Mahler, and it is perhaps no coincidence that both men were also of Jewish descent and devoutly religious, though both converted to Christianity. Mendelssohn wrote to Ferdinand Hiller in a letter dated 10 December 1837 — like Bernstein over a century later — that

> two months of constant conducting takes more out of me than two years of composing all day long . . . . At the end of the greatest turmoil if I ask myself what I have actually been doing, after all it is hardly worth speaking of . . . . I often think I should like to retire completely, never conduct any more, and only write; but then again there is a certain charm in an organized system, and in having the direction of it . . . .

There must also have been a similarity in temperament and gifts between Mendelssohn and Bernstein. As for the outer appearance, we

Bernstein conducting the Vienna Philharmonic in Mahler's Ninth Symphony

have a description of Mendelssohn from J.C. Horsley who wrote to Sir George Grove: 'You had only to be in his presence for a few moments to feel how completely his appearance and manner represented the genius he possessed . . . . He had a lithe figure, was very active and had a great deal of what may be termed sinuous movement in his action, which was inimitably in harmony with the feeling of the moment' (see Jack Werner, in *Music and Letters*, vol. XXVIII, p. 316). Horsley goes on to quote Mendelssohn himself:

> Ever since I began to compose, I have remained true to my starting principle: not to write a page because no matter what public or what pretty girl wanted it to be thus or thus; but to write solely as I myself thought best, and as it gives me pleasure . . . . People talk much about music, but really say so little. I fully believe that words are insufficient to express thoughts; and if they were sufficient, I think I should leave off composing music.

And on the problems of national music Mendelssohn is said to have exclaimed: 'No national music for me! Ten thousand devils take all nationality!'

Gustav Mahler, whose manifold artistry and fanatic zeal in bringing out the content and meaning of a musical composition when conducting are found again in the musical creed and work of Leonard Bernstein, has also expressed how he solves the inner conflict of dividing his creative and interpretative activities: 'I need a practical affirmation of my musical talents as a counterweight against the overwhelming spiritual experience in creating music', he said in 1910; conducting provided relaxation from the feverish tensions of creative work. A contemporary, the critic Adolf Weissmann, in *Der Dirigent im XX. Jahrhundert* (Berlin 1925) describes Gustav Mahler's appearance and the impression that he made:

> The frenzy of an ethical Dionysian created for itself above all a mimic equivalent . . . . The body surrendered itself without inhibition to a picturization of what had to be expressed . . . . The high tension of the ecstatic conductor is mirrored in conjuring and magnanimous and at times violent movements while his chin pierces the air and his baton whizzes around like a weapon. But the more rises the creativeness of this man, the deeper becomes the inner satisfaction with the cosmos sounding from within, the more wants the never weakening tension to attain moderation in the outward mimic expression, an only imaginary calm that is also extravagance, and there originates a new optical image of conducting which again differs from any other one knows.

The appearance and gestures of Gustav Mahler as a conductor seem to have been very similar to those of Leonard Bernstein, but with this difference: while Bernstein's ecstatic movements produce an immediate reaction from the orchestra, it has been said of Mahler that as his sensitive creative experience of sound intensified, so too did the remoteness between himself and his players and it became ever more difficult to achieve an understanding with those who regarded the adaptation of the orchestral sounds to Mahler's own ideals as exaggerated. In his interpretations he always wished to recreate the colourful images living in his inner world.

Despite all similarity of talent and purpose, the composer-conductors Mahler and Bernstein lived in two different worlds: Gustav Mahler's contemporaries were not yet ready for his music and for his interpretations of the music of earlier periods. Fifty years after his death, Leonard Bernstein opened to his own contemporaries the door to an understanding of Gustav Mahler and his times. Again, Adolf Weissmann describes the impressive nature of the great conductor and the radiance of Mahler's personality in words that could well be applied to Leonard Bernstein: 'That anyone can interpret the sounds of a musical score by a mere effort of will to each one of a multitude of people uniformly, and how he can throw a great audience into vibrant excitement, seems a continual miracle' (Weissman, *Der Dirigent*, pp. 66–79, 196).

A conductor's talent, technique and knowledge and his efficacy do not necessarily always go hand in hand with the views of the orchestra members. It can happen that a performance that is praised enthusiastically by both public and press is severely criticised by the players who complain of insecure leadership or obvious errors by the conductor. For an authoritarian maestro manages, more often than not, to gloss over or conceal a love for detail under a covering of the richest possible, glamorous and luscious sounds from the orchestra.

It was therefore revealing to talk about Leonard Bernstein the conductor with a prominent member of the Wiener Philharmoniker and to hear him compared with other regular conductors of the famed orchestra. Professor Hans Novak, one of the first violinists with the Vienna Philharmonic, of which he has been a member since 1945, has played under Bernstein's baton over since he conducted *Falstaff* at the Staatsoper and took part in the orchestra's festival concerts, tours, and recordings. His view of Bernstein, given in a personal interview in Salzburg in August 1982, was:

He is a genuine, a sincere musician. He feels the music the way he interprets it and he interprets it the way he feels it. He consumes himself in the rehearsals as much as in concerts. He is as temperamental when he rehearses as he is in conducting for the public; he certainly does not act and gesticulate for the sake of show — people who say this just do not know, it is silly to say this. He jumps about during rehearsals when he has no public behind him. Apart from this, he is certainly not the first conductor who jumps up when the music becomes exciting. I have played under Mitropoulos and he did the same. He was Bernstein's great model and he may have unconsciously learned it from him. His other teacher, Fritz Reiner, with whom we have also often played, was different: he made very scanty movements, even at the loudest fortissimo passages, and still produced immense musical effects. Bernstein opened all doors with us because he had the courage to translate all his feelings into movements without restraint.

In contrast to the appreciation of this Viennese musician, who has played with the greatest conductors and soloists, an American musician is reported to have said, somewhat obtusely: 'Bruno Walter or Beecham, they're great men, but their traditions are not ours. When Walter conducts, you feel rococo, see old castles and Vienna; when Bernstein conducts, we feel the spirit of ourselves in the music'. One comment on this is 'Bernstein, a born mimic, can convey rococo castles in his conducting, although when he does the feeling is apt to be more of stage-sets than of the real thing. But the symbol most often evoked by his electric — and eclectic — energy is not the castle, nor even the skyscraper which is the castle's American equivalent' (Henry Anatole Grunwald, 'A Bernstein Suite', in *American Horizon*, July 1959, pp. 17–23).

What the Viennese violinist referred to as Bernstein's 'courage' in translating his feelings into movement and music, has since his early days somewhat bewildered listeners and critics who did not perceive the latent spiritual and sensual force behind the outward ecstasy. Professor Novak described to me the temperamental rehearsals; and I have often witnessed how Bernstein relived a musical work or an entire concert in the green room or at a party after the concert; he would talk about the composer and the work just played, point to this climax or the other in the music itself or the orchestra's performance and would get excited, gesticulate and even jump about as if he were still on stage conducting. It can be felt then how much Leonard Bernstein differs from some favoured star conductors whose every movement and every glance is studied to impress the audience and the television cameras and whose elegant movements produce little excitement in the orchestra. Leonard Bernstein perhaps hardly realises what he looks like when conducting, for he admires in other conductors the calm podium appearance and unobstrusive elegance. In a cable on the occasion of Karl Böhm's death (14 August 1981) he actually wrote:

> What always attracted me about Maestro Böhm's performances especially of German opera, was the combination of elegance and eloquence with which he was able to delineate musical characterization. His powers of communication, to both vocal and instrumental colleagues, seemed to me all the more striking because of the minimalism of his physical movements. His communicative gifts blazed across the orchestra pit and up to the stage from his eyes and from the somehow electrified tip of his baton. He would conduct sitting down; but in those infrequent moments when he would rise ever so slightly to a half-standing position there were climaxes worthy of the Day of Judgment'.

Hans Novak remembers Bernstein's first Vienna opera performance, 'an unforgettable *Falstaff*':

> There he came, very modest, with a small suitcase in which he had all he needed. And then even before he stepped up to the podium to greet us, he demanded that in the first bar of the opera the first violins should play one octave higher than noted. I heard one of my colleagues say, well, he seems to want to make a musical of this opera, but we were soon to understand what he wanted. The change concerned only the very first bar and we found that it was really for the better. Since the C major chord as scored by Verdi originally, sounds somewhat thick in the middle register, and when the first violins play one octave higher, the sound is immediately brighter. The entire *Falstaff* was a great success, it belongs to the best performances we did with him, apart of course from the Mahler symphonies in the later years.
>
> At the time of his first visit in Vienna he got through — as also on almost all later occasions — an enormous schedule. There was *Falstaff* at the opera house, there were orchestral concerts and recordings — Mozart's Piano Concerto, K.450, which he played himself, *Das Lied von der Erde*, Mozart's 'Linz' Symphony K.425. *Das Lied von der Erde* was sung by James King and Dietrich Fischer-Dieskau (who also sang Falstaff); all this was accomplished though Bernstein did not feel very well at the time, he came to the rehearsals with a temperature — but in the end he was healthy and well. I remember that when he started work on the 'Linz' Symphony, a colleague said he asked himself how an American conductor would take the beautiful slow introduction to the first movement, surely rushed . . . . And he began in a wonderfully relaxed tempo and we all felt what a wonderful musician he is.
>
> Then he came back in 1968 with *Rosenkavalier* and later *Fidelio*. We also got excited in his rehearsals and he can never in rehearsals get himself to finish. Normally an orchestra — this is the same the world over — gets anxious when the rehearsals should end and the conductor does not want to stop. But

Bernstein always kept us in tension and we remained a quarter of an hour, sometimes half an hour longer without a grumble till he was satisfied. With any other conductor the orchestra would have rebelled. Not so with Bernstein: We have also played some of his own compositions and we liked playing them; everything he does is genuine and comes from his heart.

We also very much appreciate his humanity. Not all conductors are like him. In 1947 or 1948 one of our colleagues died. In the morning a great conductor comes to rehearse with us and sees that a double bass player is missing. He asks the stage assistant to 'phone and he returns and says he regrets to report the colleague died last night. The conductor immediately reacted. 'Well, we must find a substitute at once!' And Bernstein? In the year 1970 we played *Fidelio* at the Theater an der Wien; space is very narrow in the orchestra pit there. At a rehearsal Bernstein lost his balance in the heat of conducting and slipped down from the podium falling onto the second desk of a violinist. It must have been very painful, blood was streaming from his face. Yet before anybody could help him he asked my colleague whether he had hurt him, whether he was all right . . . . This is Bernstein's personality!

Summarizing his impressions, Professor Novak said that his humanity and musicianship communicate themselves to the orchestral players and this influences their performance: 'We feel his love, his own enthusiasm for music, which he expresses on the podium as well as in words in his books'.

One of the younger members of the Israel Philharmonic Orchestra, Meir Rimon, principal French horn, described Leonard Bernstein's work with the musicians in a brief sentence: 'After a rehearsal and after a concert with Bernstein you are completely exhausted, completely tired out. But you are satisfied, you are happy!'

American observers speak of Leonard Bernstein's phenomenally reliable ear, so that an orchestral musician maintained that while he may not have absolute pitch his sense of relative pitch is so keen that having heard the oboe's A-440 in the morning, he could retain it in his ear for the rest of the day (Briggs, *Bernstein*, p. 106). To show his magnanimity towards his musicians, the story goes that a musician worn out with concerts and midnight recording sessions dropped off to sleep during a concert, just before a brief but important solo. He expected a severe reprimand, but there was not a single word. At the repeat performance however, when the musician played his solo brilliantly, Bernstein opened his eyes very wide and spread his left hand in a gesture which said as plainly as words: 'Where were you last time?' (ibid.).

Leonard Bernstein has devoted much thought and research to problems of the deeper significance and correct interpretation of great masterpieces and each of their parts and sections; the outcome of his studies is exemplified in his performances as well as in his theoretical writings and lectures. Tempo belongs among the fundamental problems of each interpretation and on this question he had the experience of a discussion in his youth with Arturo Toscanini. The 82-year-old Toscanini had invited Bernstein, fifty-one years his junior, on an October afternoon in 1949 to visit him at his New York villa. The two conductors talked about various professional matters, among others the love scene in Hector Berlioz' *Roméo et Juliette* — a work that has fascinated Leonard Bernstein throughout his career; in his Harvard lectures he points to the derivation of motifs and themes in Wagner's *Tristan und Isolde* from the music of this Dramatic Symphony by Berlioz. He asked for the veteran maestro's opinion on the tempi in various parts of the work, which he was to conduct in the near future. He had heard a radio broadcast and a gramophone recording both conducted by Toscanini, and found that the tempi were very different. Toscanini, who was famous for his incomparable and unfailing memory, protested categorically — it was impossible, there could not be different tempi in his two performances because there was only one possible speed at which to play the 'Love Scene', the correct, or Toscanini, tempo. However, he promised (ibid., p. 134) to compare the transcript of his broadcast with the Victor recording and on 13 October 1949 wrote to Bernstein that he had compared the recording with the broadcast and confirmed that the recorded performance was much faster. 'And I confirmed another fact', wrote Toscanini, 'namely — that every man, no matter the importance of his intelligence, can be from time to time a little stupid . . . So is the case of the old Toscanini.' And the great maestro continued, 'Your kind visit and dear letter made me very, very happy . . . . I felt myself forty years younger'.

On the allegedly infallible Toscanini, John Briggs tells another illuminating story. On the ship returning from a South American concert tour with the NBC Symphony Orchestra, Toscanini was listening to a short-wave broadcast from London. Toscanini's face darkened as he heard a performance of Beethoven's 'Eroica' Symphony: what *porco* of a conductor could be taking the music at that insane speed? When the performance ended, he was livid with fury and ready to smash the radio. Then a bland British voice announced: 'You have just heard a recording by the BBC Symphony Orchestra, conducted by Arturo Toscanini' (ibid.).

Leonard Bernstein and Dietrich Fischer-Dieskau

Impressions of orchestral players who have worked with Leonard Bernstein may fittingly be followed by appraisals of his conducting and piano playing by two of the most prominent singers who have often performed with him. In a letter dated 20 June 1982, Dietrich Fischer-Dieskau writes:

Only a few have represented the United States in the fifties and sixties in so striking a manner and at his own risk as Leonard Bernstein. It could happen that an air traveller was handed a prospectus on America's 'On and About' and Bernstein's head adorned the cover page. One took this as a matter of course.

Lenny, as his friends and colleagues love calling him, has now matured and overcome the stage of the Adonis-like omniscient, radiant triumphant youth. Tragic blows of fate and an almost superhuman accomplishment in mastering innumerable tasks he set himself — one has just to think of his lectures at Harvard which he formed and presented in a superior way — threw into relief some traits that could rather be regarded as untypical for America: melancholy, creative wrestling with the last final situation of music (which is synonymous with a fanatic collecting of all 'ultimate' possibilities of the tones), despair, and — also magnificently erring in the interpretation of Wagner.

But he still does everything with the full power of his artistic nature, before all with his love for the cause. And this has become very rare in our world. It was characteristic already for Bernstein's Mahler — the series of over-whelming experiences in which I was privileged to participate as soloist in New York. All important works of his Moravian spiritual kinsman, were performed with a burning intensity that was faithful to the score yet born out of creative sympathising freedom. His studio recordings, produced at the same time, led to rediscovery of Mahler, even to a world-wide popularity of the composer, that was undreamt-of before.

Bernstein shares with *his* composer the unconditional, the desire for a new kind of listening, for discovery, for painful struggle on the path to an achievement that for all men of genius can always remain but partially successful.

One-sidedness one could never find with him. He has conducted anything and everything that a musician can conquer for himself. Without neglecting the famous American perfection of orchestral playing he brought to the concert stage new qualities of ecstatic expression both visible (in the person of the conductor) and audible. Young people have benefitted for life from the experience, old traditionalists were shocked out of their complacency, well-disposed sympathisers responded lovingly to the depths of their musical heart.

Many people have found fault with Bernstein for seeking the broadest possible dissemination by means of all modern media and his use of novel and effective ways to get the music across. But such petty criticism was

Christa Ludwig and Leonard Bernstein

forgotten in the face of the artistic encounter.

In his early years as opera conductor in Milan Bernstein met with Maria Callas and never forgot her. I have never received a happier acknowledgement than Lenny saying in the sixties that Maria and Dietrich were his favourite singers.

Fischer-Dieskau wrote these lines after having himself tried his hand at conducting for a number of years. In a conversation with him some weeks after receiving his letter, I asked him for his evaluation of Bernstein as piano accompanist.

To have Bernstein at the piano in the concert hall behind you or at the recording studio in front of you [said Fischer-Dieskau], this does not mean accompaniment in the usual sense, but rather the tiger in the piano — between his hands and the keyboard there is something like an electric zone; it seems as if he is grappling with a dangerous element which has to be joined in battle or else it will put the pianist to flight. As if to prepare himself, he runs his hands over the keys a few times during the initial applause. And then one surge of current follows the other and the singer must show that he can match him, for if he does not, he fails. His continually paraphrasing *rubato*, surprising colours of sounds, the whole intimacy, yet reaching far across the footlights — this is fascinating for everyone who has had his trouble with normal accompanists.

Having performed Mahler *lieder* with Leonard Bernstein in recitals in New York and Philadelphia, Fischer-Dieskau regrets that a similar opportunity has not presented itself so far in European concert halls. Bernstein has often accompanied Christa Ludwig, especially in recitals and recordings of Brahms and Mahler; she has sung in opera performances and symphonic recordings conducted by him and a cordial friendship developed ever since 1968, when she sang in *Der Rosenkavalier* in Vienna. Bernstein frequently chose her for the vocal solos in his own compositions. Christa Ludwig told me about their collaboration in a conversation in May 1982:

We first met in New York when I sang in the opening season of the new Met in September 1966; Karl Böhm conducted Richard Strauss' *Die Frau ohne Schatten* and I was the Färbersfrau. Lenny Bernstein attended the performance and when I later went to hear a piano recital of Wilhelm Kempff I met Lenny in the green-room and told him who I am whereupon he said spontaneously: Ah, you are my new Marschallin! I never forgot this, because at that moment he must have thought of me as a soprano. And I had never given any thought to the Marschallin in *Rosenkavalier*.

And then I sang with him the solo in Mahler's Second Symphony —

before the Marschallin. I was so fascinated by him — and you know I had already sung the Mahler Second with most of the marvellous conductors — because he always approaches a piece afresh so that one thinks he discovers it anew, and so *we* too discover it with him. He is not one of those conductors who have 'phoned directly with Mozart or Mahler in heaven and say: This must be that way! No, he is always searching, I think this is just wonderful that he does not hesitate, saying: How should I do this? or he ponders how a certain passage could best be interpreted. It is a sign of self confidence that he admits searching. Thus he also finds musical details that other conductors would perhaps not find at all — this fascinated me from the first day we worked together.

His constant discovery of something new in a musical work is profoundly exciting; one starts on a voyage of discovery with him and hears things one has never heard before. The other day I listened to a broadcast transmission of the Second Act of *Tristan und Isolde* which he conducted and there were musical details in his performance that I had never noticed in Wagner's music before. It may be possible that there is sometimes a lack of homogeneity, yet there is excitement in everything he does. And also you always feel that he is human; he is a genuine human being and not a musical Pope, and his high intelligence makes him different from many other conductors.

He does not only love music, he *is* music. His whole body is music. He is criticised for jumping up and down and singing — music is in him and he is not ashamed of showing it. This is wonderful, I feel, especially in our times where knowledge, competence, perfection are valued above all; and there comes an artist who has the courage to say: Well, let's see, how should I do this? or I believe this passage should be done in such a way, and here it should be a little deeper. He is a creative in the very same moment in which he interprets and this is very rare today indeed.

Das Lied von der Erde — I can compare his rendering with the performances I have sung with Solti, with Klemperer, with Karajan, wonderful performances; but with Bernstein one can only really shed tears. Or *Missa Solemnis*, I always found it beautiful but somewhat strange and reserved and there came Bernstein and explains it in his own manner and style and conducts it so that it touches my heart and *Missa Solemnis* became one of my favourite works of music.

We also talked about Leonard Bernstein as accompanist in a *lieder* concert. Erik Werba, the prominent lieder accompanist, once said that Bernstein remains a poet even when performing 'symphonic cataracts' on the piano keys. Christa Ludwig remembers that her first rehearsal with Bernstein at the piano was 'horrible':

It was awful, I was not accustomed to a piano accompanist like that and I asked myself what is he doing? He should accompany and not make music independently. He seemed to approach *lieder* from a symphonic point of view: we rehearsed Brahms' 'Immer leiser wird mein Schlummer', the theme of which comes from a piano concerto, and he played in a tempo he was used to from the concerto but this was much too fast when sung with the words. We tussled and fought over every song, as everything he did was unfamiliar to me. But his kind of musicality was so natural and convincing that many habitual prejudices melted away and I grew happy in the discovery. In the end the results were beautiful. Even at the piano he always searches how to get the meaning of the music out in the best way; he never accompanies the same as all the others.

'Have you ever heard him sing?', I asked. 'How he sings the blues on one record with his *Fancy Free* music? How he managed to perform a number from Schoenberg's *Pierrot lunaire* in Sprechgesang in his Harvard lectures, more convincing than most of the singers who try to interpret this work?'

'Have I heard him sing?', Christa Ludwig laughed, 'Well, he sings all the time! I have even forbidden him to sing. This was in the Second Mahler Symphony, in the "Röslein rot", I had to say to him, "Either you or I".' And on Bernstein as conductor, she went on:

> I know conductors who are out to give an impression of being terribly modest and are not modest at all. And the others who always say: It has to be done this way and that's it, and these are the conductors who show no modesty and are probably insecure and hide their insecurity this way. Bernstein stands in the middle between them: he is sure enough to be able to permit himself a moment of insecurity.

After Leonard Bernstein has convinced himself that he has come to understand the nature and content of a musical work, having studied the score intensely, not even a famed and authoritative colleague can persuade him to conceive it differently. Arthur Rubinstein recollects (in his book *My Many Years*, New York, 1980) his first meeting with Bernstein at the rehearsal for a concert in Montreal. One work they were to give was Edvard Grieg's Piano Concerto and Bernstein's tempo for the orchestra in the melancholy first theme was somewhat fast and lively. Rubinstein interrupted and whispered that this should be taken in a more deliberate way because of the sadness in the theme. Rubinstein remembers that Bernstein reacted very sharply, saying that this music was worthless anyway and that the *Nuits dans les Jardins d'Espagne* by Falla, the second piece in Rubinstein's programme, was no better. The great pianist was deeply offended and, proposing that Bernstein should conduct orchestral music to his liking in the first part

[115]

of the programme and leave the second part to him alone for a programme of solo piano music, left the hall.

When the organisers of the concert heard that the young Bernstein, who had been engaged in place of another conductor who had fallen ill, had so bluntly offended the great Rubinstein they were extremely annoyed and unwilling to accept the change of programme. According to Rubinstein, however, Bernstein seemed to regret his impulsiveness and brought a beautiful cashmere scarf to his hotel, where he presented it to the outraged pianist with an apology for his behaviour. Rubinstein was ready to make peace but asked how they could give a concert that same evening without a single rehearsal. Bernstein had no doubt that they would succeed, as he knew both works by heart. The concert, in fact, turned out very successful and Bernstein finally admitted that he had begun to like the two 'worthless' compositions. A warm friendship developed between the two artists and they often performed together after that, always in complete musical understanding.

European musicians and critics in the countries of Mozart, Beethoven, Schumann, Brahms and Mahler, Debussy and Ravel, Verdi, Tschaikovsky and Richard Strauss had admired Leonard Bernstein's musical understanding and feeling for the styles and means of expression of the classic and Romantic European masters ever since his first appearances in their musical capitals; with few exceptions, they praised his sensitively stylish performances of German, French and Russian music, and of Italian and Austrian opera. However, many American critics denied his ability to perform European music in what they called 'the right way'. Harold C. Schonberg noted in his book *The Great Conductors* (New York 1967) that when 'he suddenly took Europe by storm, creating a sensation conducting *Falstaff* in Vienna and Mahler in London, even in New York some of the critics began to discuss his work in respectful terms instead of looking upon him as a perpetual *Wunderkind*, "the Peter Pan of Music", as the *New York Times* said in 1960' (Schonberg, *Great Conductors*, pp. 352–3). He went on:

No greater-publicized figure than Bernstein ever appeared on the American musical scene . . . . That was one of his problems. Many thought he came up too fast, and for years he had to fight to overcome the suspicion, actual hostility and jealousy, too — created among many professionals by his fantastic success at so early an age. Too much attention was paid to him; and professionals, who knew only too well how a career can be built by publicity, have a tendency to look with suspicion on a big publicity build-up . . . . So do many intellectuals. Bernstein was popular, was written up in mass magazines — ergo, there had to be something wrong with him. A man of

[116]

supreme confidence in himself, Bernstein stepped on toes and made enemies; and there could be no denying that some of his extra-curricular activities caused a great deal of unfavourable talk: his lofty pronouncements, the kiss he gave to Jacqueline Kennedy on television, even his flamboyant clothes. He was described as having a pre-Copernical ego, i.e. seeing the whole world revolve around him . . . (ibid., p. 354).

When Bernstein took over the New York Philharmonic, the orchestra was 'sullen and badly disciplined', says Schonberg:

Within a season the orchestra began to thrive. There were mutters about the 'show business approach' that Bernstein represented, but there was no disputing its success . . . . Some members of the orchestra, especially the older men, mumbled about Toscanini and Mengelberg doing things differently. But Bernstein made the Philharmonic a happy orchestra . . . . The musicians of the Philharmonic, a temperamental collection of primadonnas who have worked under every great conductor, are all but unanimous in proclaiming Bernstein's gifts. They think he is a superlative technician, they admire his ear and his musicianship, they claim that rhythmically he is the equal of any living conductor. Some of the musicians have less regard for the way Bernstein approaches the eighteenth- and nineteenth-century repertoire; but that, they say, has nothing to do with his natural gifts (ibid., pp. 356–7).

Schonberg argues that Bernstein's 'performances of the classics through Brahms have never been fully accepted' — in America, he should have added; for European critics have always admired his congenial approach to classical and Romantic music. They would agree that 'his ideas about Stravinsky, Strauss and Bartók can be brilliant and sure-footed'. Schonberg also says that 'his ideas about earlier music have impressed many as mannered and wayward' but this would not be the European view (ibid, p. 357). Of course, Schonberg's book appeared in 1967 and Leonard Bernstein has since amply proved his mature insight into the world of the classics, especially when conducting the Vienna Philharmonic, and it cannot be said of him that, as 'the most choreographic of all contemporary conductors' his 'wild motions juxtaposed against a Beethoven symphony convince many that there is more to the choreography than to the music'; Schonberg also concedes that 'even listening to Bernstein on records, where choreography is not a factor, illustrated a kind of musical approach much different from that of today's predominantly literal conductors'.

The American observer and critic sees in Leonard Bernstein 'essentially a throwback, a romantic'; a romantic he most certainly is, as may be sensed also in his own compositions. In orchestral interpretation, Schonberg regards as romantic a 'considerable fluctuation of tempo' as he 'often slows down for second subjects, underlines melodies, is constantly using a full palette of expressive devices that are generally scorned today'. Quoting an early verdict of Virgil Thomson that Bernstein as 'a child of the twentieth century was uncomfortable in a nineteenth-century repertoire and thus had to counterfeit an emotion he did not really feel', Schonberg thought Bernstein's romanticism somewhat 'calculated', 'breaking the line', something the 'authentic exponents of a romantic tradition — Walter, Furtwängler' almost never did. The critic attributes certain 'excesses' in Bernstein's inter-pretations to his desire to educate his public, to 'explain music to the multitude': 'he seemed to think that unless he made a big thing out of a specific passage, audiences would miss the point', would not dis-tinguish between a first and a second subject in a symphonic movement unless he emphasised their entries. Schonberg notes that this was his criticism in Leonard Bernstein's early career. When he returned from his sabbatical to the Philharmonic during the 1963/5 season, the critic detected in him 'a new kind of confidence': 'The choreography was still present — that is a permanent part of Bernstein — but there also was a greater reliance on the taste of the audience, a more direct approach to music, less of the obsessive exhibitionism that had so marred his work'. His operatic conducting also had a great impact, as he 'has always had a dramatic flair': 'Bernstein and opera would appear made for each other' (ibid., p. 358).

It is certainly true that classical and Romantic music interpreted by Toscanini or Bruno Walter sounded as if they almost never 'broke the line'; they gave musical expression to the prevalent notion of classicism as the sublime realisation of unity of idea and form, and Romanticism as a poetic, profoundly personal art surmounting purely musical forms; this they did while suppressing their own individual feelings and emotions. It could never be expected of Bernstein to suppress his own feelings, to become an impersonal exponent of music. In every epoch of history, in every country, in every cultural environment, the creative artist has accomplished his work while struggling with problems of structure, form, technique and style; no great work of art has ever been created in a facile way, putting things together superficially. The interpreters of a masterpiece approach it either by way of intuition, or they follow distinguished models, or they try to reconstruct for them-selves the birth-pangs of the work. The erudite listener to a musical performance may follow an interpretation, simply surrendering himself to the experience of hearing beautiful or stirring sounds, or he may feel

[118]

Northampton Central Library (NC1)

Customer ID: *******1347

Items that you have checked out

Title
Leonard Bernstein: The Infinite Variety of a Mus
ID: 00400177
Due: 06/10/2018

Total items: 1
Account balance: £0.00
15/09/2018 16:22
Checked out: 3
Overdue: 0
Reservations: 1
Ready for collection: 0

Items that you already have on loan

Title
Science of meditation: how to change your brain
ID: 00401143768
Due: 29/09/2018

Title: Simone Weil: a modern pilgrimage
ID: 80002357914
Due: 29/09/2018

that a composition hides other values than those spread before him or that its sounds should have a different colouring. In the course of time, historical understanding and ideals of interpretation constantly change; the interpreter, too, grows with every new experience and deeper study. Leonard Bernstein admits that when analysing a composition before a lecture or a performance, he tries first of all to conjecture what was in the composer's mind when planning and when writing it. From one performance to the next, he may detect new traits even in the most familiar work and, in the course of an orchestral concert, changes of tempo, mood or style may occur. For this reason, particularly in Bernstein's case, a gramophone recording will have only a limited documentary value, all the more so when it is made in a studio and the final outcome represents a patching-together of various taped passages; a live recording of a performance has a much greater chance of preserving the spontaneous experience of great music even though its technical quality may well fall below that of a studio recording.

The fact that Leonard Bernstein always follows the 'chief requirement of all', that the conductor 'be humble before the composer; that he never interpose himself between the music and the audience' is evident when he discusses a musical work or speaks of a performance just given. Clearly, the orchestral players are aware of this. As an example, the members of the Israel Philharmonic tell of the final rehearsal of Tchaikovsky's *Francesca da Rimini* before a concert tour. So exhilarated were the musicians that they spontaneously rose as one man and applauded. Bernstein thanked them, adding, 'But you should have heard this from Koussevitzky — that's where I learned it'.

The importance of the conductor's personal charisma and the influence on his musicians of the inspiration of the moment was to be seen at an Israel Philharmonic concert in Jerusalem in May 1981. Bernstein had conducted the first half of the programme (with his *Musical Toast* and with Beethoven's *Choral Fantasy*). After the interval, he handed over to two young Israeli conductors, asking one of them to conduct a performance of his own *Divertimento* of 1981 which he himself had for several days rehearsed and already performed with the orchestra. He sat in the audience and watched the young Israeli conduct the orchestra through the *Divertimento*, which was already thoroughly familiar to them. Those present heard a faultless, clean rendering of the work, but missing was the irresistible charm and wit of the lighter passages, where, with a mere twitch of the shoulder, twinkling eyes and a smile, Bernstein

[119]

would have indicated the exact musical expression to the players. It might be thought that just his presence in the concert-hall would have sufficed; but there was a world of difference between the earlier performances and recording under Bernstein and the performance that evening.

As to Bernstein's way of working with an orchestra, the conductor himself has explained:

> I think that teaching is perhaps the essence of my function as a conductor. I share whatever I know and whatever I feel about the music. I try to make the orchestra feel it, know it, and understand it, too, so that we can do it together . . . . It's a kind of chamber-music operation in which we are all playing together. I never think that they are there and I am here. The whole joy of conducting for me is that we breathe together. It's like a love experience (Gruen and Hyman, *Private World*, p. 27).

Does he think that his method differs very much from that of other conductors? He spoke at length to John Gruen about this during his Italian holiday in 1967:

> I don't think I have as much of a ritual as other conductors. Most conductors I've observed dress in the tailcoat they wore at the last concert. They just hang it up after a concert at the hall and put it on again to go on stage. I could no more do that than I could walk out in a bathing suit. Everything must be new — clean from skin outward. It is a sign of the general feeling I have before a concert . . . . There is something ritualistic in the act of preparation itself, which is almost priestlike — before I approach the altar. I don't know where this comes from. But there is something about getting scrupulously clean, squeaky clean. It's a becoming-worthy-of-entering this holy of holies, that everything you put on must be absolutely spotless, like priestly garments' (ibid., p. 35).

Speaking of rituals, Bernstein mentioned one semi-superstitious practice:

> When Koussevitzky died, I was given a pair of his cuff links. I wear them always when I conduct. This has developed into something like a superstition — the only one I have . . . . They are very precious to me . . . and I always kiss them before going out on stage. Rodzinski, I believe, never conducted without a revolver in his back pocket. I don't know what that meant. Also, one was asked to kick him backstage before he entered. I was asked several times to do this. A good luck kick . . . . Toscanini always used

to appear hours in advance. He'd dress there — bring everything — because he wanted to be in the hall, to know that he was safely there and sit and think and whatever. I don't arrive in my dressing room and have an absolutely quiet period of meditation, or anything like that. On the contrary, there are usually all kinds of people waiting for me, either to greet me, or with problems that must be solved, decisions that must be made'(ibid., p. 36).

Before the concert begins, Bernstein has a last look at the score of the first piece he is to conduct. While studying the music at home he has scrupulously marked every detail that the musicians must copy into their parts even before the first rehearsal but there will certainly be new discoveries and new divergencies in the course of the performance. While conducting, 'the audience may disappear from consciousness. But the men remain with me. The orchestra never disappears. I mean, one is not alone with Brahms or whomever. We are all alone with him'. Once a performance is over and the public calls him back to take his bow, he feels rather empty.

In his conversations with John Gruen he also answered the question whether his performances were ever affected by his own moods. 'Not in the easy sense that when you're feeling depressed, it will show. Or that's a good time to conduct Tchaikovsky's Sixth, because it's depressed music . . . . As a matter of fact, when you're in a very strong mood, a very positive mood, it may be exactly the right time to conduct Beethoven's Funeral March' (ibid., p. 37).

After the concert Bernstein never rests. He loves to receive friends in the green-room, discusses the concert with them, often goes into every little detail of the interpretation he has just given and of the various musical works in the programme. He cannot go to bed after an exciting concert, and each concert is exciting for him. He may go out to a restaurant, even see a film. Nor, when he gets home, does he always lie down and sleep. More often than not, he will take down from the shelves or the piano desk one of the musical scores to be played in a forthcoming concert and sit down to study a new work.

When a conductor is capable of analysing the works of the great symphonists of the past with deep insight into their underlying secrets, can he also examine his own composition so minutely? That is to say, when Bernstein conducts one of his early symphonies — say, *Jeremiah* or *The Age of Anxiety* — after an interval of many years, or the more recent *Halil*, can he analyse them as objectively as a Brahms symphony? During our conversation of April 1982, Bernstein confirmed that after not having seen or heard a work of his for some time, he can approach it afresh. He quoted the example of the Deutsche Grammo-

[121]

phon recording of his *On the Waterfront* suite, *Halil,* and 'Three Meditations from *Mass*'. He first heard a sample pressing on a poor-quality
old-fashioned record player, but *Waterfront* still felt as if it were a new
piece for him. He saw the work in a new light and realised that it had
been performed differently from the way he did it years before; its form
had become clearer to him.

Bernstein has given on television illuminating analytical comments
on a number of great symphonies of the past — the works of Beethoven,
Mozart and Brahms, for instance. To the question, 'Do you approach
repeat performance of such works you have grown to know so well,
always in the same spirit?' he replied:

> Certainly not. Every performance is a new experience. A new analysis. I just
> had this experience with the Wiener Philharmoniker. We toured Germany
> last year and played the Brahms First and the Mozart E flat major — only
> Brahms and Mozart. And this was like the first time. The freshness and the
> invention of each piece happened to the greatest degree on this tour. We also
> went to Copenhagen and Helsinki, and then Berlin, Hamburg, Frankfurt,
> Stuttgart, Hanover, we made an immense tour and played Brahms and
> Mozart at each place. And each night, instead of becoming repetitions, the
> performances brought a new experience, I really was able to come so close to
> the composers.

The reasons and background for the differences that occur in repeat
performances of one and the same work have been dealt with at length
by Leonard Bernstein in a letter to Franz Endler, then music editor
and critic of the Vienna daily *Die Presse.* This was a contribution to the
centenary celebrations of the Gesellschaft der Musikfreunde; the letter
was printed in *Die Presse* and appears in the original English text in
Leonard Bernstein's book *Findings* (New York, 1982). The main points
made relate to two performances of Beethoven's Ninth Symphony,
given one after the other at only a few days' interval, yet which turned
out completely different in interpretation and spirit.

> In the case of Beethoven's Ninth, it is not a matter of reverting, in
> performance, to one or another extreme of conception [Bernstein argues], but
> rather a matter of emphasis, leaning toward one extreme or the other . . . .
> The one is a highly literal, faithful, rhythmically and dynamically accurate
> reading of the score, free of orchestrational changes or additions, without
> gratuitous pauses or retardations or rubati, faithful even to the highly
> controversial (sometimes even impossible) metronome markings, and with
> no dynamic adjustments in the cause of orchestral balance. Let us call this
> Approach Alpha. The other, Approach Omega, would be a highly romanti-

cized conception, based on extramusical ideas such as Formless Chaos (the opening bars), Germinal One-cell creation (the first motive), culminating in The Development of Man in Full Reason and Spirit, complete with fermate, rubati, dynamic exaggerations and/or changes, vacillating tempi, poetical meanderings, and personal, subjective indulgences. Somewhere between Alpha and Omega lie all the performances of the Ninth we have ever heard; but I have rarely heard two performances from any one conductor that tended so divergently toward the two alphabetical extremes as these two I heard myself conduct.

One of these performances took place at the Konzerthaus in Vienna, the other at the Symphony Hall in Boston. 'The Vienna performance leaned more in the Omega direction, almost like a Mahlerian adumbration — more sostenuto, perhaps more romantic', says Bernstein, while 'the Boston performance favoured clarity, immediacy of attack, what some might call a more classic approach', adding: 'Yet it was I, with no premeditation or cause, who performed them both.'

Bernstein sees a number of reasons for his almost diametrically opposed interpretations of one and the same work. One is the vast difference in the accoustic qualities of the various concert halls which a conductor has to consider in order to transmit the sounds he wishes to come from the orchestra. Another is the particular quality of the orchestra with which he is working, and still another are the personal qualities of the orchestral players who perform solo passages in a symphonic composition. The type of instruments the musicians are using must also be taken into consideration, American brass instrument sound different from the German. But all these are exterior conditionings, he says,

these are forces that impinge on the conductor, who to some extent must take his cue from them . . . . The truth is that in both cases the performances essentially came from the podium, based on my relationship with that mighty score, as of that moment. Although there had been only four days between the last Vienna performance and the first Boston rehearsal, I had again gone through a crucial re-examination of the score in those four days, as I had in the days preceding the Vienna rehearsals, and as I have always done before any performance of a major score, no matter how often I have previously conducted it. And each time there is a difference, even if it is only a difference between Mu and Nu. And with Beethoven, the difference tends to be greater than with any other composer.

Following deep meditation on the many spiritual and musical aspects of Beethoven's art and on the secrets behind the notes that have

Leonard Bernstein at the piano, September 1953

ever to be detected anew, Bernstein says that

> to play Beethoven's music is to give oneself over completely to the child-spirit which lived in that grim, awkward, violent man. It is to be seduced by a ravishing innocence. Without that utter submission it is impossible to play the Adagio of the Ninth. Or, for that matter, the Scherzo. Or, Heaven knows, the first movement. And the Finale? Most of all! It is simply unplayable unless we go all the way with him, in total, prepubescent faith, in that certainty of immortality which only children (and geniuses) really possess — to go all the way with him as he cries out 'Brüder!', 'Tochter!', 'Freude!', 'Millionen!' 'Gott!'. But especially 'Brüder!' That above all is his child-inspired cry. We must believe it in order to play it.

The answer to the riddle of the Vienna and Boston performances lies in the 'ratio of hope to despair' that he felt in Vienna or in Boston:

> How long were my arms in one city or the other — long enough to embrace my brothers, the orchestra; or only the cello section; or everyone including the chorus? How childlike was I capable of letting myself become? How trusting? How willing to suspend disbelief? How desperate about Vietnam, Israel, the Soviet Union, a newly-lost friend? How hopeful for new music, for Kreisky, for the black American, for peace? *Brüder!*' (For full text, see Bernstein, *Findings*, pp. 291–8).

A great deal has been written about Leonard Bernstein's doubling as soloist and conductor in the performance of classical piano concertos; in the Mozart city of Salzburg especially there has been, as well as public enthusiasm, much criticism of his Mozart interpretations. The conductor Nikolaus Harnoncourt, regarded as a stylist of rare insight and famed for his epoch-making opera performances (with Jean-Pierre Ponnelle as producer) of Mozart and Monteverdi, has in a number of articles and interviews expressed the opinion that Bernstein's perform-ances of Mozart piano concertos are more congenial to the composer's style than many others he has heard; he finds them profoundly moving. He has compared Bernstein's interpretations of Mozart symphonies and concertos with the opera performances that Fritz Busch conducted in Glyndebourne (as preserved on exemplary recordings) and to the spirit of Pablo Casals' conducting Mozart's G minor symphony. In Salzburg, many concert-goers and critics argued that Bernstein did not play 'in Mozart style', but, says Harnoncourt, 'anyone who can say what is genuine Mozart style should let me know'. In his book *Musik als Klangrede* (Salzburg, 1982), Harnoncourt says we often hear that people want to enjoy Mozart, 'to experience just the fascination of his music's beauty. However, Mozart's contemporaries described his music as dazzling and harsh, full of contrasts, it upset and aroused them, and this led to severe criticism at the time'. Harnoncourt argues that 'people who attend a concert in order to enjoy *Mozart-happiness* and instead are offered *Mozart-truth*, feel disturbed; many listeners may not want to be confronted with the *real Mozart*'.

In March 1983, when in Salzburg, I asked Nikolaus Harnoncourt why Leonard Bernstein's playing of Mozart came so near his own ideals of interpreting the real Mozart. In his book, Harnoncourt speaks of music as 'dramatic tonal speech': all music talks, and interpretation has to render that language intelligible.

Bernstein's playing makes me happy because it conveys the basic dramatic musical speech. I believe that Mozart composed his piano concertos as spontaneous dialogues and often there is even a dialogue of the piano with itself. As Bernstein has a genuine, profound insight into the art of composition, he makes these dialogues sound really spontaneous and he sometimes creates an impression as if he invents the music himself while playing — I have never heard anything like it and it has always been like this in my imagination.

What are the special features of his playing — how does it differ from that of other pianists?

Bernstein's playing never sounds smooth, never polished. The normal practice is *jeu perlé* on the semiquavers, as smooth and as uniform as possible, avoiding contrasts while remaining truthful to Mozart's written instructions — that is what I am accustomed to hear. With Bernstein the difference is clearly felt between — to put it simply — legato and staccato, between the dramatic and the lyrical phrases which frequently alternate in quick succession; there are often two or three dramatic bars followed by a lyrical questioning or reply, and this Bernstein can convey, breathing with the music. There are commas representing breathing; the listener feels how a musical statement is answered and participates in an extremely gripping event. In many other, ordinary, performances we are offered a beautiful kaleidoscope without deep content — that is superficial Mozart only. Bernstein's interpretation is exciting and I feel a personal kinship to his way of playing.

Did Harnoncourt think that his performance creates so congenial an impression because he is himself a composer?

'I would certainly think so. The insight he has does not easily come to a musician who is a performer only.'

Is it good practice or bad (as many critics maintain) for a soloist to conduct a concerto from the piano?

> In the particular case of Leonard Bernstein this has not disturbed me at all. I had the feeling that the impact of his playing transmits itself to the orchestra and each musician knows how to play his Mozart, so the outcome was quite harmonious. In general I am not in favour of this practice especially as regards Mozart, for his piano concertos in particular contain a maximum of symphonic music and most piano-playing conductors do not completely fulfil the demands of either the solo part or the orchestral score of the works. Only Bernstein satisfied me in this respect. But I am really not generally in favour of this practice.

Harnoncourt went on to say that, in conducting, he particularly likes Bernstein as an interpreter of Mozart

> because his performances penetrate into the music much more deeply than those of other conductors. But I have also heard exceptionally beautiful — rather than beautiful I'd like to say moving — performances of *Fidelio* in Vienna and of Beethoven's Ninth in Salzburg. It makes me so angry when people, even professionals, speak of showmanship in his conducting. You can hear that everything he does is genuine, he lives the music. And if someone in Salzburg said he does not play Mozart in Mozart style, I can only reply that nobody in the world can know what *is* and what *is not* Mozart style. If a musician has such an insight into Mozart's world as Bernstein has and interprets his music so convincingly as he does, then in that moment that is Mozart style.

Nikolaus Harnoncourt here confirmed what Bernstein himself has said about the music in Mozart's Piano Concerto in G major, K.453. On television on 22 November 1959 from Venice, where he was playing with the New York Philharmonic, he called the Andante movement his favourite piece of all time, in which Mozart rose to the greatest heights of expression, his music uniting serenity, melancholy and tragic intensity in one great lyrical improvisation.

The Mozart concert which had so impressed Nikolaus Harnoncourt had taken place during the Salzburg Festival, on 13 August 1975. Bernstein conducted the London Symphony Orchestra in a programme consisting of the Largo movement from the Fifth Symphony of Dimitri Shostakovich, in memory of the composer who had recently died, the Sibelius Fifth, the *Chichester Psalms*, and the Mozart Concerto.

[127]

Among the critical opinions Harnoncourt remembered was Peter Cossé's description of Bernstein's conducting that

> at first seemed to be fluttering, encouraging, beckoning, as if music were more a brisk greeting than a matter for serious reflection . . . . Thus the pianist Bernstein dissolved the concerto into small clouds with distant thunder, wanted to show graceful keyboard work with attentive ritardandi, adorned by curious trills . . . . In the Andante movement everything was directed towards emotion, the ritardandi at times brought movement to a standstill, closing phrases withstood all progress . . . . The final movement sometimes hit the essence of the matter, but then again it gave more information about the interpreter than about the score: fireworks with quite a few misfires (*Salzburger Nachrichten*, 16 August 1975).

Karl Löbl wrote in the Viennese *Kurier* (15 August) that he felt that Bernstein 'strove to make music with all his might, with a total effort and a personal commitment of each participant . . . . Music is in him and urges to be communicated. As a composer he could hardly write enough to activate this communication constantly anew so he turns to the music of other composers, with due consideration for its content and message. For style, he cares less: style is something for a museum and real life is not always stylish'. 'Classical relations seem suddenly revoked', wrote Karlheinz Roschitz in the *Kronenzeitung* (15 August 1975): 'Subjectivity is carried to extremes, but Bernstein's personality makes it possible. In this way too, it is possible to interpret Mozart excitingly.' Franz Endler said in the Viennese *Presse* of 16 August that Bernstein's Mozart interpretation is 'wilfully personal', but this is 'legitimate and something that has become rare in the museum routine of our days'. The critic felt 'at every second that he does not simply play Mozart, but mirrors him in his own personality'.

In 1948, Bernstein at twenty-nine had been expounding what makes the ideal conductor. In an essay for the magazine *Theatre Arts* of February 1948 (vol. XXXII, no. 2, pp. 14–16), his task was to review some new recordings; but in addition he analysed Bruno Walter's art of conducting and for the first time eloquently discussed Gustav Mahler's music, which he was later to promote in unprecedented fashion.

His article was entitled 'Music that Sings' and in it he praised the recording of Mahler's Fifth Symphony by Bruno Walter for its 'singing' from beginning to end. 'It is remarkable, indeed puzzling', he wrote, 'to find that the singing quality is a rare commodity in our time'; a singing interpretation of music should be the foundation and essence of each performance. He then began to speak of Mahler:

Mahler is primarily a singer. They say he is long, and sometimes trivial; they say he is pretentious, and uses the same tune-patterns to the point of exhaustion throughout nine symphonies. I don't know; I simply don't find it so. But I do know that he never writes an unsinging note. He sings not only with his strings, but with tom-toms, basses, piccolos and celesta. He sings whether he is feeling Schubertian, Bachian, choralish, Yiddish, *fastoso*, orgiastic or funereal.

Walter is also a singer. He may sometimes arrive short of the ultimate precision; he may not exercise the rhythmic lash of Toscanini; but he never conducts an unsinging note.

The result of this combination is fascinating. Mahler in other hands can wear down with banality, through a treatment of its dance elements with the 'energy' method. Walter's tempi, on the other hand, never seem slow; and yet there is always room for every last 32nd note to breathe, and to exert its particular inner energy. This is a private magic of Walter's, and every artist can learn something from it. There is a general sostenuto, even in the most hectic passages, which makes what I call the 'singing quality'. And with Mahler's music this becomes the ideal.

What is it, to get down to fundamentals, that makes a 'singing' conductor? After all, an instrumentalist is the 'onlie begetter' of his result; there is no one or nothing else responsible in influencing the contact between human tissue and mechanical instrument. But a conductor has a round hundred of mediators, moderators, ameliorators and transmogrifiers. What can possibly happen between the impact of Walter's baton and the perceived sonority that can determine the sonorous quality? For certainly Walter had not verbalized his intention with respect to every note. In most cases verbalization of these performing subtleties is utterly impossible, or if achieved, hopelessly misunderstood.

Let us say that the basic attribute of the conductor is the authority he represents. If this authority must be shown by conductorial gesture (which so often is the root of the 'energy method'), I doubt that it would allow for much singing. But if the authority emanates from the conductor, is unconsciously apprehended and unequivocably observed, then the baton is free to mold the phrase, to take its own time *between* the beats, to fall lovingly on an *ictus*, allowing it to unfold, live its full life, however short, and to sing out its meaning.

This is apparently the case with Bruno Walter. I have never detected a moment's insecurity in his rehearsals or performances. He has nothing to prove; he has only the music to make. The battle is half won before he begins to rehearse because his singleness of purpose and uncluttered devotion are unarguable. There is no barrier between his baton and the player, or — more important — between himself and his baton. Then whatever communication is possible between one musician and another is free to transpire.

[129]

After discussing the merits of some other recent record releases Bernstein returns to the subject of Mahler's music. The album of the Fifth Symphony, he says,

> shows again the peculiar ambivalent quality of the man. Just as he marks, for so many hearers, the end of the whole nineteenth-century romantic movement, so does he initiate, especially for many present-day composers, the new drive which has superseded it. Mahler is a threshold man; and it is obviously with great regret that he says farewell to the room behind him. It is with equal misgiving that he faces the bright, bare room he is about to enter.
>
> His ambivalence is usually seen in terms of his conducting–composing conflict. Many critics claim to find traces in each new work of the concerts he had conducted during the preceding year. If this is true, these influences may constitute his real link with the past; but what is fresh in his works is still as fresh as a Schubert song.
>
> In the Fifth Symphony, for example, the opening funeral march and parts of the finale may be relegated to the sphere of imitation, if you will. But of the opening of the second movement, I can humbly say that I only wish I had written it.

Not only the remarks on the ideal conductor but also the evaluation of Mahler, the man and his music, by the 29-year-old Leonard Bernstein have remained characteristics for his own interpretative and creative work throughout his life and career. In the opening of the second movement of Mahler's Fifth Symphony — which Bernstein so much admires (*Stürmisch bewegt. Mit grösster Vehemenz*) — is to be found a technique of composition that became a fundamental trait of Bernstein's treatment and development of musical motifs and themes. Mahler begins the movement with a five-note motif that at first is repeated several times; out of this germ cell he then develops a longer melodic phrase, which he spins out and develops further; it later appears combined with a theme from the first movement of the symphony. This method of building themes from a nucleus, letting them grow and develop, and combining motifs and themes from various parts of the work is a hallmark of Leonard Bernstein's technique and style of composition in his symphonic music as much as in the dramatic music in *West Side Story*.

4

From Juvenile Songs to Broadway

I am a serious composer trying to be a
songwriter . . . . I wrote a symphony before I ever
wrote a popular song.
Leonard Bernstein, May 1954

In the forty-five years between 1942 and 1987 Leonard Bernstein has written some fifty compositions, among them three symphonies, the symphonic suite *On the Waterfront*, the Serenade for solo violin and small orchestra, three orchestral works, four ballet scores, solo and choral pieces, the short opera *Trouble in Tahiti*, the comic operetta *Candide*, *Mass*, piano and chamber music, and a series of songs with piano. The years 1982–5 were devoted to the writing and rewriting of his opera *A Quiet Place*. His three musicals he composed in 1944, 1953 and 1957 — each with fifteen to twenty numbers. These musicals first made Leonard Bernstein's name familiar to the wider public; the third, *West Side Story*, established his world fame as a composer.

The first Broadway musical, *On the Town*, based on the ideas and content of the earlier ballet, *Fancy Free*, contained music of a particular kind of originality unknown on Broadway before. Yet his first characteristic Broadway song had already been heard as a prelude to *Fancy Free*; this was the blues song 'Big Stuff' with the composer's own lyrics. However, as Bernstein says, his first symphony, *Jeremiah*, completed in 1942, preceded his first popular songs and even before that he had written piano music, chamber music and a Psalm. The 'Jeremiah' Symphony, the work of a 24-year-old composer, reveals many musical traits later to be found in Bernstein's mature compositions, in his serious music and lighter songs. It is obvious that no musician without a thorough musical training could have written a musically complicated song such as 'Big Stuff'.

'Lenny Amber', the arranger and pianist of the New York publishing house of Harms Inc. in 1942–3, had had a close look into the world of pop music and learned to improvise tunes of his own. But he had only recently graduated with distinction, both at Harvard University, in 1939 and at the Curtis Institute of Music, in 1941. It was his professed aim and purpose to become a serious composer as well as a conductor.

As early as 1935, when he was sixteen, Bernstein had composed his first important work and, as though presaging things to come, it was based on a biblical Psalm. His text, in English, was a free and rhymed version of the Hebrew Psalm 148, and he composed an expressive, at times dramatic, musical interpretation of it for voice and piano. Though a youthful piece of music with echoes of Wagner and Brahms, it is much more than just a juvenile composition exercise, since it already shows several 'Bernsteinish' features. The singer starts after a 'grave' succession of Wagnerian chords on the piano vacillating between C sharp minor and C sharp major, which returns in shortened form as an interlude between sections of the work and again as Coda; in the Coda it leads in pianissimo chords into A major tonality. After the piano introduction, the vocal melody develops at first in tender mood, in pure A major, accompanied by harmonious chords — 'Andante moderato' — after the interlude the vocal line starts one note higher, now very agitated — 'Allegro agitato' — accompanied by D minor harmonies, and becomes more expressive and more dramatic until the climax on 'Hallelujah', after which the work ends with pianissimo piano chords. While this *Psalm* shows only a limited individuality in style and expression, it undoubtedly indicates an innate talent for melodic invention and for melodic–dramatic intensification. Moreover, the *Psalm* shows a flair for clear formal design and melodic variation: in particular, it includes one expressive means of dramatic progression that reappears in all Leonard Bernstein's vocal compositions throughout his creative life, the rise from a low E to the higher F sharp, that is, a progression of a ninth.

PRAISE YE THE LORD MONSTERS OF THE SEA PRAISE HIM YE VA-GRANT FLOCKS OF THE LEA

Two years later, in 1937, he composed a large-scale work, the first in a series of instrumental compositions which he himself regards as juvenilia, yet they have provided themes or even entire passages or sections for use in later works. It is a Trio for violin, violoncello and piano, which he performed with some fellow students at Harvard. He

[132]

also started writing a piano concerto, 'in C minor, very romantic, very Tchaikovskyish', as he recalls while singing its first theme. The Trio started with a slow introduction marked 'Adagio non troppo', a characteristic Bernstein procedure: it is written in a chromatic free-tonal idiom, a cello motif consisting of six notes is taken over by the violin and spun out in canonic polyphony by the two string instruments. After the lyrical Adagio, there follows a lively and pronouncedly rhythmical section, 'più mosso', in which violin and violoncello continue to emphasise their lyrical propensities. The second movement, 'Tempo di marcia', also foreshadows some characteristic Bernstein features of later creative periods. The least original of the movements is the Finale, a vivid piece after a slow introduction in post-Romantic colouring.

From the same period dates *Music for Two Pianos*, with a Largo introduction, Blues and Foxtrot, the latter written in typical Bernstein rhythms — indeed he used them seven years later for dance scenes in the musical *On the Town*. The work was first performed in summer 1938, played by the composer together with Mildred Spiegel, a fellow student of Heinrich Gebhard. For Gebhard his piano teacher, Bernstein composed a two-movement Piano Sonata and for Mildred Spiegel two dance movements for piano; these also reappeared in the ballet music for *On the Town*.

Bernstein's most original work in his early years was a Violin Sonata, composed in 1939 and first performed in 1940 by himself and the violinist Raphael Hillyer, to whom it is dedicated. The form invented for this work returns with many interesting variants in a number of his important later compositions. The Sonata has two movements, the second being a variation on the first. Five years afterwards, the theme of the first movement, marked 'moderato assai', was used by Bernstein in the ballet music for *Facsimile*; the variation movement is recalled in the third variation in the First Part of *The Age of Anxiety*, written ten years after the violin sonata. Clustered chords in the first variation and the melodic transformations in the second variation come near to twelve-tone chromaticism; structures and techniques of composition at work here became hallmarks of Bernstein's style. It was no mere passing whim to incorporate music from the juvenilia in some later, more mature works. The 'Jeremiah' Symphony, too, includes memories of earlier works: in its first movement Bernstein used a 'Chorale' taken from the third of four movements of a woodwind quartet for two clarinets and two bassoons with piano (1940).

Leonard Bernstein began serious composition with *Psalm 148* and in his vocal works and music on sacred themes may be seen his most significant contributions to both contemporary American and neo-Hebrew music. His characteristic style as a mature composer stems from musical inventiveness and imagination, and from a melodic resourcefulness rooted in his provenance and upbringing as an American and a Jew. Psalmody, cantillation melos and *song* inflexion reverberate not only in his vocal music, but in the instrumental melodiousness of ballet scores and symphonic compositions as well. The First Symphony reaches its climax in the concluding vocal movement; the Second Symphony is melodically shaped in adherence to a literary-melodic work; the Third Symphony is a choral symphonic composition. Like the Second Symphony, the Serenade for violin solo and small orchestra originates in a literary work and is thus connected, at least latently, with verbal expression. It is one of the most attractive features of Bernstein's music that his symphonic experience — gained as a conductor and as composition student at college and university — has been amalgamated with his innate sense for vocal expression in his musical works of all kinds and descriptions.

Two years after his Psalm composition of 1937, Bernstein began sketching music to verses from the *Lamentations of Jeremiah*, the prophet's threnody on destroyed Jerusalem and his prayer to God to lead His people back into the Holy City. The psalmody of the vocal line is moulded after a traditional melody from Hebrew liturgy; it is chromatically enriched and out of its melancholy mood the composer develops a plaintive motif in descending thirds, which often reappears in later works either identically or in recognisable variants. The original composition of 1939 was written for soprano; in 1942 Bernstein rewrote it for mezzosoprano and orchestra incorporating it in his First Symphony, which also uses Judaic liturgical motifs in its other two movements. Because of his father's adherence to religious tradition he was thoroughly familiar with synagogue chants and the Jewish heritage; he dedicated the 'Jeremiah' Symphony to his father.

When, two years after the Symphony, Leonard Bernstein's first musical, *On the Town*, appeared on Broadway, alert music lovers in the audience may well have found the opening music somewhat astonishing: the musical did not begin with the plushy instrumental or vocal introductory number traditional in Broadway shows, but with an unusual and original song for solo voice and orchestra, 'I Feel Like I'm Not Out of Bed Yet' in the form of an operatic recitative echoing both Jewish liturgical chanting and the kindred inflections of negro spirituals. Then, very surprisingly, this breaks quite suddenly into a rousing rhythmic hymn to New York. This opening contains all the characteristic Bernstein features: the psalmodic melodiousness, rhythms strikingly developed from Stravinskyan models, and New York as the centre of pulsating joy of life and enthusiastic love. 'For me Lenny does not just embody America in general, but New York — Lenny *is* New York', says Yehudi Menuhin.

Jerusalem was the theme of Leonard Bernstein's first major composition, the 'Jeremiah' Symphony: New York was that of his first music for the theatre, the ballet *Fancy Free* from which *On the Town* was derived. For *Fancy Free* he had written the lyrics and music of his first Broadway song, 'Big Stuff'; with it he proved that he is 'a serious composer trying to be a songwriter', having written a symphony before producing a popular song. The statement was made in one of his 'Imaginary Conversations', entitled 'Why don't you run upstairs and write a nice Gershwin tune?' (in Bernstein, *Joy of Music*). This particular imaginary conversation is with a professional manager (P.M.) who asks Bernstein why he does not write popular tunes rather than 'interesting' music:

> Your songs are simply too arty. That's not for the public, you know. A special dissonant effect in the bass may make you happy, and maybe some of your highbrow friends, but it doesn't help to make a hit. You're too wrapped up in unusual chords and odd skips in the tune and screwy forms: that's all only an amusing game you play with yourself . . . . You just have to learn how to be simple, my boy . . . . I'll bet my next week's salary that you can write simple tunes if you really put your mind to it.

Bernstein was aware of the fact that he does not write 'commercial' songs yet he nevertheless found it 'a little depressing' that he never hears 'someone accidentally whistle something of mine, somewhere, just once'. But he explains to P.M. that 'composing is a very different thing from writing tunes . . . . Composition means a putting together, yes, but a putting together of elements so that they add up to an organic whole'.

Bernstein's first Broadway song, 'Big Stuff', contains all the traits condemned by P.M. in the imaginary conversation. The song begins with a chromatically interesting melody: its first two-bar phrase is made up of seven of the twelve semitones of the octave, followed by a second two-bar phrase, a variant of the first, based on four semitones not used in the first melodic phrase. The note B flat that would complete a twelve-note series but is not sounded in the two two-bar phases dominates the middle section of the song and returns in the instrumental coda as A sharp. Another feature departing from ordinary

Broadway numbers and popular songs is a certain asymmetry. The melody of 'Big Stuff' does not have the customary eight-bar regularity. After two main melodic strains of six bars each, there follows a six-bar middle section; when the main tune is repeated after this it is melodically enlarged to eight bars. The chromaticism of the melody is mirrored in an unusual harmonisation which becomes rich and condensed in the course of this original piece.

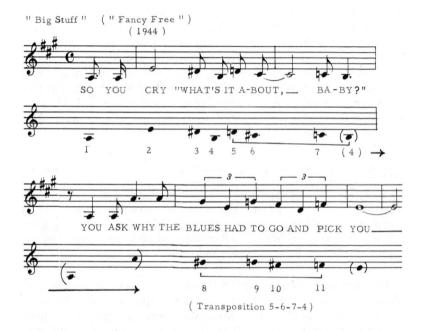

(Transposition 5-6-7-4)

There have been melodies of rich chromatic character in American music before Bernstein, especially in the music of George Gershwin and Marc Blitzstein. But the invention of tunes on seven-note or twelve-note chromatic progressions, though not bound to strict dodecaphonic treatment, was a real novelty, just as much as the departure in 'Big Stuff' from the eight-bar regularity of 'normal' songs. It is true that the originality of Bernstein's tunes and their rich harmonisation and sophisticated rhythms were and are an obstacle to their becoming hits in the Tin Pan Alley sense: nevertheless, his shows as a whole with their record albums have achieved world-wide success.

In the nine years between Leonard Bernstein's first and second Broadway musicals — *On the Town* (1944), and *Wonderful Town* (1953)

— he composed four choral pieces: one Hebrew liturgical chorus and three arrangements of popular Hebrew tunes, three song cycles, two separate solo songs and seven vocal pieces for Sir James Barrie's play *Peter Pan* (performed 1950); by 1943 he had already written his first song cycle, *I Hate Music*. These were the nine years in which he was employed at the New York music publishing house, became Koussevitzky's assistant at the Berkshire Music Center, was appointed assistant conductor of the New York Philharmonic, made his sensational debut stepping in for Bruno Walter, saw his First Symphony and *The Age of Anxiety* first performed (1944 and 1949 respectively), conducted for the first time in Europe and in Israel (1946 and 1947 respectively) and in 1951 married Felicia Montealegre Cohn. His short opera *Trouble in Tahiti*, premiered in 1952, was the last in the series of vocal compositions during this period.

The instrumental works of the early period mirror Leonard Bernstein's preoccupation with vocal music, each in its own way. The most important of these is the Sonata for clarinet and piano (1941/2), dedicated to David Oppenheim and first performed by himself with the clarinettist David Glazer at the Institute of Modern Art in Boston on 21 April 1942. The Sonata opens with an animated, melodious clarinet solo, accompanied by the piano in contrapuntal fashion recalling the style of Hindemith — Grazioso — till the piano takes up the melody and spins it out in typical Bernstein fashion helping to turn this into a playful movement. In listening to the song 'Lucky to be me' from *On the Town*, written two years after the Sonata, a striking similarity is felt between the first motif of the song refrain and the basic two-bar melodic motif in bars three and four of the clarinet part at the beginning of the Sonata. The second movement of the two-movement Sonata consists of a slow introduction — Andantino — and a lively main part — Vivace e leggiero. After an introductory five-note phrase, the clarinet plays a lyrical seven-note motif extending through three bars; the opening five notes and the next seven combine with the piano accompaniment to make a structure employing eleven of the twelve semitones of the octave. As in 'Big Stuff', one note is missing from a complete twelve-note melodic and harmonic texture. Here the missing note is E flat = D sharp and the composer leaves this for the second section of the introduction, using it to start the melodious theme of the Vivace which by itself is developed out of the opening theme from the Andantino introduction.

The song-like themes characterising the style of the clarinet sonata,

[137]

often recalling Bernstein's theatre music, also leave their mark on the various pieces for brass instruments composed in 1948. *Rondo for Lifey* (named after Judy Holliday's Skye terrier) for trumpet and piano opens with a three-note descending motif resembling 'Lucky to be me' and the clarinet motif in the sonata. *Elegy for Mippy I* for French horn and piano, *Elegy for Mippy II* for trombone, *Waltz for Mippy III* for tuba and piano are all dedicated to the composer's brother Burton and named after the latter's mongrel dog. They too are conceived in a chromatically song-like instrumental fashion and contain the kind of 'odd skips in the tune' with which the P.M. in the imaginary conversation found fault. Particularly notable are the melodic jumps of a seventh and ninth, the ninths abounding in *Elegy for Mippy II*. In this interesting piece, Bernstein demands that the trombonist 'should accompany himself by tapping one foot, *mezzoforte*, four to the bar', the piece being written in 12/8 metre, and thus the rhythmically complex solo becomes infinitely more sophisticated in rhythm.

'As gracefully as possible under the circumstances' opens the C sharp minor *Waltz for Mippy III*, like the other pieces composed in memory of Burtie's dog, with an expressive tune for the tuba, accompanied by the piano in four-note broken chords that are continually repeated and combined to form contrapuntal figures. The fifth and last work in the series (commissioned by the Juilliard Musical Foundation) is entitled *Fanfare for Bima* and written for a quartet of trumpet, horn, trombone and tuba (the soloists in the four preceding pieces). Bima was Sergei Koussevitzky's black cocker spaniel and a footnote in the score mentions that the Fanfare 'is based on the theme whistled in the Koussevitzky household to call the pet'.

The remaining instrumental compositions of the period are Bernstein's three cycles of piano pieces entitled *Anniversaries*. The first series, *Seven Anniversaries*, was composed in 1943; they are dedicated to the birthdays of Aaron Copland (No. 1), Leonard's sister Shirley (No. 2), the composer Paul Bowles (no. 4), the conductor Sergei Koussevitzky (No. 6), the composer William Schuman (No. 7). The other two recall the memory of a friend, Alfred Eisner (No. 3) and Koussevitzky's first wife Natalie (No. 5). *Four Anniversaries* followed in 1948, as birthday presents to Bernstein's bride Felicia Montealegre, his friend Johnny Mehegan, the composer David Diamond and Helen Coates, his revered piano teacher and later organizing secretary. In 1954 came yet another series, *Five Anniversaries*, for Elizabeth Rudolf, Lukas Foss, Elizabeth B. Ehrman, Sandy Gellhorn and Susanna Kyle. All these piano pieces show the mark of Leonard Bernstein's musical style: chromatically conceived melodious themes, multicolour rhythms, rich harmonies. 'In memoriam Natalie Koussevitzky' contains an elaboration of the mournful theme dominating the conclusion of the 'Jeremiah' Symphony. Musical quotations can be detected in the birthday dedication to Sergei Koussevitzky. An alluring portrait of his young bride Felicia is built up out of a quiet lyrical section and another which is vivid and motivically related to the first. In all instrumental compositions of the time, especially for the piano, the influence of Igor Stravinsky and Aaron Copland are strongly felt, the latter in melody and rhythm and the former in rythmical drive.

The few single vocal compositions of the early creative period are the liturgical synagogue chorus *Hashkivēnu* of 1945 (with organ accompaniment), the arrangements of Hebrew folksongs 'Ssimchū na' (after Mattityahu Weiner, a popular Israeli composer), 'Re'ēna' (both dating from 1947), 'Yigdal' (1950), and the two solo songs 'Afterthought' (1945) and 'Silhouette' (1951). 'Afterthought' — words and music by Leonard Bernstein — is described as a study for the ballet *Facsimile* (composed in 1946). The markedly expressive melody of this song opens with the typical leap of a ninth, a motif continually repeated. The rising ninth followed by a descending major third form the opening of a characteristically expanding melody which in its variants becomes richly chromatic. 'Silhouette', subtitled 'Galilee', is dedicated to Jennie Tourel 'on her birthday in Israel'; it also has a text by Bernstein and contains a passage imitating the sound of Arabic sing-song.

Weightier and more original than the separate songs are the three song cycles *I Hate Music* (1943), *La Bonne Cuisine* (1947) and *Two Love Songs* (1949).

I Hate Music is the cycle of *Five Kid Songs* which brought Jennie Tourel and Lenny Bernstein together for the first time, its New York premiere on 13 November 1943 preceding Bernstein's spectacular debut with the New York Philharmonic. Intellectual wit and humour pervade the text and music of these Bernstein 'kid songs', in which a naive unaffected girl gives rein to her feelings. 'My mother says that babies come in bottles; but last week she said they grew on special baby bushes' are the opening lines of the first song. 'Jupiter has Seven Moons' introduces the second of the girl's wondering questions. 'I hate music! But I like to sing: la dee da da dee' is the central song of the cycle. It opens with the typical Bernstein rising ninth — E–F sharp — followed by descending fourth and fifth. The syllables 'la dee da da dee', sung without piano accompaniment, could be some sort of a parody of dodecaphonic music, and they are sung 'freely, rather tonelessly and carelessly'. Then 'in tempo' she continues: 'But that's not music, not what I call music. No, sir', becoming more and more agitated. The remaining songs of the sophisticated cycle are 'A Big Indian and a Little Indian' and 'I'm a Person too'.

As lively and amusing as the *Kid Songs* are the four songs in the cycle *La Bonne Cuisine, Four Recipes for Voice and Piano* (1947), dedicated to Jennie Tourel, 'the onlie begetter of these songs'. In humorous style, Leonard Bernstein took the texts from Emile Dumont's *La Bonne Cuisine Française* and set them to music using both the original French and his own English translation, under the titles 'Plum Pudding', 'Queues de Boeuf', 'Tavouk Guenksis', 'Civet à toute Vitesse'. The first perform- ance was sung at New York Town Hall on 10 October 1947 by Marion Bell with Edwin MacArthur at the piano. The 'Two Love Songs' from English versions of poems by Rainer Maria Rilke ('Extinguish my eyes' and 'When my soul touches yours'), were both composed in 1949 and both first publicly performed by Jennie Tourel, although the one was given at a Town Hall recital on 13 March 1949 and the other not until 13 March 1963, fourteen years later, at the Philharmonic Hall, with Alan Rogers as accompanist.

For performances of *Peter Pan* in 1950, Bernstein composed inciden- tal music and a series of vocal numbers. In keeping with the play and its young audiences, he wrote simple catchy tunes, among them 'Who am I?', 'My House', 'Peter, Peter', and 'Never-Never-Land'. 'Pirate Song' and 'Plank Round' are set for male chorus.

The vocal and instrumental works of the early creative period were written between the two musical comedies *On the Town* and *Wonderful Town*, two paeans to Bernstein's New York.

On the Town, which opened in Boston on 13 December 1944 with a New York premiere on 28 December, resembles *Fancy Free* in telling of the adventures of three sailors on shore leave in New York. Each of them has his own idea about conquering the city and getting a girl. Gabey is a sentimental romantic, Chip is cooler-headed, Ozzie just wants to enjoy himself. By sheer chance it happens that Chip and Ozzie must carry out Gabey's wishes, for he sees a pretty girl's picture on a subway poster, and falls head over heels in love with her. His friends are called on to help him find the girl in the vast city. They separate and plunge into the hectic life of 'New York — New York', each starting in a different direction and encountering his own adven- ture. Chip succumbs to the wooing of a passionate young woman cab-driver; Ozzie meets a girl, an anthropology student, at the Museum of Natural History; Gabey systematically searches for his idol and at last finds her at a music school where she is taking singing lessons. The uncomplicated story of the search for life, yearning and love is set against the background of the vigorous, intoxicating life of New York. The writers were Betty Comden and Adolph Green, who based the comedy on Jerome Robbins' original concept, with Leonard Bernstein adding some lyrics of his own to those of his friends Comden and Green, who also appeared in the Broadway production.

The work includes twenty musical numbers. After the introduction, with its resemblance to operatic recitative, and the paean to New York, comes the 'Chase Music' that sets the sailors on their road. Gabey's song about his dream girl, 'She's a Home-Loving Girl', was used by Bernstein for the first of *Three Dance Episodes* which he put together for orchestral concert performances in 1945. A comic number, written by Betty Comden and Adolph Green for themselves, with cynically witty music by Bernstein, is 'I Get Carried Away'. The central lyrical number, 'Lonely Town', one of the composer's loveliest tunes, describes the loneliness of someone who is lost in a great city and finds no love — longing for love brings loneliness whether on Main Street or on Broadway. The wide expressiveness of the melody demands the lengthening of the main melodic strain to twelve bars, instead of the 'normal' eight, a trait often encountered in Bernstein's songs. 'Lonely Town' became the second of the *Three Dance Episodes* in the orchestral Suite. Cheerful and sentimental numbers alternate in the score for *On the Town* until Act I concludes with the rhythmically sophisticated 'Times Square Ballet', the last of the *Three Dance Episodes* of 1945. In Act II the most original numbers are the song 'Ya got Me' and the two ballets, the 'Imaginary Coney Island Ballet' and 'Real Coney Island Dance', containing motifs taken from the composer's *Music for Two Pianos* of 1937. The orchestration was completed by Leonard Bernstein together with Hershy Kay; its style, as with the composer's later Broadway shows, differs as does the music itself from the stereotyped luxurious orchestral sounds usually accompanying commercial musical comedies. Bernstein's music demands individually sharp contrasts between purely lyrical and rhythmically accentuated melodies; its jazzy elements have to be emphasised and strengthened by orchestral colouring.

Five years after *On the Town* was staged, a film based on the same plot was produced, but using only four of Bernstein's songs. For the rest of the music another composer was engaged by the producers.

The second musical comedy, *Wonderful Town* (New York, of course) begins in Greenwich Village. In *On the Town*, the explorers of this city of cities had been three sailors: in the new work, two sisters come from Columbus, Ohio, to try their luck in the metropolis. Ruth wants to

[141]

become a writer, Eileen an actress. They find a one-room basement apartment in Greenwich Village, but there is no peace for them from the many odd characters who pass their windows, and in a mock tearful duet, they lament that they 'ever left Ohio'. The sisters find it extremely difficult to fulfil their ambitions. Getting used to New York life is easier for the dark-haired, witty and attractive Ruth than for the blonde, gentle, wide-eyed Eileen who even manages to get arrested and ends up charming all the policemen. She experiences a series of misadventures until finding a job in a night club. Ruth too fails at first in her attempts at a writing career, but at last she writes a successful story and is taken on by an important newspaper. Rosalind Russell as the intelligent and highly temperamental Ruth and Edith Adams as the more naive, sweet-natured Eileen, together with George Gaynes as the ubiquitous editor, starred in the production of *Wonderful Town* at New York's Winter Garden Theatre, where it opened on 26 February 1953 — after a New Haven preview on 19 January — to a run of 559 performances; *On the Town* ran for 463 performances at the Adelphi Theatre.

The music for *Wonderful Town* is still more jokey, grotesque and original than that in *On the Town*. The first musical numbers — 'Christopher Street' and 'Ohio' — set the mocking tone of the entire comedy. 'One Hundred Easy Ways to Lose a Man' establishes Ruth's characteristic bubbling wit, while the newspaper editor's 'What a Waste' is no less comic in its ironical commentary, pointing the moral that out-of-towners should stay at home and not invade New York to seek their fortunes. A climax is reached by writers and composer in the sophisticated comedy of 'Conversation Piece', in which the main characters desperately try to start a conversation, but whenever one of them begins telling an anecdote, the others simply make him stop, while the music, in cynical commentary on the emptiness of the scene, bridges the gaps. When in the end all the characters talk and sing at once, drowned by shrill coloratura trills, it sounds like a biting New York version of a comic episode in one of Jacques Offenbach's Parisian operettas.

Among the sixteen numbers of *Wonderful Town*, some are markedly grotesque: 'Swing', the ballet 'At the Village Vortex' and 'Wrong Note Rag' with its repeatedly disturbing dissonant 'wrong note'. The vivid action is interrupted only rarely by lyrical, romantic music such as the plaintive duet 'Why, oh Why, oh Why, oh, Why Did We Ever Leave Ohio?' (Ruth and Eileen); 'I'm a Little Bit in Love' (Eileen); 'I Love a Quiet Girl' (The Editor) and 'It's Love' (Eileen, The Editor and chorus). The 'Ohio' duet has a middle section in which a more lively

orchestral interlude forms the background for a melodramatic dialogue, a practice Bernstein often follows as a means of introducing
musical contrast. 'I'm a Little Bit in Love' counts with 'Lonely Town'
(from *On the Town*) as one of Leonard Bernstein's loveliest tunes in his
early theatrical works. The long line of melody is unusually rich in
rhythmical scansion and its modulations also add interest. 'A Quiet
Girl' has a melody accompanied by a kind of pedal point for ten bars; it
seems at first to be of an almost folk-like simplicity, but this is enriched
with colourful harmonies. 'It's Love', from Act II, opens with a variant
on a quotation from 'A Little Bit of Love' and the new tune developed
here uses identical harmonies: its hearer may well feel that this is the
art of a 'songwriter who wrote a symphony before he ever wrote a
popular song'.

It is strikingly evident from the thematic foundations of Leonard
Bernstein's compositions over his entire career that each of them, from
the lightest to the profoundly serious, reveals a common trait: an
element of loneliness, of doubt and sorrow which communicates itself
in the mood and feeling of his literary themes and of his music.
Following his youthful *Psalm*, the biblical prophet's lament for Jerusalem was Leonard Bernstein's first important composition, as it
appears in the 'Jeremiah' Symphony. *On the Town* and *Wonderful Town*
show how lonely and frustrated people may feel in bustling New York.
In the song cycle *I Hate Music* a child rebels against society. In
Facsimile, symbolic choreographic scenes centre on the lives of lonely
and disappointed men and women. The Second Symphony is inspired
by a poem on *The Age of Anxiety*, which has as its theme the instability
and emptiness of modern society and the fears and dreams of people
who no longer understand each other. The operetta *Candide* is based on
Voltaire's bitter satire on the ways of life, the philosophy and optimism
of society. The short opera *Trouble in Tahiti* shows a young married
couple whose life is empty and unfulfilled. With the film *On the
Waterfront*, his music accompanied a presentation of tragical conflicts,
West Side Story became the first musical ever written based on tragic
confrontations, on dissatisfaction and frustration among young New
Yorkers. Plato's discourses on the passion, power and longing of love
form the basis for Leonard Bernstein's *Serenade*. The crisis of belief and
religion of modern man is the theme of the 'Kaddish' Symphony and in
Mass, which Antal Dorati has termed a 'modern mystery play'. Like
earlier Bernstein compositions, Jerome Robbins' ballet *The Dybbuk*
deals with traditional Jewish motifs of belief, mysticism, and liturgy. In
the later symphonic music we find very different foundations — though
the difference is perhaps more apparent than real — in the light-

hearted *Divertimento* of 1981–2 and the 'Nocturne' entitled *Halil. Divertimento*, with all its gaiety, contains movements which raise fundamental questions, such as 'Sphinxes' and an 'In Memoriam' before the rousing Finale. *Halil*, written in memory of a young Israeli killed in battle, is deeply affecting in its underlying drama of struggles and hopes.

Leonard Bernstein cares deeply about the struggle between good and evil, joy and misery on earth, love and destruction, lust for life and adversity, and his concern finds expression in all his theatrical and symphonic music, indeed in almost everything he has written. In his most mature compositions it is reflected musically in the juxtaposition and coalition of alternating diatonic and chromatic melodies, of sharply dissonant and romantically harmonious sounds, of diversified complex and metrically scanning rhythms. Even the early song 'Big Stuff' manifests this trait quite clearly; in *Halil*, thirty-seven years later, conflicts are contested in symphonic form. In his Harvard lectures, Bernstein has dealt with 'the unanswered question' — tonality, free- or non-tonality, the central concern and problem for the composers. In his compositions, this musical problem is equated with the struggle of man in our times.

Leonard Bernstein's musicals have been influenced by his profound musical knowledge and symphonic thinking to such a degree that he has not produced song *hits* in the accepted sense, rather he has been able to create a novel style of music for the theatre that in turn has had a marked impact on his symphonic compositions.

5

Symphonic Works

Are symphonies a thing of the past? No, obviously,
since they are still being written in substantial
quantity. But yes, equally obviously, in the sense that
the classical concept of a symphony — depending as it
does on a bifocal tonal axis, which itself depends on
the existence of tonality — *is* a thing of the past. . . . If
I may be pardoned for a quasi-existential paradox, I
suggest that the answer is in the questioning.
Leonard Bernstein, September 1965

'Are symphonies a thing of the past?' — Leonard Bernstein himself has composed three symphonies proper and written two symphonic Suites; the series of symphonic movements derived from his film score *On the Waterfront* and the *Serenade* which is a kind of solo concerto for violin in symphonic suite form. In each of these works he has tried to imbue the traditional concepts of symphony and suite with a new meaning as each composition is based on an extra-musical idea and develops in a pure musically-conceived form that is especially adapted to suit the primary inspiration. Within the frame of the symphonic compositions are mirrored religious traditions, poetic drama, philosophic meditations and social conflicts out of which emerge the unmistakable character of a musical style deriving its effective impact from an agitated lyrically-minded or dramatic, at times theatrical expressiveness. The stylistical means and formal structures are derived from many model compositions in classical, Romantic and contemporary music; Leonard Bernstein is an eclectic in the same sense that most significant music is eclectic in the original meaning of the word, 'selective'.

The all-too-often misused term 'ecleticism' should be reexamined for the purpose of analysing the musical style of Leonard Bernstein — as much as for an appraisal of the music of Gustav Mahler, whose personality and compositions have so much in common with the conductor-composer of modern America. Any musicological study reveals two diametrically opposed sorts of eclecticism. A great many composers have continued to write, without adding much individuality, in forms and styles developed by earlier masters; true epigones, their contributions to world music are of little importance historically or aesthetically. Others have enriched the melodic, rhythmic, harmonic and structural models of preceding historical periods through a novel approach, a new perspective and original imaginative ideas and have created a synthesis of tradition and innovation that surpasses the artistic achievements of other contemporary composers, and ensures that they will be of enduring interest. To recall only the greatest and most ingenious masters of eclectic synthesis and innovation: Johann Sebastian Bach, who took over and summarised what was best in the Italian, French, English and German music of his time, creating a style that we recognise as 'unmistakably J.S. Bach' today; Wolfgang Amadeus Mozart tried his hand at adapting current fashionable Italian, French, German and Austrian musical styles, and even mannerisms, and was regarded as a successful composer for as long as these musical roots remained intelligible. In his mature works, most especially in his operas, piano concertos and symphonies, the brooding, passionate and dramatic depth beneath the refined and charming surface overshadowed the eclectic beginnings. The music of most of the great composers can be viewed in a similar way; Richard Wagner and Gustav Mahler most certainly belong to the ranks of those masters whose erstwhile eclecticism formed the basis of an innovating and unique musical art.

Leonard Bernstein has not created a single symphonic work that is independent of an extra-musical idea, thus each of them has a musical form quite its own. The underlying literary, dramatic or religious incentive rarely influences the structure and style of an entire composition, so that each of the symphonic works can be listened to and evaluated as an independent musical work without any knowledge of the extra-musical foundations. Where the music follows a text, as in the 'Kaddish' Symphony, Bernstein has arranged it in such a way that it easily adapts itself to his conception of musical form. Thus his symphonic music is dramatically effective and exciting because it is always possible to perceive and follow the development of small motivic and rhythmic germ cells into enlarged and intensified melodious and rhythmical structures. This style of composition may be found in many of his early works and it links his chamber music with the symphonies and the symphonies with his music for the theatre. A keen perception of the foundations of the great symphonic music of the past — demonstrated both in Bernstein's interpretations as a conductor and in his analytical

The composer at work

lectures and television broadcasts — has surely influenced his own creative work; his study of the music of J.S. Bach, Mozart, Beethoven and Brahms has left its impact on his process of elaborating a musical idea in the logic, consistency and imagination demanded of symphonic composition.

A unifying theme connects his three symphonies; it could be termed 'man, his beliefs and doubts in the modern world', and this crisis of faith is mirrored for Bernstein in the critical situation of contemporary music. 'The crisis in faith through which we are living', wrote Bernstein in his preface to *The Infinite Variety of Music* 'is not unlike the musical crisis.' There is much talk of the 'death of God' and 'the death of tonality': 'I humbly submit to you the proposition that neither death is true, all that has died is our own outworn conceptions. . . . We will, if we are lucky, come out of them both with new and freer concepts, more personal perhaps — or even less personal: who is to say? — but in any case with a new idea of God, a new idea of tonality. And music will survive'.

The First and the Third Symphony have explicitly religious backgrounds, though striking deviation from orthodox tradition is noticeable in both works: Leonard Bernstein has set the 'Lamentation of the Prophet Jeremiah' in the First Symphony for a female voice and in the 'Kaddish' Symphony (No. 3) it is again a female soloist who gives expression to man's faith: in the premiere performances he chose Hannah Rovina (Israel's First Lady of the Theatre) for the narration of his text in Israel, and it was later given by Felicia Montealegre Bernstein; only for the revised version of the work and its new recording, he transferred the part to a male speaker (Michael Wager). In the Second Symphony, based on Auden's *The Age of Anxiety*, the 'speaker' is a solo piano: 'The pianist provides an almost autobiographical protagonist, set against an orchestral mirror in which he sees himself, analytical, in the modern ambience' (Bernstein). In the *Serenade* the composer lets a solo violin interpret philosophical meditations.

The main themes are of a different tonal character in the symphonic compositions: some are stated in simple diatonic fashion, others have modal tonality or are chromatically conceived, being built on a succession of twelve notes, none of which shows predominance over another. In Bernstein's work, such twelve-note chromatic themes are usually divided into two phrases of seven and five notes respectively or a seven-note or five-note motif is accompanied by harmonies supplementing the 'missing' notes. In contrast to strict dodecaphonic development, these twelve-note themes always aim at a tonal solution. A characteristic of all Leonard Bernstein's musical themes is their rhythmical variety — their metres and rhythms are either scanned asymmetrically or they give an impression of asymmetry through steadily shifting accentuation; the composer reveals his intimate familiarity with jazz. Another distinctive trait of Bernstein's symphonic structures is his practice of dividing individual melodic cells into new patterns by breaking them up and combining them in the formation of new motifs and themes. This practice of fission and combinative elaboration can be noticed within a symphonic movement as well as in the sequence of a number of movements. An early example of such a method was the Violin Sonata of 1939, in which the second movement is a variation of the first; similarly each variation in Part I, B, of *The Age of Anxiety*, written ten years later, takes up a characteristic musical trait of a previous one and develops out of it a new figure which serves as a foundation for yet another variation. In all his symphonic works the composer is able to create an astonishingly diversified and rich variety of musical content sometimes from extremely concise basic motifs. He uses not only the traditional means of repetition and varied repetition employed by composers of all preceding epochs, with transposition, inversion and transformation by means of rhythmic and harmonic variation or changed instrumental colouring. In his music the pregnant motivic cells are continually expanded, combining with split and varied cells to grow to larger and more elaborate themes, and each of the new structures lives a musical life of its own until superseded by yet another, similarly built derivation or changed instrumental colouring.

Leonard Bernstein has frequently analysed his own methods of composing, as well as those of the great masters. His remarks on J.S. Bach, in a television talk of 31 March 1957, may be fittingly applied to his own creative practice: 'Once the theme is stated at the beginning, the main event is over. The rest of the movement will be a constant elaboration, reiteration, and discussion of that main event, just as the architecture of a bridge grows inevitably out of one initial arch' (repr. as 'The Music of Johann Sebastian Bach', Bernstein, *Joy of Music*). In Bernstein's symphonic music a decisive role is also played by contrast in orchestration: in the First Symphony there is a constant juxtaposition of instrumental colours, in the Second Symphony orchestral soloists are used to contrast with the piano solo, and in the 'Kaddish' Symphony solo and choral voices, instrumental solos and orchestral groups of sound vary in constantly changing combinations and contrasts.

At a press conference in Berlin in August 1977, Leonard Bernstein repeated and expanded the words of his 'Letter to the Reader' in *The Infinite Variety of Music*:

The work I have been writing all my life is about the struggle that is born of the crisis of our century, a crisis of faith. Even way back, when I wrote *Jeremiah*, I was wrestling with that problem. The faith or peace that is found at the end of *Jeremiah* is really more a kind of comfort, not a solution. Comfort is one way of achieving peace, but it does not achieve the sense of a new beginning, as does the end of *Age of Anxiety* or *Mass*.

Making a logical connection between the spiritual foundations of all his works Bernstein says: 'I suppose I am always writing the same piece, as all composers do. But each time it is a new attempt in other terms to write this piece, to have the piece achieve new dimensions, or even acquire a new vocabulary'.

This statement can easily be tested by noting the similarity of the motifs, themes, sounds, imaginative elaborations and moods from Leonard Bernstein's earliest compositions to his latest works. Melodic formulas can be recognised in his songs and theatre music, which are not basically different in his symphonic themes. It is obvious indeed that a composer who has never succeeded in writing a symphony could not possibly have devised a score like that of *West Side Story*, while only the composer of *West Side Story* was able to create a complex musico-dramatic symphonic work like *Kaddish*. The imaginary professional manager in Bernstein's essay in *The Joy of Music* found fault with the theatre composer Bernstein in that his tunes are too arty and too highbrow; *Kaddish* was censured for its 'theatricality'. Leonard Bernstein himself acknowledges that he always leans towards the dramatic in all his music, a trend exemplified even in the titles of each movement in the 'Jeremiah' Symphony: 'Prophecy', 'Profanation', 'Lamentation'.

As for 'programmatic meanings', the composer says of the 'Jeremiah' Symphony that

> the intention is not one of literalness, but of emotional quality. Thus the first movement ('Prophecy') aims only to parallel in feeling the intensity of the prophet's pleas with his people; and the Scherzo ('Profanation') to give a general sense of the destruction and chaos brought by the pagan corruption within the priesthood and the people. The third movement ('Lamentation'), being a setting of poetic text, is naturally a more literary conception. It is the cry of Jeremiah, as he mourns his beloved Jerusalem, ruined, pillaged and dishonoured after his desperate efforts to save it.

There remains the hope that Israel will be led back to the Holy City: 'Turn Thou us unto Thee, O Lord', the prophet prays.

The symphony opens — Largamente — with a French horn playing a motto-theme which recurs in all the three movements in various guises and variations. Like many of Bernstein's themes, from his earliest works to the tunes in *West Side Story*, the melodic cadences in *Kaddish* or the nocturne *Halil*, it is characterised by a recurring descending melodic line; it uses six notes of the twelve in the octave, while two additional notes are sounded in the low strings and the 'missing' four notes of the twelve-note scale appear in the imitation of the descending motif that follows in the woodwinds immediately after the solo horn passage. All the subsidiary themes in the first movement are in some way related either to the horn melody or to the woodwind motif deriving from it; the character of the latter especially is the source of an important theme found in episodes in all three movements; it shapes the 'Lament' motif of the Finale. The opening horn theme and its woodwind counterpart have been traced to cadences from traditional Hebrew liturgy (see Jack Gottlieb's notes accompanying the Deutsche Grammophon recordings of the Symphonies): the first half from the *Amen* sung during the Three Festivals of Passover, the Feast of Weeks and the Festival of Tabernacles; and the second half from the *Amidah* prayers (the 'Eighteen Blessings') intoned in the liturgy of the High Holy Days. The Scherzo theme is paraphrased from a biblical cantillation motif intoned on Sabbath days; the vocal motifs in the 'Lamentation' are derived from the Dirges chanted on the Ninth of Av, the day of mourning on which Jews all over the world commemorate the destruction of the Holy Temple of Jerusalem by the Babylonians. Jack Gottlieb notes that one of the Dirge tunes is a variation of the *Amidah* cadence in the 'Prophecy' movement, indicating that the foreboding prophecy has been fulfilled.

The Scherzo opens with the main theme played by clarinets in unison — 'Vivace con brio'. The paraphrased liturgical chant is presented with strongly accented rhythmic variation which becomes stronger and more individual in the course of the movement. The grim Scherzo develops with rapidly increasing colours and dynamic force. In a kind of Trio a choral-like theme from the first movement and fragments from other thematic motifs recur and expand, till a horn call based on the motto-theme ushers in the Scherzo reprise, where the barbaric dance strains are set against the prophetic theme in forceful counterpoint. Jeremiah's mourning for his beloved Jerusalem takes the form of a symphonically elaborated song for orchestra and solo voice singing the original Hebrew verses from the *Book of Lamentations*, (I; 1–3, 8; IV, 14–15; V, 20–21. The prophet's call, enhanced by choral and lyrical elements, resounds in this Finale; in the Coda comes the plaintive melodic phrase in descending thirds stemming from the woodwind motif in the second half of the symphony's opening thematic cadence and also recalling the motto-theme of the french horn. Slowly and tenderly fading to pianissimo, the symphony seems to sound at its end a hopeful and confident note. The descending phrase in thirds, which reappears in *Seven Anniversaries* as part of the memorial for Natalie Koussevitzky, in the 'Scene at the Bar' in *Fancy Free* and again in *Halil*, reminds the listener of the motto-theme of Aaron Copland's Piano Sonata (1939–40) where it opens the first movement and reappears with variations in the third.

Though the 'Jeremiah' Symphony contains little of symphonic form and content in the conventional sense, the work is truly symphonic in its basic principles. Concentrated, logical development and elaboration characterise each of its movements; the relationship, and, to some extent, identity of the motifs creates a strong feeling of unity between the parts; the traditional dramatic contrasts between the energetic and lyrical have remained their foundation, even if they appear in a different order from that used in the classical or romantic symphony. The themes are pregnant and impress themselves on the ear to such a degree that their variations and elaborations are easily recognised; the rhythms draw their sharp accents from the more complicated devices of jazz or Latin-American dance; the harmony is what is aptly described in American terminology (first by Nicolas Slonimsky) as 'pan-diatonic', in contrast to the 'pan-chromaticism' of non-tonal music and the 'harmonic chromaticism' of the late nineteenth century — it always tends towards a certain harmonic and tonal stagnation.

The Second Symphony, *The Age of Anxiety*, completed in 1949 when Bernstein was thirty-one, has been described by the composer himself as 'an essay in loneliness'. It was written during a period of hectic travels, concert appearances and continual unrest. One of its movements was premiered on tour before the entire symphony was finished.

In W.H. Auden's *Eclogue* (1948), 'one of the most shattering examples of pure virtuosity in the history of English poetry', says Bernstein, a girl and three men meet in a New York bar; all of them feel lonely and insecure and try to overcome their mental conflicts by drinking. They discuss the problems and anxieties of their life and then set out on a 'dream-odyssey', singly or in pairs, exchanging partners, without finding anywhere a place or any purpose in life. The girl invites the men to her apartment for a drink; in the taxi they mourn the loss of a leader-figure to guide and help them. They seem to have a good time in the apartment, wildly drinking and dancing, but this is no more than escapism. At last, they all separate and each tries to come to terms with herself or himself. Faith in life returns, but a long way lies still ahead before they can find fulfilment.

The poem paints a terrifyingly depressing picture of post-war youth, the loneliness and despair of contemporary life: yet some irony pervades the unfolding of the young people's thoughts and problems. Leonard Bernstein has used the poem as a starting point rather than a scene-by-scene programme for his Symphony for Piano and Orchestra, the pianist representing the composer himself (so he says) 'through Auden's character Malin'. The symphony is in two parts, each consisting of three sections following each other without a break. Part One comprises a Prologue, a set of variations ('The Seven Ages') and a second series of variations ('The Seven Stages'). Part Two begins with the Dirge, the 'song of mourning for the colossal Dad', continues with the Masque, the wild Scherzo and concludes with an Epilogue.

The Prologue states the nostalgic main theme, played by two echoing clarinets, pianissimo — Lento — unaccompanied and sounding almost as though improvised. This is followed by an extended descending scale which (in Bernstein's words) 'acts as a bridge into the realm of the unconscious, where most of the poem takes place'. The variations in the two sets of seven are not based on one underlying theme, as with most classical sets of variations; each takes up a characteristic feature of the preceding variation and from it develops some new feature, which in its turn serves as foundation for its successor. 'This is a kind of musical fission', says the composer, 'which corresponds to the reasonableness and almost didactic quality of the four-fold discussion', that of the four characters in Auden's poem.

The opening of the Dirge, for piano solo, has an expressively rising eleven-note melody supported by a pedal-point providing the twelfth chromatic note, as basis for the theme; a contrasting middle section, Bernstein admits, is of 'an almost Brahmsian romanticism, in which can be felt the self-indulgent, or negative, aspect of this strangely pompous lamentation'. The Masque is 'a nightmare of a scherzo'; it is scored for piano solo and percussion, 'in which a kind of fantastic piano-jazz is employed, by turns nervous, sentimental, self-satisfied, vociferous', symbolising the bout of drunkenness. When the orchestra comes plunging into the end of this movement, it shows the emptiness and pretence of Masque. The Epilogue begins immediately; the feeling of loneliness breaks through again, but Bernstein, unlike Auden, gives his work an optimistic ending: the protagonists can face the reality of life.

As to the relationship of the music to the poem, Bernstein has said that 'no one could be more astonished' than himself 'at the extent to which the programmaticism of this work has been carried'. In the original programme notes for the first performance by the Boston Symphony Orchestra on 8 April 1949 he wrote:

I had not planned a *meaningful* work, at least not in the sense of a piece whose meaning relies on details of programmatic implication. I was merely writing a symphony inspired by a poem and following the general form of that poem. Yet, when each section was finished I discovered, upon re-reading, detail after detail of programmatic relation to the poem — details that had *written themselves*, wholly unplanned and unconscious. Since I trust the unconscious implicitly, finding it a sure source of wisdom and the dictator of the condign in artistic matters, I am content to leave these details in the score . . . .

The composer cites an example for what he calls 'details that write themselves'.

I recently discovered — upon re-examining the *Masque* movement — that it actually strikes four o'clock! Now there is no mention of four o'clock in the poem; there is only the feeling that it is very late at night, that everyone is tired, that the jokes are petering out, and that everyone is valiantly trying to keep them going. So we find the music petering out, while the celesta strikes four as naively as day and the percussion instruments cheerfully make a new stab at energetic gaiety. I was pleasantly surprised to find this in the score, since I had not really written it. It had simply been put there by some inner sense of theatricality. If the charge of theatricality in a symphonic work is a valid one, I am willing to plead guilty. I have a deep suspicion that every work I write, for whatever medium, is really theatre music in some way; and nothing has convinced me more than these new discoveries of the unconscious hand that has been at work all along in *The Age of Anxiety*.

In this way, Leonard Bernstein makes his own illuminating statement on the 'theatricality' of his music, at the same time answering many of his critics. It is interesting to compare his feeling of an 'unconscious hand being at work' in the creation of a musical composition with a maxim of the poet Jean Cocteau: 'An artist may tentatively open a secret door, without ever comprehending that behind it there lies an entire world'.

Sixteen years after completing *The Age of Anxiety*, Leonard Bernstein reassessed his 'attempt to mirror Auden's literary images in so literal a way'. He found he has 'succeeded least well in the finale, where the non-participation of the solo piano (in the 1948 version) did not so much convey the intended *detachment* as rob the soloist of his concertante function'. The final movement was therefore amended to provided the solo pianist 'with a final burst of cadenza before the coda'. When the revision was completed in 1965, Bernstein said he was satisfied that this would be the final form.

Many characteristic melodic, rhythmic, harmonic and structural means of expression combine in the musical language of this symphonic work. As in many Bernstein compositions, its melodic themes are dominated by intervals of thirds, more often than not in descending lines. There are minor and major thirds, forming melodic motifs or chord combinations; at times these are 'filled' by linking intervals in seconds. The theme sounded by the clarinets in the opening of *The Age of Anxiety* is a mixolydian-modal melody with the note G as tonal centre. It is elegiac in character and mood and inspires almost all the varied melodic developments in the course of the symphony; it especially dominates the Prologue and Epilogue. In some themes derived from this basic melody it is in the second phrase that it appears most clearly. The twelve-note melodic ascent that opens the Dirge is made up of major and minor thirds; a characteristic, yet here unexpected, melodic leap of a seventh returns in the main theme of this movement, a theme developed out of the four last notes of the twelve-note row. In a later development another twelve-note series appears, comprising intervals of a fourth and fifth. Bernstein's method of forming melodic combinations of motif cells had already characterised much of his procedure in the 'Jeremiah' Symphony, but in this earlier work it was followed less persistently than in the Second Symphony and chromaticism did not go so far as to lead to twelve-note progressions. In the Epilogue of *The Age of Anxiety* the yearning for faith finds musical expression in another succession of fourth and fifths. The coexistence and juxtaposition of twelve-note melodies, of themes in major or minor thirds interrupted by fourths or fifths, and modal structures fulfil similar functions in all Bernstein's compositions. Where his music becomes strongly dramatic, its melodies are dominated by expressive rises in sevenths or ninths.

In his three symphonies and in *Serenade*, Leonard Bernstein has succeeded in giving a musically apprehensible form and content to extramusically inspired compositions. He does this by variously expanding motif cells into melodies, then creating sections through further amplifications and finally joining sections together into the shape of a symphonic movement. The process of deriving larger formal units from motifs and melodies — Bernstein's method of evolution through fission and concatenation, the interrelation of various musical ideas in a work — has rightly been described as the most important

[155]

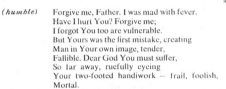

(*humble*)   Forgive me, Father. I was mad with fever.
Have I hurt You? Forgive me;
I forgot You too are vulnerable.
But Yours was the first mistake, creating
Man in Your own image, tender,
Fallible. Dear God You must suffer,
So far away, ruefully eyeing
Your two-footed handiwork — frail, foolish,
Mortal.

⊡ At the point where *all* voices reach their ostinato, and before the Speaker starts, the conductor should signal the chorus to sit down slowly and continue their ostinati, reaching silence at the words: "—frail, foolish, mortal."

From the score of *Kaddish*

basis of his music, with the factors of rhythm, dynamics, texture and orchestration reinforcing or augmenting the evolutionary process (see Jack Gottlieb, 'The Music of Leonard Bernstein', MA thesis, Univ. of Illinois, 1964; David E. Boelzner, 'The Symphonies of Leonard Bernstein', MA thesis, Univ. of N. Carolina, 1977). In Leonard Bernstein's stages of developing these characteristic features of his musical style, *The Age of Anxiety* may be seen as a distinct landmark.

The Third Symphony, *Kaddish*, for speaker, soprano solo, mixed chorus, boys' choir and orchestra, was composed in 1963 and first performed in Tel Aviv on 10 December 1963 under Leonard Bernstein's direction. In 1977 he revised the text and music, making some cuts: he conducted the Israel Philharmonic in the final version in Mainz on 25 August 1977. There is a CBS recording of the original version, with the composer conducting, Felicia Montealegre Cohn-Bernstein as speaker, soprano Jennie Tourel, chorus and boys' choir directed by Abraham Kaplan and Donald Bryant, and the New York Philharmonic Orchestra. The new version, too, was recorded by Deutsche Grammophon Gesellschaft in 1978; the composer again conducted, but the orchestra was the Israel Philharmonic. Other participants were Michael Wager (speaker), Montserrat Caballé (soprano), the Wiener Jeunesse Chor (chorus-master Günther Theuring) and the Vienna Boys' Choir (chorus-master Uwe Christian Harrer).

Between the composition of the Second and Third Symphonies lies an interval of fourteen years. During this time Leonard Bernstein wrote *Prelude, Fugue and Riffs* for clarinet solo and jazz ensemble; the music for *Peter Pan*, *Trouble in Tahiti*, songs and piano music, the Broadway show *Wonderful Town*, *Serenade* based on Plato's philosophy, the symphonic film music for *On the Waterfront*, the operetta *Candide* and, the peak of this creative period, *West Side Story*. It was surely no accident that after *West Side Story* (1957) Bernstein wrote no important new work for five years. He composed only two works to special commission; incidental music for Christopher Fry's play *The Firstborn* — music for voice and percussion (1958) — and two Fanfares (1961). One of these was for the inauguration of John F. Kennedy as President on 19 January 1961, the other for the twenty-fifth anniversary of the New York High School of Music and Art. There is a tragic link between the Kennedy Fanfare and the 'Kaddish' Symphony: as Bernstein was orchestrating the final 'Amen' of the symphony on 22 November 1963, he heard of the assassination of President Kennedy. *Kaddish* is dedicated to 'the beloved memory of John F. Kennedy'.

[157]

(above) Leonard Bernstein with Hanna Rovina at a rehearsal of *Kaddish*, Tel Aviv, December 1963
(below) Felicia and Leonard Bernstein with Michael Wager, who was the speaker in the revised version of *Kaddish* (Hanna Rovina and Felicia had been the original speakers)

The title *Kaddish* is taken from a traditional synagogue prayer, the origins of which date back to the first or second century of the Christian Era, a song of praise in honour of the Almighty and a plea for peace. Its antiquity is evident from its very language; the main part is in Aramaic, a language closely related to Hebrew, formerly spoken in various dialects in Near Eastern countries. While Hebrew was the language of the educated, Aramaic was spoken by the common people; this is why Jesus addressed the people in Aramaic and why a large part of the more popular biblical books and many prayers and religious documents of the Jews were written in Aramaic and have come down to us in that language. The original *Kaddish* was augmented — probably several centuries after it was first formulated — with Hebrew verses: these are the final phrases expressing man's desire for peace and his prayer to God to grant him life. *Kaddish* is recited in daily Jewish worship near the end of the service. Although the prayer centres around the praise of the Eternal and His kingdom on earth — 'May He establish His kingdom during your life and during your days . . . . May there be abundant peace from heaven, and life for us and for all Israel' — and belongs to the rite to be performed every day, it is widely believed that it is only recited at funerals. It is indeed the main prayer at a graveside but its content is a plea for life rather than grief for the dead. Leonard Bernstein, conscious of the significance of this hymn to the glory of God and its traditional use at times of mourning, has given expression to both aspects of *Kaddish* in his symphonic work. Mourning allows Man — symbolised by the Speaker — to 'say *kaddish*, my own *kaddish*, there may be no one to say it after me . . . . I will sing this final *kaddish* for you, for me and for all these I love'. The end of the world may come, for Man, whom God has created in His image, has disappointed his creator, while God has turned away from His creatures and faith is shattered. But God and Man must become reconciled again, peace must defeat chaos, life be victorious over death. The Speaker, in Bernstein's words, 'represents Man, or that part of Man God made to suggest his immortality . . . the part that refuses death, that insists on God'. Originally, Leonard Bernstein thought of a woman as speaker 'because she represented *das ewig Weibliche* [the eternally feminine], that part of man that intuits God', but in the final version gave the role to a man, because he 'realised that his former idea was too limiting'. Later still, he considered that it was possible to cast the speaker as a man or a woman.

The problem occupying Leonard Bernstein's thoughts ever since his first compositions based on the Bible, is the crisis of faith. He has endeavoured to present it in words and music in many different ways, and it became the main theme of the 'Kaddish' Symphony. The impressive context of poetry and music throws the problem into relief and the work expresses a tragic doubt in belief and redemption as well as eternal hope. Religious circles both in America and in Israel have taken offence at the struggle of Man with his God as put into words in Bernstein's own lines of text, and at the doubts of divine creation hinted at in the debate with the Creator. Moreover, it is thought blasphemous to set a sacred liturgical prayer in a confrontation with vigorous jazz as part of a dramatised choral and instrumental symphony for the concert hall. The charge of blasphemy has been answered by reference to the Bible, which testifies to a certain intimacy between Jews and their God; Moses strove with God, Jacob wrestled with the angel, Job reproached God. In *Kaddish*, Leonard Bernstein seeks to set the necessity for a return to genuine belief and to faith against the modern loss of faith and devoutness; and in so doing mirrors the spiritual element in the musical struggle of contemporary composers, torn as they are between the rejection of tradition, a parallel to the dissonance of modern life, and the acceptance of a new belief in a tonal redemption, the musical counterpart of the hope that faith will be renewed being the belief in the never-dying validity of tonality.

In his philosophy of religion and of music, Leonard Bernstein is by no means alone. Among contemporary composers, Arnold Schoenberg in particular, from early youth onwards grappled with the problem of Man who prays and yet is in conflict with God. When in the spring of 1911, he first planned a dramatic musical work, he contemplated using as a text August Strindberg's *Jakob ringt* (*Jacob wrestles*), but then took as a theme 'The prayer of Man in this time'. He sketched out a symphony with vocal solos, chorus, and orchestra, in which one part was to be entitled 'Dissatisfied. The common man's God does not suffice' and another 'The belief of the disillusioned'. Some of the sketches, dating from between 1912 and 1914, were used for the (unfinished) oratorio *Die Jakobsleiter*. It is interesting that, for the first time, Schoenberg expressed dissonance in this work in the shape of a twelve-note melody — paralleled in the music of Leonard Bernstein. The struggle of Man with God runs throughout Schoenberg's entire life and work, from the dramatic text *The Biblical Road* (not set to music) to the opera *Moses and Aaron* and down to his last meditation — published against his express desire as *Modern Psalm* — where the composer broke off on the words 'Und trotzdem bete ich' ('And yet I pray'): That could well be the title and epigraph for Leonard Bernstein's 'Kaddish' Symphony: after Man has called God to account ('you ask for faith, where is your own?') he reconciles himself with his Creator.

The Symphony develops in three parts: Part One consists of an Invocation and a first *Kaddish* prayer; Part Two is entitled 'Din-Torah' (Trial by God's Law) and contains Man's first accusation and a second *Kaddish*; Part Three comprises a wild Scherzo, the Speaker's second dispute with God, a third *Kaddish* and the reconciling Finale.

'Invocation', recited by the Speaker, is the first plea that God will listen to the prayer that could be the last *Kaddish* ever: 'I want to pray, and time is short'. The chorus then chants 'Kaddish I' in Aramaic with its last verse in Hebrew. In 'Din-Torah' the Speaker brings forward the squabbles and doubts of Man and his disbelief in the validity of God's 'eternal covenant'. He asks: 'Where is faith now, yours and mine?', and the chorus responds 'Amen'. The Speaker then asks for forgiveness, he 'was mad with fever' and forgot that God too is vulnerable — 'My sorrowful Father, if I could comfort you, hold you against me, rock you and rock you into sleep . . .'. 'Kaddish II' follows as a soprano solo with boys' choir: the music takes on the character of a lullaby — Andante con tenerezza. This has a doubly tender, warm effect, as the choral 'Amen' interrupting the Speaker's 'madness with fever' leads into a tumultuous eight-voiced pell-mell texture in which each voice sings in a different rhythm, metre and tempo, starting 'forte' and dying away to 'pianissimo' before 'Kaddish II'. In the 'Scherzo' the Speaker paints a vision of the Kingdom of Heaven just as the Creator planned it, but 'there is nothing to dream. Nowhere to go. Nothing to know', recalling the dream-odyssey in *The Age of Anxiety*. The Speaker here ends in calling on God to believe in Man: 'Father! Believe!' The boys' choir begins to intone 'Kaddish III' and the Speaker repeats his entreaty to God to believe in Man so that he may find the Kingdom of Heaven on Earth. 'Kaddish III' continues, to the words 'while the rainbow [of the covenant] is fading, our dream is over. We must wake up now; and the dawn is chilly'. The mood of the Finale turns to reconciliation: 'Beloved Majesty: my Image, my Self! We are one, after all, you and I'; and 'Forever will recreate each other! Suffer and recreate each other!' The work ends with another *Kaddish* by soprano solo, boys' choir, full chorus and orchestra, on a dramatic and forceful 'Amen'.

Comparison of the 'Kaddish' Symphony with Bernstein's earlier symphonic compositions reveals some novel features in the development of the musical structure and form. The method of fission and concatenation of motifs and the interrelation of the various themes formed in the course of a work, in this third Symphony often gives way to a continually changing combination of melodic motifs subjected also to rhythmic variation. The composer demonstrates the manifold shapes and meanings of his melodic motifs yet throughout they retain their identity — even when a twelve-note series is turned into a tonal melody. The latter transformation is possible in Bernstein's music as his twelve-note rows invariably incline toward a tonal harmony. A most distinctive example in the earlier works was the 'Dirge' in *The Age of Anxiety* with its ascending twelve-note theme formed of thirds. In *Kaddish*, thirds also dominate a twelve-note theme opening the main part of the choral 'Kaddish I' — Allegro molto — which accompanies the chorus as a kind of ostinato; it was evolved from the basic three-note cell heard at the very beginning of the symphony — a rising minor second and a minor sixth, while in typical Bernstein fashion a counter melody mirrors the ascent in a descending line composed of the same intervals; a second phrase, ascending, repeats the three intervals starting from another tone and it is enlarged by ascending sevenths. Extreme chromaticism and latent diatonic leanings ultimately leading to tonal simplifications characterise the *Kaddish* score; the dodecaphonic melody line from 'Kaddish I' is transformed into a tonal theme in G flat when the Speaker demands 'Believe!' at the opening of 'Kaddish III'.

Where the 'Kaddish' Symphony assumes dramatic character, Bernstein heightens the tension — as in all his music — by melodic leaps in sevenths and ninths. The melodic phrase developed at the beginning of 'Kaddish I' out of the germ cell at the very beginning of the work — a five-note phrase to which chords with additional six notes of the chromatic scale provide harmony — introduces the opening choral 'Yit'gadal v'yit'kadash!' in which the melodic phrase crescendos to a climax in an ascending minor seventh; in the ostinato of the Allegro molto immediately afterwards, the twelve-note theme is based on the thirds and fifths from the motif cell and a rising major seventh. The 'Kaddish melody', designed by the composer as melodic climax, the G flat major 'singing' theme that starts on the Speaker's 'Believe!' and provides the musical material for 'Kaddish III', is an extension of the basic motifs of the symphony; it is composed of minor and major thirds and ascending minor sevenths. This harmonious melody of 'Believe!' echoes the tender melodic strains of 'There's a place for us/Somewhere a place for us' in the dream sequence of *West Side Story*.

The 'Kaddish' Symphony has startled and even offended a considerable number of listeners and critics because of the unusual text, the humming, singing and at times (in the eight-voiced 'Amen') chaotic babbling constrasted with the purity of a boys' choir, the melodramatic recitation, the vacillations between pan-tonality and tonality, chromaticism and diatonic melodies, the daring orchestral colours and the boldly introduced jazz elements in an oratorio-like song of praise derived from religious sources. It has been argued that theatricality is out of place in a religious paean, but this is to ignore the fact that the centre of the work is the dramatic dialogue betwen Man and God on the renewal of mutual faith and confidence. Leonard Bernstein has worked more intensively on this Symphony than on any other composition, apart from the opera *A Quiet Place*. He began *Kaddish* in the summer of 1961 and continued to work on it during the summers of 1962 and 1963, finishing it in August 1963. A further three weeks sufficed for the orchestration, completed in November 1963. Some critics expressed regret that this important music was at all connected with a text, yet religious inspiration and musical form are here so closely intertwined that it is difficult to dissociate one from the other. When the work was first performed in America, certain reviewers described it as a climax to the concert season, whilst another called it 'the worst tearjerker since the heyday of the Second Avenue Yiddish melodrama'. In Israel, where the world premiere took place in December 1963, fears of controversy with Orthodox zealots proved unfounded and the symphony was generally well received. In America, some Jewish critics severely censured what they termed irreverence and blasphemy, while Christian voices were much less critical of the religious background and appreciated the overall seriousness and the composer's thought-provoking literary and musical intentions.

In 1954, five years after *The Age of Anxiety* and nine years before the Third Symphony, Leonard Bernstein wrote two important compositions: the music for Elia Kazan's film *On the Waterfront* and the *Serenade* for violin solo, string orchestra, harp and percussion, the one a predominantly dramatic, the other a basically lyrical work. The film was first shown on 28 July 1954; the *Serenade* was premiered by Isaac Stern on 12 September, with the Israel Philharmonic Orchestra conducted by the composer at the Teatro Fenice in Venice.

The Symphonic Suite from Bernstein's music for *On the Waterfront* originated in his wish 'to salvage some of the music that would otherwise have been left on the floor of the dubbing-room': conceived symphonically, the work could not possibly reveal its full stature if it were left as mere background music. The first performance of the Suite (dedicated to the composer's son Alexander) was given by the Boston

Symphony Orchestra conducted by Bernstein at Tanglewood on 11 August 1955. As with the Broadway shows, the scene of the film is New York and the bustling, exciting life in the great city is again set against the loneliness of the characters. The plot concerns the young longshoreman, Terry (played by Marlon Brando), who rebels against the racketeering among the dockworkers and against the dictatorship of brutal union leaders; his girl Edie (Eva-Marie Saint) stands by him in his struggle. The Suite, from a wider point of view offering a musical portrait of life and love in New York, not unlike that in *West Side Story*, is so eloquent in its dramatic music that the listener hardly needs to know anything of the film.

The Suite opens — Andante, 'with dignity' — with a broad melodious theme fashioned in the typical Bernstein mode: a two-note melodic germ cell (an ascending major third) is repeated as a sequence of two minor thirds, the four notes are expanded into six ascending notes; the sequence is then imitated in descending notes and something of a melodic cadenza, also composed of thirds, concludes this main theme of the Suite, now grown to a length of six bars. A French horn solo first gives out the theme, woodwind and brass develop it contrapuntally. The short opening motif in thirds becomes part of a theme for variations in the following Presto barbaro (the five-part suite is played without a break) which uses percussion, at first softly, then rising to violent outbursts and in the course of the variations always dominating the orchestral sound. The variations, too, assume an ever denser character with their themes and counter-themes, recalling the brutal background to the film's action. The third part — Andante largamente, more flowing — expands the main theme, 'Terry's Theme' into a lyrical movement suggesting Edie's love for Terry. In striking contrast — Allegro non troppo, molto marcato — there follows a fierce Scherzo taken from the film's climax, the hero's fight with the racketeers. The return of 'Terry's Theme' leads from the short Scherzo into the final movement — a tempo — symbolising Terry's path to victory and, as the music rises to a double fortissimo, his position appears secure. However, the score does not end in complete happiness and, as in most of Bernstein's work, a feeling of uncertainty and bitterness leaves many questions still open: some discords at the conclusion of the Suite hint at the suffering that preceded triumph, and that may still lie ahead. It is the eternal question of whether happiness can last, which is also asked in *The Age of Anxiety*, and in *Kaddish*, in *West Side Story* and to some extent in *Mass*. An interesting sidelight may be seen in Bernstein's stark juxtaposition of contrasting musical colours parallelling director Elia Kazan's choice of black-and-white photography in his film, a technique which is still capable of a much greater impact than colour, especially in reproducing the expressiveness of the actors.

Elia Kazan's film and Leonard Bernstein's music for it have won many international prizes. In London, the critic Hans Keller, well-known for his sharp observations and poignant reviews, described this music as

> about the best film score that has come out of America. In sheer professional skill, it surpasses everything I have heard or seen of the music of his teacher, Aaron Copland (himself one of the very few contributors of musical music to the American film), while in textural style and harmonic idiom it is more daring even than many more individual film scores by our own [British] leading composers (*The Score and IMA Magazine*, vol. XII, 1955, pp. 81ff.).

Hans Keller notes the influence of Stravinsky and Schoenberg, Copland, Hindemith (via Piston?), of Puccini's epigones, folkish elements, pentatonicism, jazz, and various European sources (perhaps even the 'Dawn' interlude from *Peter Grimes*, 'with its waterfront atmosphere into the bargain'). However, although

> on the rarer occasions when Bernstein does approach Hollywood's usual suppliers, his eclecticism becomes strikingly inconsistent, unity flags, his art becomes artificial, his synthesis synthetic . . . . [it is] the largely contrapuntal texture of the *Waterfront* score that constitutes a momentous historical event in the realm of the most modern of all arts, which, on the musical side, has hitherto shown a predilection for the most outmoded homophony.

He also declares that 'the field in which, after much antithesis, Schoenberg and Stravinsky have finally shown their common historical function is that of polyphony:' before Bernstein, no composer of incidental music for films or, for that matter, for the theatre had seen the importance of polyphony in enhancing the dramatic qualities of a musical score. Keller goes on:

> From the single thematic line with which the title music opens and the ensuing two-part canon at the octave, it is clear that Bernstein is determined to subject the Hollywoodian sound track to a radical spring-cleaning. Parallel to the contrapuntal method runs a panchromatic harmonic style that seems to derive from the new expressive chromaticism which Gradenwitz notes in *The Age of Anxiety* [Peter Gradenwitz, 'Leonard Bernstein', in *Music Review*, vol. X, no. 3, Aug. 1949], whereas the pan-diatonic approach (Stravinsky, Copland) in sections where the contrapuntal method is relaxed would appear to stem from earlier procedures (Jeremiah Symphony, *Fancy Free*) . . . . At the same time, the panchromatic motive power does not confine

[165]

itself to the contrapuntal stretches, but also promotes some chordal developments. There is, for instance, an atonal build-up which, without availing
itself of all the twelve notes, is unmistakably influenced by dodecaphonic
technique . . . . The contrapuntal method largely determines the anti-
Hollywoodian instrumentation, which is in the Mahler-Schoenberg tradition
inasmuch as it throws contrasting parts into relief at the expense of conventional sonority, and in the Stravinsky tradition in that, with one or two
exceptions, expressive suppression is at a premium, despite the fact that
Bernstein's is a more sentimental creative character. Wind and percussion
(including the piano) are treated as the new instruments which they have
become through Stravinsky, and even the jazzy and swingy elements have
travelled via Stravinsky . . . .

In summarizing his evaluation of Leonard Bernstein's creative
achievements, Keller points to his gift for a combination of 'manifest
thematicism with generous melodic development' and keeping his
music from monotony: 'Bernstein's downright Schoenbergian thorough-
thematicism [Keller's translation of the German *Durchthematisierung*]
comes off with flying colours'. He also praises the 'extreme variation
technique which may derive from the fourteen variations of the first
movement from *The Age of Anxiety*, and with the intermittent support of
an elaborate and un-mechanical *ostinato* technique which, unlike most
Stravinskyism, honours rather than insults the master of the *ostinato*.
The variation forms themselves are stratified, in that variations become
themes: an ideal cinematic answer to the Schoenbergian demand for
developing variation'.

Leonard Bernstein's method of developing one variation out of a
preceding one (even his juvenile Violin Sonata displays this trait) is
also the musical foundation for his *Serenade*, in which each of the five
movements originates from elements in a preceding part of the work. In
the traditional violin concerto, the orchestra presents the main theme
or themes before the entry of the soloist, Mendelssohn's E minor
concerto being one of the few exceptions; Bernstein's *Serenade*, on the
contrary, assigns to the solo violin the role of 'chief speaker' in the first
four movements: only the last movement begins with an extended
orchestral introduction. The composer wrote explanatory notes on this
work soon after he completed the score (dated from 'Vineyard Haven,
June 28, 1954'): 'There is no literal programme for this *Serenade*, despite
the fact that it resulted from a re-reading of Plato's charming dialogue
The Symposium. The music, like the dialogue, is a series of related
statements in praise of love, and generally follows the Platonic form

through the succession of speakers at the banquet'. As for the musical relation of the movements Bernstein explains that 'it does not depend on common thematic material, but rather on a system whereby each movement evolves out of elements in the preceding one'. 'For the benefit of those interested in literary allusions' he says he 'might suggest some points as guide posts':

I. Phaedrus and Pansonias: In Plato's *Symposium*, Phaedrus, a hypochondriac literary man, opens the dialogues. He is the guest of the 'tragic poet' Agathon who, with his colleagues and friends, wants to celebrate his victory in a drama competition. Among his guests are the philosopher Socrates, the widely-travelled geographer Pausanias, the comic poet Aristophanes, the physician Eryximachus and Alcibiades, the disciple and friend of Socrates, a brilliant and opportunist statesman. Some others appear in the *Symposium*, but not in Bernstein's work, where in the first movement the opening by Phaedros takes the form of a lyrical strain in praise of Eros, god of love, the solo violin starting 'a fugato', taken up by the string orchestra. 'Pausanias continues by describing the duality of lover and beloved. This is expressed in a classical sonata-*allegro*, based on the material of the opening *fugato*' (Bernstein).

II. Aristophanes (Allegretto): Plato makes the physician Eryximachus speak before Aristophanes, because the poet has hiccups, but Bernstein lets the poet appear first: 'Aristophanes does not play the role of clown in this dialogue, but instead that of the bedtime story-teller, invoking the fairytale mythology of love'. Musically speaking, the thematic material for this playful movement is developed out of the themes of the *Allegro* part of the first movement, itself based on a motivic phrase in the *lento* and *fugato* introduction. Bernstein plays around with this newly-developed theme in manifold contrapuntal settings; melodic expansion of the motifs from this theme provides a lyrical middle section before the return of the light-hearted world of the opening.

III. Eryximachos (Presto): 'The physician speaks of bodily harmony as a scientific model for the working of love-patterns', writes Bernstein: 'This is an extremely short *fugato scherzo*, born of a blend of mystery and humour.' The movement vacillates dramatically between fortissimo and pianissimo, virtuosity and simple playfulness; it takes up in canonic imitation a very tuneful melody, originally from the middle section of the preceding movement, elaborating it in unrestrained vivacity. The musical themes of this Presto go back to the two germ cells from the beginning of the *Serenade*: the three-note motif formed of a third and a sixth expanded into a five-note musical idea and the melodic rise immediately following it.

IV. Agathon (Adagio): In the contribution to the *Symposium* made by the host, Agathon, Bernstein sees 'perhaps the most moving speech of the dialogue. Agathon's panegyric embraces all aspects of love's powers, charms and functions. This movement is a simple three-part song'. The Adagio begins with the orchestra murmuring pianissimo, while above it the solo violin plays a lyrical cantilena; only later in the movement do the motion and the dynamics intensify into passion, with the solo violin constantly singing muted until the cadenza is reached, fortissimo, when the mute is removed. There follows a varied, and abridged, repetition of the first part of the movement, with the violin again playing 'con sordino'. The chromatic theme developed.in the middle section of the movement out of previous motifs assumes great importance, in a renewed variation, in the following, and final part.

V. Socrates and Alcibiades (Molto tenuto and Allegro molto vivace): On this final movement, Leonard Bernstein's comments are the most detailed:

> Socrates describes his visit to the seer Diotima, quoting her speech on the demonology of love. This is a slow introduction of greater weight than any of the preceding movements; and serves as a highly developed reprise of the middle section of the Agathon movement, thus suggesting a hidden sonata-form. The famous interruption by Alcibiades and his band of drunken revellers ushers in the *Allegro*, which is an extended *Rondo* ranging in spirit from agitation through jig-like dance music to joyful celebration. If there is a hint of jazz in the celebration, I hope it will not be taken as anachronistic Greek party-music, but rather the natural expression of a contemporary American composer imbued with the spirit of that timeless dinner-party.

When the orchestral introduction to the final movement elaborates the cantilena melody of the middle section in the 'Agathon' Adagio the texture becomes more dense in chordal harmony than anywhere else in the work; the many-coloured harmonies, while strongly chromatic, remain within the bounds of tonality. Before the solo violin enters to take up the cantilena theme, it gives a reminder of the germ cells underlying the various themes; the cantilena is played pianissimo, and then begins the stormy Rondo. Here material that has become familiar returns in various guises to reassert the basic unity of all the musical ideas developed in the course of the *Serenade*, so emphasising the unifying subject of the talks at the Symposium, on which personalities of differing character and standing have tried to shed light and express opinions. In 'presto vivace' tempo, the *Serenade* is brought to its conclusion: the orchestra plays the main theme heard at the very beginning in a most concentrated quotation, then the solo violin leads to the ending, accompanied by the reiteration in the orchestra of the familiar motif in thirds.

Leonard Bernstein has sometimes said that he regards the *Serenade* as the composition most satisfying to himself. Undoubtedly it is one of his most original works both in subject and in structure. There is little here of the exciting theatricality governing Bernstein's three symphonies; the philosophical theme could hardly have been expected to inspire a dramatic fervour like that of the symphonies, which here gives way to a lyricism now tender, now passionate. The lyrical moods are often interspersed with episodes of refreshing liveliness and humour, and the orchestral colouring of the work is especially attractive. As counter to the solo violin, the score calls for a string ensemble, harp, xylophone, glockenspiel, triangle, drums, cymbals, bells, tambourine and kettle-drum. As in most of his compositions Bernstein here uses ever-changing combinations of sound colours to lend specific character to the different themes and, to some extent, to the various characters involved. The easily recognisable formal structure and the interrela-tionship of the musical themes combine to establish *Serenade* as a symphonic piece of music whose hearers can appreciate it without necessarily knowing anything of the composer's philosophical and literary inspiration. Those who do know something of Plato's work and its ideological concept will discern in Bernstein's own conception and musical realization much genuine feeling and sympathy with the characters.

Serenade has been recorded by Zino Francescatti (CBS) and Gidon Kremer (Deutsche Grammophon) under the direction of the composer. The original recording by Isaac Stern was not listed in the record catalogues in 1986.

In the *Serenade*, as in all of Leonard Bernstein's music, there reigns the dualism of nostalgia and actuality, simplicity and complexity, tonal melodious emotion and chromatic pan-tonal drama. The underlying themes of the three symphonies stem from Leonard Bernstein's reli-gious background and American character; in the *Serenade*, the nostal-gia harked back to classic Greek philosophy. *On the Waterfront* and his Broadway musicals show the loving human as alone in the turmoil of the big city and the suburban couple in *Trouble in Tahiti* are lonely too; Jewish and American mentality combine in *Mass*; nostalgic memories of themes, song and dance forms pervade the only superficially light-hearted *Divertimento*.

The impact of Leonard Bernstein's music on a non-musician has been poignantly described by his younger brother Burton, himself a successful writer. Burton Bernstein has always seen his brother's career with a great deal of objectivity; indeed, as a boy he 'sneered at his world' as a rebellion against the too-frequently-repeated question whether he was going to be a famous conductor too. He describes how, aged eleven, he had to attend Jennie Tourel's recital when the *Kid Songs* were premiered in New York: 'I recall not much of the recital. I was one of those eleven-year-old philistines who are determined to ignore concert music, especially recital music, and I had to be nudged to attention by my mother for the performance of Lenny's piece . . . [Bernstein, *Family Matters*, p. 143] and 'anything connected with long-hair music and art was beneath my notice — sissy stuff' (ibid., p. 173). Asked how he feels now about Lenny's concert and Broadway music, Burton wrote:

> As a non-musician, I am eminently unqualified to discuss Lenny's work, but as a dedicated fan I can state, with some objectivity and intelligence, that Lenny's music is distinctly Lenny — as unmistakable as a moose at a dinner party. Yes, there are vague influences — Copland, Gershwin, Offenbach, whatever — but when all is said and done, the music is pure Lenny. He has given a new style and idiom to American music, which is a grand accomplishment all by itself (letter to the author, 22 December 1982).

6

Music for the Theatre

> The American musical theatre has come a long way,
> borrowing this from opera, that from revue, the other
> from operetta, something else from vaudeville — and
> mixing all the elements into something quite new, but
> something which has been steadily moving in the
> direction of opera.
> *Leonard Bernstein*, October 1956

Remembering Leonard Bernstein's own dictum that every work he writes 'for whatever medium, is really theatre music in some way' (programme notes for *The Age of Anxiety*, April 1949), it is not astonishing to note that choreographers have been inspired by his concert music. For example, in 1950 Jerome Robbins created a ballet based on *The Age of Anxiety* and in 1959 Herbert Ross used the music of *Serenade*. Bernstein himself was much concerned with music for the stage between 1944 and 1957; after *West Side Story* (1957) there was a pause until he completed *Mass, a Theatre Piece* (1971). In 1974 came the music of the *Dybbuk* for a Jerome Robbins ballet. During the seventies, he failed to attract collaborators for a new kind of musical drama and decided to give up writing for Broadway. In 1982–3, Bernstein composed his first serious opera, *A Quiet Place*, conceived as a sequel to the shorter *Trouble in Tahiti* (1951).

A great many original traits were already to be found in the early musicals *On the Town* (1944) and *Wonderful Town* (1953). In action, lyrics and music they were different from anything Broadway had seen and heard before and they displayed perfect integration of text, music and movement. Different in kind were *Trouble in Tahiti* and *Candide*, though written in the same creative period. Among Bernstein's musicals, *1600 Pennsylvania Avenue* (1976) was an unsuccessful latecomer. In the early theatrical years, most original scores were written for Jerome Robbins' ballets.

On 18 April 1944, Leonard Bernstein conducted the premiere of the ballet *Fancy Free*, conceived and choreographed by Jerome Robbins. The plot has been described in the composer's programme notes for a concert performance of the music in New York in 1946. From the moment the action begins, with the sound of a juke box wailing out the blues song 'Big Stuff' behind the curtain, the ballet is strictly young wartime America, 1944. The curtain rises on a street corner with a lamp-post, a side-street bar, and New York skyscrapers picked out with a crazy pattern of lights, making a dizzying backdrop. Three sailors explode onto the stage. They are on 24-hour shore leave in the city and on the prowl for girls. How they meet first one girl, then another, how they fight over them, lose them and in the end take off after yet another girl makes up the scenario of the ballet.

The blues number 'Big Stuff', which was originally recorded by Billie Holliday, opens the ballet and sets the tone with its unusual melodic line and its rhythmic and harmonic texture (see page 131, above). The 'Pas de deux' based on this leads to the 'Competition Scene', where the friends and rivals scuffle over who is to dance with the two girls. The preceding instrumental movements of the ballet music are an 'Opening Dance', a 'Scene at the Bar' (in which may be discerned the lyrical descending thirds from the 'Lament' in the 'Jeremiah' Symphony) and the 'Girls' Entrance'. After the 'Competition Scene' follow three variations in which each of the three contestants for the two females presents a solo. The first sailor (in the 'Galop') aims to appeal with a kind of acrobatic, vaudeville showiness; the second (in the 'Waltz') shows a mock gentility, abruptly shifting to bumps and dance-hall devices; the third (in a 'Danzon', modelled on a Cuban pattern) grotesquely parodies seductive Latin-American gestures. The term 'variations' is used in the ballet sense, but the music is also in variation form, and the composer points to the opening three notes of 'Waltz' as the nucleus of the three dances. Echoes of one of the main motifs of the ballet as a whole are also heard in various passages.

Characteristic means of linking the movements closely together are piano solos, which play an important role in the instrumental texture of the jazzy score, a method again used by Bernstein in his later ballet score for *Facsimile*.

The originality of scenario and music, the virtuosity of the choreography and the topical wartime associations secured for *Fancy Free* an immediate success both in America and in Europe. A Suite arranged by the composer for concert performances acquainted concert audiences and record collectors with a kind of American music entirely new to music-lovers of every kind. 'This is no Gershwin', joked Israeli composer Menahem Avidom when Leonard Bernstein conducted *Fancy*

Free in Tel Aviv. 'I should think so', retorted Bernstein.

The music for *Facsimile*, as for *Fancy Free*, was commissioned by the Ballet Theatre (later the American Ballet Theatre) and Bernstein wrote it for Jerome Robbins in 1946. The ballet opened on 24 October 1946 at the Broadway Theatre in New York; on 5 March 1947, the composer conducted the first performance of a concert version, with some changes in the Finale, describing the work as a *Choreographic Essay*.

The theme of *Facsimile*, like that of many Bernstein works, is loneliness. The mood of the music is thus predominantly lyrical, beginning poetically with an oboe solo whose melodic theme is taken up by a solo flute and violins. The score then developes in four episodes paralleling four scenes of the ballet scenario, which opens with a woman on a beach, bored and lonely, who encounters first one man and then another, but in the end is alone again. The four episodes included in the *Choreographic Essay for Orchestra*, in which piano solos feature prominently, are 'Solo' (the Woman), 'Pas de deux' (the Woman and the First Man: flirtation and disappointment), 'Pas de trois' (amusing games followed by a romantic triangle involving the Woman and the two Men, ending with her cry 'Stop!') and the 'Coda' (the Woman alone again, still unfulfilled). The fleeting flirtations had offered nothing but a 'facsimile' of friendship; the music developed from the opening melodic phrases ends as inconclusively as the stage action — the kind of triad which closes the score mirrors emptiness and leaves every question open.

Among Leonard Bernstein's stage works there is a composition which originated as a commissioned instrumental concert piece but came into its own only after it was used in a choreographic production. This is *Prelude, Fugue and Riffs* for clarinet solo and jazz combo, composed in November 1949. The jazz musician Woody Herman, who had already commissioned Igor Stravinsky to write *Ebony Concerto*, asked Bernstein for a composition, which proved the instigation for an unusual work. However, unlike *Ebony Concerto*, it was never performed by Woody Herman, although his excellence as a clarinettist had caused Bernstein to give the leading part to the clarinet. The first performance of *Prelude, Fugue and Riffs* did not come until October 1955, when it was presented by Benny Goodman and his jazz ensemble in Bernstein's television programme 'What is Jazz?'. Before that, aware that Woody Herman's band would not play the piece, Leonard Bernstein had reorchestrated it to suit a Broadway show orchestra and incorporated it into a ballet sequence for *Wonderful Town*, but it was only performed before the show reached Broadway, not after.

In its original virtuoso orchestration, *Prelude, Fugue and Riffs* is very difficult to perform and there is little chance of hearing it except on the CBS record (of 1964?) by Benny Goodman and the Columbia Jazz Combo. The composition presents an astounding combination of classical forms and contrapuntal structures with jazz themes and swinging jazz rhythms; both the contrapuntal and the rhythmical elaborations are so complex and contrasted that it sometimes sounds as though the players were improvising. On 15 May 1969, the New York City Ballet presented John Clifford's choreography of this music: another entirely new choreography was created by Michael Uthoff for the Hartford Ballet, who gave it on 15 July 1978 at the Fine Arts Center Concert Hall of the University of Massachusetts at Amherst, under the title *Patrasolifutricatramerifu*.

Leonard Bernstein's two stage works of the 1950s were the one-act opera *Trouble in Tahiti* and *Candide*, which he calls *A Comic Operetta*. For *Trouble in Tahiti* he wrote his own libretto, while *Candide* was Lillian Hellman's adaptation of Voltaire's romantic satire on society. To appreciate the composer's approach to musical theatre, it is worth reading his television talk, 'American Musical Comedy', given on 7 October 1956 and published in *The Joy of Music*. He distinguishes between variety show — music-hall, vaudeville, etc. — revue, operetta, light opera, opera buffa, opera comique, grand opera and Wagnerian opera. In this way, he describes the whole range from shows whose sole aim is to entertain to works with an artistic intention 'to enrich and ennoble the audience by inducing lofty emotions in them'. For him, the musical comes somewhere in the middle between variety and opera; historically it has gradually shifted from one pole to the other, from simple entertainment to an artful blend of various theatrical elements.

The history of American music provides early examples of musical plays resembling the early German *Singspiel* and even opera. According to Bernstein, the first American musical was an extravaganza entitled *The Black Crook* which opened in New York in 1866, a mishmash of melodrama, ballet and variety acts. It lasted five and a half hours and had a 'melange of uninspired music and a loosely strung together plot'. But it ran for eighteen months in New York and toured for a further twenty-five years. While American, French and German characters and musical-elements accounted for the plot and music of *The Black Crook*, Bernstein sees the 'first step in the direction of native roots' in the musical *A Trip to Chinatown* (1890); the story had an American background and the songs were characteristically American. Yet 'songs were stuck into the plot arbitrarily with no regard for what is known as integration'. Then the comic operas of Gilbert and Sullivan and later Franz Lehar's *The Merry Widow* came to America: their influence was felt in American operetta, whose first great representative is Victor Herbert. Operetta plots were dramatic and the composer tried to establish a relationship between action and songs, giving his music as elaborate a finish as he would to an opera. In contrast came the development of revue and burlesque; in these shows American jazz came into its own.

The American musical owes to the revue the element of entertainment and to the operetta the integration of action and music. The troublesome political and economic developments of the 1920s brought about the introduction of social themes and other problems into the plots of musicals: America's musical theatre suddenly became 'adolescent', says Leonard Bernstein. Musical comedies did not abandon the aim of amusement and entertainment, but plots and lyrics were now spiced with satire and topical comment. Bernstein sees in George Gershwin's *Of Thee I Sing* (1931) the most serious satire of the times, which served as a model for several musical comedies in the 1930s: 'It has a marvellous story, serious and funny in a way no show had ever been before: glorious songs, perfectly integrated into the scheme; a highly American subject; natural American speech; sharp, brilliant lyrics; an all over unity of style embodying wide variety — in other words, this show marks a point of culmination in our history'. Moreover, 'the characters are not remote or exotic . . . and it is, both verbally and musically, in the vernacular'.

In the further development of the American musical theatre, Bernstein admires the original way in which ballet scenes were used for the first time by Moss Hart and Richard Rodgers in *On Your Toes* (1936) with 'Slaughter on Tenth Avenue', a ballet with its own action clearly integrated into the plot of the musical comedy. Kurt Weill and Marc Blitzstein gave the American musical theatre a new direction, while in George Gershwin's *Porgy and Bess* the song style of the musical comedy was artfully transferred into the world of opera. Some stylistic trends have found their way from opera and operetta into later American musical comedies, mainly in the works of Oscar Hammerstein III and Richard Rodgers.

These historical reflections occupied Leonard Bernstein's mind while he was writing his own operetta *Candide*; his short opera *Trouble in Tahiti* had been written six years earlier. According to the composer's own definitions, this one-acter is poised between operetta and opera; the main difference being that *Trouble in Tahiti* though divided into operatic 'numbers', is *durchkomponiert*, the music is uninterrupted, and the relationship of motifs and themes closely links the separate musical sections.

Trouble in Tahiti, an opera in seven scenes, words and music by Leonard Bernstein, has been described by the author as 'a light-weight piece. The whole thing is popular-song inspired and its roots are in musical comedy, or, even better, the American musical theatre'. It is dedicated to Marc Blitzstein, whose flair for the ironic, critical approach to the way people live, their feelings and social traditions has had an impact on Bernstein's libretto and music. The opening of *Trouble in Tahiti* immediately introduces us to a new world of opera: it begins with an elegant vocal Trio, in a dance-band ensemble style, dressed in smart evening clothes and singing 'in a whispering, breathy *pianissimo*, which comes over the amplifying system as crooning . . . . The Trio is refined and sophisticated in the high-priced dance-band tradition' (Bernstein's directions). The Trio 'extols the virtues of life in the American Suburbia of the 1950s. One by one they list the advertising media's requirements for happiness' — in stark contrast to the seven scenes which are about to unfold. From the beginning there is a clear discrepancy between the commercial atmosphere of the Trio, which accompanies throughout as a modern version of the Classical Greek Chorus, and the mood of the stage action: this is felt as the easy, swingy rhythms introducing and interrupting the Trio scan a twelve-tone melody, the first six notes of which form two major triads, the first phrase ending in a downward leap of a ninth.

The characters are Sam and Dinah, a young couple in their thirties, well off materially but unhappy and dissatisfied with each other. Breakfasting in their 'little white house' in the supposed Utopia of surburbia, they quarrel about anything and everything: Sam, successful in business, wants peace and quiet at home, Dinah would like a more eventful, romantic life. The second scene is set in Sam's office where he is still worried by the argument with his wife; he is not even cheered up by the thought of playing in the coming handball tournament. Meanwhile, Dinah, close to a nervous breakdown, has gone to see a psychiatrist; the doctor can do nothing to help her in her marital difficulties. In the next scene, Dinah and Sam accidentally meet in the street but pass by with no attempt to communicate. In an Interlude with the jazzy twelve-note melody and the Trio, the formulas for

[176]

happiness and success heard in the Prelude now sound even more ironical and illusory. In complete contrast, Sam is shown in Scene Five gloriously happy: he has won the handball championship and sees himself as embodying an 'American success story'. In Scene Six Dinah, having meanwhile seen the much-advertised film *Trouble in Tahiti*, talks about it to another woman at the bus stop. She becomes so muddled in comparing the exotic film plot with her own life that she can no longer distinguish between fantasy and her personal reality. In the second part of this scene Sam and Dinah return home and in Scene Seven vainly seek a solution to their troubles. At last Sam suggests that they should go to the cinema; but only one film is showing in their suburb, the 'terrible' *Trouble in Tahiti*.

The moral of Bernstein's story is obvious: social status and material success are no recipe for a happy life. In the quarrels between Sam and Dinah may be seen the reflection of the arguments the young Bernstein possibly overheard in his own home; it is no accident that the successful businessman in the opera bears the same name as Lenny's father, while the name Dinah is also known from the Bernstein family. 'Men are created unequal' is the essence of Sam's monologue in Scene Five: all a man needs is victory and success.

Bernstein has been criticised for having set to music a libretto with a simple moral and a sequence of everyday scenes, and employing a style that does not quite disclose whether the aim was musical comedy, operetta, comic or tragicomic opera. Indeed all these are touched on in this short work, nor do we know whether words and music should make us laugh or cry. An intense study of the score provides an insight into the rich inventiveness and artistic craft of composition invested by the composer in this seemingly light-weight work, which nevertheless in artistic terms is on a level with some of his major compositions.

The twelve-note row made up of thirds, fourths, fifths and seconds (which reappears with the singing Trio) and concluding with a typical Bernstein ninth, and on the repeat with an ascending seventh, is a hallmark of this opera's style as in his symphonic works. Seventh and ninth intervals dominate the ostinato accompaniment, in chords and broken chords, to Sam and Dinah's dissonant dialogue. In Sam's first solo scene, the telephone monologue in Scene Two, the composer plays around with thirds and sevenths; at the same time, in the unlighted area of the stage, Dinah can dimly be seen on the psychiatrist's couch, as a reminder that Sam is always thinking of her. Content with his success, Sam here, as in his handball triumph later, expresses his thoughts in thirds; with his troubles, come dissonant sevenths. In Dinah's scene following Sam's monologue the music turns after a

[177]

dissonant B minor tonality to a romantically coloured, diatonically harmonised G minor. After the short street encounter scene and the ironical 'Interlude' with the Trio comes Sam's proud 'success' monologue. The orchestral accompaniment is in 'punch-ball' rhythm, in strongly scanned 6/8 metre; the tonality changes from C major to G major, F minor, and returns after numerous modulations to C major again. Mellifluous thirds dominate the melodies and chords of this scene, for Sam is happy in his own world. In Scene Six Dinah tells the story of the film in a now famous aria, 'Oh, what a movie! What a terrible, awful movie!!!'. Leonard Bernstein has here succeeded in writing a witty satire on Hollywood scenarios and music of the 1950s. At the conclusion of the area, the Trio comes in again with its 'Island Magic' harmonics. Dinah interrupts herself and the singing Trio — she is terribly late and if she doesn't rush home, there'll be no dinner for Sam. The opera ends on vague, indeterminate harmonies, with all questions left open. The longing for a romantic, quiet, happy life cannot be fulfilled; in Scene Four the two sang of the 'way to peace and life' and 'the garden with a quiet place', but neither has been found. This is the theme the composer took up thirty years later for the opera *A Quiet Place*.

The chamber opera character of *Trouble in Tahiti* is underlined by the instrumentation, which calls for the small ensemble of fifteen wind instruments, percussion, harp and string quartet. The orchestra usually plays an unobtrusive accompanying role; the composer asks the conductor that it 'should be held down carefully', because 'every word and idea must be projected clearly . . . especially since there is no plot in the ordinary sense, and very little action. If the words are not heard, there is no opera' (Leonard Bernstein's *Notes on Production*).

The composer conducted the first performance on 12 June 1952, at the Festival of Creative Arts at Brandeis University, Waltham, Massachusetts. Two days later he led a performance there of Marc Blitzstein's version of Brecht–Weill's *Dreigroschenoper*.

Between *Trouble in Tahiti* and *Candide*, Leonard Bernstein wrote incidental music for two plays. In 1955 he composed three choral pieces with drum accompaniment to French texts and five choruses in Latin with bells for *The Lark*, an adaptation by Lillian Hellman of Jean Anouilh's *L'Alouette*. The play was first performed in Boston and New York in the winter of 1955; the choral pieces later also found their way into the concert hall. In the same year, Bernstein produced incidental music, consisting of instrumental pieces for chamber orchestra and vocal solos for Oscar Wilde's *Salome*; this has so far (1987) not been published, performed or recorded. At the same time, his cooperation with Lillian Hellman on *Candide* began to take shape. The idea of writing a comic operetta using Voltaire's satirical fantasy, which had fascinated Leonard Bernstein ever since he had read it as a student, emerged in 1954, but now work began in earnest, with Dorothy Parker, Richard Wilbur and John La Touche writing some of the lyrics; Bernstein himself also contributed texts for his music.

Voltaire's satire, published in 1759, ridiculed the optimistic philosophy of Gottfried Wilhelm Leibniz, who in *Théodicée* (1710) declared that God had created the most perfect of all possible worlds. In Voltaire's novel, Candide's experiences are a test of this proposition and ultimately demonstrate its absurdity. Voltaire took only a few weeks to write *Candide* at the end of 1758. In March 1759 his book was burnt publicly in Geneva and banned in Paris; three years later the Vatican put it on the Index of prohibited writings. Nevertheless, its first publication was followed by thirteen editions in the next two years: by the time of Voltaire's death in 1778, there had been forty editions. *Candide*'s message to humanity, that the world always has catastrophes in store, has never lost its cruel significance, as we still see today. The devastating Lisbon earthquake of 1755, which originally inspired Voltaire to write *Candide*, stunned the world at a time when people believed themselves most happy and secure; the satire held up a mirror to the complacent and called on them to wake up to life's realities. It is this message that probably first attracted Leonard Bernstein to the work; it corresponds in many ways with the latent pessimism that again and again is seen in his writings, his opinions and his creative work. Madame de Staël called Voltaire's satire a work of 'Infernal gaiety' and some of this character may well be felt in many parts of Leonard Bernstein's congenial operetta score.

In the first scene of the operetta, Dr Pangloss explains the optimistic doctrine to his pupil Candide who is about to be married to the young Westphalian girl, Cunegonde; the young couple sing a lyrical marriage duet, but a catastrophe soon destroys the country and Candide believes that his Cunegonde has perished. He cannot believe that this means God's world is really not good and embarks on a journey to other countries. In the various scenes he finds himself in Lisbon, Paris, Buenos Aires and Venice, but finally returns disillusioned to the ruins of Westphalia. In the second scene, set in Lisbon, an Arab conjurer predicts direful experiences for him; two ancient Inquisitors threaten Dr Pangloss and Candide with hanging. An earthquake interrupts the proceedings, Dr Pangloss apparently perishes, but Candide manages to escape. In an Interlude, he meditates on the tragic loss of teacher and beloved, yet still believes in the philosophy of optimism, arguing that if all went wrong it was surely his own fault. The third scene finds him in Paris and to Candide's astonishment Cunegonde is there alive, a demi-mondaine in a house shared by a Marquis and a Sultan. An Old Lady, Cunegonde's duenna, tells her to put on her most precious jewels to meet Candide. In a duel, Candide kills both the Sultan and the Marquis, and then, with Cunegonde and the Old Lady, joins a group of pilgrims bound for the New World. In Scene Four they reach Buenos Aires where all the pilgrims are arrested and enslaved, apart from Cunegonde and the Old Lady. After a warning about the future by a pessimistic street sweeper, Candide learns that Cunegonde and the Old Lady have moved to the Governor's palace. He escapes and sets out to seek his fortune in the fabled Eldorado, hoping to return one day to find his Cunegonde. This scene concludes the First Act of the operetta.

The Second Act opens with the Governor in Buenos Aires trying to get rid of the Old Lady and Cunegonde who have begun to get on his nerves. Candide, who has in fact made a fortune, returns with his pockets full of gold and asks the Governor where to find Cunegonde. Although the Governor has had them tied in sacks and given orders that they be taken to a ship, he tells Candide that Cunegonde and the Old Lady have sailed to Europe. Our hero thereupon buys a ship to follow them, but it is leaky and sinks. In an Interlude after Scene One, Act Two, Candide and the prophetic street sweeper are floating on a raft, but the latter is eaten by a shark. Dr Pangloss now makes a miraculous reappearance and tries to reassure Candide and revive his hopes. Scene Two is set in Venice where Cunegonde is now a charwoman in a palace, while the Old Lady is a woman of fashion. Drink and gambling lose Candide all his remaining gold and possessions and he finds himself penniless, friendless and without hope. In the final scene he has returned to the ruined country of Westphalia. Dr Pangloss, Cunegonde and the Old Lady are also there, but Candide no longer believes in the optimistic view. The only aim in life should be, he says, adopting Voltaire's own philosophy, to plant one's garden, cultivate it and make it grow.

To write a 'comic operetta' founded on philosophical doctrines turned out a somewhat taxing intellectual undertaking and even while working on it, the collaborators were doubtful whether an audience would accept such a complex story with its unusual lyrics and music. The lyric writer Richard Wilbur later ascribed their failure to several causes: 'There was no single villain in the story, the audience forgot what was happening to the characters' and he himself 'was inclined to be too literary and stubborn' (Briggs, *Bernstein*, p. 196). The music constantly shifted between the various forms of musical theatre: Bern-

stein's score was sparkling and light, elsewhere it was rather sophisticated. In a 'dialogue with himself' (*New York Times*, 16 November
1956), published about halfway between the first performance of
Candide in Boston and the New York premiere, Bernstein named as 'one
of the knottiest problems of the score' the question: 'Does this F sharp
sound as if it belonged in a Broadway musical?'

His alter ego asks, in the person of 'Id': 'Have you forgotten that in
front of millions of Americans viewing *Omnibus* on October 7 you
committed yourself forever to a definition of American musical comedy
as being what it is largely because of the American elements in it? Your
only problem is that you have betrayed your own definition. Now let's
have that F sharp'. Defending *Candide*, Bernstein replies:

> Voltaire's satire is international. It throws light on all the dark places,
> whether American or European . . . . The matters with which it is concerned
> are as valid for us as for any — and sometimes I think they are especially
> valid for us in America. And they are also the charges made by Voltaire
> against his own society.
>
> *Id:* *Candide* is beginning to look to me like a real old-fashioned operetta.
>
> *Bernstein*: If that's all you're worrying about, then our argument is con-
> cluded. You remember I said that one of the most obvious attributes of the
> operetta is the exotic (to Americans) atmosphere in which it exists, and that
> the music of the operetta is more serious in musical content, more highly
> developed, less like Tin Pan Alley — gay though it may be? I guess *Candide*
> follows in this tradition, rather than in the pure musical comedy tradition of
> *Guys and Dolls* or *Wonderful Town*. And now, demon, I hereby exorcise you,
> and command you to lie down again in peace. Good night.
>
> *Id* (who always has the last word): Good night. And now, what are you
> going to do about that F sharp?

Leonard Bernstein clearly felt that *Candide* was not destined for
success — the F sharp, which can be seen as a recurrent means of
creating dramatic tension in all his music, was surely not the only
stumbling-block to the operatta's acceptance by Broadway audiences.
'The eighteenth-century philosophical tale is not ideal material for a
theatre show', wrote Brooks Atkinson in the *New York Times*, expressing
New York public opinion. *Candide* was withdrawn after seventy-three
performances. It was, however, not only the libretto which the Broadway public found hard to swallow: the music was charming, amusing
and spirited, but there were no light tunes which anyone could hum,
whistle or sing, and its sophisticated artistry and wit appealed to only a
few. The overture, however really delighted the public and it became a
favourite opener in symphony concerts.

A concert version of the operetta was performed by a touring ensemble in many American cities. In April 1959, *Candide* reached the London stage and there both audience and press showed more understanding for the special brand of wit and humour in story and music than had the Americans. On 20 December 1973 a new version of the operetta, with a revised libretto by Hugh Wheeler and lyrics by Richard Wilbur, John La Touche, Stephen Sondheim and Leonard Bernstein, appeared at the Chelsea Theatre, Brooklyn, New York. Some numbers had been cut, others changed, and the orchestration was reworked by Hershy Kay to suit a thirteen-player ensemble.

What is it that has attracted Leonard Bernstein since his youth to Voltaire's critical, sarcastic, anti-optimistic novel? Is it the juxtaposition of pessimism and love of life that finds expression in so many of his own texts, as well as the literary works inspiring his music? In the music he wrote for *Candide* there is less indication of these divergent moods than in his major works, even in the early 'Jeremiah' Symphony. The *Candide* Overture is one of the most light-hearted pieces Bernstein ever wrote, as full of fun as Mozart's *Figaro* overture or the opening of an operetta by Offenbach or Sullivan; not even the ominous F sharp disturbs its course. Yet this Overture not only introduces some of the vocal themes of the operetta, but puts at the beginning the characteristic Bernstein interval of a seventh followed by a major second, the germ cell of most of the melodic ideas in the entire work. In the framework of a classical sonata form, themes and counter-themes are artistically contrasted and elaborated; separate parts of motifs and themes whirl around in ever-changing orchestral colours. In the second scene of Act One the duet 'Oh, Happy We' takes up the second subject theme from the Overture. In the third scene Cunegonde sings her great virtuoso Jewel Aria, 'Glitter and be Gay', starting in slow waltz tempo and continuing in lively Allegro movement with its final section derived from the Codetta at the close of the Overture.

One of the musically most astonishing parts in *Candide* is the Trio that opens the Second Act, sung by the Old Lady, Cunegonde and the Governor. It starts with a fortissimo orchestral introduction — Adagio — in widely spaced octaves, consisting of a twelve-note row including all possible intervals, ending in the downward leap of a seventh on to 'that F sharp'. The phrase is repeated in a slightly faster tempo — Andante moderato, ma trattenuto — now played 'pianissimo, senza espressione', the phrase transposed a whole tone lower, followed by spoken lines. Another recapitulation of the chromatic theme follows with mirrored intervals and then comes more dialogue. For a fourth and last time the orchestra intones the chromatic theme with changed intervals, 'sempre pianissimo'. The Old Lady then embarks on an aria, which Cunegonde later joins, complaining of the boredom in the palace and infuriating the Governor. The twelve-note theme expresses the ennui of the women prisoners; it returns in the opening strains of the aria and concludes 'violente', 'fortissimo', answering the Governor's angry shout of 'Quiet!'. The main part of the aria has a declamatory melody revolving around continually repeated intervals of minor and major seconds, with dissonant D major harmonies giving dissonant effects, and moving from middle to high melodic registers. The Governor's first, spoken, 'Quiet!', still in a low tone of voice, is followed by Cunegonde's part of the aria, shifted to D minor; this time the Governor's 'Quiet!' is a little louder. The Old Lady continues in D major again, ending wittily: 'I'd rather be in a tempest at sea, or a bloody North African riot, than . . . put up with this terrible quiet'. 'When are we going to be married?', asks Cunegonde, and the Old Lady repeats 'Comfort and boredom and quiet', whereupon the Governor, now singing 'fortissimo', in a falling D major third, the all-important F sharp–D, ends the scene with 'QUIET!'. The recapitulation of the twelve-note theme concludes with the downward seventh followed by the dominant-tonic cadence of D major.

It was indeed too much to expect a Broadway audience to comprehend the wit of such a scene: there is hardly any stage action, the words are commonplace and, to grasp its originality, the hearer must be aware of the intellectual interplay of words and music, even of the significance of chromaticism and tonality. Leonard Bernstein had a premonition that composition to an ambitious literary libretto would not earn the desired success, nor would it give him inner satisfaction. But nevertheless he was disappointed at the reaction of those critics who had earlier given him moral support and praised his works only now to show harshening towards *Candide*. However, he was not discouraged from making just one more effort to create something entirely new for the Broadway stage. Ten months after the *Candide* première, the new work was performed. It was a breakthrough, confirming Bernstein's ideas, providing Broadway with a musical completely novel in text, action, and music. It was a tragedy with music, a play with a message that startled and even alarmed the public, and music which was daring, complex and full of surprising twists. *West Side Story* made theatre history and with it modern American musical production and choreography conquered the world.

'And now, what are you going to do about that F sharp?' This note, on which Leonard Bernstein's *alter ego* comments so critically, again assumes a dominant role in *West Side Story*. No doubt Bernstein stressed it in his 'dialogue with himself', realising that from his very earliest compositions, at the most expressive and dramatic passages in a musical work, he has allowed a melody to skip a ninth — mostly ascending — to reach an F sharp. In his composition, when he was seventeen, of *Psalm 148*, the vocal melody jumps to 'that F sharp' from the note E at three climactic points of the song in the frame of a harmonic texture. Since that time Bernstein has consistently used the energy-laden expressivity of ninth skips — and the only somewhat less stirring sevenths — to imbue a vocal or instrumental theme or variation of a theme with a strong dramatic accent.

In vocal music these jumps in ninths have a much more poignant effect than in instrumental works and it is not easy for a singer especially to reach 'that F sharp' from middle E. The contralto Ursula Mayer-Reinach explains:

Every singer knows that this F sharp is an *angle tone* in the ascending scale. For soprano, mezzosoprano and contralto voices it is the decisive transition note for reaching a genuine vocal summit; for a baritone, too, it is a note he must be able to master in order to attain the dangerous G and G sharp. For the bass it is the glorious coping-stone of his voice. The emphatic accentuation of the F sharp in Lenny Bernstein's music always implies a challenge to the singer, and the dramatic emphasis communicates itself to the listener in a natural way.

7

West Side Story

> At this very moment I have just ended a performing
> period and started a creative one again . . . . Now the
> conducting's over and will be over for seven months
> while I write another show, a rather serious and tragic
> musical comedy for Broadway — figure that one
> out . . . .
>
> *Leonard Bernstein*, February 1957

Leonard Bernstein's intensive work on the score for that 'rather serious
and tragic musical comedy' occupied him from February to August
1957; on 26 January, he had conducted his last concert with the New
York Philharmonic before the break and his programme had included
the first performance of the *Candide* Overture as a concert piece. Like
most of his musical works, *West Side Story* was completed just in time for
rehearsals before the premiere at the National Theater, Washington,
DC, on 19 August. The first New York performance followed on 26
September at the Winter Garden; the original production ran for 732
performances and a 1960 revival for 249.

It was in the period 1949 to 1950, while Jerome Robbins was
preparing the choreography for *The Age of Anxiety*, that he first thought
of an operatic type of musical in which drama, singing and choreographic action would be of equal importance. He suggested to
Leonard Bernstein that the plot of *Romeo and Juliet* should be adapted to
a modern environment. In Shakespeare's romantic tragedy the lovers
belong to two bitterly hostile families. Robbins and Bernstein considered situating the plot in the East Side of Manhattan where lovers
belonging to different religious creeds live among vicious street fighting
by hooligan gangs; this was to be called *East Side Story*. As both men
were busy with other projects in the early 1950s, the plans were shelved
for almost six years. When they reverted to the story in 1955, having
brought in the writer Arthur Laurents, race hatred and adolescent
crime had become more pressing American problems than religious

[185]

antagonism; the growing number of Puerto Rican immigrants on New York's West Side in particular was exploding into social and racial conflict. So the title was changed to *West Side Story*; Arthur Laurents wrote the book, Stephen Sondheim the lyrics. Leonard Bernstein put much thought into the role of music in such a work, in which brutal reality and poetic lyricism, street slang and words of love, musical drama and volatile ballet scenes overlap in constant change and variation. All four collaborators, author, lyricist, choreographer and composer, sought to integrate these diverse elements into a unified whole.

The story of two lovers suffering tragically through the irreconcilable enmity of their families had been a literary subject long before Shakespeare. It appeared in late Hellenistic literature as well as in a classical Indian drama by the Brahman Bhavabhūti, written over a thousand years ago: in his *Mālatī-mādhava* a minister's daughter (Mālatī) loves a minister's son (Mādhava), with another love story as sub-plot. Shakespeare, who wrote *Romeo and Juliet* in the mid-1590s when he was in his early thirties, probably took his inspiration from Italian authors of the sixteenth century. The story was told by Matteo Bandello (circa 1520), by Salernitano a little later and by Luigi da Porto (died 1529). Luigi da Porto's version had in England been versified by Arthur Brooke (1562) and retold in prose by Paynter (1567). Four hundred years later, in 1956 to 1957, Jerome Robbins, Arthur Laurents and Leonard Bernstein took the love story and the clash of two hostile factions as the starting point of their musical drama. Ultimately, however, *West Side Story* goes deeper, showing the tragedy of a modern society in which the gulf between the generations and between authority and disobedience has become so deep that unbalanced and friendless youngsters turn to crime, while unrequited love produces violence.

In Shakespeare's drama the social order and the authority of the family remain incontestable despite the hatred between the Montagues and the Capulets. In *West Side Story* the street gangs not only fight against each other; they also revolt against the adult world, against the guardians of law and order, against society. 'We never had the love that ev'ry child ought-a get', complain the young street urchins in 'Gee, Officer Krupke'. 'We ain't no delinquents, we're misunderstood/Deep down inside us there is good! There is untapped good.' A boy who does not get an honest job is 'sociologically sick'; 'we got troubles of our own!', they concede. 'We're down on our knees,/'cause no one wants a fellow with a social disease . . . . What are we to do?' The satirical song addressed to the police sergeant reveals the genuine roots of the tragedy that evolves around the love of Tony and Maria. The older generation cannot really comprehend why there should be so much terror, fighting, murder and tragedy; in the end 'the adults are left, alone and useless, on the stage'. Shakespeare's drama closes on a note of reconciliation; the tragic death of the lovers has brought their families together. In *West Side Story* love triumphs over hatred and violence; Maria follows Tony's funeral procession proudly and full of hope that they will meet again 'somewhere, somehow, some day', the gangs join in hoping for a better world, a world of love and understanding, but the adults are excluded, they remain 'alone and useless', having been unable to forestall or halt the tragedy.

The authors of *West Side Story* have consistently stressed the fundamental difference between their concept of the background to the tragic love story and that underlying *Romeo and Juliet*. The alert observer will notice the first indication of the diversity at a very early stage. In both *Romeo and Juliet* and the Laurents–Bernstein musical play the hatred of two hostile factions leads to a street fight. In Shakespeare's first scene, first the servants and then the young noblemen of the hostile families quarrel with each other, and out of a quarrel in words a battle develops. But when the Prince of Verona enters and entreats the 'rebellious subjects, enemies to peace' to depart, they lay down their swords; the authority of the ruler has restored law and order and for the time being quietened hot tempers. However, in *West Side Story* the young native Americans, the Jets, and the Puerto Rican immigrants, the Sharks, do not stop their street fight when two policemen try to enforce order; the gangs mock the guardians of the law and only calm down after they are out of sight. These young people recognise no authority; the wretched product of New York's racially divided West Side, they will bow only to the authority of love and hope in their own future.

In Shakespeare's play the lovers foresee that there may be misfortune in store for them; when the Montague Romeo goes to attend a feast in the house of the old Lord Capulet his 'mind misgives/Some consequence yet hanging in the stars/Shall bitterly begin his fearful date/With this night's revels'; Juliet, too, has forebodings of tragedy. In *West Side Story*, on the contrary, Tony and Maria optimistically foresee a fulfilment of their love: 'Something's coming, something good — if I can wait!' sings Tony in his first solo scene and Maria echoes their first happiness in the lyrical 'Tonight'. Shakespeare's lovers cannot escape from the destiny in their stars; the moral of their story is that love will heal adversities. *West Side Story* does not attempt to moralise; love triumphs, but the bitter lack of understanding between the generations, the young driven to the streets, and their uncomprehending elders,

[187]

remains unresolved. Just as in *Facsimile, The Age of Anxiety, Candide, Trouble in Tahiti* and *Kaddish*, the ending of *West Side Story* puts a question to the protagonists as well as to the spectator. The longing for earthly love and happiness remains unfulfilled and the music, too, concludes with the 'unanswered question': against a pianissimo C major triad with the ninth added between the major third, 'that F sharp' is sounded in the lowest octave, ominously marring the harmonious peacefulness.

Never before had there been a musical whose protagonists were 'youths of the street whose speech is acrid and ugly, and whose conduct is neurotic and savage', whose 'tribal code of honour . . . is the code of hoodlums and gangsters . . . , rooted in ignorance and evil . . . . It is part of the hideousness that lies under the scabby surface of the city' (Brooks Atkinson, *New York Times*, 6 October 1957). Broadway audiences undoubtedly understood the accusations implied by the aggressive play and the no less aggressive music; this was not a show meant to entertain and to amuse with a romantic story and lifting music but one of revolt, struggle and tragedy. That it became such an astounding success all over the world is due to the breathtaking sequence of scenes of an ever-changing character and mood, in which melodrama, solo and ensemble singing, dialogue, ballet, and instrumental interludes follow each other in stark dramatic succession. Each faction is musically characterized, as is each major character; nevertheless the composer has maintained a homogeneous score in which each passage is derived from motific elements first heard in the instrumental 'Prologue'. American and Latin-American dance rhythms underline the different roots of the warring Jets and Sharks; the ballet scenes are not designed as extravagant lavish interludes, as in most musical shows, but are integrated into the drama. *West Side Story* thus demands remarkable talents from all the cast: not only must they act their roles but also be accomplished singers and ballet-dancers. The fact that it was possible to find such all-round talent for the New York and London productions as well as for the film, made a very considerable contribution to the work's world-wide success.

The orchestral 'Prologue' opens with three chords, each built on the interval of a minor second and minor third, against which is heard a descending figure of C–A–G sharp — a progression using the same intervals: minor third = minor second. As the upper two notes of the chords and the bass notes add up to a major triad, it may be thought for a moment that tonality, though disturbed by the dissonant minor

UNITY THROUGHOUT
THE WORK

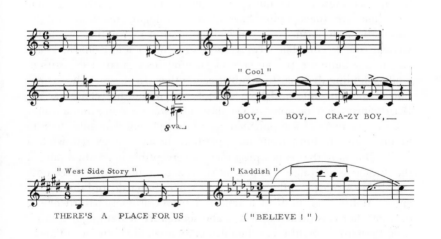

second, might claim superiority; however with the third chord in the sequence the melodic succession from the top of the chords to the bass — G–D–G sharp — which is a descending fourth and tritone, underlines the motivic seventh G–G sharp. This is one of Leonard Bernstein's principal intervals — with the still more dramatic ninth — where he aims at increasing the musical tension. The chords and intervals as sounded in these first four bars of the 'Prologue' are the cells, in the melodic, rhythmic (with their syncopation) and harmonic sense of motifs, themes and melodies, throughout the colourful score of *West Side Story*.

The 'Prologue' serves on the one hand to present the musical material for this almost operatic composition and on the other hand introduces on stage the leaders of the hostile gangs, the Jets and the Sharks. They meet in the West Side streets which the Jets claim are wholly American, their own territory. They tease the Puerto Ricans, show off their strength, and soon two groups of youths start a scuffle. The three-note chord and its variants are recognisable as the fight motif of the Jets. Out of its intervals emerges a four-note melodic theme — a broken major triad and a tritone — that in typical Bernstein manner grows with its first repetition to a six-note phrase and is then further elaborated in conjunction with the motivic chords and their bass lines. In the opening bars of the 'Prologue' ten notes of the chromatic scale formed the musical material of the motifs; two notes were missing to complete a twelve-note structure, F and F sharp. These two notes dominate the accents of ensuing instrumental exposition, while sounding dissonantly against each other. In the melodic formation of the four-note and then six-note theme another characteristic Bernsteinism may be noted: a vacillation between a major and a minor triad — the two notes supplementary to the opening four notes turn to minor — and the jump from the upper note through the triad down to a ninth. One note that is not prominently perceptible in the first part of the 'Prologue' is B flat; it is only of transient interest in the three-note chords (as A sharp). B flat sets the tone when Bernardo and the Sharks enter. At first the motif of fourth and tritone from the third of the opening chords is turned upwards and set against A flat major harmonies; Bernardo's motif takes the form of an ascending tritone B flat–E, followed by the figure B flat–C flat–A (minor second–major second) and this is expanded into a continually growing melodic line, accompanied and supported as a motif by an ostinato in rigid rhythm. In mime and in music, the Sharks take the upper hand for some time, till the reappearance of the three-note chords and derived melodic phrase bring the Jets back, while the entry of the police leads to the beginning of the stage action proper.

The opening of the 'Prologue' is recalled as the opening of the first vocal number: the 'Jet Song' led by the Jets' leader, Riff. The octave upbeat of the theme is dramatically widened to a ninth upbeat, the three-note chords with added bass line become the orchestral accompaniment to Riff's song in an ambiguous G minor–B flat major. In the middle section of the song, there reappears the descending motif of two thirds and a tritone. During the scene-change after the 'Jet Song' the musical material of the 'Prologue' is recapitulated. Tony enters; he had been a founder of the Jets but has not been with them for some time. Riff wants him to return and come to a dance at the Gym where Sharks and Jets are to meet. The second scene concludes with Tony's hopeful song 'Something's Coming — Something Good' . . . 'Could be, who knows?' Minor second and major second with a tritone upbeat form the motif of the first, D major, part of his song; in the refrain the tonality is C major, disturbed by 'that F sharp' in its harmony. D major returns after indeterminate, modulating chords. In the third scene, Maria, the sister of the Shark leader Bernardo, appears for the first time: she and Anita, Bernardo's fiancée, work in a bridal shop. Anita makes a dress for Maria to wear at the dance she is going to with her brother and her suitor Chino. The music of Tony's hopeful song leads from one scene to the other. At the Dance at the Gym which follows Maria's proud thought, 'To-night is the real beginning of my life as a young lady of America', Tony and Maria fall in love at first sight; Bernardo furiously demands that Maria should leave immediately, while Tony fears an impending fight. The six numbers of the Dance at the Gym — 'Blues', 'Promenade', 'Mambo', 'Cha-Cha', the 'Meeting Scene' between Tony and Maria, a melodrama, 'Jump' — are musically developed out of the basic motif material and also using the melodic intervals of Tony's 'Could be, who knows?'. After Maria and Tony have seen each other for the first time, the short 'Cha-Cha' — Andante conrazia — is derived entirely from Tony's motif in seconds with tritone upbeat, followed by a five-note melodic descent, with an ascending second as cadence. This complete melodic phrase is later to supply the first line of Tony's love song 'Maria'; it also accompanies the dialogue in the couple's 'Meeting Scene'. The crowd of youths breaks into the tender scene and the dance ends with a 'Jump' in a sinister pianissimo, with music based on the Jets motif. The dancers are interrupted by interludes entitled 'Promenade'; they are in a misleadingly primitive F major made dissonant by a recurring G flat, which is nothing else but 'that F sharp'.

Tony's song 'Maria', in E flat major enriched by chromatic devia-

West Side Story: beginning of the Fugue ('Cool')

tions, opens with the tritone-minor second motif (E flat, A, B flat) and continues with the descending melodic line in seconds and the cadence to a higher second interval, as first heard in the 'Cha-Cha' music. With mounting commitment and expression in Tony's song, the intervals of the melody become more widely spaced, ascending and descending; his germ cell motif, the ascending second — harmonised with a major third to create a tritone sound — concludes the song, the orchestra contemplating 'pianissimo' on Tony's 'The most beautiful sound I ever heard'.

There follows the romantic 'Balcony Scene' by the fire escape to the apartment of Maria's family. The music opens 'pianissimo' under the whispered dialogue of Maria and Tony who fear they will be discovered. This is the music, with its four descending intervals followed by ascent and new descent, that recalls the 'Good Night' in Benjamin Britten's *Rape of Lucretia* where, as in *West Side Story*, a lyrical scene is overshadowed by ominous foreboding (see page 49, above). In a melodically expanded form — with wider-spaced intervals — the 'Maria' motif becomes the theme of the haunting 'To-night' duet; its melody is accompanied by three-note chords derived from the character of the chords that opened the 'Prologue'. A counter-melody hinted at in the orchestra expands significantly into a new variant of the basic motif — ascending seventh–descending minor second–minor third––major third (A flat–ascent to G flat–descent F–D–B flat): this will later become the theme of the lyrical dream song 'Somewhere — There's a Place for Us'.

Tony has to disappear as Bernardo and the other Puerto Ricans arrive. As a boisterous intermezzo between the tender love scene and the violence to come, the Puerto Rican girls amuse themselves by comparing their homeland with 'the island Manhattan'. Only Rosalia thinks of Puerto Rico nostalgically, Anita and the other girls like everything in America. Leonard Bernstein here juxtaposes two Latin-American dance rhythms: Seis for the verse and Huapango for the refrain; melodically the music is based on motifs connected with the Sharks.

Scene Six is set in Doc's drug store where a council of war has been called to prepare the forthcoming 'rumble' between the two rival gangs. The atmosphere is tense; the danger of an immediate fight is averted by the appearance of the plain-clothes policeman Schrank against whom the hostile gangs unite as against a common enemy. One of the most astounding numbers of the score is the Jet leader Riff's 'Cool': Riff admonishes his boys 'to keep coolly cool/Breeze it, buzz it, easy does it'. The opening melodrama and the song 'almost whispered' are kept pianissimo and piano; the music derives from the Jet motif, C–F sharp–G (tritone–minor second). After the song there develops a genuine fugue, accompanying a frenetic dance and rising dynamically from gentle sound to a wildly orgiastic outburst. The fugue opens with the tritone cell of the Jet motif with the lower fourth as upbeat: upbeat and tritone G–C–F sharp (F sharp again!) adding up to the typical seventh-skip G–F sharp. This is followed by an ascending minor seventh and a descending minor second, recalling the 'Somewhere' motif. The entire phrase is repeated with some variation. The fugue then develops out of the motif figures; it is so transparently orchestrated that the entries and elaborations of motifs and themes can easily be followed by the listener. The climax is reached when the Jet theme is heard unisono-fortissimo, excitedly interrupted by a yelling Jet rushing in joining the gang. The dance continues with unabated force; a sudden diminuendo leads to a recapitulation of Riff's song, which is again excitedly whispered pianissimo under his breath and the fugal theme peters out, so to speak, to a rhythmic background of drums in a double pianissimo. This scene precedes the entry of the Sharks into the drugstore. The council of war itself is not accompanied by music. The scene ends with the 'To-night' music accompanying a dialogue between the enamoured Tony and the frightened Doc.

The six scenes so far have provided something of a preparation for the coming drama. When the curtain rises on the first street scene, the time is 5 p.m. on a late summer afternoon; the drugstore scene in which the conditions are set for the intended once-and-for-all battle for the control of the district finishes soon after midnight the same day. The second part of the First Act, opening at the bridal shop and ending with the deadly Rumble, unfolds between 5.30 p.m. of the day after the drugstore scene and 9.00 p.m. 'Under the Highway'.

At the bridal shop, in Scene Seven, Tony comes secretly to see Maria and they enact an imaginary wedding ceremony. During their dialogue the music recalls the 'Cha-Cha' dance themes; the 'Somewhere' motif leads on to the love duet 'One Hand, One Heart', in which most of the dissonant motifs of the score are harmonically softened. Scene Eight is set in a neighbouring street barely an hour later: the gangs are making final preparations for the fight. They face each other singing in ensemble, led by Riff and Bernardo respectively. Anita and Maria are with their group, Tony with his. The five-voiced 'To-night', based on the music of the romantic Balcony Scene, now becomes of a sinister and foreboding character; it ends in furiously dissonant chords.

Scene Nine ends the First Act with the 'rumble' itself. Tony vainly attempts to reconcile between the gangs but Bernardo challenges him to fight it out. Riff is the first to open his knife and attack Bernardo; seeing Riff mortally wounded, Tony picks up his friend's knife and stabs Bernardo in self-defence. The music has now risen to a fearful pitch, with Jets and Sharks motifs wildly mixed: it is abruptly stopped by a police siren off stage and 'the gangs disperse in panic and confusion'. The stage empties: only Tony stands mute and dumb-founded before the bodies of his friend Riff and Maria's brother Bernardo. Fragments of the themes linger on confusedly till a Jet girl tugs Tony away before the police find him. Off-stage, a clock strikes nine as the curtain falls on the tragic end of Act One.

The six scenes of Act Two are set between 9.15 p.m. — opening immediately after the closing scene of Act One — and midnight. Ascending major thirds and minor seconds open the first number; knowing nothing of what has happened just a quarter of an hour before, three girls are helping Maria to try on her wedding dress; her song 'I Feel Pretty' develops out of the intervals of the opening motif. The scene ends abruptly with Chino storming in and telling Maria her brother has been killed by Tony. He takes a gun from Bernardo's room and ominously pockets it. He has hardly left when Tony climbs in through the window from the fire escape. 'Killer, killer, killer!', Maria shouts at him while the music, pianissimo, but in an agitated tempo with incessantly syncopated drum beats, gives out the tragic motif in minor second intervals. It continues softly as Maria becomes aware that Tony did not mean to kill; the boy wants to surrender to the law, but Maria pleads with him not to leave her but to flee away from the world of hatred that surrounds them. Tony's song 'I'll take you away, take you far, far away out of here' is derived out of the minor-second motif. Maria joins in with 'Somewhere there must be a place we can feel we're free'; this is not yet the romantic 'Somewhere', but a transition to the orchestral ballet sequence in which Maria and Tony dream of a place where the rival groups would unite in peace, where there would be no violence and hostility, only quiet and peace and forgiveness. The motifs are turned into harmonious phrases and at the climax of the dream scene a girl's voice is heard expressing the lovers' feeling: 'There's a place for us, Somewhere a place for us . . . . Some day! Somewhere . . .'. The melody, whose appearance has been care-fully prepared throughout the entire score is accompanied by the orchestra in a soft, artistic counterpoint of great beauty; it ends in full diatonic major chordal harmony, but with the 'Somewhere' motif in a bass voice sounding in a minor mode that again concludes on 'that F sharp'. The emotional impact of the scene is greatly enhanced by the device of Tony and Maria being seen but not heard in the dream

[195]

procession where gangs now walk together in friendly harmony; after a girl's voice has sung the 'Somewhere' vision song, it is repeated 'pianissimo' by the 'entire company' in two-voiced canon. However, it stops abruptly after the first line and the dream sequence turns into a nightmare. To the full orchestra's wildly dissonant sounds, there reappear the sombre shadows, gaunt fire escapes and dark streets of the big city. The figures of Riff and Bernardo are seen, Jets and Sharks interchange, Tony and Maria are separated, chaos reigns. Reality seems to appear unreal. As abruptly as it began the nightmare ends. Tony and Maria come together and dreamily sing the last lines of the 'Somewhere' melody; the music concludes the scene with the question mark of the ascending major second.

A little later that same evening, the Jets gather in an alley for further action when Police Sergeant Krupke enters, threatening them all with arrest. As soon as he has gone they stage a mock trial of the kids before Officer Krupke, a 'Judge', a 'Psychiatrist' and a 'Social Worker'; the blame for the tragic misery of the uncared-for, unloved, troubled youths, for the juvenile delinquency is laid at the door of the uncomprehending adults faced with an unloved and bitter generation.

The song 'Gee, Officer Krupke' begins 'fast, vaudeville style' and superficially sounds like a satirical cabaret number. In melodic variation and shifts of harmony as well as in its ironical comment on the text this music is a gem of artistic parody. It has a can-can like accompaniment underlined by the opening eight bars with syncopated triads. The harmony wanders through many keys together with the melody line which always starts with a tritone interval. It was E sharp–B at the beginning of the first verse, the E sharp being take over from the downward ninth jump (from F sharp to E sharp) at the conclusion of the eight-bar B major instrumental introduction. There are many calculated shocks in melody and harmony throughout the song, underlining the bitter feelings of the performers; from one couplet to the next the keys change harshly, each time with a dissonant linking note: it is 'that F sharp' when B major is followed by C major without transition; it is G when C major changes into D flat major and G sharp at the turn from D flat major to D major. In the last lines of the song F major suddenly follows a full D major triad chord.

This masterly-composed mocking scene ends with a young girl rushing in to warn the group that Chino is looking for Tony to kill him, and the Jets set out to find Tony and try to protect him.

Tony has meanwhile stayed with Maria; an instrumental interlude introducing the next scene first recalls the vicious fights and then turns into the 'Somewhere' melody. When Maria hears Anita coming to her

West Side Story: draft of 'Mambo'

room, Tony quickly climbs out of the window. In a dramatic duet, Anita implores Maria to forget Tony who has killed her brother but Maria reminds Anita of her own deep love and asks for her understanding. Again, the entire piece is built out of the contrasting, and yet motivically related, themes of strife, love and hope. In conclusion, the policeman Schrank enters and questions Maria who refuses all information.

The Fourth Scene is set in the drug store. Maria has promised Tony to meet him there but sends Anita to tell him she may be late. The Jets have come to watch out for Chino while Tony hides in the cellar. A 'Mambo' is heard from the juke-box as Anita enters to deliver her message. The assembled Jets see in Anita only the despised Puerto Rican enemy. They provoke and attack her and only Doc's intervention succeeds in stopping the wild youths. Anita, her blood boiling, forgets herself and shouts at them that Chino has killed Maria: this false information, which Doc passes on to Tony in the cellar, is meant to parallel Friar Laurence's miscarried message to Romeo. Romeo's belief that Juliet is dead is the starting-point for the final tragedy of Shakespeare's play, exactly like Anita's message in *West Side Story*. Before Anita's furious outbreak the juke-box 'Mambo' stopped suddenly; the refrain of Anita's praise of America from the First Act is recapitulated by the orchestra fortissimo, in dissonant variants; the G major harmonies of the Coda to this scene disturb an ostinato chord composed of the tritone B flat–E and an abrupt ending is provided by a furious downward leap, A Flat–G flat–A flat, stressing the seventh interval of the concluding notes.

The tragic end of the action develops without any musical comment: after Doc's dialogue with Tony, the boy runs out into the darkness so that Chino can find and kill him; then, amazingly, he meets the Maria he had thought dead. At this point, Chino finds Tony and shoots him. Maria cannot believe her lover is dying; she wrenches Chino's gun away but she cannot fire, feeling there should be an end to hatred — Maria and the dying Tony unite in their hope of peace and love, 'Somewhere . . . some day'. As in the dream sequence, a procession forms, while two Jets and two Sharks carry Tony's body away and only the baffled adults remain, 'alone and useless'. The musical reminiscence of an expanded final cadence from the 'Somewhere' tune ends the work, played pianissimo, slowly; the omnipresent questioning ascending major second is embedded in a C major fifth while 'that F sharp' is sounded in the basses, underlining, in musical terms, 'the unanswered question' of the world's tragic complexity, as well as the ambiguity of musical statements.

It seems astonishing and may even perhaps appear unnecessary to regular show-business habitués that it is possible to dissect and analyse the music of a Broadway show in the same way as a symphonic composition. The *West Side Story* score virtually invites musical and structural analysis, since it can make the listener feel that the many different numbers are closely linked by common underlying motifs, even though the passages vary in lyrical or dramatic mood, in warm diatonic or robustly chromatic melodic lines, in romantic flow or stark rhythmic accentuation. In the astounding variety of its music — songs, ensembles, accompaniments of speech, ballets — created out of a basic motif cell, *West Side Story*, leaning towards operatic music drama, is far in advance of other Broadway shows. Unity through variety, the fundamental principle of the great composers' craft, is exemplified in this richly diverse score; it proves the extent to which the skill of inventive change, contrast and variation is combined with the original inspiration and craft of elaboration. The imprint of the symphonic composer is felt throughout the music of *West Side Story* and in letting small motifs grow into phrases and phrases into melodies and themes Bernstein follows the same procedures as in his symphonies and theatre music. The ballet sequences especially are veritable symphonic movements and the development of a song motif — itself derived from an instrumental idea — into a complex fugue had no equal in show music before. Leonard Bernstein has been criticised for his 'experiment in linking drama with entertainment' in *West Side Story* and for a 'blue-eyed attempt to smooth down the momentous social problems of the American big city . . . with a *naiveté* that would have been condemned even twenty-five years ago' (Rudolf Klein, in *Osterreichische Musikzeitung*, XXXVII, 1982, nos. 7–8, p. 425). This verdict has also been put forward elsewhere, both when *West Side Story* was first performed and when it was presented in other countries far from America. However, not only are drama and entertainment contrasted in many works of art past and present, but the authors and composer of *West Side Story* made a special point of stressing the tragic conflicts within society and between the generations; the work provides much more food for thought than an average evening in the theatre.

The tragic theme for *West Side Story* has undoubtedly remained topical in its own way although times and situations have changed since 1957 and the problems of youth are different in the various countries in which the work has been and is being performed. The theme of love threatened or tragically thwarted in a hostile environment is central to many great dramas and operas. Unruliness, rebellion against law and order, moral decadence, battle and murder have sadly been seen in all ages and have provided dramatic scenes for operas to which the Viennese critic could not possibly say that 'embittered entertainment commodities were salvaged down to our times'; are such problems, he asks, a fitting theme for song and dance? Similar questions had already been asked after the New York premiere in September 1957.

To put this central aesthetic problem of 'mixing tragedy and entertainment' into proper perspective, it should be remembered that any dramatic work gives a naturalistic, realistic or symbolic representation of human thoughts and situations. The degree of sensitivity shown by a writer in putting on stage the eternal contrasts of grief and happiness, misery and hopes, laughter and tears, is the measure of his greatness; it is not easy to show doubt underlying a scene of merriment or awaken a glimmer of hope in a tragic situation. In Shakespeare high-spirited comedy is used to enhance the power of tragic scenes and the same is true of opera. How sparklingly Don Giovanni sings at his last supper while the music already darkly hints at his doom. In *La Traviata*, the ailing Violetta feels death approaching while the music lightly plays; while she is on her deathbed carnival revellers sing under her window. Monterone hurls his deadly curse at Rigoletto at a feast with gay ballet music. In *La Bohème*, there is Musetta's suggestive waltz, sung in the presence of the fatally ill Mimi, much cheerful choral singing in the same act, and, in the sadly lyrical love duet between Rodolfo and Mimi, overshadowed by the premonition of death, the sound of the flirtatious laughter of Musetta and Marcello. In the erotic scene of Salome's 'Dance of the Seven Veils' before Herod, which will lead to the beheading of the Prophet, the orchestra plays in waltz rhythms. In Benjamin Britten's *Death in Venice*, the intermezzi are seemingly light-hearted in spirit but hardly create a gay mood; the last scene of *Wozzeck* shows a child playing and singing happily in the street, unable to grasp that his mother has just died. These are just a few examples from the great operas, where outward merriment and latent tragedy are joined to underline the drama of a situation or the characters' perplexity at what is happening to them. Music is the perfect means of comment on stage action as well as on the feelings and thoughts of the characters, and there need be no hesitation in ranking *West Side Story*'s mixing of 'drama and entertainment' with the operatic scenes in the musical dramas of Mozart, Verdi, Puccini, Richard Strauss, Britten and Alban Berg.

West Side Story may perhaps be best seen as a 'period opera', to be compared with a work like Brecht-Weill's *The Rise and Fall of the City of Mahagonny* (1930). In both works, a mirror bearing an almost ludicrous image of contemporary social conditions is held up to society as a whole: in Leipzig (1930), Berlin (1931) and Vienna (1932) an elegant audience enthusiastically applauded *Mahagonny*, the critical, sarcastic dramatisation of the evils of contemporary life. As in *West Side Story*, the melodic and rhythmic language of contemporary jazz idioms determined the style of a piece of serious entertainment in opera style, designed to reflect the spirit of the times; and, as in modern America, the audience could not possibly imagine that the social censure referred to them, that they might be part of the society depicted on stage. Musically there are also parallels in the way the composers have shaped the vocal numbers. Kurt Weill followed the prosody of Brecht's biting lyrics so faithfully that every word and the content of each song could be clearly articulated. Leonard Bernstein was lucky to have in Stephen Sondheim a lyricist no less pungent than Brecht; and Bernstein set these texts to music which, despite more complex rhythms than those of Weill, enables the singers to enunciate every word with clarity. Kurt Weill's instrumentation effectively underlined the biting character of the music; Leonard Bernstein, himself a master of orchestration, in *West Side Story* had two collaborators especially versed in Broadway music, Sid Ramin and Irwin Kostal, who succeeded in giving a perfect sound painting of the locale of the play. In earlier Broadway musicals, Bernstein had collaborated in the orchestration with Hershy Kay and Don Walker; for *Mass* he was assisted by Jonathan Tunick. In the case of purely orchestral works, such as symphonies or ballet scores, Leonard Bernstein did his own orchestration. But where local colour was of special importance, or where little time was available, he thought it best to enlist the help of professional jazz musicians.

The colourful instrumentation which set the scene so authentically for the ballets, and the virtuosity of the actors–singers–dancers, gave the ballet music of *West Side Story* a prominent place in the stage action as well as in the score. It has rightly been said that the depth of Leonard Bernstein's insight into the demands of speech in song is matched by his ability to create perfect rhythms for ballet sequences, enabling the dancers to take their place as real actors in the plot. Lady Diana Menuhin, a professional ballerina in her youth, has said, 'I know no contemporary composer who so well writes for movement, understands so well the movements of the body.'

Though the plot of *West Side Story* and its treatment were at first

[201]

thought to have little 'popular' appeal in the accustomed sense, success grew with every performance. Critics, however, remained divided on its artistic merits: the prominent John Martin argued that 'with such superb craftsmanship and a medium of such potentialities' it was a pity that it

> never actually says anything, but only trades on the urgency of the subject it has chosen. . . . Whether the gang wars of delinquents is a legitimate subject for the shallow song-and-dance treatment of a Broadway show or, whether on the other hand, the whole thing is either an example of social irresponsibility or merely an exhibition of bad taste, are issues that are being widely and even angrily debated (*New York Times*, 27 October 1957).

Brooks Atkinson, on the other hand, made two important points concerning the essential qualities of the work: 'The subject is not beautiful', he wrote, 'but what *West Side Story* draws out of it is beautiful. For it has a searching poiht of view.' (*New York Times*, 27 September 1957). Later, he gets to the roots of the authors' intentions: 'The fundamental distinction of *West Side Story* is the courage with which it adheres to its artistic convictions and its unwillingness to make concessions to popular taste' (ibid., 6 October 1957).

After *West Side Story*, it was not until the 'Kaddish' Symphony (1963) that Leonard Bernstein again found ways to integrate his meditations on the times we live in, and on the meaning and significance of life and belief. *Mass* (1971) and the *Dybbuk* ballet (1974) were the next searching works in which he found ways to integrate literary content, the vocal expression of an enquiring mind, action and movement within musically imaginative forms, while imbuing new texts with new literary sense and meaning. He has always, in all his texts and compositions, tried to speak a language that is comprehensible to everyone, not only to connoisseurs. As Brooks Atkinson understood, Leonard Bernstein has never fallen below his true artistic convictions in order to make concessions to popular taste.

8

Musical Synthesis in the Later Compositions

There it stands — the result of my pondering,
Two long months of avant-garde wandering —
My youngest child, old-fashioned and sweet,
And he stands on his own two tonal feet.
Leonard Bernstein, September 1965

In June 1964 Leonard Bernstein took a fifteen-month sabbatical leave from the New York Philharmonic in order to be able to compose. He interrupted this creative vacation only once — in July 1965 — to conduct the first performance of his *Chichester Psalms*, which he had completed in May of that year. His last large-scale work had been the 'Kaddish' Symphony, centring around the crisis of faith of modern man and the crisis of tonality in modern music; since he had written this symphony, which counts with his boldest orchestral compositions, he had asked himself time and again in what direction contemporary music should go and how the manifold problems could be solved that arise out of the necessity of a novel organisation of tonal and non-tonal forces in music. He devoted the period of his sabbatical to two main activities: the attempt to create a new work for the music theatre and the study of all the trends in most recent contemporary music.

After the success of *West Side Story*, which had opened on Broadway nearly seven years earlier, Leonard Bernstein wanted to apply and further develop the experience gathered in his novel kind of musical theatre piece and, above all, to get still nearer to opera. But the first half year of his vacation from conducting passed without his making any progress in the desired direction. His literary collaborators failed to provide him with material corresponding to his musical needs (see pages 81–2, above) and he had reluctantly to give up the plans for a musical play based on Thornton Wilder's *The Skin of Our Teeth* and for another from Bert Brecht's *The Exception and the Rule*. He read more

[203]

theatre plays but did not find a drama or a comedy that could inspire him to write music. He has cast his experiences during the sabbatical and his feelings of disappointment into the form of a witty, partly ironic, partly satirical poem for the *New York Times* (repr. in Bernstein, *Infinite Variety*).

In the chronicle of his sabbatical year Leonard Bernstein writes on the many unconventional developments in contemporary music and the new terminology which he calls 'Physicomathematomusicology'. He has studied aleatoric music, musical dadaism, works composed for 'nattering, clucking sopranos', music for 'squadrons of vibraphones, fleets of pianos played with the forearms, the fist and the palms', mourns 'the dearth of romance' in new music. For him, only a very few composers rise above the fashionable experiments: 'the phenomenon Pierre Boulez and the incredibly imaginative Lukas Foss' — 'two geniuses in a shaky musical moment'. As a conductor Bernstein, looking back at his meditative period, admits that he is fascinated by each new and original work and by new sounds, as a composer he can never completely leave tonality. In each of his later compositions he has tried to accomplish a synthesis between the conflicting tonal and non-tonal forces in music; in each work he has solved his own problems in a different way.

His 'major sabbatical act — at least, the most tangible', was the composition of the *Chichester Psalms*: 'These psalms are a simple and modest affair, tonal and tuneful and somewhat square, certain to sicken a stout John Cager with its tonics and triads in B-flat major'. Although the melodic lines in this work abound in characteristic Bernstein leaps, the music always retains a tonal basis and is dominated by triad harmonies. This style was partly surely also determined by the commission of a religious composition from Chichester Cathedral in England: it was to be sung by the cathedral choirs of Chichester, Winchester and Salisbury at their traditional summer festival in 1965; the three cathedral cities are sited within some sixty miles of each other. The church authorities agreed to Leonard Bernstein's condition in accepting the commission that the Psalms must be sung in the original Hebrew. He chose for his composition the second verse of Psalm 108 and the whole Psalm 100 for the first of the three movements; in the second, Psalm 23 and the first four verses of Psalm 2 are sung; the final movement, the most extensive of the three, is composed on Psalm 131 and the first verse of Psalm 133. It is interesting to note that Leonard Bernstein did not return to Psalm 148, which he had set to music, in a free English paraphrase, at the age of seventeen.

The score of the *Chichester Psalms* was completed on 7 May 1965. The composer conducted the first performance in New York on 15 July with the Camerata Singers led by Abraham Kaplan and members of the New York Philharmonic; the boy alto solo was sung by John Bogart. In this performance the choral parts were rendered by a mixed choir. Leonard Bernstein's original conception had been a performance by a four-part chorus of boy sopranos and boy altos, tenors and basses, and at Chichester Cathedral the work was performed in this form on 31 July. There are in the score some solo vocal parts which can be sung by members of the choir and a long and expressive boy alto part that must be sung only by a boy or (possibly) by a counter-tenor. The orchestral accompaniment is for an original combination of instruments: six brass instruments, timpani, percussion including bells, xylophone, glockenspiel, two harps, and strings. The *Psalms* had been commissioned by the Very Rev. Walter Hussey, Dean of Chichester Cathedral, and are dedicated, 'with gratitude', to Dr Cyril Solomon.

The composer has written that his *Psalms* 'are a simple and modest affair', 'tonal and tuneful', dominated by 'tonics and triads', but this music is in fact not so 'simple' at all. It can best be described as being of a complex simplicity, comparable in some way with the music of the operetta *Candide* written in a similar sophisticatedly simple style. As in most of his works, Bernstein develops his music out of a short basic motif: it is made up of five notes and the extended motif becomes a melodic phrase, which in its turn serves as a theme. The melodic lines, though based on tonal centres, use uncommon intervals and the harmonies are enriched by chromatic progressions. The basic initial motif opens with a descending fourth followed by a descending seventh and then comes a repetition beginning one note higher; the rhythm is varied in order to fit the text. In a varied sequence the pure B flat harmonies give way to more chromatic textures; in a one-bar interlude (bar 6) one hears F sharp ('that F sharp' again) sounded in bar 5 in the bass voices and the orchestra — which assumes an important function, providing a ninth interval to the note G that dominates for a number of bars. The descending melody also underlines a ninth interval — here G descending to F — while in the lower voices, singing in sevenths and ninths, F sharp remains an element foreign to tonality. Thus even in the *Chichester Psalms*, conceived as a predominantly tonal composition and impressing the listener as a tonal work, the conflict between tonality and pan-tonality, triad harmonies and chromaticism is evident. It becomes sharper and gains a more outspoken expression in most of Bernstein's later compositions.

The composer sees in *Chichester Psalms* the 'most accessible' tonal piece he has ever written: 'If one is trying to find optimism versus pessimism in my music; the closest musical equivalent is tonality versus non-tonality', he said at a press conference with Deutsche Grammophon in Berlin in August 1977, and maintained that 'in most cases I use tone rows, manipulating them with some (as you would say) pessimistic or disturbing element in mind'. In the notes accompanying the Deutsche Grammophon recording of the *Psalms*, Jack Gottlieb comments on Leonard Bernstein's remarks by listing some of the dodecaphonic passages alluded to, music expressing mourning ('Dirge' in *Age of Anxiety*), anguish ('Din-Torah' in *Kaddish*), foreboding (second theme in the first movement of *Jeremiah*), violence (*On the Waterfront*), the occult (*Dybbuk*), drunken abandon (*Fancy Free*), mechanistic ideology ('Credo' in *Mass*), missed love and lost love (two songs in *Songfest*), boredom ('Quiet' in *Candide*), and repressed hostility ('Cool' Fugue in *West Side Story*). To this partial list could be added some of the macabre and stormy scenes in the 1983 opera *A Quiet Place*.

The five-note motif of descending fourth, ascending seventh, descending fifth and again ascending major second serves as germ-cell for the entire music of *Chichester Psalms*. Ever-new variants and derivations form principal and subsidiary phrases and themes; at the conclusion of the first movement its original figure is strongly confirmed in fast intensification from pianissimo to fortissimo in expanded tones by the choir and all instruments. The second movement begins with the solo of the boy alto. After the B flat major tonality of the first movement — to which the music returns after each modulatory episode — A major dominates the second movement. The melodious theme of the solo ('The Lord is my Shepherd') is based on a variant of the germ-cell motif, the interval of the fifth now being replaced by a sixth. The boy's voice is accompanied by two harps, with three trumpets and three trombones softly adding their sounds at the climax of the solo, intoning a sort of organ point. Where the words of the lyrical Twenty-third Psalm change over to the beginning of the Second Psalm ('Why do the nations rage, and the people imagine a vain thing? The kings of the earth set themselves, and the rulers take counsel together against the Lord?', the quiet mood is abandoned for a 'wild' Allegro in A minor; the expressive melodiousness is followed by a musical declamation in small-step intervals in scanned rhythms and chords of sevenths and ninths underline marked verses and exclamations. Two-note chords that had accompanied the boy's voice at the beginning of this movement reappear while the A minor episode is led back to A major and the question 'Lamah?' ('Why?') is repeatd softly. In the Coda of the movement there combine the boy's voice — with the first and the last verses of Psalm 23 — and a soft-singing choir with the also softly-playing orchestra, while a trumpet and the xylophone recall — playing *misterioso* — the 'Lamah' motif.

The third movement opens with an orchestral prelude, the music of which is derived from the motivating germ-cell and develops in a polyphonic texture, as did the choral singing in the beginning of the entire work. The B flat major tonality can be recognized and dominates till a three times ascending melodic phrase of the violins reaches the note F sharp and there follows the choral intonation of Psalm 131 — sostenuto molto, peacefully flowing — in G major: 'Lord, my heart is not haughty, nor mine eyes lofty'. In the slow and soft Coda the choir sings unaccompanied, in long notes, the first verse of Psalm 133: 'Behold how good, and how pleasant it is, for brethren to dwell together in unity'. The theme of the music is the motto-motif, which is sung four times starting on different steps of the scale. A low-voiced 'Amen', sung on G, concludes the work, while a muted trumpet and a harp intone the five notes of the germ-cell motto-motif.

In 1980, Robert Gladstein, assistant director and resident choreographer of the San Francisco Ballet and a former member of the American Ballet Theatre, presented a choreography on *Chichester Psalms* with the San Francisco company. The ballet was called *Psalms* and was based on motifs from Jewish religious ceremonies and Jewish history. The company performed it both in America and on state-sponsored tours abroad.

In the *Chichester Psalms* there is hardly a hint of traditional Hebrew musical material — despite the Hebrew text — which comes somewhat as a surprise after *Jeremiah* and *Kaddish* and in view of the later *Mass* and *Dybbuk* compositions.

Mass, a 'Theater Piece for Singers, Players, and Dancers', was completed in 1971, six years after the *Chichester Psalms*. It was composed at the request of Jacqueline Kennedy for the opening of the John F. Kennedy Center for the Performing Arts in Washington, D.C., and first performed there on 8 September 1971. With *Mass* Leonard Bernstein has created a work beyond ordinary religious conceptions. The text is taken mainly from the liturgy of the Roman Mass, with additional texts by Stephen Schwartz and Bernstein himself; there are passages from the *Book of Genesis*, Hebrew benedictions and modern lyrics, intertwining Jewish, Christian and Budhist thinking. In this strange work words and music strive towards a synthesis of religious traditions and there is throughout the piece a feeling of mysticism. Much criticism has been levelled against the idea and the form of *Mass*,

MASS

Text from the Liturgy of the Roman Mass
Additional Texts by
Stephen Schwartz and Leonard Bernstein

Leonard Bernstein

I DEVOTIONS BEFORE MASS

1. Antiphon: *Kyrie Eleison*

In total darkness a Quadraphonic tape is heard, coming from four speakers placed in the four corners of the house.

The opening of *Mass*

its blasphemous aspects, and its mysticism. Bernstein's own leanings towards mysticism have often been noted; it came to a climax three years after *Mass*, when he composed music for Jerome Robbins' *Dybbuk* ballet in which he used traditional Hebrew liturgical chant and Jewish folklore. It is of singular musical interest to follow Leonard Bernstein's development as a religious traditionalist from the *Psalm 148* of the seventeen-year-old up to the *Dybbuk* music — with *Jeremiah, Kaddish, Chichester Psalms,* and *Mass* as stations.

The 'Kaddish' Symphony had already been severely criticised in many circles as 'blasphemous' because of its underlying theme that modern man 'wrangles' with God in a crisis of faith. *Mass* offended some critics and religious believers even more; it was argued that the fusion attempted in *Mass* of liturgical ceremonies and pure *show* was simply unacceptable. One of the most outspoken critics was Cyrus Gottwald, the German choir director and a prominent champion of contemporary sacred and profane music. In a remarkable analytical paper ('Leonard Bernstein's *Mass* or the construction of blasphemy', in *Melos — Neue Zeitschrift für Musik*, 1976, pp. 281–4) he brought forward a number of serious objections against Bernstein's conception of ritual, liturgy, prayer, and of sacred composition in general. Gottwald condemns the 'spectacle' made out of the liturgical ceremonies 'between cult and show'; it leads, he says, to numerous contradictions and the mass becomes in the end a veritable *black* mass: 'Popular and symphonic music, musica viva and rock music are mixed here in a style that silences all sensibility and feeling for purity'. In text and music Gottwald finds 'hardly a confirmation, a thesis that Bernstein does not at once questions and overturns. It is impossible to rely on what he exposes. What was lacerated he tries to mend again, with a *gestus* of Mahler, wishing to display consolation. But his music refuses to bring about security above doubt'.

As in *Kaddish*, the crisis of faith in our century is the main theme of *Mass* — with the only difference that Jewish liturgy provided the textual and musical foundations for *Kaddish* and the Roman liturgy inspired *Mass*. Positive criticism of *Kaddish* underlined the note of hope and confirmation contained in the final confidence of the believer; Gottwald concedes that beyond the blasphemous aspects of *Mass* there is 'an affirmative canon' in the entire work, in that the endangered faith and religiosity at the same time serves as a challenge to renew faith.

'A work of art does not answer questions, it provokes them; and its essential meaning is in the tension between the contradictory answers', Leonard Bernstein wrote in October 1965, and this truism may well be applied to the much-disputed *Mass*. The conductor and composer

[209]

Antal Dorati, at that time Music Director of Washington's National Symphony Orchestra, described *Mass* in 1979 as a 'modern *mystery play*':

The work made a deep impact upon the emotionally pre-charged audience, not least because of the re-emergence of the Kennedy name and the Kennedy tragedy. This work-up state of mind of the public was, perhaps, detrimental to a true appreciation of the work, and the fixed date of the production was perhaps detrimental to the work itself, for in my opinion it is quite outstanding and would have merited a première unconnected with any occasion whatever.

It represents a dramatic study of the drama of worship and thus also an exploration into the nature of the religious Mass as we know it.

For this reason, I think, the name of the piece is a misnomer. If the word MASS was placed within quotation marks, then the title would be correct and significant. But how many ordinary members of the public could be expected to read as carefully and thoughtfully as that? The best would have been to use in a sub-title the words that most correctly describe the nature of the piece . . . .

Dorati proposed to name it:

MASS
(A Mystery Play)

Enlarging further, Dorati says that

the work depicts, movingly, the evolution from the improvised *laudatio* to the ceremony and its subsequent decadence, ending in the hope of a revival, the return of spontaneous, wide-eyed, grateful rejoicing in life's blessing's — the true origin and true primary content of all worship . . . .

Be that as it may [Dorati concludes] the Kennedy Center Opera House succeeded in presenting as its opening a truly original work — not only an original specimen but, as I see it, a species quite new in our age and times. For mystery plays have been missing from our stages for centuries. (Dorati, *Notes of Seven Decades*, London, 1979).

Conception, jumbled-up texts, stage action and an all-too-rich variety of musical means indeed provide much ground for criticism of this 'Theatre Piece for Singers, Players, and Dancers'. Yet it remains one of the boldest pieces of musical theatre as well as of liturgy-based compositions that have ever been written — and performed. *Mass* can well be understood as an antithesis to *Kaddish* — both works, tragical as is their prevailing mood, end on a note of hope and consolation: both the

Jewish doubter in *Kaddish* and the Christian heretic in *Mass* find their way back to faith, to belief, to God. As to the mixture of sacred and popular styles, it may be argued that both the church and the synagogue have from time immemorial tried to attract people to divine service by enlivening the traditional liturgy through the introduction of popular melodies. The ban by the church authorities in the earliest centuries of the Christian church of the singing of folk music at the service shows clearly that popular songs did find an entrance into the church; Martin Luther, on the other hand, provided for the Protestant church Christian choral texts to be sung to the popular melodies of the times. In American services negro spirituals have become a natural addition to traditional liturgical chant. In Germany Heinz Werner Zimmermann (born 1930) wrote church cantatas and a *Missa profana* (1973) in jazz style; in England Michael Tippett (born 1905) composed in 1939–41 the oratorio *A Child of our Time* using negro spirituals as chorales. In Leonard Bernstein's *Mass* rock and blues and their singers express a revolt against church ceremonies that have no meaning for the broad masses: 'If I could, I'd confess', sings the first Rock Singer, 'Good and loud, nice and slow, get this load off my chest. Yes, but how, Lord, I don't know. What I say — I don't feel, what I feel — I don't show. What I show — isn't real. What is real, Lord, I don't know. No, no, no . . . I don't know'. However, in the end, worshippers singing both in Latin and in Hebrew unite with the Celebrant and the people in singing 'Laudate Deum'.

'The first time *Mass* was performed for the public', remembers the producer Roger L. Stevens (in *Bernstein on Broadway*, New York, 1981)

was the most thrilling night I have ever spent in the theatre. The production lasted one hour and forty-five minutes. There was not a sound from the audience. At the end there were about three minutes of silence and none of us knew whether we had a failure or a hit on our hands; then everyone rose to their feet and cheered for one half hour. Needless to say, there was not an empty seat during the remaining performances. *Mass* has since thrilled audiences everywhere in the world and has become another Leonard Bernstein classic.

The world premiere has been recorded by CBS under the direction of the composer; in the theatre Maurice Peress had conducted the work. Alan Titus sang the part of the Celebrant. The Norman Scribner Choir and the Berkshire Boy Choir (with Jonathan Gram as soloist) were directed by Gordon Davidson. The choreography was by Alvin Ailey, settings were by Oliver Smith, costumes by Frank Thompson, and the entire production was in the hands of Roger L. Stevens, who had cooperated with Leonard Bernstein before in the productions of *Peter Pan* (1950) and *West Side Story* (1957).

The stage for *Mass* is described as 'a square of earth suggesting a small consecrated area'; 'a continuous path that originates in the pit rises as stairs' to this area, above which is 'a raised circular Altar space' and the path 'continues as stairs that ascend to a distant summit point'. The orchestra is divided into two parts: a pit orchestra of strings and percussion, plus a concert organ and a 'rock' organ and a stage orchestra of brass, woodwind, electric guitars and two electric keyboards. The stage instrumentalists are required to wear costumes and act as members of the cast. A sixty-member mixed choir in robes appears upstage in the course of the work, and there is a chorus of street people consisting of singers and dancers. The Celebrant is assisted in the ritual of the Mass by a complement of dancers in hooded robes playing Acolytes.

Mass opens in total darkness, while a quadraphonic tape is played, coming from four speakers placed in the four corners of the house. From the front speaker a high soprano coloratura voice is heard, accompanied by glockenspiel, xylophone and a small cymbal, singing 'Kyrie eleison'. The theme of this vocal solo contains the musical material for almost the entire composition; its opening note C is accompanied by the glockenspiel and xylophone unison playing 'marcato' a tiny motif of ascending minor third and descending major second that becomes the germ-cell of expanding motifs and themes in *Mass*; the ending phrase of the solo voice confirms this motif transposed a minor third higher. The germ motif of glockenspiel and xylophone is supplemented in the second and third bar by two ascending minor thirds, thereby forming a tritone succession as in so many of Bernstein's expressive musical passages. After a vocal and instrumental elaboration the soprano 'Kyrie' is followed by 'Kyrie eleison' sung by a solo bass and coming from the left rear speaker; the singing is accompanied by five timpani and a large cymbal. The theme is a melodious embellishment of the soprano 'Kyrie'. From the right rear speaker comes the singing of a second soprano and an alto solo, accompanied by vibraphone, four temple blocks and triangle: their 'Christe eleison' is also derived from the opening 'Kyrie'; as they sing together, the distance between their voices consists alternatingly of thirds and sevenths, later branching out into different intervals. The coloratura soprano and the bass enter their solo in contrapuntal fashion, returning to their 'Kyrie eleison'. The fourth speaker, left front, adds tenor solo and baritone with marimba and wood block; a new variant is heard to 'Christe eleison', and the other speakers, with their soloists singing and their instruments playing, are added in succession till a colourful counterpoint is achieved rising to a climax of forceful fortissimo. The four speakers are suddenly cut off and there is a quick fade to complete silence. The Celebrant is seen before the closed curtain, a young man in his mid-twenties, dressed in blue jeans and a simple shirt. 'He strikes a strong chord on his guitar' and it is this sound that has wiped out the sound from the quadraphonic tapes 'at the point of maximum confusion'.

The Celebrant sings a 'Hymn and Psalm': 'Sing God a simple song. Lauda, Laudë . . . God loves all simple things, for God is the simplest of all'. While the curtain rises, he continues with the words of the biblical Psalms, 'I will sing the Lord a new song' and 'I will lift up my eyes to the hills from whence comes my help'. A solo boy from the Boys' Choir enters and takes the Celebrant's guitar; two altar boys invest him with a simple robe. An expressive cadenza ('Lauda') of the Celebrant is interrupted by six solo voices, heard from tape, singing 'Dubing, dubang, dubong' pianissimo, 'precise and swinging' to jazzy accompaniment, slowly gaining in intensity and strength up to a fortissimo 'Alleluia' climax: omnipresent is the motivic germ-cell of the work. The 'responsory' ends, while the voices subside again to a pianissimo 'Dubing, dubang'. For part of the 'Kyrie' the composer used a short piece of music he had written in 1969 in honour of the centenary celebrations of the Metropolitan Museum of Art in New York; it was called *Shivaree* and orchestrated for two ensembles of brass and percussion. In 'Alleluia' he quotes a short Round for Mixed Chorus, entitled 'Warm-Up', composed for Abraham Kaplan and his Camerata in 1970. 'A Simple Song' is based on music Leonard Bernstein had started to write for Franco Zefirelli's film *Franciscus of Assisi* — the project which Bernstein abandoned (see page 82 above.) Some of the music conceived for this film was also used in the later 'Sanctus' of *Mass*.

With the Responsory 'Alleluia' concludes the first part of *Mass*, 'Devotions before Mass'; its three sections — Antiphon, Hymn and Psalm, and Responsory — contain already all the different trends and moods of the work apart from presenting the basic musical material of the composition. The following 'First Introit (Rondo)' consists of 'Prefatory Prayers' and 'Thrice-Triple Canon: Dominus Vobiscum'. When a 'Marching Street Band' opens this Rondo, a solo trumpet intoning the basic three-note germ-cell motif, the stage is suddenly flooded with people, lights and music, and a Street Chorus on-stage sings a new 'Kyrie' to the accompaniment of stark rhythmical and jazzy strains of military music. There is a hint of canonic singing even before the thrice-triple canon of the second section; two soprano soli

[213]

singing in thirds ('Emitte Lucem') anticipate the final march movement of the orchestral *Divertimento* of 1981. The Celebrant joins soloists
and chorus, the Boys' Choir enters, there is dance music, the boys play
kazoos and the entire Chorus shouts 'Alleluia' before the thrice-triple
canon opens, sung without instrumental accompaniment. It is interrupted by the Celebrant, reciting a prayer over the last fading phrases
of the canon, and a tape is then heard off-stage continuing the prayer
sung 'fast and primitive' by Boys and Men to the accompaniment of a
'small folk band'. This opens the Second Introit, consisting of the three
sections 'In Nomine Patris', 'Prayer for the Congregation' and 'Epiphany'. While the Celebrant and the singing from tape proceed,
Acolytes enter the altar space of the stage and the Choir fills the pews.
Instrumental development of their sophistically primitive music leads
over to another prayer recitation by the Celebrant and the Prayer for
the Congregation, sung in the D major of the 'Simple Song'. 'Epiphany' follows: an oboe solo heard from quadraphonic tape — 'sound
darting about from all four speakers'. The solo opens with the three-
note germ-cell motif; it is highly chromatic and expressive and elaborates elements from motifs and themes already familiar to the listener.

 The fourth part, 'Confession', contains the three sections 'Confiteor',
'Trope: I don't know', and 'Trope: Easy'. The 'Confiteor Deo omni-
potenti' of the chorus accompanied by the pit orchestra is preceded by
a prayer of confession, in English translation, recited by the Celebrant
speaking over the last notes of the oboe solo. The chorus sings in fully
harmonised twelve-voice division supported by the orchestra. Gradually the voices subside, the instrumental orchestration becomes scan-
tier, till pianissimo unison singing to percussion accompaniment. 'The
Celebrant blesses the relics of the Acolytes' and three guitars off-stage
and finger-snapping by tenors and basses create a 'swinging' atmosphere. After this intermezzo the full 'Confiteor' chorus comes up once
more and leads over to the first 'Trope'. This is the first 'rock solo',
played by rock band on stage and sung by the rock singer in 'heavy
blues' style, expressing the doubt of man in the honesty and effectiveness of confession in the traditional way. A high male voice joins the
rock singer at the end of his song. The second 'Trope' is opened by a
blues singer accompanied by a blues combo on the other side of the
stage: 'Well, I went to the holy man and I confessed . . . It's so easy
and you feel no pain'. A second rock singer continues and there follow
two more blues singers and another rock singer, all doubting and all
insecure. In stark contrast to the rock and blues scene the chorus enters
again, with verses from the traditional Confession while the Acolytes
enrich the Celebrant's robes with ecclesiastical ornaments. The first

blues singer is brought to confess pianissimo 'Confiteor', the Celebrant blesses him and asks the congregation to pray. There is a very short pause, then there follows as fifth part 'Meditation No. 1', for orchestra alone, standing here in place of a spoken or sung prayer.

This 'Meditation', later used by Leonard Bernstein for the first of his *Three Meditations for violoncello and orchestra* composed for Mstislav Rostropovich, is musically developed out of the three-note motivic germ-cell from the beginning of *Mass* and contains elements from the 'Kyrie' sections.

Part Six of *Mass* is a 'Gloria' in four sections: 'Gloria tibi', 'Gloria in Excelsis', 'Trope: Half of the People' and 'Trope: Thank you'. At the end of the 'Meditation', a group of boys had rushed up the stage and handed the Celebrant a set of bongo drums and he now opens the 'Gloria tibi' with 'joyous excitement, half-whispered', playing the three bongos. Boys' Choir and Celebrant intone 'Gloria Patri' antiphonally, with the basic theme appearing in repetition, in inversion and in transposition. At the climax the Celebrant embraces the Boys and shouts a prayer of praise. The full choir accompanied by the pit orchestra then sings 'Gloria in excelsis Deo' in unison; this is again in jazzy style, as is the following 'Trope' on a quatrain sent as a Christmas present to Bernstein by Paul Simon: 'Half of the people are stoned and the other half are waiting for the next election. Half the people are drowned and the other half are swimming in the wrong direction . . . . They call it Glorious Living . . .'. The swinging music, sung by the Street Chorus and played by the Stage Band, is the same as for the preceding section. While it goes on, the Acolytes place an elaborate stole on the Celebrant's shoulders. The 'Trope: Thank you' is sung by a solo soprano in quiet tones, to an chamber-orchestral accompaniment. The 'Thank you' is interrupted by the Street Chorus taking up pianissimo the first verse of the preceding Trope. The Celebrant again asks the congregation to pray and 'everybody quietly sits or kneels'. The prayer, as before, is clad in the musical form of an orchestral 'Meditation'.

This 'Meditation No. 2' takes the shape of a theme with four variations. The theme opens with a descending tritone followed by a chromatic sequence of notes, which in the first variation becomes a kind of *cantus firmus* and combines with a derived melodious theme to a twelve-note series. The second variation clusters the thematic notes to chords, the third lets them ascend in fortissimo union chords from the lowest registers to the highest, and the fourth again varies them melodically, pianissimo, in widely-spaced intervals. The 'Coda', quoting the 'Brüder' chords from the Finale of Beethoven's Ninth Symphony, accompanies the entrance of two altar boys; one bears 'an elaborate Bible', the other a censer. 'The Celebrant censes the book and kisses it' and then opens Part Eight: 'Epistle: The Word of the Lord', reading from the Book and preaching. A Young Man from the Street Chorus interrupts him 'as if reading': 'Dearly Beloved: Do not be surprised if the world hates you' and another young man also rebels. The Celebrant teaches them that 'you cannot imprison the Word of the Lord', for 'The Word was at the birth of the beginning'. This entire scene of doubting reproaches and the Celebrant answering confirming the Word of the Lord is dominated by the declamatory singing of the Celebrant inspired by synagogal liturgy and the plain-chant of the Latin church; the first instance of such cantillation in *Mass* was the four-voiced fortissimo choral singing of 'Gloria in excelsis'. The 'Epistle', in the music of which the 'Kyrie' motif appears in various guises, ends with the Celebrant closing the Book; immediately begins Part Nine: 'Gospel Sermon: God Said'.

The 'Gospel Sermon' is celebrated by a Preacher. He 'jumps on a bench, surrounded by his congregants' and reminds the people of how God created the world; he uses simple language comprehensible to the masses and the chorus answers him, repeating words and motivic sequences. Dance interludes are played between sentences till the climax is reached with the Preacher's 'And God saw it was good'. In the course of his sermon he has become 'a little less pious' and then 'always a bit nastier', and his 'God saw it was good' is followed by a very rhythmical and jazzy series of stanzas sung by doubting people: God has made the world and men to be good but everything has turned out bad, is the tenor of their complaints. 'With rising arrogance and delight', the Preacher sings antiphonally with the chorus 'God made us the boss, God gave us the cross, we turned it into a sword to spread the Word of the Lord, we use His holy decrees to do whatever we please'; the Chorus dance, 'drunk with power', but they are halted by the Celebrant 'who is now even more elaborately robed'. Upon seeing him, the Preacher again takes up a a pious attitude and continues 'God said: Let there be light!'. The scene ends, slowly fading out, subsiding to pianissimo sounds.

Part Ten: 'Credo' in five sections is in the greatest possible contrast to the preceding scene. The Celebrant declaims the Credo in English till he is interrupted by choir singing coming from a tape, accompanied by percussion instruments. The four-voiced choir sings in unison, in Latin, and is in turn interrupted by a male group of singers on-stage — accompanied by the rock band — while the Celebrant kneels. A solo baritone takes up the idea of 'Et homo factus est' — man has not become what he had been supposed to be, so 'how can anybody say *Credo?*' The final words are cut off by the quadraphonic tape and the continuation of the Credo is heard. In turn a mezzo-soprano solo interrupts the music from the tape, singing on stage: in her 'Trope: Hurry' she complains that God has promised to come again — 'When?', she asks, then implores: 'Hurry and come again!' The tape continues with the choir singing 'Sedet ad dexteram Patris', which is followed by the Street Chorus in an agitated mood. The mezzo-soprano enters again, in a restless and depressed mood; her melodic lines, like those of her previous solo, are characterised by alternating melody rises and falls but they conclude with desperate chromatic descending tones. Choir and soli take up words and syllables detached from their context in a confusing mood, singing louder and quicker, breaking suddenly off on 'Amen'. The 'Credo' ends with another 'Trope'. Three soli of the Street Chorus repeat 'Amen' fortissimo to the sounds of the Rock Band, introducing a solo rock singer singing piano: 'I believe in God, but does God believe in me?' He singles out any possible thing he may believe in, but does God react to his beliefs? 'Are you listening to this song I'm singing just for you?', he asks: 'I believe each note I sing, but is it getting through?' And there comes the F sharp that has been haunting Leonard Bernstein's thoughts and musical imagination since the earliest times of his having been a creative musician: 'I believe in F sharp, I believe in G', the rock singer continues,' but does it mean a thing to you or should I change my key?' The notes mentioned and the changes of key are naturally commented on by the melodic line and the harmonisation. 'Do you believe in anything that has to do with me?', the singer finally asks, 'who'll believe in me?' There is no answer to his question. The Celebrant is seen again, speaking 'Let us pray!', and there begins 'Meditation No. 3: De profundis, part 1'.

In contrast to the previous silent prayers composèd as orchestral meditations without voices, this third prayer interlude is sung by an eight-voiced choir, accompanied at first only by low-toned brass instruments and organ, then by a large variety of percussion players. The basses of the choir first intone the theme of 'De profundis clamavi', the other voices join contrapuntally until they all shout out 'clamavi' with the highest intensity possible. The stirring piece ends on a note of hope while four altar boys bring the Celebrant vessels for Communion: Monstrance, Chalice, Lavabo-basin, and Sanctus Bell.

The Celebrant opens Part Twelve of *Mass*: 'Offertory: De profundis, part 2'. The Boys' Choir files in carrying lighted votive candles. The Celebrant blesses the sacred objects and leaves the stage. Boys' Choir and general Choir sing 'Exspectat anima mea Dominum' in antiphonal setting, becoming ecstatic, clapping their hands in rhythm, and then the ensemble are drawn to the holy vessels and there starts 'a primitive and fetishistic dance' around the sacramental objects, always accelerating in tempo; it is abruptly stopped by the reappearance of the Celebrant in rich vestments and golden Cope. 'There is a frozen silence, during which the ensemble slowly backs off and exits.' The Celebrant remains alone on the stage. He goes to the piano, picks out a melody with one finger, searching it out, and sings along with it, as if improvising: 'Our Father, who art in Heaven'.

Part Thirteen of *Mass*, 'The Lord's Prayer', consists of the Celebrant's unaccompanied solo song, during which some choir boys and some instrumentalists come in and listen, and of another 'Trope' with the motto 'I Go On'. The Celebrant lets his 'Amen' follow with a meditative solo in which he reflects on what may happen if everything collapses and the spirit falters: 'I go on right then, I go on again', he maintains, and concludes in suppressed voice with a remembrance of the 'Lauda' from his 'Simple Song'. Two altar boys enter and assist him in the washing and drying of his hands. His 'Lauda' is commented upon by the instrumental sounding of an ascending minor second — here, as in *West Side Story* and other Bernstein works — indicating doubtfulness, questionability, anxiousness.

As he is finishing his singing, the Celebrant rings the Sanctus Bell loudly thrice, shouting 'Holy! Holy! Holy is the Lord!' This opens Part Fourteen: 'Sanctus', during which the Celebrant is preparing Communion. Two sections of the Boys' Choir alternate in singing a two-part 'Sanctus' in harmony in thirds; after the 'Osanna' the boys disperse and there begins a dance, at first in a mystical mood then gradually becoming more and more lyrical, more ecstatic. 'The Celebrant joyously receives his guitar from the Solo Choir-boy' and starts playing and singing. There is a word play with musical notes on 'mi' (= E) and 'me', and on 'sol' (= G) and 'soul': 'Me with soul Means a song is beginning' — with the notes E–G opening the melody — and the Celebrant then intensifies his singing, reaching the highest registers with the Hebrew word for Sanctus: 'Kadosh! Kadosh! Kadosh!' The ensemble gathers and brings imaginary gift-offerings to him. Each member kneels, places a gift and then stands, until the entire company has surrounded the Celebrant. He is no longer visible. The Choir sings 'Kadosh' in Hebrew, alternating with the praises in English translation. At the climax the crowd breaks apart, revealing the Altar, and intone 'Sanctus' again fortissimo, once in a descending and then in an ascending major second. The Celebrant hurries downstairs to the 'consecrated square'. He kneels and, as he grasps the Monstrance, he is interrupted by soloists of the Street Chorus singing 'Agnus Dei', accompanied by electronic instruments in the orchestra pit. 'Agnus Dei' forms Part Fifteen of *Mass*. It is sung in an agitated four-part harmony, first by the few soloists, then with more singers — and orchestral instruments — joining them, until singing and playing becomes rather wild. The Celebrant tries in vain to continue the consecration. His way to the Altar is barred by the Acolytes. The singing becomes dissonant, while the Celebrant appeals to the ensemble. The ensemble then underlines the word 'pacem' in 'Dona nobis pacem' in cut-off-syllable exclamations. The Celebrant weakens; in a desperate effort to regain control, he elevates the Monstrance above his head and with a last hoarse whisper utters: 'Let us pray!' Instantly the ensemble kneels and the choir sings 'Agnus Dei' again, this time in timidly soft voices — Andante misterioso — while the Celebrant moves to the Altar: 'Non sum dignus, Domine' ('I am not worthy, Lord'), he speaks. The choir rises in intensity and 'the stage becomes gradually disorganized. Musicians wander downstage, singers appear where instrumentalists should be, the Celebrant begins to climb the upstage staircase with increasing difficulty, stumbling as if under a great burden'. He elevates the holy vessels; the choir still exclaims 'Pacem!' When he reaches the summit he remains standing there motionless while the whole stage is increasing in disarray and turmoil. Suddenly the Celebrant is heard singing above a raging choir of eight voices: 'Pacem!' and the choir breaks off, leaving him on his high note. On his last note (which is 'that F sharp'!) 'he hurls the raised sacraments to the floor. The Chalice is shattered; the Monstrance is smashed. There is a stunned silence; and throughout the entire sequence no one moves except the Celebrant, who gradually moves down the stairs. Entire company falls to the ground'. There are noises of breaking glass. The Celebrant sings — 'catatonic' — 'Look . . . . Isn't that . . . odd . . .', he snaps fingers: 'Red wine isn't red at all . . . it's sort of . . . brown . . . brown . . . and blue . . .'. Ominous tritone intervals are heard, the Celebrant's singing rises to major sevenths.

The next Part, Sixteen, of *Mass*: 'Fraction: Things Get Broken' develops tragically and dramatically. The Celebrant asks the ensemble, 'What are you staring at? Haven't you ever seen an accident before?' and picks up a smashed fragment and smashes it again: 'How easily things get broken'. He becomes more and more confused, gets wilder and wilder, hits or kicks percussion instruments, smashes Altar candles, cradles the broken Monstrance, and at last 'lunges at the Altar with a cry, wreaks violence upon it, rips up the Altar cloths, waving them like streamers, and leaps up onto the Altar and dances on it like a madman'. Then he tears the vestments from his body, throws them to the crowd, runs about in mounting frenzy and despair, and then suddenly stammers unconnected words from the prayers, kneeling down, becoming again catatonic, sings for himself, clapping his hands 'like an idiot'. He sinks to the floor, fatigued, trembling, manages to get up again, descends the pit steps and disappears into the pit. The music fades out on two triads, dissonant in combination with their highest and lowest notes sounding a tritone interval. A sustained silence leads on to the following Part.

Part Seventeen: 'Pax: Communion (Secret Songs)' opens with a solo flute, playing on stage, taking up the expressive instrumental chant of the solo oboe from the end of the Second Introit ('Epiphany'). On its last fading melodic figure — the three-note germ-cell motif from the beginning of *Mass* — a boy soprano begins: 'Sing God a Secret Song — Lauda, Laudé', to the melody of the Celebrant's 'Simple Song' from Part One. The boy meets a grown-up man from the Street Chorus and the man joins him to sing 'Lauda, Laudé' in a misterioso soft voice. The boy and the man embrace and other voices are heard, more people come up and several chains of embraces are formed, which spread all over the stage. The 'Laudate' becomes both more intensive and stronger, as the orchestra is also gradually augmented; at the climax, the Celebrant is suddenly detected — he has reappeared unobtrusively, dressed simply as at the beginning of *Mass*. The entire ensemble whispers: 'Pax tecum'. A prayer for peace is sung, pianissimo, in the D major of the 'Simple Song'; the boys descend into the house, fill the aisles, 'bringing the touch of peace to the audience'. On the last pianissimo 'Amen' a voice is heard from tape, speaking, 'The Mass is ended; go in peace'.

Mass leaves listeners and analysts with conflicting feelings. It is undoubtedly a work of bold textual and musical conception, providing ample food for thought and meditation, and a work that cannot leave anyone unmoved. However, the mixture and actual confusion of styles, logical though they are from the point of view of the ideological background, are at times embarrassing and it is easy to understand how the charge of blasphemy has been levelled against *Mass*.

Here it may be interesting to compare the work with two compositions, already mentioned, which have faced similar criticisms. Michael Tippett wrote the words and music for his oratorio *A Child of our Time* in the middle of the Second World War, taking up a tragical occurrence in order to call for a humanitarian pacifism. In 1938, one year before the war broke out, a young Jew who had succeeded in fleeing from Nazi Germany shot a German diplomat in Paris because he had refused to sign the papers that were to enable his mother, who was still in Germany, to leave and join him legally. In the wake of this act of despair the Nazis took bloody revenge and intensified the persecution and murder of Jews: the 'Kristallnacht' of 9 November 1938 marked the beginning of most cruel and wide-spread pogroms. Michael Tippett's oratorio was inspired by this tragedy; the war aroused him, shattered him and strengthened his desire to create a work exposing the cruelty of strife and struggle. He replaced the traditional chorales of the classical oratorio by negro spirituals — the last of which was 'Deep River' — and throughout the work it is possible to feel his appeal for peace and humanism. The oratorio attracted much attention at the time and is still regarded as one of the composer's major works. However, as his quest for humanitarian pacifism led him to refuse war service, he was sentenced to three months' imprisonment in 1943. Twenty-three years later, in 1966, he was knighted for his services to music and is now Sir Michael Tippett.

Among recent compositions that attempt to approach religious texts and music from a novel point of view, Heinz Werner Zimmermann's *Missa profana* occupies a special position. After having composed a number of church cantatas for the Protestant Church in Germany, with the texts of biblical Psalms sung in jazz rhythms, in his *Missa profana* he juxtaposed four vocal soloists, a choir, a symphony orchestra and a jazz combo. For his text he took the five movements of the Latin Mass and an Introit. In the 'Kyrie' movement there originates — as the composer states in his own introductory notes — 'a dialogue between the choir and the vocal soloists (supported by the traditional orchestra) and a jazz ensemble. The jazz instruments formulate with their music a rather light-hearted world of naïve optimism'. Embedded in this Allegro movement is a latent Adagio — not at all gay or playful — intoned by the choir and the soloists. In contrast, the jazz instruments get a depressive phase of their own in the beginning of the 'Gloria'.

The slow introductory section is to depict the *blues feeling* of the *lonesome masses* in the big cities . . . . But in this movement there is also a sequence of contrast: the choir and the vocal soloists sing a bright 'Gloria in excelsis Deo', which brings the happy message of peace and goodwill . . . . Many attempts have been made to combine with each other jazz ensembles and symphony orchestra, but in most cases the heart of the jazz — the chorus improvisation — was a lamentable victim. On the other hand, where jazz improvisation was retained the composer usually sacrificed the ideal of genuine integration with symphonic music and this led to the musical result of simply changing from jazz to symphonic parts and vice versa.

So far Heinz Werner Zimmermann on his *Missa profana*, the first performance of which took place at Minneapolis, Minnesota, in 1982. It is obvious that Zimmermann's approach was quite similar to Leonard Bernstein's 'blasphemous' *Mass*, especially in his letting a jazz combo express the *'blues feeling* of the *lonesome masses* in the big cities' opposite the individualists, the soloists, accompanied by the traditional orchestra, and in his inclination to call for peace and goodwill. The *Missa profana* is a characteristic link in the chain of unconventional and novel religious compositions, in line with Igor Stravinsky's *Symphony of Psalms* and *Missa*, Michael Tippett's oratorio, Leonard Bernstein's *Kaddish* and *Mass*, as well as works by Olivier Messiaen, Dieter Schnebel, Krzysztof Penderecki and Frank Martin. Frank Martin had at one time planned to compose a *Requiem* using the traditional liturgical texts to the accompaniment of a jazz orchestra. He abandoned this idea; however, in his *Requiem* (1973) he used exciting jazz rhythms and instruments in the 'Dies irae' movement.

Shortly after the world premiere of *Mass* Leonard Bernstein wrote *Two Meditations from Mass* for orchestra; the instrumentation was for organ, piano, harp, percussion, and string orchestra. A year later he wrote *Meditation III from Mass*, for orchestra. He premiered this work with the ‑Israel Philharmonic Orchestra in Jerusalem on 21 May 1972, but later withdrew this version. All three *Meditations* were rewritten five years later (1977), being scored for violoncello solo and small orchestra, and dedicated to Mstislav Rostropovich, who played the world premiere with the composer conducting the National Symphony Orchestra at the Kennedy Center, Washington, DC, on 11 October 1977. Leonard Bernstein, in a personal note, thanked John Mauceri 'for his assistance in preparing this version for Cello and Orchestra'.

The *First Meditation* is an arrangement of the 'Meditation' played by the orchestra in *Mass* between 'Confessio' and 'Gloria'. The violoncello opens the quiet, serene piece with the main theme that is derived from the 'Kyrie' motif in *Mass*; it is possible to recognise G minor as the basic key. The solo, played in the highest registers of the instrument, is accompanied by strings, percussion and organ; the organ later takes up the theme and after a succession of chords in sevenths the soloist continues with a modal melodious phrase; this is followed by a recitative on the main motif, played fortissimo. After an expressive elaboration of the 'Kyrie' motif comes a repetition of the melodious modal phrase that is derived from it and the *Meditation* closes with yet another quotation of the 'Kyrie' motif, played very quietly.

The *Second Meditation* is derived from the orchestral 'Meditation' that in *Mass* is an interlude between 'Gloria' and 'Epistle', the theme with four variations and a coda. In the original orchestral version the theme was played by the lower string instruments and percussion and the violoncelli carry the first variation; in the new version the solo violoncello performs the theme pizzicato and in the first variation it 'sings' (cantando) the variation and the lower string instruments accompany the soloist with the exact notes of the theme — the violas in expanded notes, violoncelli and basses pizzicati. As in the original version, variation and theme 'cantus firmus' combine to form a twelve-note row. In the second variation the solo cello plays a passionate trill on a high note against sound clusters which the orchestra develops out of the notes of the basic theme. In the third variation soloist and orchestral instruments alternate in playing the ascending thematic passages and these reappear in the fourth variation in widely-spaced intervals, in slow movement and in a melodious mood; in the lowest register the soloist sounds an F sharp in pianissimo tone and in the second part of this variation participates in the melodious development. In the Coda Bernstein has soloist and organ play the pure A major triad and the orhestra cellos and basses add the tritone motif of the theme pizzicato. Underneath the A major triad Bernstein has written the word 'Brü-der' alluding to the ideal of brotherhood contained in the final movement of Beethoven's Ninth Symphony; the triad is repeated twice. After all the thematic variants from the preceding variations have been brought up again in low-voiced meditative recollection, this *Meditation* closes with a quotation of the ascending thematic passages from the third variation, played in unisono by the soloist and groups of violins and cellos — in thrice pianissimo, in contrast to the variation (and to the orchestral version in *Mass*) where these passages are marked by an expressive upswing.

The *Third Meditation* is not identical with 'Meditation No. 3', the 'De profundis', in *Mass*. This work for violoncello and small orchestra is opened by the soloist, accompanied by percussion instruments, with the music from 'Epiphany' in *Mass* where this music is played by solo oboe before 'Confessio' and by solo flute at the beginning of the final 'Pax: Communion'. This is expressive, low-voiced music, derived from the 'Kyrie' motif, and richly chromatic; the formation of its intervals also reminds the listener of the music in the 'Din-Torah' part in the *Kaddish* Symphony. It is played pianissimo but as fast as possible, and it ends with the 'Kyrie' motif, a long extended note to percussion accompaniment. This carries over to the second part of this *Meditation*, beginning 'fast and primitive', then gradually mounting in strength; the soloist plays the melody of the choir in *Mass* and the orchestra intones the 'folk music' accompaniment from the Second Introit in *Mass* ('In nomine Patris'). The solo cello then takes up the simplified prayer of blessings from the final part of *Mass*, alternating with the chromatic solo melody from the opening of this *Meditation*. The piece also ends very softly; the solo cello reminds us once more of the 'Kyrie ' motif and its long expanded sounds are accompanied by a small drum, playing pianissimo, very rhythmically, slowly fading out.

Between *Mass* and the music for the *Dybbuk* ballet (first performed by the New York City Ballet, choreographed by Jerome Robbins, on 16 May 1974, at Lincoln Center, the composer conducting), memorable events included Leonard Bernstein's 1,000th concert with the New York Philharmonic (on 15 December 1971), periods of conducting operas and concerts and the six Charles Eliot Norton Lectures at Harvard University (which opened on 9 November 1973), in the preparation of which Leonard Bernstein put to himself many decisive 'unanswered questions' and tried to solve problems of how, in our time, to explain — and himself to exploit — new ways and means, techniques and styles of musical composition. In his music for Jerome Robbins' interpretation of the Dybbuk legend — which, outside the Jewish world, has become known mainly through the drama by Shlomoh An-Sky and its world-wide performances by the Israel National Theatre 'Habimah' — the composer took up a classical Jewish theme ten years after the 'Kaddish' Symphony and incorporated into the score liturgical and folkloristic Hebrew motifs.

In Jewish legend, a dybbuk is the disembodied spirit of a deceased person that longs to enter into the body of a living being. In An-Sky's drama, Channon dies as punishment for his having tried to invoke the mystical powers of the forbidden Kabbalah, which he did in order to marry his beloved Leah, who has been promised by her father to another man. He now returns to Leah as a dybbuk and Leah, totally possessed by his spirit, speaks in his voice and uses his words. A rabbinical court is summoned in order to exorcise the dybbuk, but Channon does not set the possessed Leah free and in the final exorcism he takes her with him so that they can at least be united in death.

[224]

From the music to the ballet, Leonard Bernstein has arranged two orchestral suites. The *First Suite*, composed of six movements, was first performed by the New York Philharmonic on 3 April 1975; the *Second Suite* had its premiere in New York two years later, on 17 April 1977. Preceding these Suites, an initial version was entitled *Dybbuk Variations* and was first performed by the New York Philharmonic during a concert tour in Auckland, New Zealand, on 14 August 1974. This version was accompanied by pre-recorded tape.

The music is scored for a large orchestra with an unusually large complement of percussion instruments; the *First Suite* contains vocal soli which at the world premiere (and for the recording by Deutsche Grammophon) were sung by the tenor Paul Sperry and the bass baritone Bruce Fifer, while the *Second Suite* is only for orchestra. Leonard Bernstein has intimated that the two singers are meant to embody, at various stages, voices of the community of this world and the omnipresence of another, spiritual, world. The first vocal number in *Suite No. 1*, styled 'Invocation and Trance', is inspired by the ceremony performed at Jewish homes at the conclusion of the Shabbat, the separation of the profane (the ordinary day) from the Holy (the Holy Sabbath that has ended). The Jew finds himself at that moment between two worlds (and Jack Gottlieb, in his commentary on Bernstein's *Dybbuk* for Deutsche Grammophon, reminds us of the fact that An-Sky's Dybbuk drama had originally been called *Between Two Worlds*). The second vocal solo — 'The Pledge' — is based on the biblical oath of allegiance between David and Jonathan: 'Whatever thy soul desireth, I will do it for thee'. The third vocal solo — 'Kabbalah' — quotes 'The Song of Solomon' (IV: 1): 'Behold, thou art fair, my love . . .', and Leah's name is also sounded. The three movements with vocal soli are followed by an instrumental movement, 'Possession'. 'Pas de deux' is based on a canonic setting of part of the *Kaddish* text and the *First Suite* concludes with the music that in the ballet accompanies the Exorcism scene. Jack Gottlieb has described most poignantly the impact of this music: the hollow knocking on wood, heard at the start, introduces a solemn ritual, a sound universally associated with the invoking of transmigrated souls from the world beyond. A biblical text, an actual curse on incest, is followed by music incorporating traditional Hassidic folklore and a tune to a text imploring God to 'purify our hearts to serve you in truth', to which may be added 'Cast out the demons from within'.

Suite No. 2 opens with a movement entitled 'The Messengers'; it is followed by 'Leah' and by 'Five Kabbalah Variations'. The vocal 'Kabbalah' movement, which in the choreographed ballet is the final variation, appears in the orchestral *Suite No. 1*; the last movement of *Suite No. 2* is 'Dream'.

Leonard Bernstein himself sees in the dybbuk story an allegory on the duality of 'Good and Evil, Ends and Means, Male and Female, Justice and Necessity, Self and Society . . . and especially the duality of the so-called True World as opposed to *this* world in which we seem to reside'. He speaks of the 'poetry of earth', quoting Keats, thinking of the last of his Harvard lectures (see page 267), to which is juxtaposed the poetry of 'another world', the world of the spirit. Bernstein here speaks of the same struggling forces that occupied his mind and his musical thinking not only in *Age of Anxiety*, in *Kaddish*, and in *Mass*, but also, and no less even, in the 'Dream Sequence' in *West Side Story*. From the musical point of view this again results in the clash between tonality and non-tonality, in the eternal search for an answer to the 'unanswered question'. The 'poetry of earth' is linked in the *Dybbuk* music with the folkloristic strains from Jewish tradition. The mysterious 'other world' that dominates the *Second Suite* — but is interspersed with the 'earth-based' music in the ballet score — avoids tonal centres and is characterised also by more intricate rhythms. In these passages recur themes of a highly chromatic character, as in the dramatic parts of *Kaddish*, *Mass* and *West Side Story*; panchromatic motifs and themes of five, seven or twelve notes, and the intervals of the tritone, the seventh and the ninth underline the dramatic and mysterious character frequently. *Suite No. 1* ends with a tritone, repeated several times by the lower instruments of the orchestra. *Suite No. 2* concludes with a panchromatic chord. Thus both Suites end — as do so many of Leonard Bernstein's compositions — with an 'unanswered question'.

A recording of the entire ballet score performed by the baritone David Johnson, the bass John Ostendorf, and the New York City Ballet Orchestra conducted by the composer (Columbia M33082, MQ33082) seems to have been withdrawn.

No new compositions of note appeared for three years after the completion of the *Dybbuk* ballet. This was a time when Leonard Bernstein thought anew of a novel kind of musical theatre. In November 1975 a short-lived musical was premiered in New York; old friends Betty Comden and Adolph Green had produced a revue with the title *By Bernstein*, with musical numbers that the composer had written originally for *On the Town*, *Peter Pan*, *West Side Story*, *Wonderful Town* and *Candide*, but withdrawn, and songs planned for two musical plays that were never completed. A few months later, in February 1976, there opened *1600 Pennsylvania Avenue. A Musical About the Problems of House-keeping*, with a book and lyrics by Alan Jay Lerner, the successful author of *My Fair Lady*. Leonard Bernstein himself has explained why this show was destined to fail from the beginning — he had not been able to implement his own ideas (see pages 81–2, above). Some of the musical material from this ill-fated work he later used in the orchestral piece *Slava! A Political Overture*.

'Slava' is the name fondly given to the great musician Mstislav Rostropovich by colleagues and friends and Bernstein dedicated the Overture to him as a tribute on the occasion of his being appointed Musical Director of the National Symphony Orchestra of Washington, DC, in 1977. On 11 October 1977, on Leonard Bernstein's return from two festivals of his own compositions — in Israel and at the Carinthian Summer Festival in Austria — a festive concert at the J.F. Kennedy Center in Washington was conducted by both Rostropovich and Bernstein. It was an all-Bernstein programme with the world premieres of *Slava!*, the *Three Meditations from Mass* for violoncello and orchestra (with Rostropovich as soloist), and the song cycle *Songfest*. The Symphonic Suite *On the Waterfront* was also performed. The Overture is fashioned after the classical overture form: two themes (from the unsuccessful revue) are contrasted and combined with each other and generate a colourful portrait of the temperamental and gracious great virtuoso 'Slava'. In the Coda of the Overture, in which the voice of Slava's dog Pocks is also heard, trombones intone a theme from Modest Moussorgsky's *Boris Godounov* and the salutation from the crowning chorus of this opera is also sounded — 'Hail!' is 'Slava!' in Russian. During the Overture snatches from political speeches are blended in from tape and this adds to the dramatic character of this short orchestral piece, which lasts a mere four minutes.

Another short 'occasional piece' of these years is entitled *A Musical Toast*. It was written in 1980 in memory of the popular conductor André Kostelanetz. Leonard Bernstein was inspired to write it by an American party game, in which the rhythms of George Gershwin's song 'Fascinating Rhythm' are filled in with famous names. Thus, 'An-dré Ko-ste-la-netz' can be sung to it, and later the short piece was adapted as a toast to Sla-va Ro-stro-po-vich and to Ma-yor Ted-dy Kol-lek of Jerusalem.

Yet another occasional piece of music was *CBS Music*, commissioned by the CBS Network for its fiftieth anniversary. There are five movements: 'Fanfare and Titles', 'Quiet Music', 'Blues', 'Waltz', 'Chorale', and the piece was first performed in an orchestration by Sid Ramin and an arrangement by Jack Gottlieb on CBS-TV on 1 April 1978.

Songfest: score by Leonard Bernstein, choreography by John Neumeier, in performance at the Hamburgische Staatsoper

Leonard Bernstein gave up further plans in order to devote all his thought and creativity to the writing of a real opera, a sequel to *Trouble in Tahiti*, first planned with the title *Tahiti II*, ultimately called *A Quiet Place*. While this was very slowly germinating, he composed his vocal symphony *Songfest* and his only orchestral works that have neither a literary or spiritual point of departure nor are there vocal parts in them: *Divertimento* (1980), a joyful piece with a latently meditative background, and *Halil*, a thoughtful, serious and tragic Nocturne (1981). He also wrote his first piano piece for twenty-seven years, *Touches*.

Songfest is 'A Cycle of American Poems for Six Singers and Orchestra' and was composed during 1976 and 1977. The singers are a soprano, a mezzo-soprano, a contralto, a tenor, a baritone and a bass, accompanied by a large orchestra with keyboard instruments and much percussion. *Songfest*, dedicated to Bernstein's mother, was first performed in its entirety at Kennedy Center on 11 October 1977 (see page 233, below); individual songs had been performed on various occasions before.

The poems selected by Leonard Bernstein for *Songfest* represent a cross-section of American poetry through three centuries of American literary history. The earliest poem, No. 6 of the cycle, is by Anne Bradstreet, who died in 1672 at the age of about sixty. The other authors are Edgar Allan Poe, Walt Whitman, Gertrude Stein, Edna St. Vincent Millay, Conrad Aitken, e.e. cummings, Langston Hughes, Julia de Burgos, Lawrence Ferlinghetti, Gregory Corso, Frank O'Hara and — the youngest — June Jordan (born 1936). There are thirteen poets in all; in one of the twelve songs two poems are combined in a contrapuntal juxtaposition. The Puerto Rican poet Julia de Burgos was included in this American anthology as an American citizen; her poem was translated into English by Leonard Bernstein's elder daughter, Jamie.

The twelve songs are arranged in sequence following a principle of musical alternation and variety. The cycle opens and closes with a 'Hymn', both sung by the full sextet of singers. Baritone, soprano and bass (in that order) are assigned solo songs after the 'Opening Hymn'; mezzo-soprano, tenor and contralto sing solo before the 'Closing Hymn'. The central part of the work is a sextet and between the first three soli and this sextet are sung three songs for alternating ensembles: a duet for mezzo-soprano and baritone, a trio for the three female voices and a duet for soprano and bass.

[229]

As for the content of the poems, they treat many aspects of life and love, the women's liberation movement, race, poetry, art and music; the music attempts to represent in its own way the differences in poetic approach and style and in spiritual substance. The text for the 'Opening Hymn' comes from 'To the Poem' by Frank O'Hara (1926–66), in which the poet demands of a poem that it be unpretentious, 'small and unimportant and unAmerican' but human and real. The parody on the seemingly 'something grand' is reflected in an artful six-voiced polyphony in which syllabic accents of some of the words are paradostically musically misplaced, and where the poet writes that a 'military band' is not needed for 'the real right thing' Bernstein lets brass intruments blare out ironically. The second song, for baritone, is a setting for 'The Pennycandystore beyond the El' by Lawrence Ferlinghetti (born 1919), in which the narrator recalls how as a boy he had fallen in love 'with unreality' in the cheap candystore, where a young girl bewitched his senses, but 'outside the leaves were falling and they cried Too soon! Too soon!'. This is a jazzy Scherzo-like piece, sung and played 'lightly, like a quick, dark dream', developed out of a twelve-note row in which the interval of a minor seventh is prominent; it jumps upwards from G to G flat, which is none other that 'that F-sharp' which appears in so many of Leonard Bernstein's passages of an ominous significance. In 'A Julia de Burgos', the poet (1914–53) addresses her poem to herself: singing in Spanish, she describes in an agitated mood the conflicts of her life as a devout wife and a liberated woman poet: she feels like 'a runaway Rosinante, unbridled, sniffing out horizons of God's retribution'. The music, sung 'in suppressed rage' by a solo soprano follows the angry tone of the text; the rhythms change incessantly, short orchestral interludes interrupt the singing with sharp accentuation and the tonality also changes from one verse to the other.

The first sequence of vocal soli is concluded by the bassist with the poem 'To What You Said . . .' by Walt Whitman (1819–92); the five other voices sing a contrapuntal melody in unison. 'To What You Said . . .' is a posthumously discovered poem on the secret love of the poet for 'these young men that travel with me'. It is probable that not only the content of the poet's confession but especially the line 'I am that rough and simple person' inspired Leonard Bernstein to set the poem to music in an ostentiously simple melodious, rhythmical and harmonious style. The orchestra first plays an extended prelude in C major, only rarely tarnished by dissonant sounds, among them tritone digressions and a marked and disturbing F sharp. An ostinato low C accompanies the entire song from beginning to end. The bass opens with a variant of the melodious theme that the orchestra had played after opening with some mysteriously low-voiced chords; when the humming voices take up the melody in the sixth bar of his singing, he continues in melodic recitativic declamation — a device that enables the singer to make the text even more comprehensible than does pure song.

In the first of the *Three Ensembles* two aspects of America are confronted with each other in a duet (for mezzo-soprano and baritone): 'I, Too, Sing America' by Langston Hughes (1902–67) is the song of 'the darker brother' who has 'grown strong'; 'Okay "Negroes"' by June Jordan (born 1936) is satirical and ironical: 'In the nursery of freedomland the rides are rough . . . you think who's gonna give you something?' In textual and musical irony the mezzo-soprano voice contradicts the optimism of the proud newcomer. The music of the short duet is rather complex; the baritone's part is highly chromatic and melodically expressive while June Jordan's counterpoint is composed in simpler tunefulness and takes on the style of a scherzo. At times snatches from the baritone part also appear in the melody lines of the mezzo-soprano. There is a short and turbulent interlude, after which both singers return once more to their arguments.

The next ensemble piece is the Trio of female voices on the poem 'To My Dear and Loving Husband' by Anne Bradstreet (ca 1612–72) who here sings in praise of conjugal love. Leonard Bernstein said about his way of setting this poem to music that he chose a female trio in order to achieve the effect of somehow depersonalising the sentimentality of the poet's feeling. The song opens with a canon of the three voices in D flat major, which modulates to C major in a middle section. Though there is chromaticism in the melodic theme, it is accompanied by harmonies that tend always towards a tonal centre. The melodious upswing of the voices at the climax and end of the song leads to a chord composed of major seconds: F–E flat–D flat.

The last of the *Three Ensembles* is 'Storyette H.M.', on a poem by Gertrude Stein (1874–1946), composed as a duet for soprano and bass. Gertrude Stein, the writer who used a style of language new in American literature, met the painter Henri Matisse in Paris and the letters 'H.M.' most probably signify the initials of his name. After the preceding song in praise of affectionate marital love, the 'storyette' tells of impossible marriages. Soprano and bass alternate in telling the little story, their musical motifs respond to each other and complement each other, while the narrative rhythm and the orchestral accompaniment move in perpetual motion.

As an intermezzo, there follows a Sextet on the poem 'if you can't eat you got to' by e.e. cummings (1894–1962). Bernstein's setting is based on a choral piece *A Little Norton Lecture* which he wrote in 1973 for a twelve-man choir at Harvard; it was premiered there the same year by 'The Crocodillos'. In *Songfest* the five lower voices sing in the fast rhythmical 'swing' style of the 1920s and 1930s while the soprano varies the musical theme of the song in expressive melodious interpretation in the high registers of her voice. The Sextet fades out pianissimo on a B minor chord with the added tritone C sharp–G below.

The three following solo songs are set to poems by Conrad Aiken (1889–1973), Gregory Corso (born 1930) and Edna St. Vincent Millay (1892–1950). In 'Music I Heard With You', the poet remembers the woman he loved and who has gone forever. In 'Zizi's Lament' the poet regrets that he is not given the talent of 'laughing sickness' after having had all possible experiences with men and women in exotic lands. Lost love is once again the theme, in 'What Lips My Lips Have Kissed'. The three songs follow the expression of the particular poem, each in its own style. 'Music I Heard With You' is a romantic *Lied* for mezzo-soprano, in which a lyrical A major main part is followed by a panchromatic middle section; A major then returns interspersed with recollections of the panchromatism. 'Zizi's Lament' is a grotesque song for tenor with dance-like elements hinting at exotic entertainment. 'What Lips My Lips Have Kissed', as the final solo song of the second series, corresponds to the last solo in the first set of solo songs (the Walt Whitman poem); both are by far the most extended compositions of the entire cycle — each taking about five and a half minutes in performance. The sonnet by Edna St. Vincent Millay is haunted by the memory of forgotten loves; it is sung by the contralto and represents perhaps the most sensual and most expressive song in *Songfest*; the composer once told the present author that this is the piece he himself likes best in his work. It opens with one of his favourite devices in the creation of motifs and themes: an expressively ascending four-note motif encompassing a major seventh is followed by an expansion of the motif leading to a minor-seventh chord. After this orchestral introduction the singer takes up the intervals and motifs, becoming more and more expressively intense as the song continues.

The 'Closing Hymn' of *Songfest* is the Sextet 'Israfel' on the poem by Edgar Allan Poe (1809–49). The poet quotes a *Sure* from the Muslim Koran in which the angel Israfel 'sings wildly . . . and the giddy stars (so legends tell), ceasing their hymns, attend the spell of his voice, all mute'. The heart-strings of the angel are a lute and he 'despises an unimpassioned song', 'If I could dwell where Israfel hath dwelt, and he where I, he might not sing so wildly well a mortal melody, while a bolder note than this might swell from my lyre within the sky'. Leonard

Bernstein's music opens with the six voices singing in unison in the rhythm of a 'strong waltz, with passion' to the accompaniment of arpeggio chords symbolising the sounds of the lyre; out of a short motif develop passionate melodic lines; the voices separate, singing in groups, and take up parts of the theme. The Sextet is full of virtuoso swing; at its climax the theme is elaborated by the baritone then, after a short orchestral interlude, repeated by the other singers. There follows a contralto solo passage after which the entire ensemble leads the 'Closing Hymn' to an impassioned 'finale' in the C major tonality of both the opening poem and the Walt Whitman song.

Clamma Dale, Rosalind Elias, Nancy Williams, Neil Rosenshein, John Reardon and Donald Gramm were the singers in the first performance of *Songfest* in Washington, which was under the direction of the composer; they also performed the work in European cities and recorded it for Deutsche Grammophon. 'To My Dear And Loving Husband', the Trio which the composer dedicated to Rosalynn Carter, was recorded during the performance given on 19 January 1977, at the Jimmy Carter Inaugural Gala, by Benita Valente, Nancy Williams, Elaine Bonazzi and the National Symphony Orchestra conducted by the composer.

Starting on 27 August and finishing some time in October 1980 Leonard Bernstein composed the eight movements of his *Divertimento for Orchestra*, one of the most sprightly original works of contemporary music, a light-hearted, truly 'diverting' piece of musical entertainment coupled with ingenious musical craftsmanship — the casual listener can hardly notice how artfully, how cunningly this *Divertimento* is devised. The composition is dedicated to the Centenary of the Boston Symphony Orchestra, with which the composer has worked since his early conducting days, and each of the eight short movements is developed out of the two-note motif B–C symbolising both the dedicatee and the occasion — the *B*oston (Symphony's) *C*entenary. The work is as full of humour, latent puns, allusions and wit as the legendary figure of Till Eulenspiegel, that adventurous prankster, and indeed the opening Fanfare, 'Sennets and Tuckets', which sets the tone and provides the main theme of the entire *Divertimento*, reminds the listener of the French horn solo at the beginning of Richard Strauss's eponymous tone-poem. The Fanfare theme is composed of Leonard Bernstein's favourite intervals: minor third–fourth–augmented second–minor second — the last interval step, markedly accented, is the dedicatory B–C motif and from the opening lower C to the higher B the interval is a typical Bernstein major seventh. The theme is repeated immediately and led to a higher register with a variant of the intervals. The first movement of the work develops with playful turns of the basic motif upwards and downwards and of the fanfare theme.

This first movement is entitled 'Sennets and Tuckets' after the signals and fanfares mentioned in Elizabethan literature: 'Then let the trumpets sound/the tucket sonance and the note to mount' wrote William Shakespeare in *Henry V* (IV, 2), and the terms are also found in the works of his contemporaries Christopher Marlowe and John Marston, among others; the word 'sennet' is derived from 'signet' = signal. The *Till Eulenspiegel*-like theme is only the first of a series of musical memories Leonard Bernstein seems to cherish and wishes to share with his listeners. The second movement is a Waltz in the unusual metre of 7/8; it is for strings alone and has a romantic G major melody that circles around the B–C interval. The next movement, Mazurka, is for double reeds and harp; the B–C motif begins a lilting C minor tune: it appears in descending steps C-B in the melody and the ascending B–C in the counterpoint. The Mazurka, in 3/4 time, ends with a short oboe solo and a recollection of its beginning with the descending motif C–B–G.

After these two movements so reminiscent of classical dance models, there follow two pieces in the rhythms of more modern times: the Samba and the Turkey Trot. 'Samba', in gay and vivid 4/4 metre, opens with a three-times-sounded quotation of the Fanfare theme, out of which develops a longer extended theme; memories of *Fancy Free* seem to surface during the movement. The irresistibly delightful 'Turkey Trot', an Allegretto in C major, alternates three- and four-beat rhythms. Its swinging tune contains the descending form of the germ-motif — C–B — which is already hinted at in the rhythmically complex introduction; in a G major middle section the woodwind instruments play around with the 'Turkey Trot' melody in inverted intervals. After a surprise effect — 'silenzio' — the amusing piece comes to an end.

In starkest possible contrast to this humorous dance piece comes a short movement in doleful mood — 'adagio lugubre, 3/4'. It is named 'Sphinxes' and consists of a five-bar ascending twelve-note melody on the Fanfare theme and its repetition one note lower, each time with an incongruous diatonic cadence; the first time the melody is played by string instruments and after a one-bar pause is repeated by the woodwind. For Bernstein this is, musically, a central part of the work: 'Why are they Sphinxes? — for me this is a deep joke', he said in our discussion of *Divertimento* in April 1982:

I'm laughing at the Sphinxes. But nobody else gets the joke. I take the basic motive of the *Divertimento* which everything is based on and from this I make a *Tonreihe*, two tone-rows, and the first row ends with a dominant cadence, and the second one ends with a tonic. That's the joke. You make these tone-rows out of the basic motive and in the end you have to make dominant and tonic. The question — *I* find it very funny!

Leonard Bernstein here returns, of course, to that 'unanswered question' — the conflict between non-tonality and tonality which will again come up in the later orchestral composition *Halil*.

Between the five-bar tone-rows there is a bar of complete silence but after the second row comes 'Blues' without a break. It is played in a slow blues tempo, scored for brass with jazz mutes, the C–B motif creating again a twelve-note melody; a solo tuba is heard accompanied by trumpets and vibraphone, trombones take up its theme and a solo trumpet intones the opening blues melody once more, pianissimo.

The final movement, 'The BSO Forever' (referring to the name of the best known Sousa march), opens with an elegiac canon for three solo flutes on an extended version of the B–C motif — this is an 'In memoriam' for beloved Boston musicians. Then follows the heavily orchestrated March (in which the 'Radetzky March' is fondly recalled and there is a reminiscence of marching strains from *Mass*), with two Trios and Coda. The motif with the second-interval and the full Fanfare theme dominate all parts of this rousing Finale; in the Coda the Fanfare theme is combined with themes from other movements of the *Divertimento* and provides an exciting conclusion to this colourful and diverse work with its manifold reminiscences of the composer's music for Broadway and the concert hall and of music that he has conducted during his long career and that he cherishes most.

A short time before *Divertimento* Leonard Bernstein had written *Touches, Chorale, Eight Variations, and Coda*, dedicated 'to my first love, the keyboard' — since the third series of *Anniversaries (Five Anniversaries,* 1954) he had not composed any music for the piano alone. *Touches* was written for the Sixth Van Cliburn International Piano Competition at Forth Worth, Texas, and completed at Fairfield, Connecticut, in July 1980. Keeping the object of the work in mind, the composer has incorporated every possible demand of intelligent and expressive performance, technical proficiency, unconventional virtuosity and insight into the working of a contemporary creative mind.

The theme of the variations, a 'Chorale' played slowly, with much rubato, 'with a *blues* feel', without bar-line accentuation, opens with an expressive ascending melody representing a tone-row of ten out of the twelve chromatic notes of the octave, the first interval being an ascending major seventh, a dominating interval throughout the piece. The melodic upswing subsides, ending a fourth above the opening note; the left hand provides a background with chords of two minor sevenths. The use of the pedal produces a sound reminiscent of an organ. A second expanded statement of the theme adds notes so that the twelve-note is completed. The melodic phrase is then repeated and varied three more times until the original form from the opening ends the 'Chorale' on F sharp on a long 'fermata'. The first variation is played fast and 'with elegance', it follows the notes of the thematic tone-row which appear melodically as well as combined in chords. The cadence figure, twice repeated, F–F sharp–A leads over, enharmonically changed into F–G flat–A, into the second variation, in which notes from various passages of the theme are continued into new melodic sequences and chords. At the end of this variation two runs of notes through one octave remind the listener of the seventh interval in the original theme, as do two four-note chords in the bass. The third variation is dominated by intervals of seconds and fifths from the original theme; a sprightly sequence is directed to be played 'on top of the keys'. The concluding chord of this variation is composed of the minor second D sharp–E, with the E underlined through octave doubling. This minor second opens the fourth variation melodically; short snatches of thematic motifs are put against triads in a minor tonality. The variation ends with a thematic Scherzando developed in two-part counterpoint and a variant Coda of full chords. The Scherzando theme leads over to the quiet fifth variation, a slowly-played contrapuntal piece that varies and elaborates the Chorale theme. Against this meditative contrapuntal variation Bernstein sets the somewhat faster sixth variation in which two-voiced chords in the right hand move 'legato' in 12/8 time while the left hand plays melodically, 'staccato ed un poco pesante', in 4/4 time. The seventh variation, played very fast in virtuoso octave chords, is based on figures from the third variation. The eighth variation is a variant of the first; it ends with the thematic ascending major seventh that also becomes the foundation for the Coda in which melodic formations and chords are dominated by sevenths. This Coda is very fully orchestrated with the pedal used throughout so that the illusion of a Chorale becomes even stronger than in the opening presentation of the theme. At the conclusion of the work — which lasts about nine minutes in performance — there is a return of the thematic cadence that ended the opening

'Chorale'; the movement slows down, the cadence is played softly — 'intimo, dolce' — and its last chord is a fifth with F sharp as the highest note and a chord of a seventh sounded in the bass.

In a foreword Leonard Bernstein has explained the meaning of the title, which may be pronounced either in the English or the French way:

TOUCHES = (French) the keys of the keyboard
= different 'feels' of the fingers, hands and arms: deep, light, percussive, gliding, floating, prolonged, caressing . . .
= small bits (cf. 'a *touch* of garlic'); each variation is a *soupçon*, lasting from 20–100 seconds apiece.
= vignettes of discrete emotions: brief musical manifestation of being 'touched', or moved.
= gestures of love, especially between composer and performer, performer and listener . . . .

Touches was published in 1981 by Jalni Publications, with Boosey and Hawkes as the sole selling agent.

Halil. Nocturne for Solo Flute, String Orchestra, and Percussion, was completed in score on 13 April 1981; on 27 May the composer conducted the premiere in Tel Aviv with Jean-Pierre Rampal and the Israel Philharmonic Orchestra. This final composition before the opera is without doubt one of the most personally engaged of Leonard Bernstein's works. Its origins lie in the impact made on Bernstein by the fate of a young and talented Israeli flautist who was killed in his tank on the banks of the Suez Canal during the 1973 Israeli war of defence: 'I never knew Yadin Tanenbaum, but I know his spirit', confessed Leonard Bernstein. '*Halil* (the Hebrew word for flute) is formally unlike any other work I have written, but is like much of my music in its struggle between tonal and non-tonal forces. In this case I sense that struggle as involving wars and the threats of wars, the overwhelming desire to live, and the consolations of art, love, and the hope for peace. It is a kind of night-music which, from its opening twelve-tone row to its ambiguously diatonic final cadence, is an ongoing conflict of nocturnal images — wish-dreams, nightmares, repose, sleeplessness, night-terrors — and sleep itself, *Death's twin brother . . .*'.

At the time that we discussed the 'Sphinxes' in *Divertimento*, we also talked about the musical conflicts apparent in the *Halil* score: 'It is musically like an *essay*, a *study* on the struggle between tonality and non-tonality', Bernstein said, 'almost like a Ph.D. dissertation. The question of the "Sphinxes" is exactly the same: tonal or not tonal, what is the solution?'

As in so many of his compositions, Leonard Bernstein bases his music for *Halil* on the juxtaposition of twelve-tone rows that show leanings towards tonality with tonal cadences. Lyrical and dramatic elements amalgamate in the unmistakable individual Bernstein way and are supported by a colourful orchestration with the body of strings and the percussion group alternating in dominance. The entire work is shaped by the expressive opening twelve-tone flute melody; this consists of four cells: a motif containing four notes — a descending minor third and minor sixth (making up a seventh) and an ascending minor third; a figure of three notes — descending major second and fifth — and its repetition a semitone lower; and a two-note falling conclusion — a cadence of a minor seventh. A minor seventh also marks the distance between the first note of the twelve-tone row and its last. Following repetitions of the entire theme in retrograde and then its original form, the music develops as a continuous variation of the basic motifs. It remains lyrical until giving way to an outburst of strings and percussion against which the flute enters in singing fashion. 'Shrieking' and 'crude' episodes follow before lyricism again holds sway, with the solo part marked 'childlike' in places. After another dramatic climax *Halil* ends in moving tranquillity, with the 'ambiguously diatonic' D flat final cadence.

Leonard Bernstein dedicated *Halil* 'To the Spirit of Yadin, and to his fallen Brothers'. Yadin's bereaved parents were present at the Tel Aviv premiere.

The real opera Leonard Bernstein had long wanted to write finally began to take shape when the composer met the young writer Stephen Zinsser Wadsworth (born 1953) in 1980. Bernstein's short opera *Trouble in Tahiti* (1952) had been based on the composer's own libretto; he had long been thinking of a sequel to be called *Tahiti II*, showing the characters thirty years later, but he felt that this time the book should be written by a professional librettist. By Christmas 1980 a preliminary scenario was ready but it took several more months for Wadsworth and Bernstein to arrange more frequent meetings and to begin to make progress. A year later work on the opera became serious and a deadline for its completion was set by a triple commission received by the writers: from the Houston Grand Opera for a premiere in June 1983; from the J.F. Kennedy Center in Washington, DC, for performance in the autumn of the same year; and from the Teatro alla Scala of Milan

Leonard Bernstein and the librettist Stephen Wadsworth at work on *A Quiet Place*

for the 1983/4 season. Author and composer worked feverishly on the opera, mainly at Leonard Bernstein's house at Fairfield, Connecticut, and last touches and changes were being made even when rehearsals at Houston were already in progress. Quoting a line from *Trouble in Tahiti*, the new opera was named *A Quiet Place*. The world premiere took place on 17 June 1983 at the Jones Hall for the Performing Arts in Houston, Texas, and was presented by the Houston Grand Opera. A festive audience applauded it but the work was received with mixed feelings by professionals. *Trouble in Tahiti* was performed during the first part of the evening. Both operas were directed by Peter Mark Schiflter and conducted by John DeMain.

The scene of *A Quiet Place* is the 'Suburbia, USA' of *Trouble in Tahiti*; the time is 'now', that is to say, thirty-one years later. Dinah, the unhappy wife of Sam who thought himself 'a born winner' in sport, business and in life, has died in an automobile crash that may have been intentional. The first of the four scenes of the opera is set in the funeral parlour where the family and friends come to meet. Sam and Dinah's children, forty-year-old Junior (as he was called in the earlier work) and thirty-year-old Dede, have come over from Canada. Junior, homosexual, aggressive, psychotic, has had an affair there with François, a French Canadian who is now married to Junior's sister, Dede. While Sam is standing motionless in a corner of the room, guests and mourners are arriving: Dinah's brother Bill, her friend Susie, the family doctor and his wife and the psychiatrist to whom (in *Trouble in Tahiti*) Dinah had related her dream of struggling to find a way out of a dying garden when she heard a voice promising her that love would lead her to 'a quiet place'. The macabre scene at the funeral parlour leads to a ceremony of reminiscences and of readings from the Bible and from poetry. But when the guests depart and Sam is left alone with his children and son-in-law, he explodes in grief and anger, singing an aria which gives vent to his feelings that thirty years of his life were nothing but disappointment and he comes to blows with his psychotic son.

An Orchestral Interlude links Scenes One and Two (the opera is performed without an interval). Sam, alone in the master bedroom of his house in the evening, has found a letter left by Dinah — but one never learns what the letter really contained. Dede comes in and tries on one of Dinah's dresses; another row looms. François rebukes Junior for his behaviour at the funeral parlour and this in turn provokes yet another psychotic reaction of visions of incest and abnormal eroticism which reveals Junior's need of his father. Dede and François are deeply shattered by all that happens but find comfort in their love.

A Quiet Place, Scene 3, with Timothy Nolen as Junior and Sheri Greenawald as Dede, during the Houston Grand Opera world premiere, Houston, June 1983

In a vocal Interlude in this first version of the opera Dinah's brother Bill and the Doctor's wife are seen meeting somewhere in town and exchanging feelings about Dinah.

In Scene Three it is the following morning and Dede addresses her mother while weeding the now overgrown garden that Dinah had planted. Junior appears for breakfast and brother and sister re-enact their parents' quarrelsome breakfasts, as they were recorded in the first scene of *Trouble in Tahiti*. François joins them in Trio; when Sam and some neighbours come into the garden there seems to develop a happier atmosphere. The doctor's wife even succeeds in creating a gay mood and the scene ends in relieving laughter.

An Orchestral Interlude leads into the fourth and final scene. The party has broken up and Sam and his children look forward to a few days of being together. But it needs only a disagreement on some small matter and they start arguing bitterly, divided once again by all their temperamental differences. At last François forces the family to realise that Dinah's death should teach them the importance of mutual understanding. Real communication, however, necessary as it is, is not so easy to achieve — more is needed than the superficial glamour advertised by the jazz trio in *Trouble in Tahiti*.

The libretto for *A Quiet Place* can hardly be called entertaining nor are the figures really interesting. Ann Holmes, Fine Arts Editor of the *Houston Chronicle*, was right in saying in her review of the world premiere (published 19 June 1983) that the 'inner psychological land-scape on which these misbegotten souls try to reclaim themselves and their relationships' makes the libretto 'so complex and convoluted and so delicate an emotional fabric that it lacks the very simplicity and boldness and decisive character motivations that make the ideal opera libretto'. One might add that the characters on stage, with their superficiality, their perversities and idiosyncrasies, their agonies, quar-relsomeness and lack of understanding for each other evoke no real sympathy in the audience and the composer, though affectionately trying to bring the figures to individual life, seems to have not been very much at ease with them either. The characters in this opera are in fact only superficially complicated; the music is intrinsically much more complex and revealing. This is a remarkable score on many points; however, while Leonard Bernstein appears to have been en-thusiastic about the libretto and took the family troubles very seriously — in stark contrast to their ironical treatment in *Trouble in Tahiti* — the score lacks the depth of his other compositions inspired by religious or literary subjects. Characteristically it rises to heights where religious texts are quoted and when a Chorale — most expressive in its apparent

From the manuscript score of *A Quiet Place*

simplicity — is sung in the funeral parlour scene: 'God has His ways, Who are we to judge?', sings the ensemble and the theme of the Chorale is derived from a previous passage in the dialogues, 'Dinah was kind', a line that also returns in the Chorale. Great effect is made by the Prologue to the first scene, when chorus voices are heard from off-stage giving a cataclysmic impression of Dinah's automobile crash in discordant contrapoint.

Some motifs and musical ideas in *A Quiet Place* can be traced to *Trouble in Tahiti*, especially in the garden scene, where Dede's music underlines her spiritual and musical nearness to her mother. Conflicts between tonality and panchromatism pervade the Bernstein score as they do in all of his mature works. Leonard Bernstein's setting remains masterly, even the shallowest phrases are set to music that carries some conviction; his melodic lines are so carved as to permit singers to pronounce both clearly and intelligibly.

Lukas Foss, who attended a workshop two months before the Houston premiere, when some of the music was rehearsed and performed 'and everybody was moved to tears' (Lenny Bernstein told me on the telephone), wrote in a letter (7 April 1983) on the parts he heard there: 'Once again I am struck by the way Lenny plunges into a new project making it totally his own, mixing pop and operatic elements and it turns out Bernstein. Original is the virtouosic way he handles the setting of the English language. Don't know anything quite like it'.

Looking back at Leonard Bernstein's works from the earliest juvenilia down to *A Quiet Place* — a span of more than forty-five years — one may remark a tendency that is common in the life's work of quite a few composers, especially in the latter half of the twentieth century. Bernstein has during his long development as a creative musician always tended towards borrowing in a new work from earlier — even once discarded — works and he also used complete pieces in new contexts. He has perhaps more than most composers engaged in an incessant struggle with problems of composition — its forms and styles, tonality versus free or completely abandoned tonality, lyric quality against dramatic force, blues and jazz opposite symphonic thinking in both instrumental music and operetta and opera. Some of his large-scale compositions were analysed by him and reconsidered long after their completion and after having been widely performed and 'final versions' were then prepared, published, and performed — not without being scrutinised and altered later again. It is hard to establish whether dormant insecurity or developed maturity is the reason for his frequent reverting to earlier music of his; he had never lacked in inventive imagination. In *A Quiet Place* the references to the early short opera *Trouble in Tahiti* and the borrowings from its score are somehow logical because of the intentional links between the characters in the two works. Yet in the light of the experience of the first performances and the critical reaction — regarded as justified by author and composer — *A Quiet Place* was not left in its original form but regarded by Leonard Bernstein — as compositions have lately been seen rather frequently — as a 'work in progress'.

'We are trying out a new format', Leonard Bernstein told me when he was in Salzburg in January 1984 to conduct the Vienna Philharmonic prior to a US tour: 'Whether it is going to work, I don't know but we'll know in Milan in June and in Washington in July. *Trouble in Tahiti* will remain as it is. It will be cut into two parts (instead of serving as a Prelude). There will be lots of cuts in the Third (new) Act and some rewriting of the score' — on which the composer worked in March 1984 after the concert tour. Details of the textual changes and the reasons for them were explained to us in a letter of the author, Stephen Wadsworth, dated 28 December 1983:

> We have decided — with the encouragement of John Mauceri, who will conduct the piece in Milan and Washington — to make a substantial structural change in the evening that features *Trouble in Tahiti* and *A Quiet Place*; we are going to play them interlaced at La Scala and the Kennedy Center. The order of the three-act evening is planned as follows:
>
> Act I: *A Quiet Place* —
>   Prelude
>   Scene 1 and Interlude 1
>   Scene 2 opening (rewritten)
>   *Trouble in Tahiti* — opening through 'Rain Duet'
> Act II: *A Quiet Place* — Scene 2 finish
>   *Trouble in Tahiti* — finish
> Act III: *A Quiet Place* — Scenes 3 and 4, much cut and combined.
>
> We have decided to try this configuration of the two operas to acquaint the audience better with the deep textual and musical relationship between them, also to relieve the audience of the burden of a two-hour sit through *A Quiet Place* and to provide a more convincing dramaturgy for this peculiar combination of operas. Many of the things that didn't work dramatically and perhaps musically (in the original form) are being cut or altered. Of course, everyone has different — and strong — feelings about what did and didn't work, which is all rather confusing, and there were certainly a number of clear reasons *why* whatever didn't work didn't work : a poor director (or better I should say a director ill-suited to the operas), a hall in which

everything had to be amplified and rehearsals that were therefore occupied in sound-balancing rather than in rehearsing, and also the design . . . . We certainly had a sensational cast of singing actors, but they received no direction.

At the time of writing his letter, Stephen Wadsworth admitted he was not sure yet — nor was the composer — to what extent the alterations would amount, and 'whatever changes we try can be retracted or changed back if we prefer'. As Wadsworth was engaged to direct the staging of the opera both in Milan and in Washington — he has studied both acting and stage-directing himself — , he saw the dramaturgically revised opera before his eyes already from the viewpoint of its staging. As an interesting sidelight Stephen Wadsworth points in his letter to his composer's 'surprising, chronical distrust of his instincts — surprising for a man of such original and truly great notions . . . . But then, we both are that, as we try to make a really new, fresh step in American musical-theater language. It isn't easy to know what the next step should be if no one has taken it before you'.

Lenny Bernstein added some points of his own in our Salzburg conversation:

One of the problems with the opera is that it is more important than ever to understand the words all the time because one of the things it is about — there are many things — one of the things is the American language, the way *we* speak, which I don't believe has ever been set that way before — it's not the same as the English in Benjamin Britten's operas, he makes the English language sound wonderful but it is British English . . . .

I tried to set the language to a kind of music that goes with it — it is a very hard thing to do and very few people understood.

One of the obstacles to a success of the Houston performances was, as the authors see it, that the acoustics of the hall were such that most of the text remained unintelligible: 'and in an opera you have to understand the words'.

In the new version *A Quiet Place* begins with a Prologue during which voices and noises are heard from behind the closed curtain bringing to mind the car-crash in which Dinah lost her life; a choir sings in the orchestra pit 'The path of Truth is plain and safe' after a three-bar orchestral prelude (a sixth-note flute solo with a descending ninth is continued by a pianissimo motif played by muted trumpet, completing the twelve-note series). The chorale-like two-part motto sung by the choir will be repeated throughout the opera as kind of a leitmotif; its words continue 'My Heart shall be the Garden'. When the noises behind stage are fading away, the choir intones — following the biblical 'Song of Songs' — 'Give All for Love, for Love is strong as Death'. The First Scene immediately following has not been substantially altered except for some dramatic and musical cuts; it closes with a lyrical orchestral postlude, played very softly with only one episode leading to a dramatic climax after which an expressive violin solo concludes the First Act.

Act Two opens with Sam taking up Dinah's diaries which move him deeply; while he is reading, the Jazz Trio from the opening of *Trouble in Tahiti* begins the flashback encompassing the first scenes of the earlier opera up to Dinah's dream of a peaceful garden and 'a quiet place' and the couple's inconclusive meeting in the street: 'Years have gone and what has happened to dull the mystery? And where is our garden with a quiet place? Can't we find the way back to the garden where we began?' This first half of *Trouble in Tahiti* is followed without a break by the continuation of the opening scene: Sam is still looking at Dinah's papers as the family assembles and they start quarrelling. After Junior has been quietened and fallen asleep,the chorus gives the Leitmotif chorale again, pianissimo. The second part of *Trouble in Tahiti* begins immediately, starting where it left off, with the Jazz Trio. This leads to Sam's proud description of himself as a man of success. Act Two closes with the last scene of the earlier opera — Dinah's aria on the 'awful movie' and her return home where there will be no harmony between husband and wife.

Act Three begins with an orchestral prelude, the scene in the garden that had been Scene III in the original version of the opera and the mocking imitation by Dede and Junior of their parents' breakfast quarrels. A row breaks out between Sam and his children; Sam takes Dinah's diary from his pocket and reads aloud some fragments from it — as a counterpoint Dinah's own voice is heard. This passage is without instrumental accompaniment. The imaginary duet — sentences from the diary, echoes and comments — gradually mounts in intensity and instruments add to the turmoil. Then mysterious, sinister laughter is heard pianissimo, which the chorus takes up fortissimo. Unexpectedly, Sam and the children start making plans for a happier, more harmonious future and the Jazz Trio from *Trouble in Tahiti* is heard; but the peace is not durable, the future remains uncertain.

There is no doubt that the revision of the opera represents a dramaturgical and musical improvement, in a more logical link between the two operas and a better juxtaposition of Sam and Dinah's ironically light-hearted early story with the scenes after Dinah's death. When the jazz-singers break into the serious atmosphere of Act Two, this can hardly fail to recall *Ariadne auf Naxos*, by Hugo von Hofmannsthal and Richard Strauss with its 'Harlequin' intermezzo. Did composer and writer of *A Quiet Place* perhaps also think of a similar amalgamation of the serious and comic? 'Yes, you are right', said Lenny (May 1984), 'in both works there is an opera within an opera . . . but in our work it has, of course, a different meaning . . . .'

Among the critics, Andrew Porter best perceived the intention to present a stylised portrait of American life and language in words and music. After the premiere at Houston, he wrote in *The New Yorker* (11 July 1983) that the characters' 'feelings, thinking and utterances are inchoate. They do not talk with wit and precision: sentences remain unfinished, trains of thought leave the rails and some of the language is coarse'. However, he went on, 'all this is deliberate. The opera is an ambitious, arresting attempt to fashion an orderly work of art from material lifelike in its vagueness and unruliness. The music gives shape to the piece. The underlying form is that of a four-movement symphony, with the linked nocturnal duets as a slow movement and games in the garden as a scherzo, and the score is one of the richest Bernstein has composed'. In the revised version of 1984–5, the nocturnal duets were cut as independent intermezzi. Twelve months before the revised opera was to have its European premiere, Andrew Porter concluded by saying: 'When *A Quiet Place* goes to La Scala, it can show that good American operas on contemporary subjects are still being composed'. In fact, public and critics in Milan liked the opera much better than had American audiences.

The first performance at the Teatro alla Scala took place on 19 June 1984, with Stephen Wadsworth as stage director and John Mauceri conducting. Duilio Courir headlined his review 'Drama and American Dream by Bernstein' (*Corriere della Sera*, 21 June 1984). He saw a game of mirrors in the picturing of American family life as well as in the score which was characterised by the amalgamation of many musical influences. Angelo Foletto (in *La Republica*) also spoke of 'the American dream' of Leonard Bernstein: 'Bernstein is dreaming (*ma non troppo*)' and he called the opera 'a significant success with the Milanese and international audience in the Teatro alle Scala'. William Weaver, however, said in the *International Herald Tribune* (Paris edition, 27 June 1984) that 'although the Milanese public has not evinced a great interest in the Bernstein work, the local critics have received it with enthusiasm', continuing: 'their approbation is easily understood and shared'.

At the Kennedy Center a month later (22 July) 'the incarnation of *A Quiet Place* received mixed reviews, mostly not particularly favourable' as Stephen Wadsworth wrote to me. However, there were a number of critics who had hated the work in Houston and who now found they loved it. Some of the critics, he feels, 'are still delighted to take potshots at Lenny, deriding the pretensions of the opera'. 'The music is willing but the plot is weak' ran one headline in the *Washington Post* (23 July); the reviewer, Joseph McLellan, found the music, 'tensely chromatic and deeply expressive.' The following day, John von Rhein in the *Chicago Tribune* described the opera as 'certainly . . . Bernstein's most compassionate work for the theater . . . recognizably the work of an American composer of wide-ranging musical culture'. However, he 'cannot pretend that Bernstein and Wadsworth have found the ideal structure for their creation; perhaps that will always remains elusive'. Leighton Kerner's extensive article on the opera in *Voice* (21 August 1984) was entitled 'The Fearsome Garden'; he described *A Quiet Place* as a 'hard-edged, harrowing and generously beautiful work', a piece that 'ranks among the five or six strongest American operas'. Much credit was given to the conductor John Mauceri for his ideas and assistance in the preparation of the new version of the opera and critics were unanimous in praising his work as its conductor. Following the Milan and Washington stagings of 1984, the first new series of performances beginning at the Vienna State Opera House in April 1986 saw further alterations and changes, so that it could still be said that *A Quiet Place* was a 'work in progress'.

Leonard Bernstein's new works of the year 1986 were a *Prayer* for the re-opening of the refurbished Carnegie Hall, a six-minute composition set to Hebrew words to be sung by a baritone with orchestral accompaniment, and *Jubilee Games*.

Jubilee Games, written for the celebrations of the Israel Philharmonic Orchestra's Jubilee Season in 1986/7 — to commemorate the orchestra's foundation in December 1936 — was premiered, with the composer conducting, during the orchestra's tour of the USA and Europe in September 1986, and then performed in Tel Aviv and Jerusalem for the opening of the season. As then performed, the work consists of two movements entitled 'Free-style Events' and 'Diaspora Dances'; however the composer 'hopes one day to add another movement or two'. As so often before, Bernstein has quoted passages from the Old Testament as the starting point for the composition. In Leviticus (XXV, 8–17) Moses is commanded to 'speak unto the children of Israel when ye come into the land which I (the Lord) give you' and to 'say unto them'

And Thou shalt number seven Sabbaths of years unto thee, seven times seven years . . . shall be unto thee forty and nine years. Then shalt thou cause the trumpet of the Jubilee to sound, on . . . the Day of Atonement shall ye make the trumpet sound throughout all your land. And ye shall hallow the fiftieth year, and proclaim Liberty throughout the land unto all the inhabitants thereof. It shall be a jubilee unto you, and ye shall return every man unto his possession, and ye shall return every man unto his family . . . . for it is the Jubilee, it shall be holy unto you . . . . Ye shall not, therefore, oppress one another, but thou shalt fear thy God, for I am the Lord thy God.

The English word 'Jubilee' goes back to the Hebrew 'Yovēl' which originally meant 'ram's horn trumpet'* — the *shofar* sounded on festive days and, in the passage cited above, ordained to mark the fiftieth year as a holy year. For any American verse 10 — 'ye shall . . . proclaim Liberty throughout the land unto all the inhabitants thereof' — has gained especial significance as the inscription on the American Liberty Bell.

In the first movement of this work Bernstein plays freely with seven-note scales or modal groupings and the musicians underline the significance of the number seven (*sheva* in Hebrew) by shouting or whispering this number seven times, every four bars; later they exclaim *Hamishim* (the Hebrew for 'fifty') and the brass sounds fanfare-like 'signals' imitating the traditional motifs prescribed for the *shofar*. These 'calls' are recorded on tape and serve as counterpoint to the recapitulation of a preceding chorale-like section of the many-coloured movement. The composer himself comments on this movement as follows:

> The first movement, 'Free-style Events', is musical athletics, with cheers and all. It is also charades, anagrams, and children's 'counting-out' games. But mainly it is celebratory, therefore spontaneous, therefore aleatoric, ranging from structured improvisation to totally free orchestral invention 'in situ'. It is thus inevitable that the movement will vary considerably from one performance to another, and even from one rehearsal to another. But it is formally controlled, at least in terms of beginning — middle — and end, by pre-recorded tape reprises.

The second movement opens in 18/8 time, an allusion to the traditional practice of assigning numerical values to the letters of the Hebrew alphabet: the Hebrew word *Ḥāi* (*Chāi*) equals the number eighteen: similar gematria games like those underlying the develop-

*In Genesis (IV, 2) Juval, the son of Lamech and Adah, is named 'father of all such occupied with stringed instruments and pipes'.

ment of metres and rhythms of this movement had already been used characteristically for Bernstein's *Dybbuk* ballet music of 1974. The composer has made the following comment on this movement:

> The 'Diaspora Dances' of the second movement are 'free-style' only in a socio-cultural, geo-Judaic sense, and hence necessarily eclectic in style, their musical connotations ranging from the Middle-East back to Central-European ghettoes, and forward again to a New-Yorkish kind of jazz music. Horas are strictly excluded, as is whatever could slither in under the rubric of 'Disco'.
>
> I hope one day soon to add another movement or two — 'halevay' [may it be given!] before the jubilee of Israel itself.

The *Prayer* for baritone solo and small orchestra — based on traditional Hebrew benedictions — written in 1986 for the festive opening of the refurbished Carnegie Hall, New York, is to become one of the additions devised for *Jubilee Games*.

9

Leonard Bernstein as Musical Pedagogue

The only way one can really say anything about music
is to write music.
Leonard Bernstein, December 1957

'I'm not by nature a lecturer', Leonard Bernstein said when talking
to students at the University of Chicago in February 1957 ('Something
to say . . .', *The Infinite Variety of Music*), and he added: 'When I teach I
ask a lot of questions of my students and I like very much to learn from
them'. Nevertheless, the life story and development of the conductor
and composer Leonard Bernstein show clearly that from his earliest
youth he has felt an urge to let friends, colleagues, music-lovers,
students and listeners participate in his ideas and theories on music —
and he has done this with an original talent that does not fall behind
his qualities in all the other spheres. Following his thesis that the
writing of music is the only way to say something about music, he has
tried to demonstrate and to solve the problems of creative composition
— foundations, techniques, means of expression and style, structures,
tonality and non-tonality foremost among them — in musical works of
all kinds, thereby teaching himself as well as others about 'the infinite
variety of music' and the ways of a composer to communicate with his
audience. His many lectures and analytical essays — only a few of
which have been incorporated in his books — supplement what he has
said in the language of music.

The most fruitful and simply formulated indication of his approach
to music and to the explanation of music to an audience was advanced
by Leonard Bernstein in the context of the first of his Young People's
Concerts in New York on 18 January 1958, when he answered the
question 'What does music mean?' by saying that 'music is never *about*
things. Music just *is* . . . . The meaning of music is in the music, and

[252]

nowhere else'.

The manifold aspects of musical creativeness, of creative musical interpretation, of historical and topical analysis of musical masterworks have occupied Leonard Bernstein's mind ever since his serious interest in music started to develop. In his years of study at Harvard University and at the Curtis Institute of Music he discussed problems of writing and performing music and of theory and analysis with his teachers and fellow students; he wrote concert reviews and essays for the students' journal and for the periodical *Modern Music* between the years 1938 and 1946. His Harvard dissertation had as its subject 'The Absorption of Race Elements into American Music'; it was published in Bernstein's book of memoirs and essays, *Findings* (New York, 1982). Since then he has written more than a hundred articles and manuscripts for television and delivered his six Charles Eliot Norton lectures at Harvard. *The Joy of Music* — his first collection of talks and essays — was published in New York in 1959; in 1962 followed *The Infinite Variety of Music* and the volume containing the programmes *Young People's Concerts for Reading and Listening* (enlarged edition 1970); the Harvard lectures of 1973 were published in 1976 as *The Unanswered Question*; *Findings* appeared in New York in 1982.

The lively and attractive conversational style of Lenny Bernstein's talks — also reproduced in the written and published versions in the book — cannot delude the attentive listener or reader into presuming that there is no depth to them; behind every sentence, every formulation he will detect a challenge to rethink matters, to meditate as Bernstein did, to check his own approach to music. Above all, listeners to the programmes and readers of his essays are always struck anew by the broad range of this thinking and the scope of his all-round knowledge of many fields apart from music — philosophy, psychology, the history of literature and the arts, linguistics, general history — supported by a phenomenal memory for events, dates and people. It is difficult to name any musician of past or present who can combine such a thorough knowledge of the history of music and the development of musical styles with a deep insight into the makings and the significance of the masterworks in active interpretation. In some ways Richard Wagner comes to mind, whose universal knowledge was as broad and comprehensive — and this without a formal education. Wagner researched and wrote on legends, literature, philosophy, art and music of all nations and historical periods; however, what he learned he used only to bolster his own thoughts and tendencies, his completely egocentric view of life and the world. In more recent times Arnold Schoenberg was an ingenious creative musician with a most extensive

New York Philharmonic
Young People's Concert

339th Concert — 41st Season
(Founded by Ernest Schelling in 1924)

LEONARD BERNSTEIN, *Music Director*

Saturday, November 2, 1963, at 12:00 Noon

Leonard Bernstein, *Conductor*

"A Tribute to Teachers"

MOUSSORGSKY   Prelude to "Khovantchina"

THOMPSON   Scherzo, from Symphony No. 2

PISTON   Suite from "The Incredible Flutist"

BRAHMS   *Academic Festival Overture, Opus 80

Program subject to change

*Recorded by the New York Philharmonic

Columbia Records   Steinway Piano

The telecast of today's concert will be shown on CBS Television, Channel 2, on Friday, November 29, at 7:30 p.m., sponsored by Shell Oil Company.

Mr. Bernstein plays the Baldwin Piano

THE PHILHARMONIC-SYMPHONY SOCIETY OF NEW YORK, INC.
Philharmonic Hall, Lincoln Center, Broadway at 65th St., New York 23, N. Y.
Carlos Moseley, *Managing Director*   William L. Weissel, *Assistant Manager*

Programme for a concert for young people, 2 November 1963

Welcome back to Phil. Hall

BERNSTEIN

My dear young friends: ~~It is good to be~~
~~back with you all again for another~~
~~season of YOUNG PEOPLE'S CONCERTS here~~
~~in Philharmonic Hall.~~ You may think
it strange that I have chosen to open
this new season, of Young People's Concerts with the subject of
teachers. After all, aren't these
programs always about music? And what
have teachers got to do with music?
The answer is: everything. We can all ~~imagine a self-taught painter, a writer,~~ think of paintets as being completely
~~self-taught, and maybe some writers too~~,
but it is almost impossible to imagine
a professional musician who doesn't owe
something to one teacher or another.
The trouble is that we don't always
realize how important teachers are, in
music or in anything else. Teaching is
probably the noblest profession in the
world -- the most unselfish, difficult,
and honorable profession. but It is also the
most unappreciated, underrated, underpaid,
and underpraised profession in the world.

(MORE)

The opening of the script for Leonard Bernstein's introductory talk at the Young People's Concert general knowledge; egocentrically minded in his own way, all his life he searched for an eternal truth, for a God-given order which all art must obey. Pierre Boulez is also one of the musicians who are interpreters of music and composers of the highest rank; he has also expressed himself in musical works, in writings and lectures and in conducting music but within an intentionally more restricted sphere.

'I am a fanatic music lover. I can't live one day without hearing music, playing it, studying it, or thinking about it. And all this is quite apart from my professional role as a musician', Leonard Bernstein wrote on 21 June 1966 (see *The Infinite Variety of Music*): 'I am a fan, a committed member of the musical public'. For him there is no difference between 'serious' and 'light' music: 'For me all good music is *serious* music' and serious music can be music of the classics or jazz or popular music. Music may be inspired by a story but 'stories are not what the music means': 'Music has its own meanings . . . and you don't need any stories or pictures to tell you what it means', for 'music means what the composer planned' and 'it's a *musical* plan, so it has a *musical* meaning'. Bernstein proves this is an original way: he tells his young listeners stories which might be the subject of a musical composition and then he shows that the composer has connected a completely different story to his music, so that 'whatever the music really means, it's *not* the story — even if there is a story connected with it'; the story may just give an 'extra meaning' to the music. So what does the listener need to know about music in order both to enjoy and to understand it? 'We don't have to know everything about sharps and flats and chords to understand music. If it tells us something — not a story or a picture, but a feeling — if it makes us change inside, then we are understanding it'.

Leonard Bernstein's Young People's Concerts, his Omnibus television programmes and analytical demonstrations of music have been seen and heard by millions of people in many different countries and made them familiar with music of both the past and the present. As a commentator and conductor he has succeeded in invoking the interest and understanding in a conservative public for music of our own times or, at least, has brought the listeners so far as to be ready to be confronted with new sounds. Titles, introductory chapters and chapter headings in his collections of essays, together with the media publicity for his lectures can, indeed, easily evoke the suspicion that they all belong to a species of popular writing with scholarly pretentiousness: for example, 'How to listen to music', 'How to understand music' or even 'What is music?' However, such an impression is quickly dispelled for the reader of Leonard Bernstein's texts. The first and main difference between the majority of books on musical appreciation and Bernstein's deliberations is his boundless respect for the works of the masters. This can be felt in his conducting as much as in his theoretical analyses, whereas many popular-minded authors put their own assumed importance above all.

Where the commonplace appreciation talk describes details in thematic developments and the craft of composition in a musical work, and possibly imbues it with imagined poetical or emotional meanings, Leonard Bernstein is more concerned with the totality of a work, with the *Gestalt*, and from the view of a piece as a whole looks at the 'building stones' that form its foundations: 'There have been more words written about the "Eroica" symphony than there are notes in it . . . and yet, has anyone ever successfully *explained* the "Eroica"?' Bernstein asks.

> Can anyone explain in mere prose the wonder of one note following or coinciding with another so that we feel that it's exactly how those notes *had* to be? Of course not. No matter what rationalists we may profess to be, we are stopped cold at the border of this mystic area. It is not too much to say *mystic* or even *magic*: no art lover can be an agnostic when the chips are down. If you love music, you are a believer, however dialectically you try to wriggle out of it ('The Happy Medium', December 1957, in *The Joy of Music*).

The sentences quoted contain Bernstein's Credo as a musician, a composer and a guide to the deeper understanding of the secrets of great art. His own studies of philosophy, literature and the history of music laid the foundations of his insight into the workings of the great masters' minds: 'The most rational minds in history have always yielded to a slight mystic haze when the subject of music has been broached, recognizing the beautiful and utterly satisfying combination of mathematics and magic that music is' ('The Happy Medium', op. cit.): 'Plato and Sokrates knew that the study of music is one of the finest disciplines for the adolescent mind, and insisted on it as a *sine qua non* of education: and just for those reasons of its combined scientific and *spiritual* qualities'. Principles of physics, acoustics, mathematics and formal logic are employed nowadays to explain phenomena in musical works, but the 'magic' questions are still unanswered. He sharply rejects the specious and commercial 'Music Appreciation Racket' — a term coined by Virgil Thomson — 'which uses every device to sell music — cajoling, coyness, flattery, oversimplification, irrelevant entertainment, tall tales — all in order to keep the music business humming . . . . It turns every note or phrase or chord into a cloud or crag or Cossack . . . . It abounds in anecdotes, quotes from famous performers, indulges itself in bad jokes and unutterable puns, teases the hearer, and tells us nothing about music'. There is also not much sense in 'the now-comes-the-theme-upside-down-in-the-second-oboe variety', which is 'to supply you with a road map of themes, a kind of Baedeker to the bare geography of composition; but again it tells us nothing about music except those superficial geographical facts'.

There are many other ways in which music is analysed and 'explained', but 'if we are to try to *explain* music, we must explain the *music*, not the whole array of appreciators' extra-musical notions which have grown like parasites around it'. Bernstein concedes that 'we must have intermittent recourse to certain extra-musical forces, like religion, or social factors, or historical forces, which may have influenced music', yet the extra-musical concepts can only be 'useful if they are put in the service of explaining the notes'. Bernstein feels that 'the happy medium' between the various ways of introducing music to music-lovers can only be found with the 'conviction that the public is *not* a great beast, but an intelligent organism, more often than not longing for insight and knowledge'; then 'even the road-map variety can be serviceable if it functions along with some central idea that can engage the intelligence of the listener'.

Following the guidelines he has set himself, Leonard Bernstein succeeds in formulating poignant definitions of periods and styles and detailed expositions of musical masterworks. Classical music for him is 'music written in a time when perfect form and balance are what everybody is looking for'. Now 'there were hundreds of classical composers writing at the time of Mozart — writing fine pieces, that stuck to all the rules, and were elegant and proper and all the rest of it. But their music doesn't last, for it just doesn't make the people who hear it feel something — feel the sense of classical perfection, with that extra something added. And that extra something is what we call beauty, and what we call beauty has to do with our feelings' ('What is Classical Music?', in *Young People's Concerts*). 'That's what Mozart's music has — beauty . . . Beethoven took all those classical rules of Mozart and Haydn and stretched them till his music got bigger in every way . . . . It's like looking at classical music through a magnifying glass — it's all much bigger'. Romanticism, coming after Beethoven, — 'I guess you could say that he was a classicist who went too far' — is music 'full of romantic feelings — like mystery, longing, rage, triumph, and joy'.

'What makes music funny?' asks Bernstein in another essay for young listeners, and postulates that 'music can't make jokes about anything except music itself'; it cannot tell funny stories but can imitate noises and take surprising turns, can introduce wrong notes and produce amusing effects through special orchestration. But 'all humour doesn't have to be a joke or make you laugh . . . . Humour makes you feel *good* inside. And, after all, that's what music is for'.

Further chapters in the first (1962) edition of *Young People's Concerts* deal with the question 'What makes Music American', discuss 'Folk Music in the Concert Hall', Impressionism as the music of colour, movement, and *suggestion*, characteristic ways of orchestration in a symphonic work and the key to the understanding of a symphony as a mirror of life: 'Development is the main thing in music, as it is in life; because development means change, growing, blossoming out, and these things are life itself . . . . A great piece of music has a lifetime of its own between the beginning and the end. In that period all the themes and melodies and musical ideas, however small they are, grow and develop into full-grown works'.

For the second edition (1970) the book was enlarged by two chapters: 'What is a Melody', and 'Musical Atoms: A Study of Intervals'.

The talks and essays collected in *The Joy of Music* (1959) and *The Infinite Variety of Music* (1962) elaborate most of the elementary subjects dealt with in the chapters conceived for a young audience. Among the most illuminating essays in *The Joy of Music* are an analysis of Beethoven's Fifth Symphony and a talk on 'The Music of Johann Sebastian Bach'. In *The Infinite Variety of Music* we find equally compelling analyses of Beethoven's 'Eroica', Antonín Dvořák's 'New World' Symphony, Tchaikowsky's 'Pathétique' and a talk on 'The Ageless Mozart'. Here especially Leonard Bernstein demonstrates what he means by interpreting music *through* music.

Ludwig van Beethoven's Fifth Symphony had been the subject of Bernstein's very first television broadcast (14 November 1954); idea and text were developed out of the lecture the author heard him deliver in Tanglewood in the summer of 1948 (see page 57, above). It was 'the curious and rather difficult experiment . . . to take the first movement of Beethoven's Fifth Symphony and rewrite it', by trying to establish what would have become of this movement if Beethoven had developed the first sketches he noted down for the opening theme instead of the ingenious motif he finally found. The 'experiment' served Leonard Bernstein as an example of how an artist struggles until he is satisfied that he has written down a composition that develops logically and achieves a certain stature. It is 'the key to the mystery of a great artist: that for reasons unknown to him or to anyone else, he will give away his energies and his life just to make sure that one note follows another inevitably. It seems rather an odd way to spend one's life; but it isn't so odd when we think that the composer, by doing this, leaves us at the finish with the feeling that something is right in the world, that something checks throughout, something that follows its own laws consistently, something we can trust, that will never let us down'.

The three collections of talks and essays were followed in 1982 by a volume entitled *Findings*, which contained memoirs, letters, poems, essays, lectures, speeches, and a classified list of Bernstein's compositions. The four parts of this illustrated book are: a collection of 'Juvenilia' (1935–9) culminating in the reprinting of the Harvard thesis; 'Postwar Meditations' (1946–57), in which special interest centres around 'Excerpts from a *West Side Story* Log'; 'The New York Philharmonic Years' (1959–67) includes a script for a pre-concert lecture to young people, 'A Tribute to Teachers', and a talk on 'Mahler: His Time has Come'; and 'The Last Decade till Now' (1969–80). Part Two contains two letters from Bernstein to Helen Coates written after his concerts at the DP camps near Munich in 1948, together with thoughts on right and wrong in musical nationalism in Israel and in America. Parts Three and Four contain essays on some great composers — Edgar Varèse, Marc Blitzstein, Carl Nielsen, Aaron Copland, Igor Stravinsky, George Gershwin — a moving tribute to the singer Jennie Tourel, memoirs of the conductor Victor de Sabata and of Maria Callas, and the letter to Franz Endler on the different interpretations of Beethoven's Ninth (pages 122–3, above). Leonard Bernstein wrote a Preface to the book on 25 August 1982, which was his own sixty-fourth birthday.

The talks, lectures and essays in Leonard Bernstein's books are addressed to that 'intelligent organism, more often than not longing for insight and knowledge', that public he speaks of in the Introduction to *The Joy of Music*. The depth of his knowledge and breadth of vision is perhaps best revealed in the six lectures he gave as Charles Eliot Norton Professor of Poetry at Harvard in the winter semester 1973/4, that same university from which he had graduated thirty-four years before. The lectures were televised in many countries of the world, and were published by Harvard University Press in 1976 under the title *The Unanswered Question*. Like his other books, this volume has been translated into many languages, among them German, French, Hungarian, and Japanese.

The Unanswered Question demands very intensive attention on the part of the listener and reader, and a readiness to follow Leonard Bernstein as he builds a whole universe of scientific, methodological and artistic aspects of musical knowledge. Bernstein says that the principal thing he absorbed as a student at Harvard was the sense of interdisciplinary values, the truth that the best way to know a matter is in the context of another discipline. In his own research, the fruits of which he now imparts to his students, he approaches the manifold problems of music theory and musical aesthetics with the help of such other disciplines as linguistics, poetry, elementary physics, historical perspectives, aesthetics, and philosophy. He throws light on the impact of such extra-musical fields on musical analysis; the 'unanswered question' which Charles Ives put forward in his orchestral piece of that name (see pages 11–12, above) and which serves Leonard Bernstein as the title for his lecture series, lies, for him, in the *ambiguity* of music, in the debate and struggle on tonal and non-tonal foundations of musical expression. For Leonard Bernstein the composer and the theoretician it is this central problem that dominates his thinking and re-surfaces in each of the six Harvard lectures, the headings of which are 'Musical Phonology', 'Musical Syntax', 'Musical Semantics', 'The Delights and Dangers of Ambiguity', 'The Twentieth-Century Crisis', and 'The Poetry of Earth'.

Leonard Bernstein was inspired to attempt to link the foundations of the aesthetics of music and linguistics through the teaching of the linguist Noam Chomsky who ascribes to man — and to man only — an 'innate grammatical competence', 'a genetically endowed language faculty which is *universal*'. 'It is a human endowment', adds Bernstein, 'it proclaims the unique power of the human spirit: Well, so does music'. He then asks how will it be possible to investigate musical universality by so scientific a means as linguistic analogy. He does not doubt that there exists some musical universality; there are common traits in the music of composers as different as Johann Sebastian Bach, Maurice Ravel, Igor Stravinsky, Aaron Copland — even in Hindu dance music when heard out of its genuine context — the reason surely being that music is composed from a store of notes and sounds provided by nature: language everywhere is formed from minimal speech units that arise as naturally from the physiological structure of our mouths, throats, and noses as musical sound units come out of waves produced by strings, wind instruments, membrane instruments, or vocal chords. Thus there should be analogies between the phonology, syntax and semantics of linguistics and musical phonology, syntax and semantics, between expression in words and in musical sounds. Although Bernstein remembers the sentence of Michel de Montaigne, writing some four hundred years ago, that the most universal quality of man is his diversity, he maintains that above this apparent paradox it must be conceded that grammatical similarities found between languages or families of languages have parallels in music: in music as well you can find basic traits of universal relevancy. In speech there are 'primal words' composed of the simplest sounds formed by mouth, throat, and nose. Music is 'heightened speech' and must have originated everywhere from common roots, as did language. 'I have often thought that if it is literally true that *In the Beginning Was The Word*, then it must have been a *sung* word. The Bible tells us the whole Creation story not only verbally, but in terms of verbal creation. God *said*: Let there be light. God *said*: Let there be a firmament. He created verbally. Now can you imagine God *saying*, just like that, *Let there be light*, as if ordering lunch? Or even in the original language: *Y'hi Or?* I've always had a private fantasy of God *singing* those two blazing words: Y'HI — O–O–O–R!' Only heightened speech, *singing*, could have caused light to break forth: music begins where language leaves off, argues Leonard Bernstein.

In linguistic theory many different hypotheses have been developed to prove or disprove complexities found in the universal appearance of sound and speech patterns. 'We musicians are luckier: we have the built-in preordained universal known as the *harmonic series*' — the acoustical phenomenon of overtones vibrating together with each sound produced by a vibrating string or column of air in a musical instrument or stretched animal hide. This natural phenomenon is universal, but peoples of different races and living in different regions vary in their ways of choosing or employing the tones produced by the fundamental sound. The Western world has tempered the scale of tones by not using some of them appertaining to the natural series, and has established a system of tonal controls, which was perfected and codified by Johann Sebastian Bach, 'whose genius was to balance so delicately, and so justly, these two forces of chromaticism and diatonicism, forces that are equally powerful and presumably contradictory in nature'.

'As a musician I feel that there has to be a way of speaking about music with intelligent but nonprofessional music lovers who don't know a stretto from a diminished fifth; and the best way I have found so far is by setting up a working analogy with language, since language is something everyone shares and uses and knows about', Leonard Bernstein writes in the opening statements in his second lecture, on 'Musical Syntax'. Syntax is the study of the actual structures by which sonic universals have evolved into words, and words into sentences. In examining one attempt that has been made to establish a consistent correspondence between verbal and musical elements, Bernstein starts by equating a musical note with a letter; by extension this would mean that a scale equals an alphabet. But there are so many scales of different notes used in different cultures and alphabets are so different in so many languages that this system will not work. A better approach is the equation of a note with a phoneme, a minimal sound unit such as 'mmmm' or 'sss' or 'eee'. In that case a motif, a phrase or even a theme of music would equal a morpheme, a minimal meaningful sound unit, and a phrase of music would have to correspond to a word; a musical section would equal a clause, a whole movement would be a sentence, and a complete piece of music would equal a complete piece of talk or writing.

Though such analogies may help to explain some foundations of musical syntax, they do not illuminate all the various aspects. Taking as an example the 'second theme' in the exposition of the first movement of Mozart's G minor Symphony, K. 550, its first three notes can be equalled to one word and the following unit (of six notes) constitutes another word; but the last note of the first word (played by the strings) also functions as the first note of the second word (played by the woodwinds). A linguistic equivalent would be impossible as you cannot imitate the musical technique and make 'deaduck' out of 'dead duck'. Additionally, the term 'phrase' can also lead to confusion, because it would seem more logical to have 'phrase' equal 'phrase' instead of 'word'.

While these attempts to establish analogies do not yield entirely satisfactory results, Bernstein thinks they are not in vain, for they lead us to think about music in the same way as one thinks about language, and there is some truth in the equation of 'movement' with 'sentence'; it is no accident that the German word *Satz* means both 'sentence' and 'symphonic (or sonata) movement'. 'But the fact is there *are* no sentences in music, as there are in prose, since most continuous pieces of music do not reach a full stop until they end'. It is in the nature of music to be ongoing: 'it seems as if all music is made up of relative clauses, all interdependently linked by conjunctions and relative pronouns; and therefore, it seems that the closest we can get to a prose sentence in music is an entire movement'.

[263]

Leonard Bernstein concludes that there do exist some equations 'that will stand the test'. A musical motto, a motif, can be equated with a grammatical substantive or noun, as for example the three melodic notes that make up the so-called 'Fate' motif in Richard Wagner's *Ring* music dramas: these notes are like three letters that make up a word which is a noun, a self-naming entity. That Wagner intended the motif to signify Fate is a semantic consideration; it is a musical noun all by itself no matter what it stands for or is intended to mean. Going further, Bernstein equates a chord, a harmonic entity, with a grammatical modifier such as an adjective, because obviously the chord modifies by descriptive colouration the noun to which it is attached. The next step can be to see the verb as an analogy to rhythm, which 'activates or motorizes the substantive just as a verb does'.

Many parallels can be drawn between the elaboration and development of a word or verbal statement and the workings of musical syntax. In linguistics the term of 'transformational grammar' has been coined for the change in meaning when sentences are changed by rearrangement and the inversion of words, turning statements into questions, positive sense into negative, active meaning into passive, and combinations of all these. 'Language leads a double life: it has a communicative function *and* an aesthetic function. Music has an aesthetic function only .... Musical surface structure is not equatable with linguistic surface structure .... Language must reach even higher than its linguistic surface structure, the prose sentence, to find the true equivalent of musical surface structure. And that equivalent must of course be *poetry*.' Bernstein then turns again to Mozart's G minor Symphony in order to discover the 'deep structure out of which its marvelous surface structure has been generated', what parallels verbal and musical languages and what differentiates between them.

In the third lecture Bernstein summarises the results of his probing into the foundations of a musical phonology and the workings of musical syntax and discusses 'Musical Semantics'. Semantics, the meaning or significance of musical statements, has already played some part in the preceding deliberations: discussing phonology, 'we dealt with the ordering of phonemic elements out of the harmonic series so as to produce meaningful tonal relationships, *meaningful*, ergo *semantic*'; discussing syntax, 'we were dealing with the ordering of those tonal relationships so as to produce meaningful structures'. So what meanings are there left to deal with, Bernstein asks, and answers: 'Obviously, the musical meanings that result from the combination of both, of what we might call phono-semantics plus morpho-semantics — meanings derived by the various transformational procedures with which we've been playing'. Bernstein uses a series of examples from classical and romantic musical master works to show the abundance of ways and means at the disposal of composers who wish to organise their tonal material and structural order in their works in a meaningful way — by constant change, repetition and antithesis, development and elaboration, imaginatively, and in a poetic language — all this independent of any possible intention of a composer or the wish of listeners to add some extra-musical meanings to the work.

The three remaining lectures reveal Leonard Bernstein's own central problems as a composer and his attempts to come to terms with what he calls, in the fifth lecture, 'The Twentieth-Century Crisis' — on which he has commented most eloquently in musical compositions such as *Kaddish* and *Mass*, using music instead of words. In these pages he meditates on 'The Delights and Dangers of Ambiguity' in music, on the crisis of tonality initiated by Richard Wagner, on 'The Poetry of Earth' in music, and on the nature of the 'unanswered question'.

The growing chromaticism in musical history, based on the accretion of more and more remote overtones of the harmonic series as they were gradually accepted into common practice, led to an ever growing ambiguity of music: phonological ambiguity, syntactic and semantic double meanings. As Bernstein sees it, there was, at the end of the nineteenth century, such a sharp increase of both quantity and intensity of these three strains that a state of sheer vagueness is reached: 'And that's where the aesthetic delights of ambiguity start turning into dangers'. Immediately after Beethoven 'a new aesthetic world' came into being, 'new freedoms affected formal structures, harmonic procedures, instrumental colour, melody, rhythm — all of these were part of a new expanding universe, at the centre of which lay the artist's personal passions'. The more ambivalent the music became, the deeper its expressive capacity, but quantitive changes and the deepening of expressivity have no bearing on the qualitative valuation of a composer or his work. 'Chopin is more chromatic than Mozart but that doesn't make him a greater composer', Bartók is not greater than Beethoven because of the more strongly felt ambiguity of his musical statements. An interesting digression leads Bernstein to poetry, where he cites examples of 'poetic chromaticism', of poets who 'exploit the alphabet to its sonic limits'.

The analysis of the 'delights and dangers of ambiguity' shows the development of chromaticism from Ludwig van Beethoven through musical Romanticism up to Claude Debussy whose music is 'pointing in the direction of total ambiguity': after Debussy's *Prelude à l'Après-midi d'un Faune* 'it was to be only one short decade before the crisis did in fact arrive' — the 'twentieth-century crisis' arising when 'the problems presented by *Tristan und Isolde* had grown to a point necessitating some radical solution'. A radical solution was Arnold Schoenberg's development of a method of composition derived from themes using all the twelve semitones of the tempered scale, related only to each other and not to any dominating tonal centre. Leonard Bernstein feels, however, that over most of Schoenberg's dodecaphonic series of notes 'there hangs . . . a strong feeling of *tonality* . . . and this kind of tonal feeling haunted Schoenberg's music right up to the end of his life'. Alban Berg however, succeeds in producing 'a *positive* ambiguity out of the same tonal–atonal contradiction', he 'had an uncanny gift for dramatizing that ambiguity, for making drama out of dodecaphonic procedures within universal tonal relationships'. In his very last work, especially, the Violin Concerto of 1935, Berg 'solved that agonizing ambiguity, to-be-or-not-to-be-tonal', in a most satisfying way. 'The most beautiful things in Schoenberg are always alluding to tonality, in a nostalgic way', Lenny Bernstein said in one of our conversations on the topic, 'and those are the most beautiful things in Alban Berg, he sort of yearns for tonality. And think of Mahler: when he begins to go away from tonality, he always comes back to it.' Talking on serialism: 'I don't mean that tonality is the only solution, but tonality is basic. That's where the serialists make a mistake, they believe that one has supplanted the other — that tonality has gone and serialism was here to stay. That's not so. The one is here to stay, but the other one has not gone'.

While restudying Mahler's Ninth Symphony, and especially its final movement, Leonard Bernstein realised 'that ours is the century of death, and Mahler is its musical prophet'. But he asks '. . . haven't all centuries, all human histories been a long record of the struggle to survive, to deal with the problem of mortality?' However 'never before has mankind been confronted by the problem of surviving global death, total death, the extinction of the whole race. And Mahler was not alone in his vision; there have been other great prophets of our struggle. Freud, Einstein, and Marx have also prophesied, as have Spengler and Wittgenstein, Malthus and Rachel Carson . . . that the Apocalypse is at hand'. Both 'Schoenberg and Stravinsky, Mahler's two continuing prophets, utterly different as they were, spent their lives struggling in their opposite ways to keep musical progress alive, to avert the Evil Day'. In 'all the truly great works of our century' Bernstein sees traits of 'protest or despair, or of a refuge from both': he names works by Jean-Paul Sartre, Albert Camus, André Gide, Ernest Hemingway, Thomas Mann, Vladimir Nabokov, T.S. Eliot, W.H. Auden, Boris

Pasternak, Pablo Neruda, Sylvia Plath, Samuel Beckett, Pablo Picasso, Giorgio de Chirico, Salvador Dali, Alban Berg (*Wozzeck, Lulu*), Schoenberg (*Moses and Aaron*), and Bertolt Brecht (*Mother Courage*). All of Gustav Mahler's last pieces are 'kinds of farewells', making us feel his forebodings of death: of 'his own imminent death of which he was acutely aware . . . , the death of tonality, which for him meant the death of music itself, music as he knew it and loved it . . . and finally, his third and most important vision: the death of society, of our own Faustian culture'.

Leonard Bernstein sees the real reason for the fifty years of neglect that Mahler's music suffered after his death in the agonising message it contained — it is not 'the usual excuses we always hear: that the music is too long, too difficult, too bombastic. It was simply too true, telling something too dreadful to hear'. But we are still here, struggling to go on: 'This is the most fascinating ambiguity of all: that as each of us grows up, the mark of our maturity is that we accept our mortality; and yet we persist in our search for immortality'. This is because 'we believe a future. We *believe*'. Mahler's final farewell, the Adagio concluding the Ninth Symphony, 'takes the form of a prayer, Mahler's last chorale, his closing hymn, so to speak; and it prays for the restoration of life, of tonality, of faith'. This symphony 'is a sonic presentation of death itself, and paradoxically reanimates us every time we hear it'.

The last of the six Harvard lectures, 'The Poetry of Earth', quotes John Keats' poem:

> The poetry of earth is never dead . . .
> The poetry of earth is ceasing never

and demonstrates how composers search for possibilities of a rejuvenation of classical values, classical forms, in the midst of the twentieth-century crisis, taking Igor Stravinsky as the most characteristic example. Leonard Bernstein speaks of the 'conjurers' bags of tricks' in resuscitating tonality, of eclecticism, of 'neo-classicism', and of Stravinsky's way of establishing 'objective expressivity'. Again, Bernstein, as incumbent of the Chair of Poetry at Harvard, draws illuminating parallels between poetry, painting, and music, all tending towards an avoidance of 'self-expression', towards an anti-romantic attitude. He believes that in the 1970s there began 'a new period of fresh air and fun . . . , an ebullient renewed will to survive the apocalyptic, and to make musical progress in friendly competition, or even — as Stockhausen would have it — in communal effort'. Bernstein maintains that this has been made possible 'by the rediscovery and the reacceptance of tonality, that universal earth out of which such diversity can spring. And I believe that no matter how serial, or stochastic, or otherwise intellectualized music may be, it can always qualify as poetry as long as it is rooted in earth'.

On the last two pages of *The Unanswered Question*, Leonard Bernstein summarises the main points of his musical Credo as well as the theses propounded in the talks:

> I also believe, along with Keats, that the Poetry of Earth is never dead, as long as Spring succeeds Winter, and man is there to perceive it.
> I believe that from that Earth emerges a musical poetry, which is by the nature of its sources tonal.

He restates his belief in the existence of a phonology of music evolved from the universal known as the harmonic series, in an equally universal musical syntax, and in

> particular musical languages that have surface structures noticeably remote from their basic origins, but which can be strikingly expressive as long as they retain their roots in earth . . . . All particular languages are innate ones . . . they bear on one another, and combine into always new idioms . . . and can ultimately all merge into a speech universal enough to be accessible to all mankind, [while] the expressive distinctions among these idioms depend ultimately on the dignity and passion of the individual creative voice.
> And finally, I believe [concludes Leonard Bernstein], that because all these things are true, Ives' Unanswered Question has an answer. I'm no longer sure what the question is, but I do know that the answer is Yes.

10

The Infinite Variety
of Leonard Bernstein's Personality

> When Lenny enters a room, its temperature changes.
> He changes the climate of a room.
> *Shirley Bernstein*, Summer 1967

As conductor and composer, pianist, lecturing and writing music pedagogue, Leonard Bernstein himself personifies that 'infinite variety of music' of which he speaks in his writings. It is his manifold talents, his ever-searching mind, the lively spirit of his creative and interpretative work that fascinates friends and admirers as well as professional listeners and readers. He loves to talk on his work, to answer questions, to discuss musical problems, and enables those interested to see, hear and observe him at work — he is surely not one of those artists that seek ivory-tower seclusion. If it is at times difficult to get into close contact with him, this is because of an entourage of assistants, helpers, friends accompanying — and trying to shield — him on his travels. But — as Christa Ludwig said in our conversation — 'he is a person who needs human nearness. He is not the type who secludes himself — as does Karajan who always secludes himself because he is shy of contact with people, absolutely shy, and for this reason is believed to be supercilious or arrogant while it really only seems so that he is reserved. Bernstein is completely different, he always gives, gives, gives'. Probing deeper, it is possible to add that Herbert von Karajan is communicative mainly through his interpretation of music while Leonard Bernstein cannot but communicate, to 'give', in all possible media of art and human relationships. And yet it is often felt that, in the depths of his being, he is lonely, sceptical, unfulfilled like the personages in his works. He feels most happy in his family circle or with friends and colleagues. A talk, an interchange of ideas, memories or discussions with an old friend may go on for many hours, sometimes

[269]

The conductor

into the early hours of the morning.

While Leonard Bernstein will make no concessions to public taste where he wants to deliver a spiritual or musical message — witness the score of *West Side Story*, the conception and realisation of *Kaddish* and of *Mass*, and the demanding texts of his lectures — he does have the listener in mind while writing a work. He has talked at length on the process of creative composing in an 'improvised lecture' at the University of Chicago in February 1957 — its reconstructed text may be found in *The Infinite Variety of Music*. Under the heading of 'Something to say . . .' he admits: 'I know that I always think of an audience when I write music — not as I plan to write music, not as I am actually writing it — but somewhere in the act of writing there is the sense haunting this act of the people who are going to hear it'. There is a world of difference between a composer whose creative act is 'haunted' by the sense of an audience — and who may therefore try to express what he wants to say in as intelligible a musical language as possible — and another composer who writes only for the sake of public success. When a bowing to public taste and commercial interest was demanded from Leonard Bernstein by his collaborators, he refused to cooperate; the single instance where he had initially consented to write music for a theatre show and then could not prevent the performance of the work in a form he could not agree to — *1600 Pennsylvania Avenue* — resulted in the catastrophic failure he had himself foreseen and in a deeply-felt disappointment.

The dichotomy in the mind of the creative musician, who is the recipient of a message in his imagination as well as its prospective interpreter to an audience, is paralleled by the dominantly introvert nature of his character in contrast with the seemingly extrovert behaviour of the conductor on the concert stage. 'When you see Lenny after a concert in the Green Room or you sit opposite him in the suite of his hotel — and he is still overheated, totally worn out', says Ursula Mayer-Reinach (Gradenwitz), the singer, 'he speaks *only* on music, it gushes out of him: the music the sounds of which he has just celebrated for us is commemorated and recreated once more. He never speaks about *himself*, only of the music, of the composers, as if he wanted to render account on all that he feels, what he believes he owes the composers. It's almost an invocation the way he relives the musical experience again. And one who knows [how] to read in a person's eyes, sees his looks oscillate between doubt and a touch of preserved child-like innocence and above all a little fear he might not be understood.'

He enjoys having people around him, goes to parties — where he immediately becomes the centre of interest — sits down at the piano

[271]

wherever there is one at a party or in a hotel suite, plays, sings, and improvises. Or he goes over a piece of music he has just performed with an orchestra, sings and explains its themes while talking about it. His recollection of events, situations, encounters, dates, and people is phenomenal. On these counts Leonard Bernstein is the perfect sociable party entertainer. But his party appearance is countered by what you feel when you look into his artist's room or hotel suite or visit the study of his apartment. There are no framed autographed photographs of famous contemporaries, no diplomas, no laurel wreaths as in the private studies of other great artists. In Lenny's study you see photos of his wife Felicia and their children and other family photographs and these accompany him on his travels around the world. Next to music he likes best of all to talk of his children, their work, their progress, their success in their chosen professions. At the annual Jewish Passover Festival, when families gather to commemorate together the liberation of the ancient Hebrews from the yoke of Egyptian slavery, God's covenant from Mount Sinai and the emergence of Israel in the Holy Land, the entire Bernstein family usually assembles.

Since his earliest youth Leonard Bernstein has always been sure of his aims and had a sense of purpose in whatever he did. Imperturbable strength of will was always combined in him with an enquiring mind, energetic struggle with doubt, resolute intent with meditation, a plunge into the turmoil of social life with the longing for solitude and intimate dialogue. As a young man he already impressed by his sympathy for the problems of others, his wish to understand people, his magnanimity, his love of his fellow-men, his humanity.

'Leonard Bernstein, for as long as I have known him, has always been a dramatically special person', wrote Fredric R. Mann, the musically educated philanthropist, Maecenas, donor of the Tel Aviv concert auditorium named for him, founder of the Mann Music Center in Philadelphia and early patron of the young Bernstein, whom he supported with a scholarship,

and this observation dates back to when he was only twenty-one years old. Lenny and I were then students at the Curtis Institute of Music in Philadelphia, and he was living with acquaintances of mine. He and I became good friends and over the years I grew to know his entire family intimately. Then as now, Lenny possessed the rare combination of great intellect and talent, and a kind nature. When meeting him for the first time, his astounding mind was immediately in evidence but so was his warm personality.

[272]

Lenny and I remained friends over the years. When I became president of the Robin Hood Dell [summer home of the Philadelphia Orchestra, now known as the Mann Music Center] in 1948, Lenny conducted the opening concert of the next season — thirty-one-year-old Lenny with the likes of Helen Traubel and Lauritz Melchior in a concert version of Tristan und Isolde (the entire opera)! This was at a time when such fare was considered too *highbrow* for summer audiences, but this production was a huge success. This was the first of many performances for Lenny at the Mann Music Center: He has been heard as pianist and conductor, often collaborating with greats such as Milstein and Piatigorsky. In 1977, he came full circle with another concert version of Tristan, this time with Ingrid Bjoner and James King, and in 1979, his Mahler Ninth was one of the highlights of the season.

It is difficult, if not impossible, to say in which area Lenny's greatest talent lies. His talent, like his interests, seems unlimited, both in and out of the arts. In music, he is equally proficient with the classics, jazz and musical theater, and within classical music, he has been able to master many forms: symphonic, chamber, choral, song and ballet. The entire world of music has always been his home.

In all that he does, Lenny is thoroughly and uniquely American, and yet he has always been true to his heritage, being involved as creator and interpreter with Jewish and Israeli culture. In 1957, he conducted at the dedication of the Mann Auditorium in Tel Aviv.

For me, Lenny has always been a constant inspiration, a consistently loveable, real person whom success has not spoiled. He is today basically the same as he has always been, as kind as ever, just more mature. But even in his youth he was mature, being ahead of his time in that area as in so many others (Fredric R. Mann in a letter to the author, 17 January 1983).*

Some of his prominent friends and collaborators have written on their joint work with Lenny in the introductory notes for the album *Bernstein on Broadway* (Amberson Enterprises and G. Schirmer, New York, 1981), which contains songs from Leonard Bernstein's musical stage works. George Abbott, director of *On the Town* writes that

if you think that he was at that time [1944] an insecure novice, feeling his way carefully in the new medium, you quite misjudge the man. He was almost arrogantly sure of himself. Not that he was conceited. It didn't take that form: he didn't brag, his conversation was not laced with I's; but he knew what he wanted for his music, and that point of view he defended, often vehemently . . . . So here we have a handsome young man (looking a good deal as I imagine Lord Byron would have wished to look), the possessor of a

---

* Frederic R. Mann died in February 1987, aged 83.

fine intellect and a talent recognized even at that point; and would one not expect such a man's life to go from one day to the next in serenity and security? But it was not all that smooth. His life, like yours and mine, was full of annoying problems.

George Abbott also recounts that Lenny often interrupted his work and 'would seemingly overcommit himself', to make a speech for a good cause somewhere, to conduct an orchestra far from New York. 'Why', asked George Abbott. 'Why is waving that stick so important?' Lenny's reply: 'But it's the most fun of anything in the world. I love to make music'.

Evaluating Lenny's personality, George Abbott continues: 'Leonard is a very complicated man. He was and is a smart fellow. I mean about everything, from crossword puzzles to politics. If some fate had forced him to be a lawyer or a broker, he would, I think, have been highly successful. However, he did what he liked: he made music. Wonderful music, original music'.

With regard to Lenny's versatility it is appropriate to make the point that he inherited from his father quite a number of qualities that have contributed to forming his personality. Not only the deep-rooted religiosity and faith, a mainstay of Leonard Bernstein's thinking, but also the flair for enquiry, search, research, investigating and seeking the truth behind appearances are all attributes of a descendant of Talmud scholars. But there has also always been a sign of Leonard's having inherited something of his father's commercial talents. He had, at an early stage of his career, secured for himself the rights in his own compositions and founded an organisation named Amberson Enterprises (Amber = Bernstein) to serve his artist's and publishing interests. From his considerable income he has established a foundation which bears his name; it supports Amnesty International and other institutions of public benefit. For a series of his later compositions he has assigned rights to Jalni Publications — the name made up of the names of his children, Jamie, Alexander, and Nina. He magnanimously lends assistance to young talents and even during a period of hectic travel, rehearsals, concerts, meetings, interviews, recording sessions and television broadcasts he will always find time to listen to a young pianist or watch an aspiring conductor at rehearsal. For his friend and assistant of many years' standing, Jack Gottlieb, who has written commentaries for most of his works for concert and record sleeve notes and has also become known as a composer in his own right, he wrote the words for a cycle of songs. During a concert tour of Japan with the New York Philharmonic Orchestra in 1960 he noted down a series of short poems in the form of Japanese haiku and gave them to Jack Gottlieb as a present. Gottlieb composed the *Haiku Souvenirs* for voice and piano in August 1967, publishing them in 1978.

For the album *Bernstein on Broadway* contributions were written by (apart from George Abbott) Stephen Sondheim (lyricist of *West Side Story*), friends Betty Comden and Adolph Green (who wrote *On the Town* and *Wonderful Town*), Hal Prince (who took part in the productions of *Wonderful Town, West Side Story*, and a new version of *Candide*), Roger Stevens (producer of *Peter Pan, West Side Story* and *Mass*), and Jerome Robbins; it appears that the collaboration of authors, directors, producers, and choreographer often took a most dramatic form because of the inventiveness and dynamisn of the composer. Jerome Robbins, whose original ideas were the stimulus for many of Bernstein's works, relates how a working session generally developed, and in his own autobiography there are many more interesting details.

In the note published in the album Jerome Robbins tells what usually happens when he visits Lenny's studio to hear the music he has finished for a new scene they had conceived: 'He'd lead me over to a piano covered with scribbled music sheets, lyrics, pencils and erasers in various destroyed states, and the inevitable overflowing ashtrays'. Lenny would then tell him that he couldn't play himself what he has written because 'there are so many voices' and it will never sound 'like it will in the orchestra'; and 'then he'd postpone playing by giving a ten minute analytical lecture on the composition', Jerome Robbins thinks possibly for 'covering his anxiety'. But at last he would sit down and play and make the piano sound like an orchestra: 'His feet would stamp out the chords and percussion, threatening the ceiling of the apartment below. His prodigious piano technique produced second and third voices of the piece; his voice, singing in different ranges, doubled back and forth over octaves demonstrating orchestral parts, choruses, duets, and solos . . . . His excitement was contagious . . .'.

Among Lenny's oldest friends is the great violinist Isaac Stern, who has played very frequently in his concerts and for whom Bernstein composed his *Serenade* — 'a lovely work', Isaac Stern says, 'with some extraordinary beautiful moments. I never could quite understand why it did not become sort of a repertoire piece of violinists. It is, of course, difficult to play for the orchestra. The last movement, which is very Lenny, very Bernstein, is in a language that comes not easily on the tongue of most violinists — it is not easy on the players and on the audience'. What Isaac Stern most admires in his friend is the many-sidedness of his interests and his knowledge:

> With a mind as broad and as constantly curious as his is, his mind is always searching, looking, probing, trying, and with every passing moment it adds to its store of knowledge and experience, and that's on top of an enormous educational programme and a wonderfully retentive memory that he has where all the knowledge that he has found important and necessary he simply retains and it adds to this kind of overall *Gestalt* view of music. Of course, this constantly percolates in him and he has retained all this sense of sharp excitement and sense of drama, sense of contrast, sense of colour that he has, this is quite enormous. At the same time he has this now much more mellow, broader overlook while he still drives himself and his orchestras, but still there is a broader pace, a broader concept now than he had in his younger days.

Isaac Stern played with Lenny Bernstein for the first time in 1947: 'I think it was in Rochester, New York, and we played the First Prokofieff Concerto. We became close friends and played together often. We made lots of recordings together and did the first performance of *Serenade* in Venice'.

Isaac Stern and I talked in Jerusalem in April 1982 and I asked: 'If you didn't know Lenny so well, whom would you objectively most appreciate — the conductor, the composer, the writer?'

'First, I think, his mind. That's what I most respect. Then Lenny as conductor.'

'Somebody asked him one day whether inwardly he is not first and foremost a creator, a composer. And he agreed.'

'Yes, that's what he feels he is. But what he is in reality, I think, he's a man of extraordinary intelligence.'

'Do you think you could feel that when he conducts?'

'Oh yes. Because there's a tremendous spirit. Look, Lenny combines the two things which are most rare: enormously broad knowledge and profound intellectual insight, and then the third quality which is indefinable — a radiant excited mysticism. And that is what gives the whole thing quite a meaning, because he believes in a certain mystical property of life as a consequence of his education, and he also believes in random miracles . . . .'

'. . . and so many miracles happened in his life: the beginning of his career as a conductor among them. But he would have become a

(above) Leonard Bernstein's sixtieth birthday concert, 25 August 1978, with
(L toR) Yehudi Menuhin, 'Slava' Rostropovich and André Previn
(below) (L to R) Fredric R. Mann with Arthur Rubinstein and Isaac Stern

musician, a conductor anyway!'
'He is such a master in conducting, he is absolutely sure of everything', said Isaac Stern.

On more personal aspects: 'I remember so many special moments
when we were alone, just the two of us discussing music, life, people,
ourselves, our families, hopes, ideas, these have always been very
special moments — there was one night when we were creating *Serenade*
in Venice, when we were playing there, and we had dinner and we
started to talk, we talked until six o'clock the next morning, just about
ourselves, life, hopes, ideas, and there is this tremendous insight, the
compassion, and then his own uncertainty as to what, always that
looking, because he sees a lot and he looks into which way things will
go, there's always this searching, his wonders about life, about himself,
about people around him and so on — very extraordinary'.

'Do you feel when Lenny makes music that something is sensed of
the complexity of his mind and of his own feelings?'

'In art, in performance, one of the most difficult things in performing
music is — also for him — one of his greatest weaknesses — the most
difficult thing is how to be simple . . . . Don't interpret, just let the
music go free like through a glass, a clear glass, a beautiful glass. That's
for me the greatest art and that's the centre of the greatest artists'
achievements, where everything seems so simple, so right, and just
that. Now Lenny is beginning to touch some of that, and that's also
why he was always first involved with the emotional and then came the
intellectual approach, all he learned from his analyses of Brahms,
Beethoven, Mozart, Bach — Lenny knows all the cantatas and everything else. Of course, I agree with his basic ideas that Bach's music is
not in kind of a simple German style denuded of humanity — Bach was
a humble, servile figure in the service of a court or a church and had to
live the life that he lived. It took quite some time for Lenny to see
behind this music and that, say, of Mozart. But now he has this
masterly insight . . . .'

With another friend of long standing, Yehudi Menuhin, we talked
about Lenny in October 1982. Menuhin very much regrets that in
recent times he has had too little opportunity to play with him:

> But you know as soon as the conductors take wings and are composers and
> educators and lecturers, they have less and less time for ordinary soloists. I
> did play the last time with Lenny to celebrate his sixtieth birthday in
> Washington [1978]. It was a wonderful occasion — he conducted and

Rostropovich and André Previn played the Beethoven Triple Concerto with me. It was, however, just a short time after Felicia died and he was heartbroken. He is a man who feels so very deeply. There are some people, like certain women, whose emotions are precious, I mean by that: the quality of intensity, the way they come out, the spontaniety are so precious. Creative people generally must have emotions that are not suppressed. Because after all we depend on their expression for their creativity, whereas other people can afford as it were that the world does not lose too much if they suppress their emotions. But really creative people in many cases, well we know Beethoven for instance, have had a volcanic quality, the quality that erupted in the expression naturally canalized into their art.

Lenny is such a poignant, a really poignant human being who feels with everything and whose emotions even if they were to be — which they have never been — antagonistic I'd find them so valuable to the world that I would embrace them as being precious, whereas other people who indulge in emotions that have nothing to bring there is no depth to them. But I know for instance with Lenny — he feels so deeply about Israel and there was the time of the opposition of Unesco to Israel and its vote of censure against the State [1974] and my refusal to let the International Music Council (of which I was then president) break with Unesco — this must have broken his heart. He and I did not quite agree at the time but I valued his feelings, I felt them so convincing and so real. The friendship was underneath far too strong and it lasted. Since then Lenny has even accepted the highest award for contributions to music that Unesco can give, with good grace and elegance and charm because he has all of these. I was so glad he did.

Abba Eban, a former Minister of Education and Culture and former Foreign Minister of Israel, spoke in a similar way about Leonard Bernstein on the occasion of the ceremony that endowed him with an Honorary Doctorate from the Hebrew University of Jerusalem, in June 1981 — one of a number of honorary degrees and decorations bestowed on him both in his native America and abroad, and one that he especially cherishes:

Lenny has made us understand, that music is the purest and the most universal form of eloquence. And symphonic music in the hands of great masters and conductors, like Lenny, embodies the unperceived inner flow of life. In listening we perhaps overcome the insecurity, the incoherence and the incompleteness and relativity of our everyday life. And that miracle is achieved by submitting to the power of its organized flow, a submission which brings a very special enrichment . . . Lenny is not only interpreter, he is also a creator, and I think it is commonly accepted in the musical world that he already has a classic quality. I define classicism as the ability of works of art to endure and to enrich later minds, when the whole social

[279]

context from which they arose has long disappeared.

Bernstein has the power to give the catchword of 'escapism' a new meaning: 'All appreciation of art is escapism . . . escapism, to leave behind a world of fact. But the important question is always: escape into what? To escape into the true inner world of feeling is one of the most rewarding experiences that mankind can have'.

Many creative artists, both past and present, have voiced their opinion on the relationship of inspiration and artistic craftsmanship in the process of producing a work. Igor Stravinsky is quoted as saying that composing music is made up of ten per cent inspiration and ninety per cent perspiration; Arnold Schoenberg likewise demands a meaningful working together of heart and brain: an artist should accomplish his task without aiming to produce any kind of impression only, after finishing his work, he should take as an example God, the creator of the world, who looked back at what he had brought into existence and 'saw that it was good'.

How does Leonard Bernstein work as a composer?

In his talk to the Chicago students in February 1957 (see page 252, above) he spoke at length on the creative process as he understands it:

> Sometimes I compose at the piano, and sometimes at a desk, and sometimes in airports, and sometimes walking along the street; but mostly I compose in bed, lying down, or on a sofa, lying down. I should think that most composing by almost any composer happens lying down . . . . Now, this is a kind of trance state, I suppose, which doesn't exactly sound like a very ideal condition for working, but rather a condition for contemplating, but there is a very strong relation between creative work and contemplation . . . . One of the closest descriptions of the state (I should think) can be found in certain mystic Oriental writings [Bernstein then mentions Zen Buddhism and archery] . . . of the identity, the sameness of the shooter of the arrow and the target; the identification of the hitter and the hit. This is a kind of loss of ego . . . . The only way you can really digest this formulation is to experience it, because I have never yet — reading Huxley and reading the Buddhists and whoever — I have never yet found a formulation of words that really adequately describes this state.
>
> As you lie on a bed or on the floor or wherever, and the conscious mind becomes hazier and hazier, the level of consciousness begins to lower, so that you find yourself somewhere at the borderland of this twilight area, which is the area, let's say, wherein fantasies occur at night when you're falling asleep. Everybody has that experience whether he's creative or not . . . . And if the fantasy happens to be a creative one, if it happens to be taking place in

terms of notes or, if you're a writer or painter, in terms of words or design —
in other words, if it is a creative vision you are having and you are still awake
enough to remember it and appreciate it and know how to go about making
it permanent (that is, when you arrive back in consciousness to formulate the
vision into something communicable to other people) — then I suppose
you've hit the ideal state.

Leonard Bernstein points to Carl Gustav Jung's comparison of the
unconscious with the substance within the porous eggshell: Jung called
the eggshell the 'persona', the outward appearance — 'that aspect of
one's self that one hopes is seen by the outer world. In other words, if I
have an image of how I look, how I would *like* to look, that would be my
persona, as opposed to my *anima*, which is inside the eggshell. Now, a
person with a very strong ego has a very hard eggshell, which is
correspondingly unporous; and, conversely, the less ego, or the weaker
the ego, the more likelihood there is of this inner substance seeping
through'.

Now, applying this theory to creative composing, Bernstein thinks
first of Franz Schubert: 'Let's say a composer like Schubert had a very
thin and very porous eggshell. The stuff was always pouring out of it.
He constantly wrote — waking, sleeping, in between; he was always, so
to speak, in something like this trance state. His persona, the shell
itself, didn't matter very much . . .'. Leonard Bernstein concedes that
this is certainly an oversimplification . . . yet it is, at the same time, a
clear way to get a sense of the process; and 'the next step after this
would be toward the age-old discussion of the relationship between
talent and insanity, because the thinner the eggshell is, naturally, the
harder it is to live in the world . . .'.

'Now, what is conceived in this trance?', Bernstein asks, returning to
the question of how the composer works.

Well, at the best, the utmost that can be conceived is a totality, a *Gestalt*, a
work. One is very lucky if this happens. In other words, you may not know
what even the first note is going to be. You have a vision of a totality, and
you know that it's there, and all you have to do is let it come out and guide it
along . . . . The next-to-greatest thing that can happen is to conceive an
atmosphere, in other words, a general climate, which is not the same as a
totality of a work, because that doesn't involve the formal structure . . . .
Every real work of art has a world of its own that it inhabits, where there's a
certain smell and a certain touch . . . . From this may proceed, then, the
totality of the formal structure.
    Well, that's the second-best thing you can conceive, but if you're not that
lucky, you can still conceive a *theme*. In other words, it can be a basic,

pregnant idea or motive [sic], which promises great results, great possibilities of development. A theme that is fertile will immediately present itself to you as such. You know without even trying to fool with it that it's going to work, upside down and backward, and that it's going to make marvellous canons and fugues . . . . You know immediately when you get such a theme that you're going to be able to do wonders with it.

This is very different from conceiving only a tune . . . . A tune, no matter how beautiful it is, is finished when it's over. Tunes can't be developed; themes can . . . .

'So, if you are in a state of trance, can't it happen that you fall asleep?'

The fact that you do fall asleep doesn't necessarily mean that nothing has happened. Not just *nothing* has gone on in this *other world* you've been in. It may be that you have conceived some glorious visions and then have fallen asleep because you didn't remain on that border between the twilight and the waking world . . . . *All* composers pray for some kind of instrument to be invented that can be attached to your head, as you are lying there in this trance, and that will record all the nonsense going on, so that you don't have to keep this kind of *watch-dog*, schizophrenic thing going on: whereby half of you is allowed to do what it wants, and the other half has to be at attention to watch what the first half is doing.

Speaking on the nature of the 'conception' and its roots, Leonard Bernstein admits that the memory of all the music that he has ever heard before certainly lingers in the composer's mind:

This is not disparaging. I'm not talking about derivativeness or being imitative of other music. All musicians write their music in terms of all of the music that [has] preceded them. All art recognizes the art that preceded it, or recognizes the presence of the art preceding it . . . . Even those composers who call themselves *experimental* composers (and are dedicated to the idea of writing music that is different from all other music that preceded it, making their music valuable only because it is different from earlier music) are admitting their recognition of the presence of art that preceded their own, because their art is still being written in terms of the art that preceded it — only this time in antithesis instead of imitation.

The most important thing in creative work is that the good creator has 'something to say' and this comes when 'the concept is conditioned by this crazy, compulsive urge to say something'. This is what makes an artist, the urge, the compulsion to say something:

I very often feel this when I am about to enter the stage to conduct — something pushing you out on the stage, an imp at your back . . . . Something makes me have to do it. It's compulsive. There's no doubt about it. It's maniacal. There's nothing you can do about it. And a composing act is equally compulsive.

Is this *something to say* emotional? In other words, you can't state facts with F sharps. You can't write music that is going to inform anybody about anything, and, in fact, you can't write music that is even to describe anything unless I tell you what I want the music to be describing . . . . Therefore, what it is that the composer is telling is never factual, can never be literal, but *must* be emotional. But it has got to be, of course, an emotion recollected in tranquillity, and this tranquillity is, of course, the half-asleep state on the couch. I mustn't say *couch* — no. It must be recollected in tranquillity, because, to dispel once and for all that romantic notion, agitated music never gets written by an agitated composer, and despairing music never gets written by a desperate composer . . . .

Bernstein quotes William Wordsworth's lines on emotion being recollected in tranquillity 'because if you're going to communicate with people you have to communicate while in a communicating state, not while in a despairing, tied-up emotional state'.

Apart from the purely musical aspects of the concept there are also many non-musical aspects that influence 'whatever the conception is that takes place in this trance'. Basically, music tends to be so abstract that ordinarily it operates independently of non-musical matters: 'A note is a note, and there isn't much you can do about it. F sharp is F sharp; it doesn't mean anything. It's not like a word . . . in that there is no conceptuality at all. In other words, it's opaque. Music is opaque and not transparent'. Among the non-musical things that may influence the conception of the composer are

the viability of the idea — something is going to come from the outer world and condition your idea a little bit in terms of communicability — nationalism, trends of the time — swings away from tonality or toward tonality, swing toward chamber music, toward new combinations . . . , or toward certain styles — a consideration of what will fellow composers say, what will the critics say, the dictates of social structures, the influences of other arts, the inspiration from other works of art, from pictures, books, from stories of other people . . . .

There are so many extra-musical ideas that may influence a composer and often he has also got to consider a soloist or an orchestra for whom he has been asked to compose a work. All 'these are considerations that shouldn't enter into it, and yet they all do. And there's the

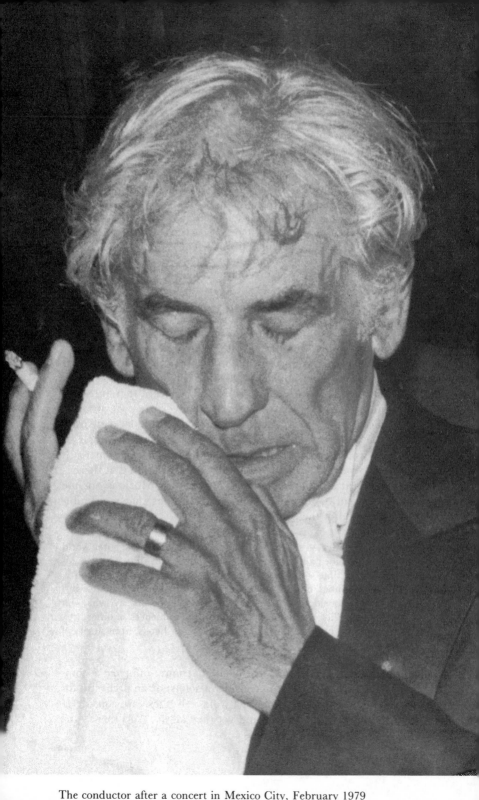

The conductor after a concert in Mexico City, February 1979

final aspect, which is self-criticism, that censor within the mind that says, *Do not do that, it's derivative* . . . . *Do not do that, it's out of style* . . . . *Do not do that, it's vulgar.* And this little fellow, whoever he is, operates whether you are sleeping or waking if, fortunately, you are a good composer'.

Leonard Bernstein's creative Credo, the essentials of which have here been summarised, permits an insight into his belief that magical–mystic powers are at work to provide the roots for an artist's inspiration and give wings to his abilities of imaginative elaboration. This corresponds with the observations of his friends who have always sensed in him inclinations towards the mystic — as they are also expressed in many of his works, such as *Kaddish, Mass, Dybbuk.* The self-analysis also proves that Leonard Bernstein is an artist who sets himself the highest aims and works on a musical piece with great artistic responsibility and with continuous self-criticism. What is true of his method of creative composing can as well be said of this preparations for musical interpretation and performance. Here is not a 'star artist' at work, a 'glamorous world favourite' out for public success, as the media and the music industry present him (no doubt for their own commercial reasons), but the devout musical servant of the great masters at the helm of an orchestra as well as a composer who wants to communicate and to be understood, but not at the price of making any artistic concessions.

'Lenny's contributions to music and musical life and his image will outlast his time', maintains Yehudi Menuhin, adding (in October 1982):

He will not only always be remembered as a composer of great weight but also as embodying something of — well, it is perhaps too banal to say — of New York. He identifies himself with New York, and New York is a great nation, a great culture, and totally un-American in many ways; the rest of the country is quite different from New York. New York is one of the great phenomena of the world and one of its jewels is Lenny. Lenny is the embodiment, the crystallization of much of the life of New York, not only the Jewish expression, but the various bases, and the quality of the town itself.

He has become an American educator. There is, I believe, no one to compare with Lenny in what he has given the people of the United States and through video tapes etc. to the world, an insight into what music really is. He has given the public an intelligent approach because so often the public who has not been raised in music has [a] most superficial understanding and reaction. I have nothing against it because music can be

Leonard Bernstein and Lukas Foss

appreciated at all levels but none the less he has given depth to the American musical appreciation which without him would have remained far less penetrating than it is now.

'In an age of specialisation, Leonard Bernstein dares to excel in performance as well as in composition, in the classical idiom as well as in the popular one', wrote Lukas Foss in his preface to *A Complete Catalogue of Bernstein's Works* by Jack Gottlieb:

> In an age of *impersonal* music, and often *impenetrable* music, Leonard Bernstein dares to be personal, human, even vulnerable. Indeed his music has the rare quality of *instant communication.*
>
> When I first knew Lenny he was barely twenty, already a young master, and his teachers (my teachers) as well as his classmates, looked up to him. Now . . . he is still a young master, and this former fellow student is still looking up to him.

Abba Eban, who described Bernstein in his Jerusalem *laudatio* as 'a classic whose work will endure' — joining Yehudi Menuhin in this verdict — said that 'there is the great consolation that art does not supersede itself, the way that science does, and therefore people like Lenny do have contact with eternity'.

Concert-goers and television viewers know Leonard Bernstein mainly as a conductor of exuberant temperament who travels around the world and as an entertaining proponent of deeply penetrating explanations of the nature, meaning and significance of music. His own music is admired for the immediate impact of its sweeping rhythms, its soaring vigourousness and its stark emotionality but attentive listeners will also perceive behind all this a restlessness, some disturbing disquiet. It is not always easy to perceive cryptic depths beneath an effervescent musical surface. One clue to the true essence of Leonard Bernstein's creative motivation, philosophy of living, and love of life he has given us in an illuminating short poem contributed in 1977 to a book of photographs by the artist Alexandra von Malaisé on the subject of her album: 'Stillness'.

Leonard Bernstein with his mother and three children in his suite at the Tel
Aviv Hilton, April 1977

STILLNESS is our most intense mode
of action.
It is in our moments of deep quiet
that is born every idea,
emotion and drive which we eventually
honor with the name of action.

Our most emotionally active life
is lived in our dreams;
our cells renew themselves
most industriously in our sleep.
We reach the highest in meditation,
the farthest in prayer.

In stillness every human being is
capable of greatness;
he is free from the experience
of hostility; he is a poet,
and most like an angel.

But stillness requires a profound
discipline; it must be worked for,
and it is therefore all the more to be
treasured.

Leonard Bernstein

Appendices

Chronology

1935 *Psalm 148*: for voice and piano
1937 Trio for piano, violin, and violoncello in three movements
Music for 2 pianos: Largo-andante and Allegro
1938 Piano Sonata: Cadenza-presto and Largo-Moderato-Cadenza
Music for the Dance, No. 1, No. 2
The Birds: music for the play by Aristophanes
1939 *Scenes from the City of Sin*: eight miniatures for piano, four hands
Sonata for violin and piano: Moderato assai, Variations
1940 *The Peace*: music for the play by Aristophanes
Four studies for 2 clarinets, 2 bassoons and piano: Prelude,
Fughetta, Chorale, Finale
1942 Sonata for clarinet and piano: Grazioso, Un poco mosso,
Andantino-Vivace e leggiero
First Symphony — *Jeremiah*
1943 *Seven Anniversaries*: piano solo
I Hate Music; Five Kid Songs: (Bernstein) for soprano and piano
1944 *Fancy Free*: ballet
On the Town: musical comedy
1945 *Hashkivenu*: for cantor (tenor), four-part choir and organ
Afterthought: (Bernstein) for voice and piano
1946 *Facsimile*: ballet
Choreographic Essay for Orchestra
1947 *La Bonne Cuisine*: 'Four Recipes', for voice and piano
Ssimchu na: (Hebrew folksong, after Mattityahu Weiner-Shelem)
for four-part choir and piano or orchestra
Re'ena: (Hebrew folksong) for choir and orchestra
1948 *Rondo for Lifey*: for trumpet and piano
Elegy for Mippy I: for horn and piano
Elegy for Mippy II: for trombone solo
Waltz for Mippy III: for tuba and piano
Fanfare for Bima: for trumpet, horn, trombone, and tuba
Four Anniversaries: piano solo
1949 Two Love Songs (Rainer Maria Rilke), 'Extinguish My Eyes'
and 'When My Soul Touches Yours': for voice and piano

Second Symphony — *The Age of Anxiety*: for piano and orchestra
Prelude, Fugue and Riffs: for solo clarinet and jazz ensemble

1950 Music for *Peter Pan* (J.M. Barrie): text for the songs by Bernstein
Yigdal: (Hebrew liturgical melody) for choir and piano
Trouble in Tahiti: opera in one act (libretto: Bernstein)

1951 *Five Anniversaries*: piano solo
Silhouette: Galilee: (Bernstein) for voice and piano

1953 *Wonderful Town*: musical comedy

1954 *Serenade*: (after Plato's *Symposium*) for violin solo, string orchestra, harp and percussion
On the Waterfront: music for the film

1955 *On the Waterfront*: symphonic suite from the music for the film
The Lark: French and Latin choruses for Lillian Hellman's version of Jean Anouilh's *L'Alouette*
'Get Hep!': marching song (Bernstein)
Salome: music for Oscar Wilde's dream, for chamber orchestra and vocal soli

1956 *Candide*: comic operetta (Lillian Hellman, after Voltaire)
'Orchestral Overture' for *Candide*

1957 Two choruses for Harvard (Alan Jay Lerner)
West Side Story: musical
Symphonic Dances from *West Side Story*

1958 *The First Born*: two pieces for voice and percussion for Christopher Fry's drama

1960 *West Side Story*: Symphonic Dances for orchestra

1961 Two Fanfares: for orchestra

1963 Third Symphony — *Kaddish*: for orchestra, mixed choir, boys' choir, speaker and soprano solo

1965 *Chichester Psalms*: for choir, boy's solo, and orchestra

1968 'So Pretty': (Betty Comden and Adolph Green) for voice and piano

1969 *Shivaree*: for double brass ensemble and percussion

1970 'Warm-Up': a Round for mixed voices

1971 *Mass. Theater Piece for Singers, Players and Dancers*
'Two Meditations from *Mass*': for violoncello and piano

1973 'A Little Norton Lecture': (e.e. cummings) for male-voice choir

1974 *Dybbuk*: ballet music and two orchestral suites

1975 *By Bernstein*: a revue with songs written for earlier shows, but not used in them

1976 *1600 Pennsylvania Avenue: A Musical about the Problems of Housekeeping*

1977 'Three Meditations from *Mass*': for violoncello and orchestra
Songfest: a cycle of American poems for six singers and orchestra
Slava!: overture for orchestra or symphonic band
CBS Music: 5 pieces for orchestra
1979 'My New Friends': (Bernstein) for voice and piano
1980 *Divertimento*: for orchestra
A Musical Toast: for orchestra
1981 *Touches*: piano solo
Halil: Nocturno for solo flute, string orchestra and percussion
1983 *A Quiet Place*: opera in four scenes (Stephen Wadsworth)
1984 *A Quiet Place*: new version, opera in three acts, with *Trouble in Tahiti* integrated into Act II (Bernstein and Wadsworth)
1986 *Jubilee Games*: two movements for orchestra
Prayer: for baritone and small orchestra

Bibliography

Leonard Bernstein's Own Writings

Leonard Bernstein has written over fifty articles and essays and some eighty scripts for television programmes, listed in Jack Gottlieb's *A Complete Catalogue*, q.v. A selection of essays and talks may be found in four books published between 1959 and 1983:

The Joy of Music, New York, 1959, and many subsequent editions — also in German, Czech, Hungarian, Japanese, Chinese, Danish, Swedish, Hebrew, Spanish, Portuguese, Slovenian

Leonard Bernstein's Young People's Concerts for Reading and Listening, New York, 1962; 2nd enlarged ed. New York, 1970 — also in German, Hungarian, Japanese, Portuguese

The Infinite Variety of Music, New York, 1962 — also in German, Japanese, Portugese

The Unanswered Question: Six Talks at Harvard, Cambridge, Mass., and London, 1976 (including three records with excerpts and examples) — also in German, French, Hungarian, Japanese

Findings, New York, 1982 — also authorised selection in German, Hamburg, 1983

Bernstein's notes on the following works have been published in the programme notes of various orchestras, on record sleeves or in accompanying booklets put out by recording companies: 'Jeremiah' Symphony; *Fancy Free*; *On the Town* — *Three Dance Episodes*; *Facsimile*; *The Age of Anxiety*; *Serenade*; *On the Waterfront* — *Symphonic Suite*; *Dybbuk Suite No. 1*; *Suite No. 2*; *Jubilee Games*

Biographical Literature

Burton Bernstein, *Family Matters. Sam, Jennie, and the Kids*, New York, 1982

Shirley Bernstein, *Making Music — Leonard Bernstein*, Chicago, 1963 (for young people)

John Briggs, *Leonard Bernstein. The Man, his Work and his World*, Cleveland and New York, 1961

Molly Cone, *Leonard Bernstein (for Young People)*, New York, 1970

Juhász Elöd, *Bernstein Story*, Budapest, 1972 (in Hungarian)

David Ewen, *Leonard Bernstein. A Biography for Young People*, Philadelphia, 1960
_____, *Leonard Bernstein*, London, 1967
Peter Gradenwitz, *Leonard Bernstein*, Zurich, 1984 (the German edition of the
    present volume — also in Spanish, Japanese, Hungarian, Hebrew)
Diane Huss Green, *Lenny's Surprise Piano*, San Carlos, Calif., 1963 (for young
    people)
John Gruen and Ken Hyman (Fotos), *The Private World of Leonard Bernstein*,
    New York, 1968
Artur Holde, *Leonard Bernstein*, Berlin, 1961 (in German)
Joan Peyser, *Bernstein*, New York, 1987
John P. Reidy and Norman Richards, *People of Destiny: Leonard Bernstein* (for
    young people), Chicago, 1967
Jack Gottlieb, *A Complete Catalogue of Bernstein's Works*, New York, 1978
Leonard Bernstein Von A–Z, a brochure issued by Deutsche Grammophon,
    Hamburg, 2nd ed., 1983. Contains an introductory essay by Klaus Geitel,
    'Leonard Bernstein — Der Musikalische Humanist'

Analytical Theses and Essays

David Ernest Boelzner, 'The Symphonies of Leonard Bernstein: An Analysis of
    Motivic Character and Form', Master of Arts thesis, University of North
    Carolina, 1977
Joseph B. Carlucci, 'An Analytical Study of Published Clarinet Sonatas by
    American Composers', Doctor of Musical Arts thesis, Eastman School of
    Music, Rochester, NY, 1957
David Drew, 'Leonard Bernstein, "Wonderful Town"', in *The Score and IMA
    Magazine*, vol. XII, 1955, pp. 77ff.
Irving Fine, 'Young America: Bernstein and Foss', in *Modern Music*, vol. XXII,
    no. 4, 1945, pp. 238ff.
Jack Gottlieb, 'The Music of Leonard Bernstein: A Study of Melodic Manipu-
    lations', Doctor of Musical Arts thesis, University of Illinois, 1964
_____, 'Leonard Bernstein: Kaddish Symphony', in *Perspectives of New Music*,
    Fall/Winter 1965, pp. 171ff.
Peter Gradenwitz, 'Leonard Bernstein', in *Music Review*, vol. X, no. 3, August
    1959, pp. 191–202
Getrude Jackson, 'West Side Story: Thema, Grundhaltung und Aussage', in
    Maske und Kothurn, XVI, pt. I, 1970, pp. 97–101
Hans Keller, 'Leonard Bernstein: "On the Waterfront"', in *The Score and IMA
    Magazine*, vol. XII, 1955, p. 81
Andrew Porter, 'Harmony and Grace (on "A Quiet Place")', in *The New Yorker*,
    1983 July 11, pp. 88–9
Mary Rhoads, 'Leonard Bernstein's West Side Story', Master of Fine Arts
    thesis, University of Michigan, 1964.
William Warner Tromble, 'The American Intellectual and Music: An Analysis

of the Writings of Suzanne K. Langer, Paul Henry Lang, Jacques Barzun, John Dewey and Leonard Bernstein — with Implications for Music Education at the College Level', Dissertation, PhD Music, University of Michigan, 1968

General Literature: Music in America, American Music, Bernstein Concerts, Bernstein's Personality; Bernstein as a Conductor, as Composer, as Teacher (a selection)

Gilbert Chase, *America's Music: From the Pilgrims to the Present*, New York, 1955
Aaron Copland and Vivian Perlis, *Copland 1900 through 1942*, New York, 1984
Henry and Sidney Cowell, *Charles Ives and His Music*, New York, 1955
Antal Dorati, *Notes of Seven Decades*, London, 1979
Ursula Gätzke, *Das Amerikanische Musical: Vorgeschichte, Geschichte und Wesenszüge eines kulturellen Phänomens*, Dissertation, Philosoph. Fakultät, Munich, 1969
Peter Gradenwitz, *The Music of Israel; Its Rise and Growth Through 5000 Years*, New York, 1949
——, 'Music in War-Time Israel', in *Horizon*, Autumn, 1949, p. 39
——, *Die Musikgeschichte Israels. Von den Biblischen Anfängen bis zum modernen Staat*, Kassel, Basle, London, New York, 1961
Henry Anatole Grunwald, 'A Bernstein Suite', in *American Horizon*, July 1959
Hans W. Heinsheimer, *Best Regards to Aida: The Defeats and Victories of a Music Man on Two Continents*, New York, 1968
John Tasker Howard, *Our American Music. Three Hundred Years of It*, New York, 1946
Charles Edward Ives, *Essays before a Sonata*, New York, 1919
Paul Henry Lang (ed.), *One Hundred Years of Music in America*, New York, 1961
Joseph Machlis, *Introduction to Contemporary Music*, New York, 1961
Claire Reis, *Composers in America*, New York, 1938
Arthur Rubinstein, *My Many Years*, New York, 1980
Harold C. Schonberg, *The Great Conductors*, New York, 1967
Nicolas Slonimsky, *Music Since 1900*, 1st ed., New York, 1937, updated in many subsequent editions
Arianna Stassinopoulos, *Maria — Beyond the Callas Legend*, London, 1980
Hans Heinz Stuckenschmidt, *Die Musik eines halben Jahrhunderts: 1925–1975. Essay und Kritik*, Munich, 1976
——, *Arnold Schönberg: Leben, Umwelt, Werk*, Zürich, Freiburg/Br., 1974
Virgil Thomson, *American Music since 1910*, New York, 1971
——, *Music Right and Left*, New York, 1951, 2nd ed. 1969
Adolf Weissmann, *Der Dirigent im XX. Jahrhundert*, Berlin, 1925

Films and Video Tapes

The Age of Anxiety, Symphony No. 2 — with Lukas Foss, piano, and the Israel Philharmonic Orchesta, Berlin, 1977
Jeremiah, Symphony No. 1 — with Christa Ludwig, Israel Philharmonic Orchestra, Berlin, 1977
Kaddish, Symphony No. 3 — with Michael Wager (speaker), Florence Quivar (soprano), and the Israel Philharmonic Orchestra, Tel Aviv, 1977
Chichester Psalms — Wiener Jeunesse Chor, Israel Philharmonic Orchestra, Berlin, 1977; RAI (Italian Radio) Orchestra, RAI Chorus, 'Concerto del Papa', Vatican, 1973
Candide Overture — with New York Philharmonic Orchestra, London and Frankfurt, 1976
West Side Story: Symphonic Dances — New York Philharmonic Orchestra, Frankfurt, 1976
'Take Care of This House', from *1600 Pennsylvania Avenue* — Frederica von Stade (soprano), National Symphony Orchestra, Washington, DC, Kennedy Center, 1977
'To My Dear and Loving Husband', from *Songfest* — with Benita Valente (soprano), Nancy Williams (mezzo-soprano), Elaine Bonazzi (contralto), and National Symphony Orchestra, Washington, DC — Kennedy Center, 1977
Trouble in Tahiti, with soloists and orchestra, London, 1973
The Unanswered Question, the complete six Harvard Charles Eliot Norton Lectures, 1973
Halil and *Divertimento* — filmed after the Tel Aviv premieres, 1982, with the Israel Philharmonic Orchestra.

Selected Discography

Most of Leonard Bernstein's compositions have been recorded. Only a few of the early recordings are still listed in current record catalogues, though they may be found in specialised or second-hand shops. Among the early discs are the first recordings of the following works:

Sonata for clarinet and piano; 'Jeremiah' Symphony; *Seven Anniversaries* for piano; *Five Anniversaries* for piano; *I Hate Music*, song cycle (with Barbra Streisand); *Fancy Free*; *On the Town*; *Facsimile*; *La Bonne Cuisine*, song cycle (with Felicia Sanders); choral pieces, *Ssimchu na* and *Re'ena*; *Elegy for Mippy I* (Joseph Eger, Yalta Menuhin); *Elegy for Mippy II*; *The Age of Anxiety*; *Prelude, Fugue and Riffs*; *Peter Pan* — selections; *Trouble in Tahiti*; *Wonderful Town*; *Serenade*; *On the Waterfront*; *The Lark*; *Candide*, complete operetta; *Candide*, highlights; *Candide*, overture; *West Side Story*, complete recording; *West Side Story*, film music; *West Side Story*, songs; *West Side Story*, Symphonic Dances; 'Kaddish' Symphony; *Chichester Psalms*; *Shivaree*; *Mass*; *Dybbuk*, complete ballet music; *Dybbuk*, Suites, no. 1, No. 2; *1600 Pennsylvania Avenue*, selections; *Songfest*, complete cycle; *Songfest*, selected songs.

Leonard Bernstein compositions currently listed in European and American record catalogues, including new re-issues of early and out-of-print recordings:

Piano and Chamber Music

Seven Anniversaries — Leonard Bernstein, piano (coupled with the Piano Sonata of Aaron Copland, which exerted great influence on Bernstein's early music), RCA Music Archive SMA 7015

Four Anniversaries, Seven Anniversaries, Five Anniversaries, Two Anniversaries — James Tocco, piano, PA (Pro Arte) 08 109 W

Touches — James Tocco, piano, PA 08 109 W

Sonata for Clarinet and Piano — Stanley Drucker, Leonid Hambro, Odyssey Y 30492

Elegy for Mippy I — Crystal; John Russo, Ignacio, Orion 79330 S 375

[300]

Theatre and Film Music

Candide — complete operetta: original cast, Columbia OL 5180, (stereo) OS 2350; original cast of new version (1973); Columbia S2X 32923

On the Town — complete musical, original cast, Columbia S31005

Dance Episodes (*see* Orchestral Works)

Fancy Free — Leonard Bernstein and New York Philharmonic Orchestra, Columbia MG 32174; Leonard Bernstein and the Israel Philharmonic Orchestra, Deutsche Grammophon DG 2531196 (*see also* Orchestral Works)

Wonderful Town — original cast, Decca DK9010 DL 9010, MCA 2050

Facsimile — ballet music (*see* Orchestral Works)

West Side Story — original cast, Columbia JS 32603; soundtrack of film, Columbia JS 2070, JST 20004; 1985 complete recording with opera singers, conductor: Leonard Bernstein, Deutsche Grammophon

Symphonic Dances (*see* Orchestral Works)

Mass — original cast of the world premiere, Columbia M2 31008

Meditations (*see* Orchestral Works)

Trouble in Tahiti — early recordings: MGM E 3646; Heliodor H/HS 25020; Columbia KM 32597; KMQ 32597; 1986 not listed in catalogues

On the Waterfront (*see* Orchestral Works)

The Dybbuk (*see* Orchestral Works)

The Symphonies

Jeremiah — Jennie Tourel, New York Philharmonic Orchestra, Leonard Bernstein, Columbia ML 5703/MS 6303; Christa Ludwig, Israel Philharmonic Orchestra, Leonard Bernstein, Deutsche Grammophon DG 2530 968 IMS

The Age of Anxiety — Philippe Entremont, New York Philharmonic Orchestra, Leonard Bernstein, Columbia MS 6885; Lukas Foss, Israel Philharmonic Orchestra, Leonard Bernstein, Deutsche Grammophon DG 2530 969 (revised version)

Kaddish — Felicia Montealegre (recitation), Jennie Tourel, Camerata Singers, Columbia Boys Choir, New York Philharmonic Orchestra, Leonard Bernstein, Columbia KS 6005/KS 6005, CBS 72265; Michael Wager (recitation), Monserrat Caballé, Wiener Jeunesse Chor, Vienna Boys' Choir, Israel Philharmonic Orchestra, Leonard Bernstein, Deutsche Grammophon DG 2530 970 (DG 2709 077: the three symphonies and *Chichester Psalms*)

Choral Works (except the Symphonies)

Mass — *see* Theatre and Film Music

Chichester Psalms — John Bogart (boy soloist), Camerata Singers, New York Philharmonic Orchestra, Leonard Bernstein, Columbia MS 6792, CBS

72374; Wiener Jeunesse Chor and boy soloist, Israel Philharmonic Orchestra, Leonard Bernstein, Deutsche Grammophon DG 2530 968/IMS (with *Jeremiah*) and DG 2709 077 (album: the three symphonies)
In the version with organ, harp, percussion — James Bowman (countertenor), King's College Choir, Cambridge, conductor Philip Ledger, Angel S 37119; His Master's Voice ASD 3035

Orchestral Works

Candide Overture — among many different recordings in current catalogues: Leonard Bernstein with the New York Philharmonic Orchestra in LP *The Best of Bernstein*; *The Bernstein Years*, vol. I, CBS Classics 60334, CB 251; see also *Bernstein conducts Bernstein*, Zubin Mehta with the Los Angeles Philharmonic Orchestra, London CS 7031, Decca SXL 6811; Eric Rogers with the Royal Philharmonic Orchestra, London, Decca 6 48 48 172; Arthur Fiedler with Boston Pops Orchestra, RCA LSC 2789; Leonard Bernstein, Los Angeles Philharmonic Orchestra, Deutsche Grammophon 2532 083

Bernstein conducts Bernstein (1) — *West Side Story* Symphonic Dances, *On the Waterfront* Symphonic Suite, with the New York Philharmonic Orchestra, Columbia MS 6251

Bernstein conducts Bernstein (2) — *Fancy Free, Candide* Overture, *Prelude, Fugue and Riffs* (Benny Goodman, clarinet, and jazz combo), New York Philharmonic Orchestra, Columbia ML 6077

West Side Story Symphonic Dances (see also *Bernstein conducts Bernstein*) — New York Philharmonic Orchestra, Leonard Bernstein, CBS 61 096; San Francisco Symphony Orchestra, Seji Ozawa, Deutsche Grammophon DG 2530 309; Atlanta Symphony Orchestra, Robert Shaw, Vox C 9002, Fono Schallplatten Münster FSM 9002

On the Waterfront Symphonic Suite (see also *Bernstein conducts Bernstein*), Leonard Bernstein and Israel Philharmonic Orchestra, Deutsche Grammophon DG 2532 051

The Dybbuk, Suites No. 1 and No. 2 — Paul Sperry (tenor), Bruce Fifer (baritone), New York Philharmonic Orchestra, Leonard Bernstein, Deutsche Grammophon DG 2531 348

Fancy Free (*see* Theatre and Film Music and *Bernstein conducts Bernstein*)

Facsimile — New York Philharmonic Orchestra, Leonard Bernstein, Columbia ML 6192; Israel Philharmonic Orchestra, Leonard Bernstein, Deutsche Grammophon DG 2532 052

Serenade for violin solo, string orchestra, percussion — Zino Francescatti, New York Philharmonic Orchestra, Leonard Bernstein, Columbia MS 7058, CBS 72643; Gidon Kremer, Israel Philharmonic Orchestra, Leonard Bernstein, Deutsche Grammophon DG 2531 196

The original recording with Isaac Stern and the Symphony of the Air,

Leonard Bernstein, Columbia CML 5144; Odyssey 434633; not listed in 1986 catalogues

Divertimento for *Orchestra* — Israel Philharmonic Orchestra, Leonard Bernstein, Deutsche Grammophon DG 2532 052

A Musical Toast — ibid.

Slava! — ibid.

On the Town — ibid.

Halil, nocturne for solo flute, string orchestra and percussion — Jean-Pierre Rampal, Israel Philharmonic Orchestra, Leonard Bernstein, Deutsche Grammophon DG 2532 051

Three Meditations from Mass for violoncello and orchestra — Mstislav Rostropovich, Israel Philharmonic Orchestra, Leonard Bernstein, Deutsche Grammophon DG 2532 051

Divertimento, arr. Lee Norris for brass quintet, Rekkenze ensemble, Disque VDE-GALLO 30–450 ('BRASS-zination')

Voice and Orchestra

(*see also* Choral Works, 'Kaddish' Symphony, *Dybbuk*)

Songfest, 12 American Poems for six singers and orchestra — recordings of the world premiere in Washington, Deutsche Grammophon 2531 044

Various songs from *Candide, West Side Story*, the Broadway shows, the films and from *Songfest*.

On DG 2531 196 (*Serenade* 'and *Fancy Free*) Leonard Bernstein sings his song 'Big Stuff' from *Fancy Free* to his own piano accompaniment and with bass guitar and percussion

Voice and Piano

Songs — Roberta Alexander, soprano, and Tom Crone, piano — Etcetera 31037, in U.S.A. Quality Records.

Jazz

Prelude, Fugue and Riffs (see *Bernstein conducts Bernstein*, under Orchestral Works)

What is Jazz? — illustrated talk by Leonard Bernstein, with the participation of prominent jazz musicians, Columbia CL 919

Index

Index